DEVELOPMENT IN THEORY AND PRACTICE

DEVELOPMENT IN THEORY AND PRACTICE
Latin American Perspectives

Edited by
Ronald H. Chilcote

ROWMAN & LITTLEFIELD PUBLISHERS, INC.
Lanham • Boulder • New York • Toronto • Oxford

ROWMAN & LITTLEFIELD PUBLISHERS, INC.

Published in the United States of America
by Rowman & Littlefield Publishers, Inc.
A wholly owned subsidiary of The Rowman & Littlefield Publishing Group, Inc.
4501 Forbes Boulevard, Suite 200, Lanham, Maryland 20706
www.rowmanlittlefield.com

P.O. Box 317, Oxford OX2 9RU, United Kingdom

British Library Cataloguing in Publication Information Available

Library of Congress Cataloging-in-Publication Data

Development in theory and practice : Latin American perspectives /
edited by Ronald H. Chilcote.
    p.   cm. — (Latin American perspectives in the classroom)
    Includes bibliographical references and index.
    ISBN 0-7425-2392-6 (cloth : alk. paper) — ISBN 0-7425-2393-4 (paper : alk. paper)
    1. Social change—Latin America.   2. Latin America—Dependency on foreign countries.   3. Latin America—Politics and government.   4. Capitalism—Latin America.   5. Socialism—Latin America.   6. Imperialism.   7. Globalization.   I. Chilcote, Ronald H.   II. Series.
    HN110.5 .A8D42   2003
    303.4'098—dc21   2003007756

Printed in the United States of America

♾ ™ The paper used in this publication meets the minimum requirements of American National Standard for Information Sciences—Permanence of Paper for Printed Library Materials, ANSI/NISO Z39.48-1992.

Brief Contents

Contents

Part IV: The Question of Transitions:
Capitalist and Socialist

Part V: Case Studies in Capitalist
Development: Impact and Consequences

Series Introduction

SINCE ITS INCEPTION, *Latin American Perspectives* (*LAP*) has worked to make its material available for classroom use. Our goal has been to introduce students to some of the important themes and issues about Latin America that have appeared in the journal and make them accessible to students. Our pedagogical plan has been to trim individual articles to their essential core, reorganize them into teachable groups—each preceded by a contextualizing commentary—and add a general introductory essay. To ensure that our material is effectively oriented for classroom use, all articles have been reviewed by three to four *LAP* editors, including the volume editor(s). Over the past three decades, *LAP* has featured major debates in its pages regarding the contentious issue of development. This volume, intended for students seeking an understanding of concepts and problems of development, past and present, includes thirty-eight selections plus the editor's introduction and conclusion along with part introductions. The volume focuses on three historical perspectives on development theory: imperialism, underdevelopment and dependency, and globalization.

Essential to the study of development in Latin America is familiarity with historical examples and experience, recognition that various theoretical perspectives affect our understandings, and a willingness to keep an open mind. This book encourages examination of different points of view, critical thinking, and a search for answers to the major unsettled questions on Latin America.

Theories of Development: Imperialism, Dependency, or Globalization?

Ronald H. Chilcote

W HAT DO WE MEAN by "development"? A clear conception is difficult to pin down. In the scholarly literature we encounter varying perspectives on existing conditions within countries or between countries and the international system. These countries may be described as advanced or backward, developed or underdeveloped, interdependent or dependent, and core or peripheral. The standard notion of development is as a gradual, progressive growth, which probably comes close to the understanding of most specialists who study development from a policy and prescription perspective. Yet this definition sees development only as moving in a linear and positive direction; in truth, it can be multilinear and even negative in its impact. Furthermore, specialists often view development selectively, through the lens of their particular academic discipline; for example, development economists are likely to emphasize economic considerations but ignore the emphasis of political scientists on democracy.

One way out of this dilemma would be to envisage development operating in multiple dimensions at the levels of individual and of society as a whole. Thus, political development would be associated with democracy in its various forms; economic development with planning for improving the standard of living; social development with people's basic needs, such as food and shelter, health care, education, and employment; and cultural development with the fostering of collaboration, solidarity, selflessness, political consciousness, and social responsibility.

Another way would be to assess these dimensions in terms of capitalism and socialism, the two principal political-economic systems of contemporary times. Until recently, the international order was thought of as a First World of advanced capitalist societies imbued with representative or formal democracy and private ownership of the means of production, the latter usually in concert with state policy and planning; a Second World of socialist societies, usually with command economies emphasizing central planning and provision of basic needs, but with limited political space for participation; and a Third World of the developing and less-developed countries that, in the case of revolutionary situations, experimented with resolving human needs through state directives, central planning of the economy, representative and participatory forms of democracy, and cultural expression for reshaping the commitment and solidarity of people in the building of a new society.

We could also look at the international order in terms of dominance and the search for autonomy, especially within the constraints of capitalism, which has come to pervade all the world, including its socialist remnants. Late in the nineteenth century and until World War II, imperialism was the general expression for these relationships. Thereafter, up to the late twentieth century, underdevelopment and dependency were prominent. During the 1990s, globalization became the dominant mode, although it has stimulated much debate and controversy. This introduction focuses on imperialism, development, and globalization and encourages students, as they seek to analyze and understand Latin America, to formulate clear conceptualizations of all three.

Theories of Development

Imperialism

Theories claiming to help us understand disparities in the world order have been in vogue since ancient times, but several stand out since the nineteenth century. The first, imperialism, dates back to Roman expansion and the Latin word *imperium*, implying command and supreme authority. During the early nineteenth century imperialism was associated with the Napoleonic empire, during the 1870s it was used to characterize expanding British colonialism, and by the end of the century it was commonly incorporated into descriptions of the dominance of one nation over another. There are three distinct periods in the history of imperialism: European extraction of raw materials such as gold and silver in outlying areas from about 1400 to about 1600; the era of slave trade and the search for commodities for the benefit of European powers, from about 1650 to 1770; and the search for markets in Africa and Asia from 1770 to 1870, after England had lost most of its American colonies. Thereafter, these traditional forms of imperialism were supplanted by the "new" imperialism at the end of the nineteenth century, characterized by European and U.S expansionism.

A theory of imperialism evolved with these experiences. Although Marx did not use imperialism in his writings and later writers did not base their understandings of imperialism on his work, Marx and Engels in the *Communist Mani-*

festo came close to a conception of the term in their reference to the expanding international market: "it must nestle everywhere, settle everywhere, establish connections everywhere." Lenin, influenced by the English liberal J. A. Hobson, shared with Rudolf Hilferding and Nicolai Bukharin a classical Marxist understanding of imperialism, which emphasized the merging of industrial and bank capital in the form of finance capital. Hobson focused on domestic underconsumption, Hilferding on finance capital, and Bukharin on monopolies of banks and corporations, while Lenin delineated a theory of imperialism that characterized monopoly as the highest stage of capitalism. All these theoretical underpinnings of imperialism were assimilated into polemical denunciations of capitalist domination and exploitation of the advanced nations over backward areas.

Dependency and Underdevelopment

After World War II, many colonies in Africa and Asia became independent through revolution or the collapse of empire. Social scientists, especially political economists, elaborated theories of development based on the capitalist experiences of Europe and the United States. Intellectuals in the newly emerging nations began to search for a new theory to explain their backwardness. Understanding imperialism as a manifestation of capitalism in an advanced phase was a starting point, but these writers also attempted to move from theories based on external considerations to analysis of why and how imperialism influenced their internal national situations—particularly social-class distinctions and struggle. The theory that emerged became known in varying forms, from the attention to economic surplus and backwardness described by Paul Baran to the theory of capitalist development or underdevelopment in André Gunder Frank or the new dependency of Theotônio dos Santos, from the subimperialism of Ruy Mauro Marini to the associated dependent capitalism of Fernando Henrique Cardoso. These theories were often labeled Marxist, even though their proponents rarely cited the early ideas of Marx and Lenin.

However, in general the new theories supplanted the old theories of imperialism and became very popular among intellectuals outside Europe and the United States, especially in Latin America. Many of the dependency theorists assumed revolutionary and socialist outcomes, based on the promise and example of the Cuban Revolution, while others envisaged a reformist path and the development of the capitalist means of production. There were similarities between the theories of dependency and imperialism, however. A similar periodization appeared in the literature. Dos Santos elaborated a scheme somewhat comparable to Marxism based on historical forms of dependency: colonial dependency when trade monopolies were established over the land, mines, and labor of colonial societies; financial industrial dependency that accompanied the period of imperialism at the end of the nineteenth century and allowed the domination of big capital in the hegemonic centers and its expansion abroad; and a new type of dependency that appeared after World War II, when capital investment by multinational corporations and industry turned to the internal markets of underdeveloped countries. Structural dichotomies also appeared within both imperialist and dependency theories: political (metropole and satellite), geographical (core and periphery), and economic (development and underdevelopment). Finally, both types of theory emphasized the international implications of unequal or uneven development. Marx observed discrepancies in the developmental process, Lenin found evidence of capitalism alongside feudalism in Russia, and Samir Amin envisaged a world of developed and underdeveloped societies, with some capitalist and others socialist, yet all integrated into a commercial and financial capitalist network on a world scale.

Globalization

An uncritical and widespread usage of the term *globalization* appears to obscure the negative impact of capitalist development and imperialism. In a general sense, globalization appears rhetorically as an ideologically and politically motivated concept implying that a harmonious and integrated world order has been evolving to mitigate the tensions and struggles that historically have disrupted the international political economy. Globalization as a concept may have roots in earlier efforts to characterize the world economy as potentially orderly and harmoniously integrated. Although it rarely is conceptualized within historical theoretical debates, globalization represents a way of describing a world today reminiscent of the thought of such writers as Karl Kautsky, who argued that capitalism eventually would transcend the problems wrought long ago by the imperialist nations. Kautsky envisaged capital as transforming into a single world entity, and he believed that a peaceful alliance of international finance capital would bring about a resolution of conflict generated by the rivalry of national finance capitals. Joseph Schumpeter believed that the world of imperialism a century ago was essentially precapitalist and would eventually disappear in a rational and progressive capitalist era. In fact, globalization might equate to how diffusionist literature since World War II has characterized the interdependent world order of nations, diffusionism here implying the assumption that spreading capitalism and technology outward from the developed capitalist part of the world would uplift and allow less-developed regions to advance on an equal level. Globalization also implies that accumulation of capital, trade, and investment no longer are confined to the nation-state. Further, it enhances the idea that capital flows have created a new world order with its own institutions and network of power relationships.

Five questions may help in a critical assessment of whether globalization is a useful concept. First, does the present stage of capitalism represent a new epoch we can justifiably call globalization or is it a continuation of the past? Obviously, the world and its conditions have altered substantially in the present era, but are we justified in postulating that a major transformation has occurred that we can call globalization? I am inclined to believe, to the contrary, that the present trends represent but a continuation of old ideas. Second, at a theoretical level, is globalization an adequate term for explaining the fact that capitalism has spread to nearly every geographical region of the world and subsumed local and regional economies under its influence? Although we can speak of global capitalism, my preference is to relate imperialism and its historical theoretical understandings to an analysis of the world today. Third, is globalization the consequence of a linear and inevitable process toward some better society? Proponents may argue for such outcomes, but the differentiation, inequality, and exploitation we see everywhere more adequately explains international economy today. Fourth, does globalization imply a new era of harmony and peacefulness in the world today? In Latin America, left revolutionary groups, especially in Central America, have negotiated political pacts allowing them to participate in electoral politics. Yet violence and revolutionary activity are evident elsewhere; for instance, in Colombia politics long has been enmeshed in violent struggle, guerrilla warfare, and the drug cartels, while the Zapatistas in Chiapas and landless peasants in the Brazilian countryside employ varying strategies of pressure and resistance. It is premature to proclaim an end to revolution and change favoring the underprivileged peasants and workers of Latin America. Fifth, does globalization suggest a new era of postcapitalism? Such an idea was inherent long ago in the end-of-ideology prophecy of Daniel Bell and Seymour Martin Lipset and their subsequent characterization of the rising postindustrial society; the idea has carried on in the various "posts" of contemporary society, ranging from postmodernism to postimperialism and even postsocialism. It would seem that ideologies counter to these trends remain conspicuous, that there is room still for ideas, and that tensions and struggle for change will carry on well into the future.

Discussion of globalization appears everywhere as polemic and controversy, in the mainstream and on the left. The mainstream tends to see an evolving process of global integration progressively bringing harmony and integration to the world community. Among left intellectuals, however, there has been debate questioning its importance. In popular and progressive magazines such as *Z Magazine* and the *Monthly Review*, the debate has carried on between those acknowledging globalization as relevant to a critical understanding of the world today and those who reject it as useless and misleading. Among critical scholars, Samir Amin sees globalization as ideology that legitimizes strategies of imperialist capital. Whereas in ancient times globalization provided opportunity for backward regions to catch up with advanced ones, Amin believes that today globalization implies expansion of capitalism with the aim to enhance inequality. He sees the model of globalization manifest today as fragile, with the inhuman conditions that affect people everywhere as inevitably spurring on fronts of popular struggle against monopolies and imperialism. In a somewhat similar dissent, Prabhat Patnaik affirms that globalization is divisive and tends to work against the unity of nations and regions. Finally, James Petras shows that globalization theory serves as an ideological rationalization for class inequalities and for obscuring present world reality.

Controversy over globalization also rages at a deeper theoretical level. Critical of but influenced by globalization, William Robinson links globalization to U.S. intervention and hegemony and argues that, today, accumulation processes transcend specific national territories and determine levels of social development among a globally stratified population. Michael Hardt and Antonio Negri accept the new world order and reject the idea of the autonomy of nation-states. In contrast, Robert Gilpin as well as Paul Hirst and Grahame Thompson remain skeptical of globalization. These writers proclaim globalization a myth and favor continuity, believing that investment and trade flows are concentrated in the core rather than the periphery and that advanced capitalist countries will remain dominant. While Robert Brenner, Roger Burbach and William Robinson, and David Held et al. provide overviews of the debate from varying perspectives, the student may wish to delve into the symposium in the theoretical journal *Science and Society*, in which the argument of neo-Marxist scholars for the existence of a transnational capitalist class is taken up by Robinson and Jerry Harris and criticized by Michael Mann, Giovanni Arrighi, and others. Just as the old notion of imperialism faded with the attention to developmental theory based on dependency and underdevelopment during the 1960s and 1970s, the idealized conception of globalization appeared in the 1980s and 1990s and has prevailed until the present as an idea that obscures the earlier theory. Yet, in reality, the diffusionist assumptions of capitalist development, manifest since World War II, have become incorporated into the presumed "new" theory of globalization seen as integrating all nations into a harmonious and stable world. Amin has argued that this theory is fundamentally ideological and can only be considered as "imperialist" globalization. Petras condemns globalization as "globaloney" and describes the arguments of the globalist theorists as vacuous, tendentious, and tautological. A comparison of the three theories below reveals important differences.

Capitalism, Imperialism, and Socialism

In my recent writings I have emphasized imperialism over dependency and globalization. Since the nineteenth century, imperialist theory generally has focused on global capitalism and its pervasive impact. The indiscriminate use of "globalization" tends to obscure analysis of the underlying economic system that dominates the world today. The concept of globalization perhaps could be useful if it were carefully defined within the context of capitalism and its evolution through history. Indeed, globalization can be understood only as a manifestation of imperialism and the devastating capitalist order. Likewise, the nebulous and elusive concept of development might be employed in a comparison of capitalism and

Figure I.1.   Contrasting Perspectives of Development Theory

Imperialism	Dependency	Globalization
Imperial states perpetuate domination and exploitation	Less-developed periphery depends on advanced capitalist core	Interdependence ensures shared benefits and equal exchanges among all nations
Multinationals and banks rule over the capitalist market	State association with domestic and foreign capital leads to underdevelopment	Diffusion of capital and technology ensures growth and development everywhere
International capital flows generate regional, national, and class inequalities	International capital flows lead to internal structural differentiation	International capital flows lead to more balanced and equal distribution of profits
Unidirectional capital flow results in concentration of investment, income, and profit	State control of investment, income, and profit offers possibility for transcending dependency	Interdependent capital flows ideally result in distribution of income and profit

socialism. For instance, the limitations of political development could be examined in light of the strengths and weaknesses of formal representational as well as informal participatory forms of democracy. Economic development usually is associated with either dominant capital through the capitalist market or state planning through the socialist market. Social development assumes that some basic needs of people are taken care of through a welfare system under capitalism or through policies ensuring that the basic needs of all people are met under socialism. Cultural development probably has something to do with preserving traditions and values in the face of capitalist penetration or nurturing them through some new awareness under socialism. The departure point in all this, as Marx reminds us in his analysis in *Capital,* is that the world today, as in the past, is shaped by a capitalism that impacts all of us and perpetuates disparity, inequality, and frustration.

My own preference leans toward imperialism as a critical way to assess the origins, evolution, and consequences of capitalism in the region. At the same time, I emphasize participatory democracy in politics and economic planning, provision of human needs, and solidarity and collaboration as means for allowing exploited peoples to rise above their miserable conditions. I favor a push toward political and economic egalitarianism through the socialization of the means of production.

Such a vision has yet to be realized in Latin America, although there have been revolutionary moments, especially in Cuba, Mexico, and Nicaragua, as well as important struggles in Chile, El Salvador, Grenada, and at this writing, in Venezuela. Since its founding in 1974, *Latin American Perspectives (LAP)* has focused on potential revolutionary change, while insisting that writers draw on theory in their analyses of concrete situations. *LAP* also describes itself as a journal of capitalism, imperialism, and socialism.

Organization of the Book

Thus, this reader is organized around these themes and also depicts the debates, issues, and theoretical directions that we have loosely defined as development. In part I, we include popular writing on the origins and evolution of empire, underdevelopment, and imperialism in Latin America. Part II delineates the four major debates on the question of dependency that have absorbed the journal's attention since its inception. Part III identifies examples of mainstream and alternative theory and practice in capitalist and socialist development. Part IV deals with the essential questions of how and when capitalist and socialist transitions have occurred in Latin America. Parts V and VI respectively offer case studies of capitalist and socialist economies and polities, bringing theory down to the practical level of lived experience.

References

Details on the ideas and authors mentioned above are in the reference section at the end of this book, which opens up the opportunity for exploring topics covered in the book more deeply. On imperialism, see Chilcote (2000, 2000a, and 2000b). On development, see Chilcote (1984), Kay (1989), Larraín (1989), and Lehmann (1990). On globalization, see Brenner (1999), Burback and Robinson (1999), Gilpin (2002), Hardt and Negri (2000), Harris (1998–1999), Held (1999), Hirst and Thompson (1996), Mann (2001–2002), Robinson (1996), and Robinson and Harris (2000).

Part I

꧁꧂

Imperialism: The Search for a Theory

A N ESSENTIAL ASSUMPTION of this volume is that an understanding of development theory and issues can begin with imperialism. Imperialism derives from the Latin word *imperium,* implying command or supreme authority; the term dates to ancient civilizations. Roman imperialism, for example, reinforced local ruling hierarchies. During the 1830s in France, imperialism was associated with those advocating restoration of the Napoleonic empire; during the 1870s it was associated with the expansion of British colonialism. Prominent theories at the turn of the twentieth century identified domestic underconsumption as the cause of British imperialism (Hobson), finance capital as the basis of imperialism (Hilferding), capital accumulation in conjunction with penetration in backward societies (Luxemburg), monopolies of banks and corporations as the source of imperialism (Bukharin), and imperialism evolved in the form of monopoly as the highest stage of capitalism (Lenin). Awareness of these theoretical tendencies provides a foundation for analysis of imperialism in theory and practice, and the student is encouraged to compare and contrast them and possibly even find a preference in studying historical examples. A useful synthesis of these trends can be found in Chilcote (2000; 2000a; and 2000b). The following seminal essay provides an overview of imperialism and development, focusing on historical conditions that have contributed to exploitation in Latin America.

1.1

Capitalism and Imperialism in Latin America: Historical Considerations

Frederick Stirton Weaver

This seminal article traces the history of empire, underdevelopment, and imperialism in Latin America. The portion included here begins with the late nineteenth century. It should help as a background and as context for formulating a theoretical approach.

I N THE LAST DECADES of the nineteenth century, the expansion of heavy (capital and intermediate goods) industries relative to consumer goods in the English economy tended to increase overall industrial concentration. This growth of heavy industry reflected the developments in industrial technology, effects of the mid-century domestic railroad boom, and, in respect to the machine tool industries, increased specialization resulting from the expansion of the market. In the early years of the Industrial Revolution, for all intents and purposes, England did not possess a capital goods industry; it was common practice for the workers recruited to work in a new plant first to build that plant and the capital equipment before operating it. Factories using machines to build machines resulted from the success of factories using machines to produce consumer goods (Marx, 1867: 382–386).

The expansion of capital and intermediate goods production worked against decentralized, economic, social, and political institutions even in England, where liberalism as an ideology and an organizational reality had attained the greatest height in Europe. Because of this context, centralization did not reach the degree

First published in *Latin American Perspectives* 11, vol. 3 (4), Sage Publications, Inc. Reprinted with permission from the Latin American Perspectives Collective. Selection from 36–50.

it did in Germany, probably to its economic disadvantage. Already by the turn of the nineteenth century, liberal institutions were inappropriate for the coordination and stimulation of large-scale industry and the liberal heritage was a definite disadvantage for England in competing with the economically more dynamic Germany. But even in England, the rise of heavy industry had several consequences: (1) rise of the corporate form of firm organization and of big financial institutions for the large firms' establishment and operation, which, as in German finance capitalism, worked to further industrial combination even among consumer goods firms; (2) promotion of a distribution of income skewed so strongly towards owners of property that it reduced the likelihood that aggregate demand would be sustained at adequate levels, thus reducing the returns on domestic investments; (3) the need by the large firms to monopolize raw material sources so as to prevent the erosion of market power by the entry of new firms into their lines; and (4) giving an organizational coherence and eventually financial resources to the largest and most profitable firms' workers, who constituted an "aristocracy of labor" which in the early years was the vanguard of a militant working-class movement. Conceptually distinct from the aggregate demand/surplus realization problem of (2) above, a large capital goods industry chronically operates at less than full capacity and is a source of economic instability: any change of demand for consumer goods has a magnified effect on the demand for capital goods, for the principal customers of produced means of production are consumer goods producers whose demand for machinery is much more volatile than is the demand for their products. The destabilizing impact of the capital goods sector on general economic activity was recognized by Marx— "the crisis of proportionality" (Sweezy, 1942: 156–162)—and figures predominantly in conventional business cycle theory (R. Gordon, 1961). Considering the market structure of capital goods, Lenin (1917: 28) concluded that "monopoly which is created in certain branches of industry, increases and intensifies the anarchy in capitalist production as a whole." The creation (or re-creation) of a strong state apparatus in England was a response to the need for managing and directing a more complex and unstable economy and for containing the workers.

Although these processes worked in very different contexts, they were very visible in both England and Germany in the late nineteenth and early twentieth centuries, and when one adds the fact that there were more than one nation with these characteristics and that the international rivalry and resulting militarism further strengthened the central state, we have encompassed virtually all of the classical explanations for the late-nineteenth-century European scramble for colonies presented in theories of imperialism. Although people continue to argue which elements were the most important in generating the imperialistic impulse at this time, it is sufficient for our present purposes simply to note their interdependence and common source in the dynamics of this stage of capitalist development. These pressures together made foreign expansion, frequently with the establishment of formal colonies, a very attractive policy. The heightened penetration of peripheral economies supplied markets for capital and intermediate goods which were utilized to produce and transport foreign raw materials and foodstuffs, and exports from the periphery enlarged foreign markets for consumer goods from the core economies as well as additional capital goods for urban trams and public utilities in the raw material-exporting nations. The resulting exports of capital and consumer goods helped maintain prosperity in the core economies sufficient to meet some of the demands of some of the domestic workers, and the whole foreign enterprise served as a vehicle to build on and focus latent nationalism and racism to control even those workers not directly benefiting from the material rewards of imperialism. Imperialism appeared to be the answer to too many problems to be resisted by governmental authorities; one need not rely on a mechanical economic theory of politics in which the most powerful industrialists and bankers are seen to control political decisions in order to explain this phenomenon.

The distinguishing feature of this stage of capitalist expansion, as Lenin brilliantly argued, was the export of capital. While there was still considerable foreign economic activity in the 1880–1914 period which had characterized previous periods (i.e., exchange of commodities for commodities; commerce, in say, sugar, where the commercial activity was the principal end; and as in England's relation to India, the extraction of tribute), the dominant and distinguishing characteristic of this period was the export of capital. When speaking of the export of capital, it is imperative that this activity not be obscured by the financial side of the operation (as in Barratt Brown, 1974: 170–200). The crucial aspect of the exported capital in the age of imperialism was not the bundling up of pound notes and shipping them overseas. When British capitalists invested in a railroad in Argentina or in nitrate production in Chile, this helped ameliorate the contradictions of British capitalism by the selling of rails, engines, rolling stock, and mining equipment abroad. The application of these produced means of production in, for example, Argentina and Chile lowered the costs of producing Argentine wheat and meat and Chilean nitrates and of transporting them to Britain, the profits from the British capital in Argentina and Chile helped the English pay for the imports of wheat, meat, and nitrates, and the foreign exchange received by Argentinians and Chileans from the exports financed imports of English consumer goods. The process cheapened industrial inputs and foodstuffs (and thereby money wages for labor power in England), thus raising the rate of return on capital operating in England. The foreign markets for capital goods thus helped the production and realization of surplus value for heavy industries, and secondarily expanded export and domestic markets for British consumer goods producers. All of this was not the consequence of financial operations in and of themselves; the central factor to emphasize is the export of capital whether that export was financed by English purchase of foreign government and private bonds, by credit extended by British banks to British capitalists, by the re-investment of profits extracted through earlier foreign investment, or whatever.

The internal logic of capitalist development proceeding in Europe underlay the momentous burst of foreign expansion in the last half of the nineteenth century, and the related advances in ocean transportation lowered costs to the point that Latin America became a profitable market for capital goods and a source of raw materials. European investment in Latin America went principally into export-supporting activities like transportation and public utilities and less typically into the export commodities' production. By the turn of the twentieth century, most of the nations of Latin America were firmly enmeshed in an international division of labor in which Latin Americans exported primary products and with those earnings, minus payments to foreigners, imported manufactured goods. Latin America's role in the global system was substantial: it has been estimated that of total world exports of particular groups of primary products in 1913, the Latin American nations exported 17.9 percent of the cereals, 11.5 percent of the livestock products, 62.1 percent of the coffee, tea, and cocoa, 14.2 percent of the fruits and vegetables, 25.1 percent of the rubber, hides, and leather, and significant proportions of various minerals (Furtado, 1970: 36).

No one denies that this tremendous increase of economic activity had far-reaching effects on the Latin American nations involved, but the persistent tendency of scholarship to focus on the commodity and exchange, surface aspects of this process, has obscured the nature and extent of the impact. Liberal scholars, using the categories of orthodox economics (which in this context means comparative advantage [opportunity cost] formulations), have argued that the integration of Latin America into international capital and commodity markets was the source of substantially increased economic resources available to the Latin American nations, resources which had at least the dynamic potential of pushing these nations into self-sustaining economic expansion. To accommodate the fact that this potential was not realized, liberal scholars employ the Rostovian tautology that these nations did not possess "the prerequisites of economic growth" (e.g., Meier, 1968: 295–299). This is more than a tacit admission of conventional economic theory's inadequate explanatory scope; it further reifies the artificial distinction between "economic" processes and social, political, and cultural dimensions of life and denies their mutual influence. The other side of the same coin is those writers who look first at the lack of long-run economic dynamism in Latin America and deduce from this that these nations' participation in world markets must have resulted in a net loss of economic resources. Even apart from the logical and empirical inaccuracies of such observations, it is simply the mirror image of bourgeois conceptions of economic processes which they see to be governed by quantitative amounts of economic resources available to the "nation," that empty abstraction of liberal theory. In fact, repatriation of profits from Latin America to the industrialized nations is frequently termed "surplus appropriation." This is an error; it is an international transfer of already appropriated surplus. The circulation of surplus is important, but this flow between nations cannot be confused with the surplus appropriation mechanism which is the key to understanding the relationship between classes.

Clearly the type of framework called for is one which relates foreign trade and investment first to domestic class structure and then to economic development and underdevelopment without short-circuiting this process in the manner of orthodox theory. This calls for a focus on the social and technical conditions of production and the manner in which foreign trade and investment affected these conditions. Thus, the researcher is in a good position to assess and explain the materially progressive or non-progressive consequences of foreign penetration in Latin America and need not construct complex and implausible explanations (as do Singer, 1950: 493–494 and Frank, 1967: 11, 56) for such historical experiences as that of Canada, which exported raw materials to and received foreign investment from more powerful, industrialized nations but nevertheless established a relatively affluent economy.

Beginning by looking at the technical conditions of export production, there are two principal facets: (1) the amounts and types of labor power and of capital equipment and other inputs required and (2) the manner in which export production related to production as a whole. In the first, one needs to know the extent to which domestic labor power was mobilized and the role of local possessing classes in this mobilization. The second facet has to do with the requirements export production placed on other dimensions of domestic production, that is, what sort of produced inputs (tools, raw materials, transportation facilities, etc.) were necessary to support export production, to what extent export production stimulated other local production in further processing the export commodity (e.g., flour mills and meat-packing sheds in the case of Argentine wheat and meat exports) which often served local markets, and to what degree those receiving income from export production and transportation create markets for locally produced consumer goods. This last point requires looking at the social conditions of production, in particular the appropriation mechanisms and employer-employee relations within the export sector, that is, the effect of export production on the dynamics of class relations.

Clearly these questions overlap in many important ways, but they are a useful preliminary device for sorting out the effects of foreign trade and foreign investment in Latin America. For instance, the enclave character of guano export in Peru between 1840 and 1879, due to its physical isolation from the centers of Peruvian life, the simplicity of its extraction and direct loading, its use of Chinese laborers and imported inputs, and the lack of involvement by domestic propertied classes, had only a slight direct impact on the Peruvian economy. In addition, although Peruvians received probably most of the income from guano, the political and social system fostered by the organization of guano production did not promote the use of the economic resources represented by these monetary flows for developing the forces of production. The Peruvian government owned and oversaw the production and sale of the guano and received most of the income from it (albeit in the form of advances against future sales with current sales credited against previous advances). Reminiscent of the Spanish Crown at the zenith of Spain's imperial glory, these revenues were derived from an activity which strengthened no domestic class, and their receipt did not require the consent of any internal constituency. Thus the major impact of the guano exports was to create a powerful central state which rose above society and was fully capable of effecting policies explicitly contrary to the interests of the planters on the northern coast (e.g., abolishing slavery) and of the *gamonales* of the interior haciendas (e.g., sharply curtailing their control over Indian labor). The major impact of the guano export boom, then, was the creation of a powerful state more like that of colonial Peru than of Peru in the immediate post-independence decades. Export production stimulated the development of neither classes nor general production until late-nineteenth-century growth in cotton, mineral, and rubber exports, which were based on domestic labor largely directed by domestic property classes and which created markets for the products of highland agriculture and employed large numbers of people in transport and commerce.

The effects of Argentine meat and wheat exports were significantly different from those of Peruvian guano, for the export bases supported coherent, powerful landholding and commercial elites and employed workers to transport, process, and market the export commodity. The wage workers directly involved in the export sector in turn were the source of markets for which production, transportation, and marketing of local commodities were directed. The complexity of the economic and social relations produced by the Argentine export economy was qualitatively different from that of Peruvian guano exports, and the sources of these differences are not accessible to studies which focus on monetary and commodity flows and ignore the material bases of class structures.

These two examples, however, are not meant to imply that particular forms of export production determined certain social consequences in linear fashion. First of all, the organization of export production only had such great effects in Peru and Argentina because export production was quantitatively so important within the nation and competing economic and social forces were relatively weak; I am not arguing that external economic relations contain some special potency. In places where domestic social forces were more firmly established, enclaves of export production did not always create a dominant state that discouraged other productive activity. Nitrate exports from what became northern Chile after the War of the Pacific did indeed strengthen the state as in Peru, but the context in which it occurred was manifestly different. When President Balmaceda initiated some significant reforms, the Chilean elite, based on agriculture, commerce, and mining and allied with English capital, was sufficiently strong to forestall such attempts. After a brief struggle in the 1890s, the domestic elites captured and reorganized the state—subordinating the executive to the legislature, which was dominated by the upper classes. The Mexican scenario was different. In the late nineteenth century, mineral exports organized by foreign capital did strengthen the central state, but it had never had the autonomy of, say, Castilla in Peru, and furthermore, it actively promoted economic growth at least as a by-product of other goals. Parallel to these two examples of qualified enclave models, Uruguayan history demonstrates that meat exports do not always create a powerful landed elite. While these exports were highly profitable for Uruguayan rural property classes and were the bases of significant urban economic growth as in Argentina, the rural possessing classes were rent by such serious divisions that they never were able to exercise the hegemony enjoyed by their Argentine counterparts. The rural elites of Uruguay were so weakened by internal strife that in the first decade of the twentieth century an alliance of urban working and white-collar classes led by Batlle established itself as the principal political force in Uruguay.

Again, the point here is that the diversity of these national experiences with foreign trade and investment was so great that it cannot be adequately encompassed by a simple model and, furthermore, that an analysis which centers on production rather than resource flows and commodity prices is capable of comprehending this variety within a unified conceptual framework.

In the years before the First World War, exports induced substantial industrial growth in Latin America, most notably in Argentina, Chile, Uruguay, Brazil, Colombia, and Mexico. But it was industrial growth with some very particular properties. Apart from export processing, the principal type of domestic industrial production was in *wage* goods, not luxury goods, which apart from some special handicraft products were imported. It was wage goods—coarse textiles, cheap wines and beers, shoes, harsh soaps, pasta, etc.—whose transportation costs offered domestic producers significant protection from foreign markets even though machinery and some inputs were imported, because transportation costs were a larger proportion of final price in these inexpensive items. Furthermore, the bulk of fiscal revenues in most of these nations was derived from import duties, and the configurations of political power within the nations meant that the duties fell much more heavily on wage goods than on other categories of imports, thus inadvertently encouraging the domestic production of these commodities.

Luxury consumption goods were not the only commodities protected neither by transport costs nor tariffs; machinery, transportation equipment, and fuels and lubricants are examples of products where transportation costs:sale price ratios were relatively low *and* where importation was not encumbered by tariffs because of their importance to the production, processing, and conveyance of major exports. In addition to the elites' decisive resistance to import duties on capital goods and intermediate inputs, once a domestic wage good firm was established, it was not in that firm's interest to have such tariffs either. Tariffs on imported machinery, fuels, and semi-processed inputs would have raised the costs of producing wage goods and reduced the locational advantage of producing locally (i.e., lowered the level of effective protection offered by the tariffs on imported wage goods). It is important to keep in mind the principle that under these conditions, general industrial growth is not necessarily in the interest of the existing industrial bourgeoisie.

Therefore, the Latin American industrial growth in the first decades of the twentieth century was dependent industrial growth *par excellence.* Those industrial activities directly linked to export production and transport obviously expanded and shrank along with the fortunes of the export commodities, but healthy foreign markets for exports were also necessary for industrial production serving local markets. Good export markets made available the foreign exchange necessary to import required machinery and inputs and also increased the markets for wage goods by raising the total (not necessarily the average) wages of workers employed in export-related activities as well as those working for the upper classes, governments, or catering to those who were so employed. With this structure of production, domestic industrial output passively grew or contracted along with export earnings and generated little of the self-sustaining dynamism necessary for widespread industrialization. The experiences of the Latin American export economies during the First World War are consistent with the dependence model and inconsistent with the deductive import-substituting interpretations of, e.g., Frank (1972: 75) and Baer (1965: 16–17). In the first months of the war, the lack of available ships reduced Latin American exports and slowed industrial growth, but by 1916 Latin American exports surged ahead and pulled domestic industrial production up along with them. The significant change during this period was that while Latin American exports, especially those from South America, continued to go mainly to Europe, their imports increasingly came from the United States (Baerrenson et al., 1965: 19–20; UN-ECLA, 1966a).

While smaller and less-industrialized Latin American nations have continued in this mode of industrial growth through the mid-twentieth century, the depression of the 1930s forced some qualitative changes in the more industrialized economies (i.e., Argentina, Brazil, Chile, Colombia, Mexico, and Uruguay). In dealing with the effects of the depression, it is customary even for people who had observed that Latin American industrial growth in the early twentieth century was clearly linked to export growth suddenly to switch over to an import substitution framework; that is, whereas earlier industrial growth was seen to be related in a dependent manner on exports, the same writers often then explained Latin American industrial growth in the 1930s as a consequence of the *lack* of export markets, which protected domestic industrialists from foreign competition. This is clearly unsatisfactory in the light of the previous analysis of the structure of industrial dependence, and a more satisfactory explanation, as usual, requires looking at the internal social relations of production and particularly their expression in the political sphere, for the economic processes of the 1930s were vitally conditioned by the pattern of national government policies.

The depression induced immediate political changes in virtually all of the South American nations, ranging from the export elites' takeover of the state in Argentina to the middle-class assumption of political power in Colombia to the short-lived Soviet Socialist Republic of Chile to the more ambiguous changes in Uruguay and Brazil. But irrespective of the class character of the new regimes, they pursued remarkably similar sets of policies. One of the most obvious was to bolster elites' declining income through a variety of measures, the most direct being price supports for export commodities as in Argentina and Brazil. Strict limitations on imports and exchange controls frequently accompanied by multiple exchange rates were necessary to protect the balance of payments and the international value of the domestic currency. Concern about the insurrectionary potential of large-scale urban unemployment fostered ameliorative social legislation and the attempt, within the severe constraints of foreign exchange availability, to enable the importation of those goods necessary for the continued operation of urban industries.

So the outcome of the various concerns was a set of policies which to a large extent countered the decline in domestic aggregate income (and therefore aggregate demand) which would otherwise have been forthcoming from the contraction in export earnings, sharply reduced imports of consumer goods, and maintained the imports of necessary inputs for domestic industrial production. All together, these policies added up to an import substitution scheme which stimulated domestic industrial growth, but it is important to remember that these schemes, first of all, required the development of a strong, centralized state capable of implementing such policies and second, were the inadvertent result of a series of *ad hoc* policies responding to different facets of the crisis and not the consequence of a deliberate industrialization effort.

Also the composition of industrial growth of the 1930s was different from that of earlier decades. The scarcity of foreign exchange confined virtually all domestic consumer demand to domestic products, while the efforts to preserve the distribution of income meant that the pattern of consumer demand was little changed. Therefore, an extremely large part of that demand was from the well-to-do consumers who had previously relied on imports for many of their consumer goods, and the leading sectors of the industrial expansion of the 1930s were those producing goods which in the Latin American context were luxury goods for upper-class markets—most notably consumer durables such as radios, appliances, and automobiles, but also including such items as pharmaceuticals and cosmetics. Some of this expansion was financed by U.S. and Western European firms attracted to these economies whose excess demand and inflationary conditions contrasted sharply with their own glutted and deflationary markets. The flow of foreign direct investment into Latin America favored industrial sectors producing for domestic markets over traditional export-oriented and public utility investments, thus beginning a new form of economic penetration which was interrupted by the intensified demand for raw materials between the beginning of the Second World War and the end of the Korean War but proceeded rapidly after the mid-1950s.

This change in the direction of industrial growth—from wage goods to luxury goods—had a profound effect on the industrial structures of those Latin American economies. As Felix (1974: 217–219) has pointed out, in the nineteenth century industrial wage goods were typically produced in factories while artisanal forms of production remained dominant in the production of custom-made luxury goods. But in the twentieth century this pattern was reversed, and even in the 1930s, upper classes' consumer goods—especially but not exclusively consumer durables—were produced by sophisticated, machine-using technologies in large-scale plants and wage goods by relatively labor-intensive technologies in smaller shops.

The foundations of a bifurcated industrial structure were thus laid during the 1930s; the consumer goods firms serving upper-class markets together with public and private firms producing their inputs (e.g., steel, glass, rubber, and chemicals, which began filling in some backward linkages), export-processing firms, and public utilities made up "modern" industry, typified by sophisticated technologies and large-scale plants, and wage goods firms continued to be characterized by small-scale plants using relatively labor-intensive technologies.

Workers in the newer portion of the industrial sector, unlike their counterparts of the wage goods firms, were able to form strong, effective unions at the plant level. This success in organizing was because, relative to workers in small firms making wage goods, they worked in larger numbers at one site, they were comparatively well paid, and the firms (and therefore the jobs) were not subject to rapid turnover. Industrial workers of the large plants joined workers with similar conditions of employment like miners, dock workers, railroad workers, and areas of the public sector and formed an upper stratum of workers who increasingly perceived their interests as being distinct from the majority of workers. This tendency was nurtured and supported by legislation which often recognized unions and the right to strike only at the level of the plant. This particular aspect of working-class segmentation was a part of the continuing process; already by the 1930s, the distinction between white-collar and blue-collar labor and between rural and urban workers had already driven wedges among different sectors of non-propertied workers who depended on the sale of their labor power for income, and again legislation had played a role.

In the first part of this section, I stressed the role of the state in promoting industrial growth during the 1930s, but I did not follow through on the consequences these policies had for the internal distribution of political power. The depression and the contraction of export earnings dealt a severe blow to the power and position of land-based export elites. As I outlined earlier, the configurations of state policies helped protect the elites' income, but in doing so the export elites became clients of the state, dependent on particular state policies in a direct and immediate way that significantly reduced these elites' independent political power. The most dramatic expression of this process was in Brazil, where Vargas maintained the internal coffee price support system for the benefit of the coffee planters. But when the planters, allied with São Paulo industrialists, attempted to exert overt pressure on Vargas to raise support prices and change some other policies, Vargas crushed the planters in a military campaign that included the aerial bombardment of the city of São Paulo. Brazilian politics were never again the same.

This same phenomenon can also be seen clearly even in Argentina, where the export elite captured the state in the 1930 coup. While their political power was assured throughout the decade, it stemmed from the control of the state and not, as in earlier decades, from their socioeconomic base. The need to regulate, guide, and mediate internal social and economic affairs within narrow external constraints, all for preserving upper-class incomes, created a formidable state apparatus. When Perón came to power, in large part due to the support of large labor unions, he created a powerful constituency by organizing the urban and rural poor whom the unions had ignored. As a part of this process, Perón turned the powers of the state against landed classes, and his ultimate failure in destroying the landed oligarchy resided more in his own fear of the forces he was unleashing and in the severity of foreign pressures than in the political strength of the rural propertied class.

The importance of the watershed changes of the 1930s has been badly overlooked by scholars of the left as well as of the right. Too often, the whole decade has been treated in a cursory fashion, employing some simplistic Keynesian schema to explain industrial growth and glossing over the structural changes within the industrial sector and the qualitative shifts in the composition of political power. In my opinion, it is in the 1930s that one must look to find the roots of current social formations in the urban areas of the most industrialized Latin American nations, and the social formations are those of monopoly capitalism.

An important characteristic of these formations is the division of the urban industrial economy into distinct parts. The number of divisions one finds analytically useful should flow from the particular applications, and I will use the most general approach and consider a single division into two parts. Therefore, I will refer to "dualism," but this is the organizational and technological dualism within the industrial sector (of Averitt, 1968 and O'Conner, 1973); it is *not* the dualism of "modern" (urban and industrial) versus "traditional" or "feudal" (rural and agricultural) which pervades so much liberal literature on economic development. The tendency towards industrial dualism was firmly established in the 1930s and became confirmed in the relatively industrialized Latin American economies by the 1950s and 1960s. Following the terminology of labor market analysis (Gordon, 1972; Reich, et al., 1973; Wachtel, 1972), I will designate as "primary" that portion of the industrial sector populated by a few large, technologically sophisticated firms which characteristically are either owned or operated by foreigners or by the state. These firms' output is largely geared to serving upper-income consumer markets or to producing inputs for making these goods. Private domestic capital predominates only in the "secondary" firms, those small units producing, for the most part, wage goods and operating in competitive markets.

The growth of the primary firms of the industrial sector depends directly on encouragement and support by elaborate, centralized, and interventionist states. These states' chronic inability to collect taxes commensurate with their expenditures has meant a continuing "fiscal crisis." Government policies promoting growth and social stability thereby breed inflations which in the face of technological and structural rigidities do little to reduce high rates of unemployment; the Latin American economies have therefore been pioneers on the frontier of "stagflation."

The working class is highly segmented even within the industrial sector, and the machine-using technology of the primary firms of the industrial sector allows expansion with little or no increase in workforce. The smaller firms increase employment roughly in proportion to output, but the largest source of new employment opportunities is in the service sector. Unskilled service sector jobs are poorly paid, unstable, and offer no prospects of advancement, and these workers constitute a large underclass, a reserve army of unemployed and underemployed workers whose presence drags down wages for workers in small firms but has little direct effect on the well-organized workers of the large firms.

A significant proportion of the economically active population is salaried, white-collar workers employed by public and private bureaucracies in managerial and clerical capacities. There are definite hierarchies of income and status among these occupations, but considerable upper mobility is possible within the white-collar group as a whole. On the other hand, getting into positions which constitute the lower rungs of this ladder from below is considerably more difficult, and requiring a degree from an institution of higher education for such a job, no matter how irrelevant for performing its duties, is important for guarding the gates against mobility into the "middle class."

With large firms controlling the markets of modern industrial products, labor unions possessing substantial bargaining power in respect to the state and the large firms, a middle class protected by social legislation covering wages, job security, and work conditions, and government regulations controlling a wide range of economic activity, the competitive market as an allocative and governing mechanism is important only for the activities and products of the poorest and most economically marginal strata of the population.

It is essential to recognize that the urban and industrial parts of these economies, in spite of the low absolute and relative levels of production, are full-fledged members of the genus Monopoly Capitalism. Once this identification is made, it is much easier to understand why industrial growth in those nations is uneven and frequently nonexistent. Monopoly capitalism simply does not contain the internal dynamics of competitive capitalism; the voracious, compulsive drive to expand productive capacity and supplant the remnants of previous modes of production that Marx attributed to capitalism was characteristic of its *competitive* phase. Monopoly capitalism requires strong stimuli from extra-market sources and conscious coordination from centralized institutions to avoid stagnation. Furthermore, economic stability is constantly threatened when mistakes or problems in key firms can deleteriously affect the functioning of the whole economy. The need for centralized direction is so strong that, as already in the case of late-nineteenth-century England, a liberal heritage is a marked drawback; the social and political decentralization crucial for economic growth in competitive capitalism is inappropriate for material advance when the organization of economic life changes. Moreover, the economic centralization of monopoly capitalism makes it compatible with, and even supportive of, a wide variety of noncapitalist social forms (Geertz, 1963).

But there are significant differences between the monopoly capitalism of the more industrialized Latin American nations and that of the United States and Western Europe. One of these stems from the sharpness of the dualism of the Latin American industrial sectors, reflecting the distribution of income. In those nations, as in all capitalist nations, the distribution of income is the outcome of struggle and negotiation among competing groups and governs the pattern of consumer demand. Latin American industrial structures, however, by themselves put severe limits on the amount of top to bottom income redistribution that can occur. In the United States, income is sufficiently high and evenly distributed that consumption patterns among different strata are not qualitatively different. Therefore, when a little income is redistributed downwards through public policy, the resulting increase in demand benefits the large, technically sophisticated corporations and stimulates general economic growth. But in Latin America, demand patterns of different income-receiving groups are so distinct (UN-ECLA, 1966b: 77–82) that Keynesian generalizations about marginal propensities to consume are not useful. Even slight changes in income distribution towards the poorest strata alter the composition of demand such that output from wage goods firms expand at the expense of profit and employment levels in large, modern firms. This shift of demand away from the more efficient to the less efficient firms disrupts established patterns, reduces average labor productivity and probably overall growth, and diminishes the incomes of the most powerful portions of the national and foreign industrial bourgeoisie and of the best organized segments of the working class. The problems attendant on all of this are exacerbated when, as in the case of Argentina, the export staple is a wage good and increased consumption by the lower classes reduces exports. But even without this factor, income redistribution leads to serious disruption and economic chaos in the urban areas and industrial sectors which then leads, with the verbal and financial backing of U.S. corporations and government agencies, international bankers, and the International Monetary Fund, to a political resurgence of those representing "fiscal responsibility," "pragmatic politics," and above all, "order." With the structure of the Latin American industrial sectors—particularly the need for high-income markets in poor countries—reform politics breaks down under the tremendous weight of its own contradictions.

This structure of industrial production is the source of another important difference between the monopoly capitalism of Latin America and that of the United States. In spite of some substantial efforts to establish backward linkage industries, the emphasis on goods for high-income consumers has worked to sustain the dependence of the Latin American industrial sectors on imported inputs of capital and intermediate goods. This means that periods of industrial growth strain a dependent nation's capacity to import, and the resulting balance-of-payments deficits frequently lead to devaluations which raise the domestic cost of imported inputs and help choke off domestic industrial expansion. Perhaps even more important are the domestic facets of this dependency. The need for imported industrial goods means dependence not only on foreign purchasers and suppliers but also on those domestic elements who produce the export staples. As a consequence, it is precisely at the time of sustained industrial growth that the economic and political positions of those who are most likely to be hostile to the success of urban industrialization are strengthened (Dos Santos, 1970a; Bodenheimer, 1971).

It may appear that we have gotten away from the essay's purpose of depicting the relationship between capitalist industrial growth in the metropolitan nations, imperialism, and underdevelopment in Latin America. But my principal argument regarding the last two is that the internal structure of the Latin American economies, reflecting the historically changing character of industrial growth and domestic class struggles, is the crucial context for comprehending the effects wrought by foreign economic penetration. Before pursuing this further, however, we should take a brief look at the sources and forms of modern economic imperialism apparent in the United States, the undisputed leader in the capitalist world throughout most of the post-war period.

As I noted earlier, U.S. direct investment in Latin America during the depression of the 1930s tended away from traditional, export-oriented activities and increasingly entered domestic industrial sectors serving domestic markets. The decline of foreign interests in Latin American staple exports and their heightened involvement in domestic markets is explained by the stagnation and declining profits in the United States, which compared unfavorably with the growing, inflationary economies in the more industrialized nations of Latin America. The Latin American tariffs which taxed even luxury consumption goods inhibited U.S. firms' serving these markets through exports from the United States, thereby leading to direct foreign investment entering the industrial sectors. The tariffs were retained in the post-war period as the middle classes fastened on governmentally sponsored industrialization as the path to more and better white-collar jobs and (along with the possessing classes) as a means to prevent social and political instability stemming from widespread urban unemployment. In the

1950s, the United Nations Economic Commission for Latin America supplied a general "national interest" rationale and policy guidelines for what became known as import-substituting industrialization. So the tariffs around good-sized Latin American consumer goods markets remained, and when this fact is connected to the changes within the U.S. industrial sector, we begin to grasp the reasons behind the persistent trend in the sectoral composition of U.S. foreign direct investment away from export staples towards domestic industry even after recovery from depression and adjustment from the Second World War. What we are considering here, of course, is the genesis of the so-called multinational enterprise.

There is continuing empirical disagreement over whether industrial concentration in the United States has increased or declined in the past, say, thirty years, but studies which distinguish between consumer goods and capital and intermediate goods have shown that, irrespective of aggregate changes, consumer goods firms have tended to become more concentrated, possibly due to the scale economies of mass media advertising, while producer goods sectors which earlier were much more concentrated have shown a definite tendency to become more dispersed (Mueller, 1967: 479; Studies . . . , 1969: 59–62). This is the empirical basis of theories which stress the oligopolistic market organizations which condition firms' needs for foreign markets which, with the post-war protectionism in Latin America and elsewhere, could be penetrated best through actually establishing production facilities within these economies (Hymer, 1960; Vernon, 1966; Caves, 1971; Moran, 1973; Levine, 1975). When a few large firms dominate the domestic market for a particular product line, they cannot aggressively compete with each other in an attempt to enlarge their individual shares of the market without endangering the set of tacit arrangements on which they all depend. These arrangements (resulting in what Schumpeter called "co-respective behavior") enable a set of firms to exercise monopoly market power jointly to maximize profits and minimize risk. Thus even when there is no threat of underconsumption and inadequate aggregate demand (in fact, especially in boom times), these large firms seek foreign markets through foreign direct investment, and in contrast to late-nineteenth- and early-twentieth-century imperialism, changing market structures have pushed consumer goods firms to the forefront of foreign expansion.

Plants in Latin America owned and operated by multinational enterprises employ technologically sophisticated, machine-using production processes, even though the equipment often has already been used and depreciated for tax purposes elsewhere. An important, often overlooked quality of this technology is that it is a *capitalist* technology which embodies a minute division of labor facilitating worker control through hierarchies of authority (Marglin, 1974; Braverman, 1974) and which reduces the number of workers (per unit of output) with whom the firm must deal (Rosenberg, 1969) and enables a scale of operation sufficient to exercise considerable market power (Merhav, 1969). From the viewpoint of the capitalist, foreign and domestic, this choice of technology and factor mix is very rational, even in economies characterized by high unemployment and apparent scarcity of capital equipment.

The large foreign corporations are an important element, perhaps the key element, in fostering the structure and institutions of monopoly capitalism in Latin America. The major deleterious impact of foreign economic penetration is to be found in its contribution to this structure and set of supporting institutions which are irrational and non-progressive economically, divisive and authoritarian politically, and corrosive socially and culturally.

In this essay, I have tried to show the manner in which capitalist growth in Western Europe and North America has governed the pace and form of economic imperialism in order to identify its changing effects on Latin America. It is important in an effort of this type to use a unified analytical framework so that seemingly diverse phenomena can be compared and analyzed consistently and fruitfully. In other words, the theory of capitalist development used for Europe and North America cannot be inconsistent with the theory of capitalist underdevelopment used for Latin America or with the relationship between these different types of capitalism.

Accordingly, my theme throughout the essay has been that the major effects of foreign economic penetration that have inhibited self-sustaining material progress in Latin America have been through the formation of domestic classes and class relationships inimical to dynamic economic growth. The Spanish organization of colonial society and the social relations of nineteenth-century export production produced social and economic configurations which closed off whatever chance there might have been for competitive capitalist industrialization in eighteenth- and nineteenth-century Latin America. Even by the early decades of the twentieth century, dynamic capitalist industrialization required large-scale plants for the production of capital and intermediate goods and centralized financial and political institutions for coordination and regulation, a role the market system was no longer capable of performing. These modern forms of capitalist industrialization necessitate a widespread commitment by those who exercise a degree of political control and ideological hegemony that is found, if anywhere in Latin America, in the authoritarian regimes of Mexico and, perhaps, of Brazil.

It follows from this that analysis of capitalist industrial growth under modern conditions of monopoly capitalism requires theoretical tools which embody an appropriate historical experience. As should be apparent from the discussion of English and German industrialization, neither English nor U.S. economic history offers suitable models to guide the study of the present. Nonetheless, these histories exercise decisive intellectual hegemony and enter scholarly works through such means as explicit historical analogy, as in stages-of-growth theorizing, abstract "universal" principles as in neoclassical theory, and simply as general understandings of what economic growth entails as in Amin (1974).

But to return to the central methodological point: Imperialism has been central in determining the shape and directions of Latin American economic history, but it has been so only because it has vitally affected the social and technical relations of production and the social organization of political power within the nations. The repeated emphasis on the drain of economic resources which many authors allege to have been the principal consequence of imperialism from the sixteenth through the twentieth centuries misrepresents fundamental causal forces in social processes. Any discussion of the magnitude of available economic resources which is not explicitly informed by the fact that the use of these resources is rooted in the social relations of production is a poor guide to political action regardless of the tradition from which it draws its language and aspirations.

Part II

The Dependency Debates

THE ORIGINS OF *Latin American Perspectives* revolved around the question of dependency and its relevance to a progressive understanding of Latin America, to its backwardness, underdevelopment, and failure to develop along an autonomous or nationalist capitalist line. At the founding of *LAP* in 1974, the literature was replete with ideas about dependency. The contemporary understandings of dependency emanated from various sources: the work of Argentine economist Raúl Prebisch and his colleagues associated with the United Nations Economic Commission for Latin America (ECLA), who after World War II advocated import substitution by placing limitations on imports and establishing an industrial infrastructure; the early writing of Argentine law professor Silvio Frondizi, who compared British commercial imperialism and U.S. industrial imperialism and attacked the assumption that a national bourgeoisie could foment autonomous development; the thought of Argentine historian Sergio Bagú, whose interpretation of colonial history assumed that capitalism rather than feudalism was accountable for the dependent relationship of Latin America to the United States; and Paul Baran's analysis of backwardness in *The Political Economy of Growth* (1960) (also see Chilcote, 1984).

Dependency was envisioned as a way of countering Western diffusionist theories about capitalist development, such as the belief that representative democracy practiced in advanced countries constituted a high form of progress and could be replicated in the less-developed countries. Dependency also was a way of looking inward at the structural weaknesses of the underdeveloped countries rather than polemicizing their condition as a consequence of expansionist imperialism. It also aimed to transcend the unproven belief that the Third World would overcome its backwardness through the nationalist bourgeois path familiar to most of Europe and the United States. Furthermore, it questioned the Eurocentric understanding of a linear path toward modernization and the possibility that the Western world could civilize the less-developed areas by spreading Western values, capital, and technology.

Various approaches to dependency appeared in the literature. First, André Gunder Frank elaborated the thesis that capitalism promotes underdevelopment in the outlying world, and he distinguished between metropolis and satellite. Second, Theotônio dos Santos offered a version called the new dependency. Third, Fernando Henrique Cardoso worked out a framework he referred to as associated dependent capitalist dependency. Each approach appears in the selections below along with relevant references for those interested in delving further into their importance and implications.

DEBATE ONE

Introduction

THE FIRST DEBATE BEGAN in the spring of 1973, when a group of young academics associated with universities in southern California met informally to debate ideas around the issue of whether dependency was a useful concept or theory for understanding Latin America. This led to a decision to publish a progressive journal called *Latin American Perspectives*. The debate evolved into the first issue of the journal, published in the spring of 1974. Several articles in this issue sparked interest, including a lead essay and overview of the literature together with an assessment of the strengths and weaknesses of dependency theory (see Chilcote, below), an exhaustive synthesis of underdevelopment and the prospects for revolution (Stavenhagen), an extensive rebuttal to critics of the thesis of capitalist development of underdevelopment (Frank), and an attack on dependency theory (Fernández and Ocampo). The overview was reprinted in many journals and languages, the synthesis was cited abundantly elsewhere, and the rebuttal to critics stimulated discussion over whether dependency was dead as a theoretical issue or deserving of ongoing attention. The attack on dependency, however, generated the most attention because it confronted the allegiance and fascination of many social scientists who were incorporating dependency theory in their own analyses of Latin America. Further, many scholars were turned off by the polemical tone of the attack and by the fact that it was inspired by a position aligned with ideas put forth by Mao Zedong. Some of their dissent appeared as rebuttals in this first issue, and excerpts are included below to give the reader the flavor of the dialogue.

DEBATE ONE

2.1

Dependency Theory: A Reassessment

Ronald H. Chilcote

This selection includes excerpts from an early attempt to identify four major theoretical directions in the extensive literature on dependency. The full text includes reference to this literature.

O VER THE PAST DECADE a new perspective of development and underdevelopment has emerged. Labelled by its advocates as dependency theory, this perspective focuses on the problem of foreign penetration in the political economies of Latin America. Generally, this theory explains underdevelopment throughout Latin America as a consequence of outside economic and political influence. More specifically, the economy of certain nations is believed to be conditioned by the relationship to another economy which is dominant and capable of expanding and developing. Thus the interdependence of such economies assumes contrasting forms of dominance and dependence so that dependent nations might develop as a reflection of the expansion of dominant nations or underdevelop as a consequence of their subjective relationship. . . .

The Dependency Model: Four Formulations

The dependency model distinguishes underdeveloped Latin America from precapitalist Europe. It does not view underdevelopment as an original condition,

First published in *Latin American Perspectives* 1, vol. 1 (1), Sage Publications, Inc. Reprinted with permission from the Latin American Perspectives Collective. Selection from 4, 12–13, 15–17, 18–21.

but instead assumes that nations may once have been undeveloped but never underdeveloped and that the contemporary underdevelopment of many parts of Latin America was created by the same process of capitalism that brought development to the industrialized nations. Latin America is underdeveloped because it has supported the development of Western Europe and the United States. When the center of the expanding world economic system needed raw materials, it was supplied by Latin America. This relationship has not basically changed, even though the United States has replaced Great Britain as the metropolis which dominates over the area, resulting in a strengthening of dependency through foreign corporate and governmental penetration of banking, manufacturing, retailing, communications, advertising, and education. Within each country the pattern of metropolis-periphery relations is replicated as the economic surplus of the countryside drains into urban areas. . . .

These premises lead *dependentistas* to a number of propositions. First, they argue that while feudalistic conditions and relationships exist, the backwardness of the countryside cannot be explained by the image of a dual society. . . .

The New Dependency

Much of the thrust of dependency theory emanates from the notion of the new dependency. Types of dependency are identifiable through periods of history, according to Dos Santos (1970a: 232). Colonial dependency characterized the relations between Europeans and the colonies whereby a monopoly of trade complemented a monopoly of land, mines, and manpower in the colonized countries. Financial-industrial dependency consolidated itself at the end of the nineteenth century with, on the one hand, domination of capital in hegemonic centers and, on the other, investment of capital in the peripheral colonies for raw materials and agricultural products which in turn would be consumed by the centers. A new dependency based on investments by multinational corporations emerged after the Second World War. Dos Santos labels this a technological-industrial dependency. An elaboration of theory on the new dependency is found in several of his writings (especially Dos Santos, 1968; 1970b; 1970c). The thrust of his argument is directed against prevailing bourgeois assumptions about development in Latin America (1970d and 1970e), and it attempts to relate traditional notions of imperialism to the internal situation of the Latin American countries. Let us explore this latter concern. . . .

Dependency and Development

The notion that capitalist development takes place within dependent situations has evolved primarily in the writings of Fernando Henrique Cardoso. Let us trace his line of argument (1972). Cardoso begins with the assumption that modern capitalism and imperialism differ from Lenin's earlier conceptions. Capital accumulation, for example, is more the consequence of corporate rather than financial control. Investment by multinational corporations in Latin America is moving away from raw materials and agriculture to industry. More often than not these corporations comprise "local and state capital, private national capital, and monopoly international investment (but in the last analysis under foreign control)" (Cardoso, 1973a: 11). Thus monopoly capitalism and development are not contradictory terms, and dependent capitalist development has become a new form of monopolistic expansion in the Third World. This development is oriented to a restricted, limited, and upper-class-oriented type of market and society. At the same time, the amount of net foreign capital in dependent economies is decreasing. New foreign capital is not needed in some areas where there are local savings and reinvestment of profits in local markets; further, dependent economies during times of monopolistic imperialistic expansion are exporting capital to the dominant economies. . . .

Dependency and Imperialism

As mentioned above, Lenin related imperialism to dependency. A recent synthesis elaborates on this relationship. According to Benjamin Cohen (1973: 15), imperialism refers to "any relationship of effective domination or control, political or economic, direct or indirect, of one nation over another . . ." This relationship involves dominance and dependence among nations which are large and small, rich and poor. Three principal forms of imperialism are evident through history. First, during the sixteenth and seventeenth centuries European mercantilism characterized the "old imperialism." Second, the European empire building of 1870 and thereafter represented a shift from informal to formal mechanisms of control and influence in the colonies during a period known as the "new imperialism" (see Fieldhouse, 1961, for a useful review of ideas on the literature on the old and new imperialisms). Third, the breakup of empires was accomplished by analysis of neo-colonialism and what today might be called "modern imperialism." Analytically, the theory of modern imperialism moves in two directions. One emphasizes the view from the metropolis and argues that imperialism is necessary for the advancement of capitalist economies. The other stresses the view from the periphery and focuses on the detrimental consequences of capitalist trade and investment in the poorer economies of the world. . . .

Some Assumptions and Issues

Our discussion has alluded to many deep issues which have influenced the various theoretical directions in the dependency literature. Let us illustrate with two examples. First is the attention given to definitions and interpretations of feudal-ism and dualism. This issue is raised by Fernández and Ocampo. Gunder Frank attacks the application of these terms to the real Latin America of today. His controversial position has been extensively debated. The curious reader might want to explore the following sources for further details: Beckford (1972), Cole and Sanders (1972), Laclau (1969, 1971), Novack (1970), Rweyemamu (1971), Seligson (1972), and Singer (1970). Second, there has been attention to the notion of uneven development, also a widely debated topic in the literature. The reader might initiate inquiry in this area by consulting Bluestone (1972) and Hinkelammert (1970).

In summary, we can suggest several assumptions which most proponents of dependency theory support, even though their work may not yet have proven their validity. We draw these assumptions from the literature in hope that they might guide the reader to further understanding, constructive critique, and refinement of dependency theory. First, it is generally believed that dependency theory provides a framework for explanations of underdevelopment and devel-opment. Second, dependency theory offers a foundation for analysis of class struggle and strategies to promote class struggle in the interest of resolving soci-etal contradictions and problems. Finally, an understanding of dependency and the adoption of certain strategies to break dependency leads to the restructuring of societies, a restructuring which limits capitalism and promotes socialism in the seeking of a new and better society.

DEBATE ONE

2.2

Between Underdevelopment and Revolution

Rodolfo Stavenhagen

The view of this prominent anthropologist covers a multitude of significant themes useful for understanding Latin America. The selection covers three future alternatives to the dilemma of underdevelopment and dependency.

Underdevelopment in Latin America

WE WILL BEGIN with the obvious by stating that underdevelopment in Latin America is not simply a question of being "behind" the industrialized nations in a manner which can be measured by comparing the gross national product, per capita product, or other such indices, but rather underdevelopment is the product of a specific historical process. Underdevelopment is the state of being of Latin American countries in modern times, just as "colonial society" was its state of being during three centuries of Iberian domination. Furthermore, the two phenomena are closely related, since underdevelopment is the historical continuation of colonization.

Given this understanding of the problem, one finds that the great task of social and economic development in Latin America is not just "technocratic" manipulation of the rates of investment and savings, modernization of business firms, or more intensive use of natural or human resources. Instead, nothing less than

First published in *Latin American Perspectives* 1, vol. 1 (1), Sage Publications, Inc. Reprinted with permission from the Latin American Perspectives Collective. Selection from 124–125, 143–146.

a profound transforming of all social and economic relations within the nations of Latin America will be necessary, as well as a qualitative change in Latin America's external relations with industrial countries, that is, with the world market in which Latin America finds itself.

It is only in recent years that the problem has come to be formulated in these terms, since for many years technicians and statesmen considered that economic development had nothing to do with social structures and political systems. In fact, from the end of the Second World War until the 1950s there was general optimism concerning the future of Latin American economies. International prices of exportable raw materials stayed high; some of the countries had accumulated considerable foreign exchange reserves; in some nations the industrialization process had made undeniable progress; and the superficial signs of a certain degree of prosperity spread through the middle classes of the growing urban centers. But this image was a mirage, made all the more dangerous since high rates of economic growth and favorable trade balances blinded the eyes of many not only to the serious problems which were still unresolved but especially to the inherent contradictions in the development process itself. In recent years early optimism has given way to more realistic appreciations and to the recognition that building the future cannot be done without eliminating the causes of past failures. . . .

Future Alternatives

Rarely in history has there existed over an entire continent, as there currently is in Latin America, such a generalized awareness among the most diverse social groups as to the necessity of carrying out major modifications of the political and social structure. Perhaps the closest approximation of this widespread consciousness was the African anti-colonial movements in the post-war years (1950s–1970s). Even though everyone is in agreement concerning the existence of a crisis, there is no possible agreement as to solutions, since ideological currents and proposed models for change are a function of the interests of social classes and of the conflicts between opposing social forces.

There is nothing in the present Latin American situation which would indicate the possibility of one single pattern of development which could be followed by all countries. Nor is there anything which would permit one to suppose that the current situation of underdevelopment, internal polarization, and external dependence can be maintained indefinitely. But it is also clear that any model for change which can be adopted will not be implemented without encountering obstacles, contradictions, tensions, and conflicts. Based on the analysis made thus far we can indicate three major alternative models for the future of Latin America.

1) *The continuation of dependent development.* Current tendencies (1970s) may

continue in some countries for some time, passing from crisis to crisis, each time sinking deeper into what has been called the "development of underdevelopment" (Frank, 1969b). Although apparently this process contains the "seeds of its own destruction," there is no doubt that the forces that maintain it have sufficient capacity and flexibility to impede the germination of these seeds, at least until powerful counterforces arise which manage to displace the forces of the status quo. If this process continues for some years the subordination and integration of America into what one author has called "the New Roman Empire" will doubtlessly be complete, and Latin American countries will pass from being satellite dependencies to being provincial dependencies (Jaguaribe, 1969). This "Puertoricanization" of Latin America, toward which present economic tendencies lead, will without doubt have unforeseeable political reprecussions.

Among the forces which support the present model of dependent development (or growth without development, or polarized expansion, as it can be called interchangeably), are of course the multinational corporations whose activities, if they were given free rein, could in a short time considerably limit the freedom of action of various national govenments. (The economic power of some of these conglomerates, measured by their sales, is larger than that of many small countries measured in terms of GNP.) And behind these economic interests one must mention the political and military strategy which the United States has manifested through various direct and indirect interventions into the internal affairs of Latin American countries during the past few decades.

To this combination of extra-Latin American forces which support the continuation of dependent development, one must add the interests of the Latin American consular bourgeoisie and the neo-fascist, "sub-imperialist" ideology of certain military regimes, notably those of Brazil and Chile. So long as there are no changes in the interests of each of these protagonists, or conflicts between them, the only forces which oppose this constellation of powers will be the nationalist and anti-imperialist ideological currents of certain sectors (including elements of the bourgeoisie and middle strata, as well as the armed forces and the Church) and popular revolutionary movements (which may or may not opt for armed struggle, according to their circumstances).

2) *Autonomous capitalist development,* based on a broad alliance of social classes and a developmental, nationalistic ideology. This model has been tried at certain times in certain countries, and its failure until now does not mean that it will not be attempted again and again in the future. This could happen if the political and social costs of the previous model become too high for the dominant national and foreign classes. This would imply the necessity of reversing some of the present tendencies of dependent development, which could only take place in the context of state capitalism and Latin American economic integration, with powerful public enterprises and state planning organizations carrying out the tasks which Latin American bourgeoisies are incapable of completing themselves.

The viability of this alternative results from the possibility which certain active elites (multiclass political parties, military groups, technocrats, and government planners) have of converting external dependence into interdependence, and polarized development into integrated development, without destroying the present class structure. In order for this to happen they would have to know how to obtain widespread mass support, active or passive, which would permit them to limit the power of the dominant classes and negotiate with foreign interests from a position of relative force. At the same time they would have to know how to manipulate and incorporate into the system these same popular forces to prevent being overwhelmed by the left. Thus, while the previous model signifies governing against the people, this model would have to govern *without* the people.

The possibilities for this model depend on a strategy which is both political and economic and which until now has not been successfully implemented in Latin America. Those that have controlled economic strategy generally have been incapable of controlling the political process, and those who have held political power have generally lacked a viable economic strategy for this model. As a consequence, it is likely that attempts at this model for development will again be transformed into the previous model of dependent underdevelopment or will be carried by their own momentum into the socialist revolutionary model, which is the third alternative we will consider.

3) *Revolutionary socialism.* Since the victory of the Cuban revolution, and especially since the socialist government took power in Chile in 1970, the alternative of revolutionary socialist development has been objectively proposed as a possible model for development in Latin America. If "socialism" in this context refers to a certain kind of political ideology and social and economic organization, the adjective "revolutionary" does not refer so much to the manner of taking power as to social changes in the modes of production and class relations. For reasons expressed previously it is hardly likely that guerrilla movements will be successful in the near future. The road of electoral politics for revolutionary parties does remain open in some countries, but as the Chilean experience showed, even before the fascist coup, revolutionary measures can be blocked by a well organized parliamentary opposition. In Latin America in the seventies it is not realistic to believe in the sudden, revolutionary overthrow of the capitalist system, either through guerrilla struggle or by electoral means, in any country. Rather, it will be necessary to envisage a "period of transition" between current dependent underdevelopment and the possible socialist development of the future. This transition will require particular political and economic strategies.

In the political area, it will require the mass mobilization of peasants and workers and large sectors of the middle classes. Under pressure of guerrilla movements and revolutionary parties (which, except in Chile, do not have mass followings), this might lead to a realignment of some traditional political forces, including sectors of the army, the "national-populist" parties, and the Church.

Again, there is as yet no successful attempt at such a political realignment, which might serve as a model. In Chile it failed; in Peru, after a weak-kneed beginning, the military backed away from this course and turned sharply to the right; some hoped that the return of Perón would herald such a course in Argentina, but it was obvious that this is not what the old leader had in mind.

In the economic sphere, the transition to socialism will require the most difficult step of all: breaking external dependency, i.e., breaking the stranglehold of the multinational corporations and of financial and technological dependence. If this can be achieved (Cuba did, Chile tried, and Mexico speaks of it), then many other measures of economic policy will come naturally: redistribution of income, elimination of structural marginality and internal colonialism, increase in standards of living of the population, popular participation in decision making, etc.

Just as there is no recipe for socialism, there is no recipe for a strategy of transition. The contradictions and the internal and external conflicts which any socialist strategy (no matter how mild) will encounter appear formidable indeed. But one of the weaknesses of those who create the future is precisely their strength: an incurable optimism and an unbreakable faith in the potential capabilities of humanity. The revolutionary alternative in Latin America cannot take place, as Che Guevara had already foreseen, without a new morality and a new kind of human being. This new human being can only arise in the crucible of revolutionary struggle.

2.3

Dependence Is Dead, Long Live Dependence and the Class Struggle: A Reply to Critics

André Gunder Frank

The author popularized his idea of capitalist underdevelopment during the 1960s and was generally accepted by North American and European intellectuals but widely criticized by his colleagues in Latin America. The reader may wish to delve into the full essay to understand the breadth of his criticism and dialogue, at the time relatively unknown to English-speaking readers. The selection offers a brief glimpse at his framework for responding to critics from the right to the left. This essay marks his shift from a dependency understanding to a world-systems perspective which was to embrace his subsequent work.

The philosophers have only interpreted the world in various ways; the point, however, is to change it.

—Karl Marx, "Thesis on Feuerbach"

The mark of an important contribution, whether in the natural or the social sciences, is not that it reveals some eternal truth. It is, rather, that existing knowledge and analysis are put together in new ways, raising questions and offering conclusions which allow and force friends and enemies alike to push their own research and analysis into different areas.

—Doug Dowd, referring to C. Wright Mills

First published in *Latin American Perspectives* 1, vol. 1 (1), Sage Publications, Inc. Reprinted with permission from the Latin American Perspectives Collective. Selection from 87, 89–93.

Rarely if ever, has the development of economies by its own force blazed the way to new perspectives. The cue to the continual reorientation of our work has normally come from the sphere of politics responding to that cue, students turn research on issues, that have attained political importance. . . . So it has always been. The major recastings of economic thought . . . were all responses to changing political conditions and opportunities.

—Gunner Myrdal, *Asian Drama*

T HE IMPORTANCE of the older dependency theory of underdevelopment is undeniable in terms of the criteria of Myrdal, Dowd, and Marx cited above. It certainly represented an important reorientation in response to changing political conditions and opportunities. It certainly allowed and forced friends and enemies alike to raise different questions and offer other solutions. It has even been co-instrumental in changing the world, though it did not revolutionize it as some of its proponents had hoped and its opponents had feared. The same may probably be said of the new dependence theory as well, both with respect to its liberal positivist grandfather and relative to its reformist developmental father before it. But implicit in the rise of "dependence" in response to changing political conditions (and those in relation to changing economic ones) is the possibility, or probability, nay necessity, of a renewed fall of the same to make way for new scientific explanations and ideological orientations as economic and political conditions change again. The more a theory has been important in view of its relation to concrete reality, the less will it be eternally true, which is a condition at best reserved for empty tautologies.

The evidence is accumulating that "dependence"—both old and new—has ended or is completing that cycle of its natural life, at least in the Latin America that gave it birth. The reason is the crisis of the 1970s in the newly changing world economic and political reality. Whatever its cause and its nature, as well as its outcome or resolution—questions and answers, precisely, that are to be co-determined by the necessary alternative to "dependence" and "Keynesianism"— the reality of the new crisis is increasingly evident in the world. Declining rates of growth and still more (and more importantly) of profits and investment in the industrialized capitalist countries as well as the intensified struggle for markets at home and abroad are evidence of renewed impasse in the historical process of capitalist capital accumulation. Recent domestic and foreign policy developments in some socialist countries indicate that the process of capital accumulation is also changing pace or direction and that these countries are intent on participating in the newly emerging international division of labor on a modified wider basis. The concomitant negotiations and the passage from the "bipolarity" of the cold war to the re-emerging "multipolarity" is accompanied by a new "dialogue" (to borrow a term from the previously unthinkable relations between South Africa and an increasing number of new African states) making itself heard around the world. Neo-social democratic movements and neofascist threats which arise when the former fail are spreading in the industrialized capitalist countries. This response is seen in the crisis-generated mass mobilization in Brandt's Germany; the difficulty in invoking the Industrial Relations Act that Labour had already failed to impose in Heath's Britain; the promotion of "Chili with spaghetti sauce," on the Chilean socialist–communist model; Pompidou's "Gaullist" reaction in France; and the Democratic nomination of McGovern and his flirtation with the Wallace vote in the United States. Moreover, there is the development of "social imperialism" (to use the Chinese terminology) and its economic and diplomatic offensive in important underdeveloped regions. An important modification of the earlier division of labor also is the subimperialist development of Brazil, South Africa, Iran, India, and perhaps other contenders along paths both similar to and different from those of Japan and Israel before them. And elsewhere in the underdeveloped world (again temporarily to borrow terms from the past), neofascist corporative trends also vie with neopopulist attempts to pave the way towards socialism from Bangladesh and Ceylon to Tanzania and Zambia to Peru and Chile. A further new or renewed dimension is the outbreak or threat of war between or among Third World states who turn their "nationalism" not only against the imperialist countries but, with imperialist backing in times of crisis, against each other.

In the face of this world crisis and the attendant critical problems in Latin America and elsewhere, the developmentalist (old dependence) theory, and indeed ideology, appears to be entirely bankrupt. It may be suggested that the once revolutionary new dependence theory as well, if not bankrupt, is at least short of ready cash to meet the immediate economic, political, and ideological demands of revolutonaries faced with the formation of strategy and tactics in the present circumstances. So it would seem in the varying circumstances of Brazil, Uruguay, Argentina, Chile, Peru, Venezuela, and Mexico, among others, and perhaps of Cuba as well. (This raises some doubt about the advisability of the belated export of "dependence" to Asia and Africa. "Third Worldism" already reached the peak of its influence in the metropolitan student revolts of 1968–1969.) Furthermore, the apparent similarity of the impasse of both the old and new dependence theories raises the question of how radically different they really were or are. Perhaps less so than some of us would like to have had it. We may observe with a reviewer of the commemorative 150th issue of *Trimestre Económico* that the erstwhile radical *desarrollistas*, who have taken over much of the still more radical new dependence analysis, now commemorate dependence in the pages of the most established journal of the continent while many of the writers themselves now occupy ministerial posts in their respective countries. So much has *part* of the new dependence analysis been accepted by the establishment that the assembled foreign ministers of Latin America, assembled in the White House, were able to reveal to President Nixon that foreign aid was flowing from Latin America to the United States. Much of the critique of foreign investment proposed by the analysts of new dependence has found its way into the restrictions on foreign investment enshrined in the code of the Andean Pact and recommended to others by the UNCTAD Secretariat. And at UNCTAD III, new dependence theory, the development of underdevelopment, and even subimperialism had gained currency in the official declarations of various delegates, grounds perhaps for considerably more concern than pride for the terms' inventors. Further reflections on the relations and differences between the old and new dependence theories we may leave to the critics below.

The new dependence theory has, of course, been the subject of various critiques and critics. We now examine, classify, and review—if not exhaustively answer—the principal tendencies reflected by those who have made special reference to me or my work. Before proceeding, however, we may observe that though my work has been no more than part of a wider current many critics have singled me out for special and often exclusive treatment as supposedly representative of the remainder, sometimes going so far as to claim explicitly or implicitly that a (successful) critique of this one example will do and hold for all. Perhaps this (inverse) preference may be traced to the critics' supposition that Frank offers a more easily vulnerable or destructible target, or a more visible one, or an earlier encountered one, or a supposedly more extreme one, or some combination of these. One thing is sure, and it has been clarified by the author and universally appreciated by friend and foe alike: the work has been internationally and consciously political and substantially inspired by the Cuban Revolution. Further, there is evident reason for the critiques, especially of the "Frankian thesis," to be reviewed by the present author.

The critiques and especially the critics seem to fall into three major groups: (1) the backward-looking right wing, (2) the traditional Marxist left, and (3) the forward-looking new left, with each of these divided into two subgroups. The belated (relative to its writing) publication of *Capitalism and Underdevelopment* in 1967 and 1969 in English and French and 1970 in Spanish was at first greeted by a favorable, if uncritical, reception in various left circles; some of this still continues (Alnin, Palloix). But the same also stimulated the critical reaction on the reactionary and liberal right (the John Birch Society's *American Opinion*) and the left liberals and social democrats of various stripes (Halperin, de Kadt, Sauvy, Mörner, Dedjer, Dalton, Alba, Pinto, the journal *Aportes*, and, in general, various contributors to the *Current Anthropology* symposium on "responsibility" and various reviewers in American academic journals).

The Critics of the Right

These critics from the right lack either the perspective, the competence, or the interest, or all three, to examine the argument on its own ground and still less, of course, to carry it forward onto higher ground. Their academic and political interest is to disqualify the argument and through their reviews to forewarn the unwary against it—by recourse to the "disqualifiers" that positivism has enshrined in the minds of its victims, empirical "error" and lack of "objectivity." With few exceptions, the critics from the conservative, liberal, and social demo-cratic right limit their reviews and critiques of the argument to highlighting minor empirical disagreements that are beside the point or steering the discus-sion all the way off the point and invectively charging that Frank's political com-mitment (but not so their own) precludes objectivity and therefore credibility or validity. They work to consider that Frank's book was a repetitive refurbishing of the imperialist thesis (which they thought dead). They accuse it of being ideo-logical rather than empirical, prophetic in tone rather than analytic in content, a particularly rigid brand of Leninism (notwithstanding the claim that the work is directed against the Communists). According to Timothy King at Queens' Col-lege, Cambridge (in *The Economic Journal*), as an objective indictment (whoever sought to indict?) the book is plainly inadequate, since the case for the defense (of capitalism) is not examined, let alone demolished. For King, only those who already know in their hearts that the capitalist system contains only exploiters and exploited are likely to be convinced of the truth of Frank's general thesis on the basis of the evidence put forward. And in his "reply" to the present author's critique of George Dalton and others' work on economic anthropology, the latter writes: "Frank hates social science that does not serve to justify revolution . . . His comment is not on economic anthropology. It is bombastic denunciation of almost everyone who does not share his revolutionary rage. There is no point in responding further to writing so full of anger and ideology." In the "discussion and criticism" section of the journal a reader observed that this sort of reply only demonstrates that the author lacks the means to meet the argument. So much for the critics from the right.

The Criticism of the Traditional Marxist Left

The major group of critics and critiques stems from the major Marxist parties and their official or unofficial spokesmen. Among these, we may distinguish par-ticularly the (A) Moscow and so inspired or aligned Communists and (B) the Maoists and Trotskyists. Among the former, the work and thesis—or the per-son—of Frank has come under the criticism, among others, of Victor Volski, Director of the Latin American Institute at the Academy of Sciences of the USSR; B. N. Brodovich, writing in *Latinskaya America* (Moscow); L. Becerra in *Problems of Peace and Socialism* (Prague); Renato Sandri, Latin American specialist of the Central Committee of the Communist Party of Italy; Ruggiero Romano in half a dozen places in Europe and Latin America; and Mauricio Lebendinsky of Argen-tina, Armando Córdoba of Venezuela, and José Rodrigues Elizondo in Chile.

These Communist Party criticisms in a way fall between those of the right wing and those of the new left, sharing some characteristics with one group and others with the other. With the new left, the Communist criticism shares the recurrent critique that Frank is not Marxist because he emphasizes distribution to the total or virtual exclusion of production or that he confuses the two in constructing the argument about capitalism. The merits of this critique, which is more seriously constructed by the new left, may more suitably be reserved for comment below, leaving for inquiry here the Communist *reasons* for this line of attack. These, in turn, would seem to be related to a second characterization that the Communist critics share with the new left: the timing of their counteroffensive. It is noteworthy that, although my articles have circulated and been the object of some isolated Communist sniper fire since 1963, the big guns were not turned on them until 1969 and especially 1970.

It may be suggested that this timing of the criticism is a consequence and reflection of the crisis referred to above and that it is designed, in its small way, to help effect a resolution one way or another. Why and how the new left responds to the crisis through its constructive critique may be examined below. Here we may inquire in what way or which direction the Communist parties wish to lead us. During much of the 1960s, the advance of the Cuban Revolution and its increasing attraction and prestige in Latin America and elsewhere obliged the traditional Communist parties—which were simultaneously battling on another ideological front with the Chinese—to adopt a relatively conciliatory attitude toward the Cuban policy and related positions in Latin America. In some cases they temporarily accepted armed struggle and in many they changed their tactical line or at least language. The by then classical formula of the "democratic" struggle against "external" imperialism and internal "feudalism" began to disappear from the Communist party programs: witness, for instance, the change as well in the electoral program in Chile from that of the Popular Action Front (FRAP) in 1964 and that of the Unidad Popular in 1970. Some Latin American Communist parties sent representatives to Havana in 1967, and others— including those of Brazil, Argentina, and Chile—sent their Secretary Generals to Moscow to make oblique but sufficiently transparent references to the effect that "petit bourgeois nationalists who deny the significance of international Marxism-Leninism have created a conception of local or continental exceptionalism . . . while accusing those parties that have remained loyal to the principles of Marxism-Leninism of being traditionalist, orthodox, and moderate." It was not until the end of the decade, and perhaps not accidentally until some time after the death of Che Guevara, that the Latin American Communist parties were again able to achieve substantial unity in "international Marxism-Leninism"— and to launch a general counteroffensive on a broad front, including targets even as diminutive as Frank.

In what direction, we may ask, is this Communist counteroffensive pointed? Politically, it is marked by the increasing economic and political rapprochement between the USSR and imperialism, marred only by potential conflict in South

East Asia and in the Middle East. The French Communist Party (the Secretary General of the Chilean Communist Party once said that it was the one that most resembled his own) declared itself to be "the party of order" during the 1968 revolt which, beyond mobilizing students, mobilized ten million workers in France. In Italy, the year-long "May" of 1969 and 1970 in Turin, Milan, and elsewhere obliged the Communist Party to follow, rather than to lead, the massive worker mobilization. More recently, as observed above, both parties have become admirers—and for their own purposes major propagandists—of "the Chilean Way." In Latin America, the Venezuelan Communist Party returned to "Democratic Peace" before splitting in two. Elsewhere, in the face of the crisis-generated increase in mass mobilization, the Communist parties have increasingly joined, promoted, and where possible led old or new popular, united, broad fronts. Are these Communist initiatives, or more accurately responses, to mobilize workers and peasants onto the road to socialist revolution, or are they to steer this objectively generated mobilization on to a peaceful road "to socialism"? The public self-criticism of the Brazilian Communist Party after the 1964 military coup was not that during the "progressive" Goulart regime it had been too moderate but that it had contributed to the coup by being too radical!

Cultural Revolution

Indeed, all these backward-looking, downright reactionary critiques, more than inviting an "answer," pose the question why this counteroffensive is in swing at all, why it is growing so fast, and why its self-appointed spokesmen dare to go so far—backward. It would be a mistake—and un-Marxist to boot—to suppose, as some of these protagonists suggest, that their latter-day reversion to the conventional wisdom of decades past is the product of divine inspiration or superior intelligence or even of plain down-to-earth realism, apparently so lacking among ordinary mortal students of "dependence." No, it is part and parcel of a reactionary political counteroffensive not only from the right but unfortunately also on the part of much of the left, which is itself the reflection of the political economic developments already alluded to and which now moves these ideological apprentices to turn the social scientific clock several decades backward.

Of course, the same economic political crisis and this same reactionary counteroffensive also sharpen the class struggle and generate political and ideological manifestations, analyses, and resolutions of the processes once discussed under the title of "dependence." These offer positive contributions to man's knowledge and liberation. The Tenth Latin American Congress of Sociology witnessed a flowering of several such critical contributions (see Olmedo, 1972). The Eleventh Congress, to be held in San José de Costa Rica in the crisis year of 1974, is likely to witness still more acute critiques of dependence after the disastrous failure of reformism in Chile and in view of the growing threat of fascism elsewhere. Hopefully some of these critiques will advance the analysis of the process of capital accumulation in the world as well as the successful pursuit of the revolutionary class struggle in Latin America.

2.4

A Theory of Imperialism, Not Dependence

Raúl A. Fernández and José F. Ocampo

The authors offer a systematic critique of dependency theory in the first part of their paper reproduced below. In their alternative, not included herein, they emphasize Maoism as a theoretical basis for revolutionary practice. This is assessed in two short rebuttals.

Dependence

THE THEORY OF DEPENDENCE has been developed as a critique of the traditional Marxist analysis and as a re-examination of the history of Latin America. In a certain sense, it has been presented by its authors as a *new* interpretation of Latin American economic and social development, and as the definitive refutation, not only of Marxists who distort historical realities, but also of bourgeois liberals who are apologists for the dependence of Latin American countries on the metropolis. There is no doubt that through this debate the most important aspects of Latin American revolutionary movements have been examined. On the one hand, the very nature of the economic system and its historical origin have been discussed. In this respect, the main attack of the *dependentistas* has been focused on the question of how to apply the Marxist conception of historical materialism, which divides history into modes of production and which

First published in *Latin American Perspectives* 1, vol. 1 (1), Sage Publications, Inc. Reprinted with permission from the Latin American Perspectives Collective. Selection from 31–39, 62–66.

establishes a relationship between feudalism and capitalism. The *dependentistas* have concentrated their attack against the interpretation that other sectors of the Latin American left have utilized, according to which Latin America had to pass through a "popular" democratic revolution to achieve national capitalism before the possibility of a socialist revolution, inasmuch as the economy had a feudal character; that is, it was not predominantly capitalistic. Through this approach, the theory of dependence sought to reject any kind of "deterministic" explanation of underdevelopment stemming from liberal bourgeois theories. On the other hand, the *dependentistas* have examined the determining conditions of the backwardness, poverty, and class domination that exist in Latin America and that have a direct relationship with imperialism.

Two themes—the character of Latin American society and its principal enemy—constitute the central aspects of a theory of the Latin American process. The first theme is related to the question of the historical development of capitalism; the second is related to the problem of imperialism. The principal merit of the *dependentistas* is that they have placed these two problems in the forefront of discussion. The great influence acquired by *dependentista* approaches in the United States and Latin America makes it imperative to carry out a scrupulous examination of the important points of this theory and to contrast it with what we understand the Marxist theory of imperialism and backwardness to be.

The Immediate Enemy

Nothing is more fundamental for revolutionary forces than the correct identification of their freinds and enemies. An error such as an alliance with enemies or an attack upon friends can determine, to some extent, the success of a revolution. Indeed, Mao placed much of the blame for the failure of pre-1926 revolutionary attempts in China on this kind of error. "The basic reason why all previous revolutionary struggles in China achieved so little was their failure to unite with real friends in order to attack real enemies" (Mao Tse tung, 1970: 13). The theory of dependence is also preoccupied with this point: every one of the main propositions of the theory has as its object the clarification of the problem of the immediate enemy and its determination in a precise manner (Cockcroft et al., 1972: 425–43; Frank, 1969b: 371–408). The conclusion which the *dependentistas* reach is an outcome of the historical and political premises upon which the theory of dependence is founded. There is a close relationship between the premises and the conclusions of dependence theory, although Frank is the only one who states it clearly:

> Tactically, the immediate enemy of national liberation in Latin America is the native bourgeoisie in Brazil, Mexico, etc., and the local bourgeoisie in the Latin American countryside. This is so—in Asia and Africa included—notwithstanding that strategically the principal enemy undoubtedly is imperialism. (Frank, 1969b: 371)

Frank clarifies this conclusion when he says that the anti-imperialist struggle through a class alliance in a united anti-imperialist front "does not adequately challenge the immediate class enemy, and generally it does not even result in a real and necessary confrontation with the imperialist enemy" (Frank, 1969b: 372).

Actually, the polemic begun by Frank revises a discussion of the relation of a revolutionary process to imperialism which was important in Lenin's political struggle in and outside of the Bolshevik party. Most directly concerned with this question is Lenin's work on the national question (especially during the Third International) and his refutation of the "imperialist economism" of Mr. Pyatakov (P. Kievsky) (Lenin, 1960; 1968; 1970). According to Lenin, imperialism is not just one among many possible foreign policies which happens to be "preferred" by finance capital (a position which he severely criticized when it was advanced by Kautsky); rather, it is the *necessary* foreign policy of finance capital. Any attempt to separate imperialism from capitalism in the present stage results in the artificial separation of the economic struggle from the political struggle, that is, "economism," or more correctly, "imperialist economism." In making a distinction between a *tactical* immediate enemy (local capitalism) and a *strategic* enemy (imperialism), Frank makes an artificial separation, similar to Pyatakov's, between capitalism and imperialism. This separation allows Frank to deny that imperialism is the immediate enemy and, consequently, to deny the need for class alliances. Although Frank ostensibly supports class alliances by the proletariat, in reality he negates any such alliances. He does this first by treating the peasantry as little more than an appendage of the proletariat without different specific interests that will influence the conceptualization of a revolution and secondly by treating the bourgeoisie as an undifferentiated class. As a result, there are only two classes left—the bourgeoisie and the proletariat—and thereby alliances for the proletariat are eliminated.[1] According to Lenin, any country dominated by imperialism has, as its immediate enemy, imperialism, and this fact makes the necessity of alliances imperative:

> The more powerful enemy can be vanquished only by exerting the utmost effort, and *without fail*, most thoroughly, carefully, attentively, and skillfully using every, even the smallest "rift" among enemies, of every antagonism of intent among the bourgeoisie of the various countries and among the various groups or types of bourgeoisie within the various countries, and also by taking advantage of every, even the smallest, opportunity of gaining a mass ally, even though this ally be temporary, vacillating, unstable, unreliable, and conditional. Those who fail to understand this, fail to understand even a particle of Marxism, or of scientific, modern Socialism *in general*. (Lenin, 1970b: 67)

Today, the *dependentistas* call imperialism dependence so as to give an explanation of Latin American underdevelopment. However, the subtle way in which they transform imperialism from the immediate enemy into the "strategic" enemy is misleading. To designate imperialism as a strategic enemy means that imperialism can only be defeated with a socialist revolution; that is, it is an enemy that cannot be confronted in the immediate battle but must wait until an initial victory has been obtained. Moreover, if the enemy (imperialism) *is* confronted immediately, the result—in terms of the dependence theory—will be the strengthening of the local dominant classes. Further, if one tries to confront imperialism in this way, in reality one *does not*.

The consequences of this theory for revolutionary practice are disastrous since they become the negation of the role the democratic struggle plays in the revolutionary process, the negation of national independence and of the right of self-determination, and the negation of the right of nations to secede. Since, for the *dependentistas*, the strategic enemy is imperialism and since the *socialist* struggle is the immediate result of the revolutionary struggle, it turns out that imperialism cannot be attacked before the revolution because it is detrimental to the struggle; and when the socialist revolution arrives, then it appears that the struggle against imperialism becomes superfluous. This is a way to deny in practice the anti-imperialist struggle.

The Character of Latin American Society

The *dependentistas* argue that Latin American backwardness is not due to the persistence of feudalism but to external dependence. The *dependentistas* refute the bourgeois theory of dualism—the traditional-modern dichotomy—and the diffusionism which is the result of this theory. But they also attack what Frank calls the traditional Marxist idea of "the need for a bourgeois democratic revolution" to destroy feudalism, to build capitalism, and then to set the stage for the socialist revolution.

By affirming that there is not, nor has there ever been any feudalism in Latin America, the *dependentistas*, and Frank in particular, can then logically conclude that there has always been capitalism from the time of the conquest in the fifteenth and sixteenth centuries. If bourgeois economists and sociologists were to say this, it would be understandable; for a Marxist who has even a cursory acquaintance with *Capital* to say this is absurd.[2] The feudal or capitalist character of a mode of production is determined by its relations of production or class; relations. It is not determined by its trade connections. The capitalist mode of production is commodity production so developed that labor-power has become a commodity and the owner of this commodity is "free" to sell it in the market. The relationship that Latin America maintained with the rest of the world during colonial times did not bring about a mode of production which divided Latin American society into capitalists and wage earners. During this time, Latin America was characterized predominantly by a mode of production whereby large aristocratic landowners extracted surplus through the enforced servitude of

Indians: firstly, in economic units characterized by subsistence levels of production and in units that marketed a surplus; and secondly, by plantations where local and foreign entrepreneurs extracted surplus through the slavery of imported Africans.

The predominant mode of production was determined by a coercive, feudal, lord-to-serf relationship similar to the situation prevalent in Spain at the time, although probably modified somewhat by Spanish contact with indigenous societies. On the plantations, the class relations were those of master-slave characteristic of a slave mode of production. A contemporary English aristocrat is a *capitalist* landowner and not a feudal lord if he employs wage workers on his lands and/or capitalist tenants who employ wage laborers and pay him rent. In the same manner, a capitalist entrepreneur who bought slaves and made them work as slaves, or an *encomendero* who enforced Indian servitude did not modify the relations of production of slave and feudal modes of production.

Responding to criticism on their characterization of colonial Latin America as capitalistic, the *dependentistas* have effected a tactical retreat: first, they spoke of capitalism pure and simple; then this became mercantile and industrial capitalism, and, finally, we have "mercantilism" and capitalism (Frank, 1969b: "Preface"; Bodenheimer (Jones), 1971; Cockcroft et al., 1972: "Introduction").

To resort to a subterfuge such as the distinction between mercantilism and capitalism to refute the feudal nature of Latin American backwardness is not a solution because, for the *dependentistas*, mercantilism is not capitalism—it is chosen precisely to dodge the criticism on the attribution of a capitalist character to Latin America in the sixteenth century—but it is not feudalism either, because this would destroy the premises of their theory. They view feudalism as ending with the incorporation of Latin America within the international capitalist system in the mercantile era. Thus, "underdevelopment in Chile is the necessary product of four centuries of capitalism itself" (Frank, 1967: 3).

This process is generalized to all of Latin America: "The present underdevelopment of Latin America is the result of its centuries-long participation in the process of world capitalist development" (Cockcroft et al., 1972: 7). And in a more recent article the position has been reformulated in this way: "Underdevelopment has been produced by the development of mercantilism and later industrial capitalism" (Cockcroft, 1972: xi). Subsequently, in Latin America the penetration of capitalism and incorporation within the world market brought about the dependence which caused and maintains underdevelopment. The interesting claim here is that from the moment of the *conquista*, capitalism penetrated all Latin American societies; and despite this penetration they were, *from the beginning*, underdeveloped and continue to be underdeveloped for the same reason. The question is, how can a society be completely capitalistic and underdeveloped?

What, then, is "underdevelopment"? There must be some reference point which allows one to determine, by comparison, the stage and degree of underdevelopment. The *dependentistas* appear to suggest such a point when they out-line the difference between *un*developed and *under*developed countries and when they define the advanced countries of today as never having been under-developed, as having gone directly from *un*development to development.[3] To jus-tify this distinction they use the notion of undeveloped countries in the sense of the *absence of market relations*. According to this logic, the *trade relations* that France—a backward country—had with England (an advanced country) in the seventeenth century would make the former *dependent* on the latter. In the case of France, this dependence relation evidently did not bring about under-development. With the exception of England, then, the whole world—in the *dependentista* sense—was dependent in the seventeenth century. Those countries which challenged their dependence upon England were the ones that were able to develop their own capitalism; and the countries that stayed dependent were the ones that did not develop their own capitalism. It turns out to be nonsense, then, to speak of dependence as a determining factor of underdevelopment since we can easily find countries that were *dependent* and are now *developed*. The theory of dependence runs into a blind alley and into its own denial as a scientific theory for its failure to resolve what it had proposed. Indeed, it has not produced anything but a vicious circle: underdevelopment is explained by dependence and dependence is explained by underdevelopment.

There are, however, two more alternatives to dependency theory. The first is that one could, in the abstract, define a model of a capitalist country: any country that did not match it perfectly would be defined as underdeveloped. But this approach is nothing more than the "bourgeois" position which leads to diffu-sionism and which has been rightly rejected by the *dependentistas*. The other alternative would be the application of historical materialism to the history of modes of production. This alternative eliminates completely the need to deter-mine development by comparison, and leads to the analysis of the nature of the development of productive forces as determinant in the appearance of different modes of production. Further, it leads to the consideration of quantitative changes leading to qualitative changes, and implies the existence of new elements in old forms and old elements in new forms. Thus, underdevelopment would be defined not in terms of dependence, which does not account for backwardness, but in terms of the strong or predominant persistence of feudal forms—in this case, the old elements—in the capitalist development of a country, as well as the advance of socialist forms of production in the contradictions that guide the development of capitalism. Without a certain amount of capitalist development in a country, socialism cannot arise; in the same manner, without the existence of capitalism in its most advanced form, imperialism, there can be no possibility of its destruction as an international system. It is this alternative explanation which we propose to develop.

Dependence and Capitalism

The basis for Latin American backwardness cannot be attributed to the capitalist character of its economies and their integration within the world capitalist system, but rather by the *lack* of capitalist development and the persistence of feudal forms in agriculture. We shall show that underdevelopment is nothing more than backwardness: a retardation brought about by feudal, semifeudal, and precapitalist remnants.

Part of the difficulty in clarifying the issue of Latin American backwardness arises from the tendency of some writers to identify a capitalist mode of production with any monetary economy. This description hides a premise which is fundamental to the *dependentista* analysis. This premise is the identification of any society which has a monetary economy as a society which has a predominantly capitalist mode of production. Historically, this premise has been an issue which has pitted Marxist historians against non-Marxist historians and one which has caused no small debate among Marxist theoreticians (Dobb, 1947: 194; Bettelheim and Sweezy, 1971; Edel, 1972). It must be made clear that this *dependentista* premise does not merely apply to Latin America today. In fact, it is a premise about the historical development of the economy of Latin America, and as such applies to economic development in general, with a number of immediate consequences.

First, is the denial of the existence of fuedalism before and during the twelfth century in Western Europe, by claiming that capitalism developed in that period. While it is true that the widespread development of a money economy eroded the basis of the feudal economy, the presence of a money economy within a society historically did not mean that the society was capitalist. One of the most fundamental principles of historical materialism is that new social and economic forms emerge from the contradictions inherent to an already existing, different social and economic form. To deny the presence of fuedalism in this period is, in terms of historical materialism, a denial of the very conditions which make the emergence of capitalism possible. In addition, to claim that *capitalism* is present during this period is to make impossible the differentiation of, for example, the system of land tenure in 1350 from that one century later.

Second, is the faulty characterization of the medieval traders as a revolutionary class. In fact, the medieval traders merely reaped the benefit of economic transformation brought about by other classes and conditions. It is easy to confuse the results of a transformation with the causes of the transformation itself. When the trade of this period is examined with scrutiny, it becomes clear that, if anything, these traders in fact hindered the development of capitalism. Trade in this period consisted almost entirely of high-profit, luxury goods; goods such as spices, wallhangings, and *objets d'art*. The landholding classes in this period invested the surplus value which they extracted from the serfs into consumption goods rather than into new and improved means of production. The traders themselves did not directly invest their profits into means of production. What profit these traders did not reinvest in trade was, for the most part, put back into the land! In Genoa during the thirteenth century, "even the greatest merchants . . . backed their commercial investments with very considerable investments in real estate" (Mandel, 1968, vol. 1: 106).

Another consequence is the denial of the revolutionary nature of the rapid industrialization of the nineteenth century. To a Marxist historian, the rapid industrialization in this period is one of the most revolutionary in the history of mankind. This is so for two reasons: first, this rapid industrialization created the most revolutionary class in modern times—the industrial proletariat; second, the process itself was not a peaceful, transitionary one, but one marked by violent, class struggle for the seizure of state power. Marx himself outlines this process with respect to France in *Class Struggles, 1848–1850* and *The 18th Brumaire of Louis Bonaparte*.

Yet another consequence is the denial of the revolutionary character of any industrial bourgeoisie (a logical outgrowth of the above consequence). It was precisely the revolutionary struggle of the industrial bourgeoisie which finally broke the political strength of the landed aristocracy.

A final consequence is the fundamental inability to make historical demarcations between different modes of production, thereby obscuring (if not in fact denying) qualitative changes in historical development. This is perhaps the most damning implication of a theory which professes to be a theory of revolutionary change. Unwittingly, the *dependentistas* have fallen into an obvious a priorism: They deny the existence of feudalism in Latin America and the revolutionary potential of some sectors of the bourgeoisie because they have assumed those two things at the most fundamental level of their premises.

The appearance of capitalism cannot be conceived as a sudden, unique act, occuring everywhere at the same time, but as a slow process of struggle against feudalism which responds to the fundamental contradiction between the forces of production and the relations of production, and which is reflected primarily in the violent class struggles that took place all over Europe between the bourgeoisie—allied with proletarians and peasants—and the feudal landowning aristocracies. In Spain, for instance, the nascent bourgeoisie was completely defeated and swept aside, leaving an open field to the feudal nobility.

The revolutionary aspect of the bourgeoisie is crucial in understanding the four-centuries-long struggle that it waged against the feudal aristocratic nobility in Europe. In Latin America, the bourgeoisie carried out a revolution against the (Spanish) colonial domination that prevented the development of their national productive forces. The wars of independence in Latin America were successful in their principal goal which was to obtain political independence from Spain. The revolution for independence opened Latin America to England (the vanguard of the world bourgeois Revolution) and this effected only a change from being tied to Spain to being tied to the capitalist monster, but it cannot be denied that it was an historically progressive movement. Spain dominated Latin America completely, politically and economically, and it thwarted most attempts at capitalist development; in this sense, it reproduced in Latin America the existing situation in Spain, where the landowning classes defeated the bourgeoisie. Although one should be cognizant of England's influence on Latin American countries during the nineteenth century—a harbinger of future imperialist development—it is nonetheless true that Latin American countries had, at this time, certain opportunities to develop along capitalist lines in much the same fashion as the United States and other countries did.

Their failure to do this stemmed generally from two causes: first, the bourgeoisie that carried out the fight against Spain was not an industrial bourgeoisie, but a commercial bourgeoisie; second, the landed feudal aristocracies—in alliance with the commercial bourgeoisie—retarded—in alliance with the incipient native manufacturing bourgeoisie. Thus, Latin America became accessible to the imperialist advance that began toward the end of the nineteenth century, and which we still witness today. This new attack was qualitatively different from the influence England exerted on the world during the early nineteenth century inasmuch as imperialism is an *advanced stage of capitalism*. If we apply the same concept of "dependence" to sixteenth-century Spanish domination, to the early nineteenth-century worldwide influence of England, and to contemporary imperialist domination, we are arbitrarily utilizing an historical concept which, in explaining everything explains nothing. According to Lenin,

> Colonial policy and imperialism existed before this latest stage of capitalism and even before capitalism. Rome, founded on slavery, pursued a colonial policy and achieved imperialism. But 'general' arguments about imperialism which ignore, or put into the background the fundamental difference of social-economic systems, inevitably degenerate into absolute empty banalities, or into grandiloquent comparisons like "Great Britain!" Even the colonial policy of capitalism in its *previous* stages is essentially different from the colonial policy of finance capital. (1967: 740)

The specific differences between classical capitalism and imperialism are discussed below.

Latin American underdevelopment can be historically explained by the failure of Latin American bourgeoisies to develop capitalism and to incorporate the area into the world capitalist system on a competitive footing. These bourgeoisies were first stymied by the national landowning class and then easily bought off by extranational imperialist forces, and this arrested the process of capitalist development. From the historical failure of the Latin American bourgeoisie, the *dependentistas* infer that the bourgeois democratic tasks have disappeared entirely from the revolutionary process. Our contention is that these tasks remain, and that the proletariat, rather than the bourgeoisie, must accomplish them.

The Methodological Critique

While most *dependentistas* have expounded upon the external forces causing dependence, new concept, the infrastructure of dependency, is used to describe the internalization of values which helps create and maintain dependence. This internalization is peculiar to "all classes and structures in Latin Society" (Bodenheimer (Jones), 1971: 164). Through this concept, the theory of dependence continues to perpetuate the artificial separation between tactical and strategic enemies and to insist on the notion of the local bourgeoisie as the immediate enemy. This theory of internalization is an attempt to explain the internal process of dependence which had been neglected by the original *dependentistas*. The problem of the relation between "external" cause—dependence—and the "internal" process is resolved with the creation of an infrastructure which enables the dependent countries to internalize the "need" to be dependent—a sort of social inferiority syndrome. Thus, even if the external cause—the dominant countries—were to disappear, the reality of dependence and the inferiority complex would persist. This *dependentismo* has consequences that are pernicious. Dependency would be recast as if Latin American people are dominated and dependent because they want to be, because they have assimilated the wish to be so. Does this mean that an "ideology of subjugation" has been created? The notion of "infrastructure of dependence" is a logical complement to the theory of dependence. Its emphasis on the penetration of "values of underdevelopment," without giving any indication of where revolutionary values might come from, is one-sided and can easily lead to a politics of quietism or desperation.

Although the relationship between the *dependentistas* and Marxist social theory is not clear, it is evident that they frequently utilize terms and modes of thinking borrowed from this tradition. The backbone of Marxist social theory is that the critic arrives (by way of the theory of successive modes of production) at a correct analysis of classes in a concrete situation which forms the base of an adequate strategy (and tactics) for the transfomation of society. Marxism, then, provides a coherent view of world history, and its categories have been tested and developed in practice in at least two major successful revolutions. Social hypotheses based on Marxist social theory can be examined against a theoretical background of revolutionary theory and practice. If there is no connection between the notion of metropolis-satellite—which is the cornerstone of Frank's argument—and Marxist social theory, his conclusions on the strategic and immediate enemies can only be tested by their immediate application to revolutionary practice.

Gunder Frank fails to relate his view of Latin America to the experience of other revolutions in the Third World. He places the Latin American revolution at the crossroads. Either the Latin American revolution coincides with the principal aspects of the Chinese revolution (anti-imperialist and antifeudal struggle) in which case his theory is destroyed or the Chinese revolution is denied; or, Latin

America is considered essentially different from China, in which case one has to reject Mao's analysis of imperialist domination and semifeudal structures, which Frank does do very effectively. It is inconceivable that the Latin American people could be asked to risk all in an effort to validate a theory that takes the lessons of revolutionary theory and history very lightly or not at all.

The theory of dependence does not explain the internal process of underdevelopment, arbitrarily attributes backwardness to external causes, says next to nothing about the contemporary nature of imperialism, and constitutes a good example of a careless use of Marxist theory. In view of these weaknesses, we feel that the theory of dependence should be rejected.

Maoism: An Alternative to Dependency Theory?

Timothy F. Harding

The importance of the critique of dependency theory by Ocampo and Fernández is twofold. First, it represents an attempt to counterpose a position which we can loosely call Marxist-Leninist-Maoist to both dependency theory as well as to the traditional theoretical approaches of the Communist parties allied with the Soviet Union. While Maoism is an important revolutionary current in Latin America, the creative application to Latin America by Latin Americans of the experience of the Chinese revolution as abstracted theoretically by the Chinese leadership is still in a beginning stage. As Cardoso and Frank point out, dependency theory had its roots in critiques both of traditional Communist analyses and of bourgeois-nationalist "structuralist" *desarrollismo*, but it was developed within a largely academic environment. This academic birthplace helped condition certain aspects of dependency theory: the implicit rather than explicit use of Marxism, the preference for jargon from bourgeois social science over Marxist terms (for example, imperialism is usually avoided and *marginalization* becomes very common). The relationship between Marxist revolutionary theory and academic dependency theory became unclear, particularly as a generation of students in the United States and Latin America who had not themselves carefully studied the classic Marxist writers assumed that dependency theory *was* revolutionary Marxism, and yet they did not find in dependency analysis any theory of action.

Furthermore, dependency's premise that dependency began with the conquest in Latin America conflicted with Lenin's insistence that imperialism represented a qualitatively different stage in capitalist development and the relationship between advanced capitalist countries and colonial areas and that this phase began in the late nineteenth century. Impatience with dependency theory drove many involved in praxis back to Marx, Lenin, and Mao and in Fernández and Ocampo's case to their critique of where they think *dependentistas* went off the Marxist trail.

Fernández and Ocampo see feudalism as the major cause of backwardness in Latin America and imperialism as the main reason for the survival of feudalism with which it is allied. This leads them to see the national bourgeoisie, or some sector of it, as a potential ally in the revolutionary process rather than as what the *dependentistas* call an instrument of imperialist domination. Although they direct their attack against dependency theory, their main disagreements with the traditional approach of the Moscow-oriented Communist parties in Latin America seem to be over how to build a revolutionary party, who the national bourgeoisie is, and what the nature of the alliance with it should be. Fernández and Ocampo might be willing to concede that most of the bourgeoisie is now supporting imperialism, but they seem to think that even some of these pro-imperialists are potential allies in the case of wars of national liberation against U.S. intervention. Since it is not within the scope of their argument, they do not give us any concrete evidence of significant sectors of the Latin American bourgeoisie, frustrated as they are by imperialism, breaking ranks with their foreign ally. Is it more dangerous for revolutionaries to damn the whole bourgeoisie as irredeemably dependent (the tendency of the *dependentistas*) or to feature the hope of a nationalist bourgeois revolutionary ally which would only appear in the case of large-scale foreign military intervention (as in China or Vietnam)?

Some of the *dependentistas* (Cardoso excepted) argue that neither the backward nor the advanced sectors of the economy can develop without a socialist revolution because of imperialism. Fernández and Ocampo agree that imperialism maintains backwardness, but they argue that because imperialism maintains feudalism, the only successful revolutionary strategy involves an alliance with the bourgeoisie. They do not tell us how they then propose to deal with the advanced capitalist sector of the economy after the seizure of power by a movement led by a revolutionary party based on the working class. We can presume it would be by socializing the advanced sectors. If a revolutionary party makes clear that it will expropriate the advanced capitalist sectors upon seizing power, how can it ally with the bourgeoisie? Does not this mean that during the struggle for power revolutionaries can only ally themselves with the most backward sectors of the urban bourgeoisie and the petty bourgeoisie, the intellectuals, and the peasantry? If this be the case, then could not the progressive sectors of the middle class and the peasantry be won by a frankly socialist program which points out to them that their aspirations would be won by a socialist revolution more effectively than by a movement which compromises with their direct and most visible oppressors, the national bourgeoisie?

The Paper Enemy

Fernando Henrique Cardoso

There are two polemics: that which clarifies, refines, and advances understanding and that such as the Fernández-Ocampo article, which is dogmatic and reaffirms positions which political practice has made obsolete. The authors unjustly lump all the *dependentistas* together and do not refer to the vast Latin American literature on the subject. Weffort (1970) made an opposite (and equally erroneous) critique to that of Fernández and Ocampo, accusing the *dependentistas* of ignoring the internal enemies and concentrating only on imperialism. The mistake in both cases artificially separates imperialism from its internal allies in the dominated country. The authors also ignore the context in which Frank set his position on the capitalist character of Latin America since the conquest, and they do not make any contribution by characterizing Latin America as semifeudal or with strong feudal remnants. The main contribution of dependency theory has been to get beyond the generality of imperialism and describe specific mechanisms and ties between the local and international structures. *Dependentistas* do not substitute for or invalidate the theory of imperialism. Nor do they claim that dependency produces only underdevelopment, for indeed there can be dependent *development*. Dependency must be analyzed historically to see how colonial slave dependency is different from feudal dependency. Some countries were never underdeveloped or dependent since both processes began only with the development of a world market and the exploitation of some states by others. Most Latin American agrarian economies are not capitalist or feudal but rather are colonial-latifundist. Thus the authors create *paper enemies* in the feudal lords and their imperialist allies. Further, they invent a growing gap between city and country while in fact industrialization, urbanization, and dependent capitalism follow developmental lines with great unevenness and regional differentiation. The principal enemy is not imperialism seen as something separate from local domination. The struggle against imperialism implies identifying its internal face, which is the local monopoly industrial-financial sector and the local bourgeoisie to which it is allied in both city and countryside.

Notes

1. Even though Frank's comments on the petite-bourgeoisie are vague, he appears, at least, very definitely opposed to any alliance with such groups by the proletariat.

2. *Dependentistas* such as Cardoso, dos Santos, and Frank are commonly regarded as social scientists in the Marxist tradition.

3. In this connection, Frank feels that "(t)he new developed countries were never *under*developed, though they may have been *un*developed" (Cockcroft et al., 1972: 3).

DEBATE TWO

Introduction

THE CONTINUING DEBATE over the relevancy of dependency theory appeared in another issue of *Latin American Perspectives* (no. 11), published in the fall of 1976. This effort was coordinated by Timothy Harding, who revisited the problems of nationalist development and the weak role of the nationalist bourgeoisie. Harding was interested in the extent to which radical *dependentistas* were returning to a Marxism based on Lenin and Trotsky, who saw imperialism as spreading capitalism throughout the world without permitting local bourgeoisies to play a major role. Harding's introductory synthesis was complemented by the criticism of Agustín Cueva. Frederick Stirton Weaver looked at the historical trajectory of capitalist development in Latin America by emphasizing U.S. imperialism as an underlying basis for underdevelopment in the region (see part I).

2.5

Dependency: Nationalism and the State in Latin America

Timothy F. Harding

In this brief review of traditional and contemporary interpretations of dependency, the author reveals the weakness of both sterile and mechanical Marxism and inadequate bourgeois theory of nationalist development. He stresses the relevance of imperialism and internal class struggle as opposed to the bourgeois dependentistas.

OUT OF THE MEETING of a sterile and mechanical Marxism and a plainly inadequate bourgeois theory of nationalist development, in the context of mass upsurge against the effects of imperialism, grew the variety of theories of *dependencia.* These theories should be seen not as a common set of firm conclusions, but as an intensive dialogue in which the Marxists, freed of the pressures of orthodoxy, had a chance at winning over the more radical bourgeois reformists in the face of experiences which consistently dashed the hopes for national capitalist reform in country after country, leading to the rapid radicalization of ever-larger numbers in a variety of groups from Aprista-type movements to Christian Democratic parties. The language of the debate has frequently been confusing, as Marxists replaced their terminology with *metropolis, periphery, marginalization,* and so on, borrowed from bourgeois social science in order to facilitate the dialogue. Students unfamiliar with Marxist writing on imperialism

First published in *Latin American Perspectives* 11, vol. 3 (4), Sage Publications, Inc. Reprinted with permission from the Latin American Perspectives Collective. Selection from 4–5, 7–9.

frequently assumed that all dependency writers were Marxist since they all shared a common terminology and a concern with opposing the negative effects of foreign investments and since some of them were Marxists. On the other hand, some Marxist critics of dependency theory, emphasizing the differences between dependency theories and traditional Marxism, said that none of the *dependentistas* were Marxists. The debate within dependency was between those whose primary objective was the defense of the national bourgeoisie against imperialism and those whose objective was a socialist revolution led by the working class. The instability of the bourgeois–working-class alliance against imperialism was reflected in the debate as well as the confusion within dependency theory (Cueva, 1976; Fernández and Ocampo, 1974; Laclau, 1971; Ocampo, 1975; Frank, 1974).

The new writers using terms of dependency frequently did not make clear the relationship between their theory and Marxist-Leninist theory of imperialism, and when they attempted to do so they sometimes misrepresented or distorted Marxist-Leninist theory. This led to considerable confusion about whether those who used dependency terminology were Marxist. Were those who, in different language, used dependency terminology expressing Leninist concepts of imperialism, or had the Leninist concepts been dismissed as irrelevant without being tested in the light of current empirical research? Some Marxists rejected the dependency terminology because they felt it implied that all power and initiative was located in the advanced imperialist countries, when in fact the advanced countries *depended* on the backward countries for their surplus value. In addition, dependency concepts ignored the fact that imperialist strategies were frequently responses to initiatives from forces in the exploited countries. Domination was never complete, and the history Latin America reflects is a constant struggle against outside exploitation as well as an internal class struggle. Dependency was thus seen as a misleading euphemism for the violence of domination which could lead to hopelessness and passivity. . . .

Lenin argued that imperialism spread capitalism to the whole world, and, as a result, a certain capitalist development continued to take place although it was characterized by great unevenness and concentration in certain geographic areas and economic sectors. Some precapitalist forms were reinforced by imperialism, but at the same time the spread of capitalism was constantly undermining them. Thus the alternatives were not necessarily imperialism and stagnation on one side and socialism and development on the other. Some countries experienced prolonged stagnation and decay under imperialism while others had periodic booms. The question for those that did experience economic growth under imperialism was, what was the character of this growth and whom did it benefit? How would it affect the welfare of the great majority of the people? (Lenin, 1970; Cueva, 1976). As Girling (1976) points out for Jamaica, capitalist growth is accompanied by serious deterioration in the living conditions, health, and well-being of the majority of the population. There is a considerable body of literature on the negative effects of the Brazilian and Mexican "miracles" on the majority of the population.

The current within dependency ideas distinct from Marxist-Leninist theories of imperialism is essentially that held by the technocrats, intellectuals, and military officers identified with what is left of the national bourgeoisie in Latin America. When it became evident in the 1950s that the application of import substitution industrialization (ISI) had led not to independent national development, but to a more incisive penetration of Latin America by multinational corporations, the technocrats who had held the ISI position divided into those who accepted, welcomed, and facilitated a closer amalgamation with foreign capital, like Roberto Campos in Brazil or Milton Friedman's "Chicago boys," who advise the military junta in Chile, and on the other hand those like Celso Furtado who moved toward radical "dependency" positions. At the state level, the national bourgeois dependency theory was articulated by the Peruvian military government after 1968 (Quijano, 1975), the Ovando and Torres political regimes in Bolivia (Zabaleta Mercado, 1974), and the more conservative thinkers within the Allende coalition in Chile. Perhaps Fernando Henrique Cardoso represents this position in Brazil (Myer, 1975), and the Chilean Osvaldo Sunkel (1970) is also a leading exponent of this position. The Andean Group strategies are based on this current of dependency ideas (Droucopoulos, 1976; Vaitsos, 1973; 1974).

The central question for this group of national bourgeois *dependentistas* is how to build a national capitalism within an overwhelming imperialist framework. The assumption here is that socialism is not on the immediate agenda (even in Chile under Allende) and that reforms of capitalism based on a thorough understanding of "dependency" can lead to independent national development. Many different facets of society are analyzed to show how the foreign controls operate inside the underdeveloped country in the fields of credit, industrialization, technology transfer, and culture (architecture, education, mass media, science). In the process of trying to design a strategy to overcome dependency within capitalism, these theorists concentrate on a frequently very enlightening description of symptoms. They avoid an analysis of the cause of these phenomena: how surplus value is extracted by imperialism and distributed (O'Brien, 1973). They play down the importance of class struggle, portraying the majority of workers as passive, "marginal," and misled. For them, the division of society into classes is less important than the subdivisions within classes into "dependent" and "autonomist" sectors (Sunkel, 1970; Cardoso, 1973b and 1973d). Just as the underdeveloped country is seen as passive victim, so the workers and peasants are seen as passive, marginal outsiders without a history of struggle. As Droucopoulos (1976) points out, bourgeois nationalist dependency theorists stay within the framework of capitalism. Thus they have no adequate strategy for resisting imperialism. (The Marxist view, on the contrary, sees the history of Latin America as one of class struggle stretching from native resistance to European colonization to the contemporary land seizures, strikes, etc.)

This nationalist dependency view looks to the state or grouping of states as the instrument of struggle against dependency (Fernández and Ocampo, 1975). Examples of such instruments include the Andean Pact, the Caribbean Free Trade Association, the Peruvian and Bolivian (under Ovando) oil nationalizations, Juan Perón's policies on his return to power in 1973, the attempt of Mexican President Luís Echeverría Alvarez through the Sistema Económico Latino Americano (SELA) to lead a Latin American movement to renegotiate terms with the United States, the attempt to build raw material export cartels like OPEC for oil, and the pressure to expand the state sector and reduce the role of multinational corporations. Studies of how the multinationals extracted profit and used financial transactions between affiliates to transfer profit abroad, avoiding state control, were circulated, leading to demands by national bourgeoisies for a larger share of profits (Droucopoulos, 1976). It was found that all Latin Americans depended on the U.S. Chamber of Commerce for their information on U.S. corporations. Centers have recently been established in Mexico and Colombia to provide this information (Wionczek, 1971; Vaitsos, 1973; 1974). However, as Galli points out (1976), international agencies such as the UN are transformed into agents of foreign private corporations, and thus may provide no defense for national capitalism.

A contradiction developed between the increasing knowledge of the harmful effects of foreign investment and the constant undermining of well-meaning attempts to control it through the national state. Each high point of national or regional control (Ovando and Torres in Bolivia, Peruvian and Venezuelan oil nationalization and mineral extraction laws, Article 24 of the Andean Pact, the law to nationalize credit in Argentina) was followed by an erosion of the nationalist position through the "discretionary" clauses which allow the local government to make exceptions to the general rule. Thus the technicians of nationalist safeguards who see the answer to dependency in carefully constructed regulations are doomed to failure when temporary economic difficulties pressure a precarious regime in need of credit and good World Bank and IMF ratings to make concessions (Girling, 1976). The government boards safeguarding against foreign control are usually made up of local representatives of the very foreign corporations they are supposed to control. If these mechanisms are not sufficient to protect the foreign corporations from nationalist pressures, the CIA is used to influence the political situation in the country, and the corporations themselves can use bribery. At the same time there are indications that the multinational corporations, in the face of nationalist pressures, are beginning to prefer funneling their investment through the state or regional grouping instead of directly investing in production. International banks are an increasingly important mechanism through which foreign capital and foreign pressures operate (Galli, 1976). The result is that government enterprises in credit, extraction, or manufacturing directly exploit the worker, and profit is returned to the foreign corporation through repayment on loans, licensing fees, management contracts, etc.

(Fernández and Ocampo, 1975). This gives the foreign corporation more security against expropriation, but the state is then transformed from a defensive mechanism against foreign capital into a disguised instrument of foreign control, with the private and international banks acting as intermediary instruments (Girling, 1976; Hayter, 1971). Galli (1976) shows how the UN agencies function as instruments of multinational corporations in underdeveloped countries. Without a revolutionary party which can make clear the connections between what would otherwise seem to be separate processes, it is very difficult to expose the state as a mechanism for imperialist penetration and mobilize workers and their allies against these facets of imperialism.

Perhaps the most serious weakness of the bourgeois *dependentistas* is their tendency to ignore class conflict internally in the backward as well as the advanced countries (Cueva, 1976). Bourgeois dependency theorists naturally view the basic contradiction as dependency vs. national development, not workers vs. the owners of the means of production. They tend to view workers as passively manipulated and co-opted and to view the radical intellectuals as the only force capable of effectively combating dependency (Droucopoulos, 1976). This view has been discredited by the resurgence of labor militancy in Argentina, Bolivia, and Chile in the 1968–1973 period, as well as by the growing racialism of labor all over Latin America (*Latin American Perspectives,* 1976).

2.6

Problems of Dependency Theory

Agustín Cueva
Translated by José Villamil and Carlos Fortín

This critique suggests that dependency theory conflicts with mainstream sociology and traditional Marxism. This ambiguity allows understanding of the weaknesses of dependency theory.

DEPENDENCY THEORY has developed from two different perspectives. On the one hand it is a repudiation of bourgeois sociology and its interpretations of Latin American history, opposing such theories as that of structural dualism, functionalism in all its interpretations, and, of course, the "desarrollista" approaches. It has served a positive critical function without which it is impossible to imagine the current orientation of academic sociology in Latin America. On the other hand it emerges in conflict with, and as an alternative to, what has been called "traditional" Marxism.

A certain paradox exists in that dependency theory criticizes bourgeois thinking from a perspective near to Marxism, while at the same time it criticizes Marxism-Leninism from a perspective full of concepts taken from bourgeois social sciences and the "desarrollista" approaches. The best example of this confusion in dependency theory is the discussion on feudalism and capitalism in Latin America: to make sense of André Gunder Frank's thesis that Latin America has been capitalist since the Spanish-Portuguese conquest one has to abandon Marx's notion of capitalism and equate capitalism simply with money economy.

First published in *Latin American Perspectives* 11, vol. 3 (4), Sage Publications, Inc. Reprinted with permission from the Latin American Perspectives Collective.

Dependency theory has in fact sought to become a "neo-Marxism" without Marx.

The ambiguity which arises from this has even weakened the criticism made of bourgeois theories of development and underdevelopment in that the critics remain very much within their frames of reference. An example is provided by Frank's polemic on whether Parsons's universal values are more characteristic of underdeveloped than developed countries (Frank, 1969c). This overlooks the main problem with Parsons's analysis, which is that of substituting superficial effects and their consideration for the analysis of the underlying structures. The same could be said of Rodolfo Stavenhagen's treatment of structural dualism (1968). Although he criticizes the use of this concept, he merely transposes meanings and continues to utilize it. Thus, no longer is the traditional sector responsible for underdevelopment, but rather the modern sector. This is the basis of the "internal colonialism" idea, although he later modified it somewhat by reference to the Marxist notion of "combination of modes of production." In these authors there is a replacement of exploitation and class conflict by an *indeterminate* system of national and regional contradictions which pose serious problems from a theoretical point of view. This substitution, which makes nations and regions the ultimate actors, confers on dependency theory a nationalist character. This is not to say that there are no international contradictions, but that the class nature of these contradictions should be emphasized: they are derivative, and only under certain specific conditions can they become the principal ones.

Notwithstanding its criticism of traditional development thinking, dependency theory is still very much within that tradition and suffers from an "economicista" perspective. Traditional development thinking in the 1960s substituted the search for the obstacles to "rapid and balanced socio-economic development" for the previous and more crucial question of class conflict and exploitation. It thus assumed that such development *can* be achieved under capitalism. For a Marxist, of course, the basic question is what *kind* of development, capitalist or socialist.

Theotônio dos Santos argues that the dependency view extends the theory of imperialism and contributes to its reformulation (1970: 41–42). Dos Santos holds that Lenin did not study the impact of foreign investment in the colonies, wrongly assuming that it would lead to economic growth (1972: 80). The fact is that dos Santos confuses the worldwide expansion of capitalism with economic growth in the periphery. Lenin referred to the former and not the latter, further emphasizing the unequal-development effect of capitalism.

The problem seems to be that dos Santos assumes that had it not been for dependency Latin America would have had a much more rapid and balanced economic growth. The fact is that dependency theory exponents possess a nostalgic longing for a frustrated autonomous capitalist development, which is precisely what makes dependency theory so nationalist in its ideology.

Although the dependency theorists have made notable contributions and the concept of external dependence is essential in order to understand Latin American history, it is also true that the concept of dependence has very serious short-comings, especially when it is isolated from basic concepts such as forces of production, social relations of production, class, and class conflict or when these are replaced by ambiguous categories such as "outward growth," "colonies of exploitation," "colonies of population," "traditional groups," "modern groups," "social integration," and others.

We have, of course, in mind Cardoso and Faletto's book *Desarrollo y depen-dencia en América Latina* (1969), a book whose main points are difficult to orga-nize and discuss because it utilizes two theoretical frameworks, Marxist and "desarrollista," and it lends itself to two interpretations depending on what you emphasize and what specific meaning you attribute to the concepts used.

Beyond the ambiguity of theoretical concepts used, this book has many gaps in its historical analysis due to the failure to apply fundamental concepts such as those mentioned above. For instance, in the chapter called "The Fundamental Situation in the Period of 'Expansión hacia afuera'" (externally oriented growth), the following basic elements are omitted: first, the precapitalist charac-ter of the Latin American economies at the beginning of the period, implying a certain concrete articulation of modes of production and thus of classes, which would in turn determine the way in which these countries became linked to world capitalism; second, the process of original accumulation in Latin America resulting from the break of colonial ties; third, and most important, the class conflict which developed as a consequence in the post-colonial experience. The book does not even mention the invasions in the Caribbean by the United States, creating colonial or semi-colonial situations without which it is impossible to understand that region's history and which are ill-described by the ambiguous term "enclave."

In general, it is the analysis of classes and class conflict which is the Achilles' heel of dependency theory. To begin with, the most important actors, and almost the only ones, are the oligarchies and the bourgeoisie and, in the best of cases, the middle sectors. When the popular sectors make an appearance it is only as passive and manipulated masses. Yet, there are many events which cannot be explained without introducing them as active actors. It is symptomatic that there have been no studies on the subordinated classes arising from the dependency theory perspective.

But even the study of the bourgeoisie suffers from the theory's inadequate understanding of Marxism. Thus the analysis of the national bourgeoisie starts by lamenting its lack of revolutionary qualities and ends by denying its very exis-tence. The same can be said about the studies on the oligarchy, a term which is also ambiguous. It is claimed by writers of the dependency school that one of the unique aspects of dependent capitalism is the fact that this traditional oligarchy is not in antagonistic contradiction with the industrial bourgeoisie, as is the case in "classical" capitalism. But this is a spurious argument, since the development of capitalism, whether classical or otherwise, does not eliminate the landlord sector but converts this group into a nonhegemonic sector of the bourgeoisie, and this has certainly happened in Latin America.

But this suggests another problem, the attempt by dependency scholars to distinguish between classical and dependent "models" of capitalism. Although it is undeniable that the history of Latin America differs significantly from that of the advanced countries and from the classic development pattern, it is confusing to argue that there are two ideal types of capitalism. In fact, from a Marxist point of view, what you have is not "patterns" or "models" but laws, such as the law of development of capitalism, which hold true in Latin America and elsewhere, to be sure within particular historical conditions. Yet, one has to be careful that one does not define each particular case as a theoretically unique one. What happens is that the particular conditions speed up, for instance, the passage from competitive to monopoly capitalism, or spare Latin America the "industrial revolution." This is the "particularity" of Latin American development, which is clearly not "uniqueness." It is wrong to make the distinction between classical and dependent capitalism the main axis of the analysis of Latin America's problems. The substantive element is capitalism; "dependent" is the adjectival element. We must therefore rely on the analysis of the laws of capitalist development. Even somebody as rigorous as Ruy Mauro Marini (1973: Ch. 5 and 6) falls into error by his insistence on differentiating classical and dependent capitalism. He argues that in the latter it is the consumption by the high-income groups which provides dynamism to the economy, whereas in classical Marxism it would be the consumption of the masses. But this appears as an exaggeration on Marini's part; certainly in Latin American countries there is some popular consumption which is responsible for some dynamism of their economies. Recognizing the obvious differences in the development of Latin America and the development of the "advanced" countries, it is also necessary to recognize that these differences are not sufficient to call forth a new theory with its own laws. Dependence does not constitute a unique mode of production or a particular phase of another mode of production. It is merely the concrete form of existence of some societies. Our conclusion is that there is no theoretical space within which to locate a "theory of dependency."

In addition to the problems already mentioned, there is the additional one of the treatment of external and internal factors in dependency theory. This frequently leads to mechanical schemes in which external factors are determinant. Frank, although he defends himself from the accusation, has been the main exponent of the view that external factors are determinant (1970: 14). Thus, he points out that in the case of Chile, it is only when it became disengaged from world capitalism in the period 1940–1948 that its industrial production grew most rapidly (1967). But this view that the crisis in the center was responsible for a policy of import substitution which permitted the Chilean economy to grow overlooks very important developments within Chile, such as the establishment of a Popular Front government in 1938. All of this demonstrates the limits of a theory which seeks to supplant Marxism by substituting import substitution for class conflict as the motor of change (understandable in terms of the political limitations of ECLA [Economic Commission for Latin America] analyses). Of course, some writers such as Cardoso and Faletto have attempted to overcome the limits of this mechanical approach (1969). But even they fall into the error of studying the state without reference to the class structure. Thus, one cannot analyze the contradictions between an independent national state and a dependent economy without reference to the class nature of the state. This is a point made by Weffort (1971) in his criticism of Cardoso and Faletto.

In conclusion, dependency theory holds that the nature of our social formations is dependent on how they are integrated with the world capitalist system. But, is it not more correct to state the inverse? Is it not the nature of our societies that determines their links with the capitalist world? It seems to us that this is a more correct formulation. Thus, for example, if Bolivia after the 1952 revolution had followed a similar course to that of the Cuban Revolution, it would not today be a dependent country. It is interesting to note that not a single study has been done on the Cuban Revolution from the dependency theory perspective and that Cardoso and Faletto fail to mention the Cuban case in their book.

The Cuban Revolution, however, is at the very root of the sociological emergence of dependency theory; it contributed to the radicalization of large sectors of middle-class intellectuals, both inside and outside Latin America, who did not have organic ties with the workers' movements (and in some cases were, in fact, proud of it, as with the *Monthly Review* group). As these intellectuals convinced themselves that they could replace the proletariat in its revolutionary task (a proletariat that had been "co-opted" by the center) it is consistent that they should reject the notions of "exploitation" and "class" and place all the emphasis on "dependence" and "nation." If this hypothesis is correct, it could also help explain the relative decline of dependency theory at the end of the 1960s. This would coincide with a resurgence of proletarian struggle in Latin America: the *cordobazo* in Argentina, the Bolivian experience of 1970–1971, the Unidad Popular in Chile.

But, does this mean that dependency is dead? It isn't, and no one has tried to deny its existence for it represents a salient feature of our societies. The many studies which have been made on it are still relevant and will continue to be relevant. What has perhaps stopped being relevant is that something called the theory of dependency. It represented a set of ideas linked by the central concept that all our history can be explained by the contrasts "center-periphery," "metropolis-satellite," or "classical capitalism-dependent capitalism" and one which could accomodate writers from the ECLA school to neo-Marxists.

It is this sociological movement which is in decline. Some, like Aníbal Quijano (1973), have completely broken with it and returned to Marxism-Leninism, returning to relevance the contributions of one of its most important Latin American exponents, José Carlos Mariátegui.

DEBATE THREE

Introduction

FROM THE INCEPTION of the journal, it was clear that there were problems with the dependency approach. There was no universal theory. Yet dependency had opened up new questions and areas of investigation and stimulated interest in new ideas about the failure of capitalist development in Latin America. There was concern about theoretical weaknesses, confusion over terminology, undue emphasis on market rather than production, and so on, but a major concern of the editors was the relevancy of dependency to Marxism. The theorists of dependency rarely referred to or cited Marx, Lenin, or other important writers of earlier generations. Yet in their writings these theorists often implied that their thought was founded on Marxist premises, and many of them envisioned revolution and socialism as outcomes for the impoverished nations of Latin America. Thus, it was appropriate to launch a third effort examining dependency. Initially, it was probably the assumption of the editors that the ensuing debates in issues 30 and 31, published respectively in summer and fall 1981, would bring resolutions to old and new questions. In fact, these debates opened up new considerations, as the dependency idea continued to permeate submissions to and articles published in the journal. A portion of the introduction to the debate appears below, along with an update on sources at the time of publication. Some of the content of this issue appears in part III (below, see Barkin and Henfrey essays), and all of it appeared in book form in a series of monographs published by *LAP* (Chilcote, ed., 1982).

2.7

Issues of Theory in
Dependency and Marxism

Ronald H. Chilcote

*The essay below searches for dependency theory in the writing of Marx and classical
Marxism in an effort to assess the relationship, if any, of dependency to Marxism.*

W HAT ABOUT THE RELATIONSHIP of dependency to a theory of Marxism?
The idea of dependency is suggested in the writings of Marx. In chapters
24 and 25 of the first volume of *Capital,* Marx describes the relationship between
rich and poor countries. In chapter 20 of volume three he states that merchant's
capital "functions only as an agent of productive capital. . . . Whenever merchant's capital still predominates we find backward nations. This is true even
within one and the same country . . ." (Marx, 1967, vol. 3: 372). Kenzo Mohri
(1979) writes that until the late 1850s Marx strongly believed British trade and
industrial capital would destroy monopolistic societies and establish the material
foundations of Western capitalism in Asia; this view is evident in a passage from
the *Communist Manifesto,* in his writings on India (in 1853), and in numerous
passages from *Grundrisse* (1857–1859). Mohri argues that Marx shifted ground
in the middle 1860s, in particular in his writing on the Irish question; one passage in chapter 15 of the first volume of *Capital* resembles the idea of development of underdevelopment: "A new and international division of labor, a

First published in *Latin American Perspectives* 30 and 31, vol. 8 (3 and 4), Sage Publications, Inc. Reprinted with permission from the Latin American Perspectives Collective.
Selection from 13–15.

division suited to the requirements of its chief centers of modern industry, springs up and converts one part of the globe into a chiefly agricultural field of production, for supplying the other part which remains a chiefly industrial field" (Marx, 1967, vol. 1: 451). Mohri concludes that Marx was moving toward a view in which British free trade was transforming the old society into the world market system so that "the resulting transformation of this society would determine a course of development of its economy and a structure of its productive powers completely dependent upon England" (Mohri, 1979: 40).

Lenin also referred to the idea of dependent nation and periphery. In *Imperialism: The Highest State of Capitalism,* he stated, "Not only are there two main groups of countries, those owning countries, and the colonies themselves, but also the diverse forms of dependent countries which, politically, are independent, but in fact are enmeshed in the net of financial and diplomatic dependency . . ." (Lenin, 1967, vol. 1: 742–43). Cardoso suggests that Lenin provided the first systematic analysis of capitalist development in backward nations when he "formulated with simplicity what would be the core of the dependency analyses" (Cardoso, quoted in Palma, 1978).

A systematic review of the writings of Marx and Lenin may demonstrate support of contemporary dependency theory. Gabriel Palma (1978) devoted some attention to such a review but concluded that approaches to dependency have not really succeeded in building a formal theory and assessment of concrete situations of dependency. Carlos Johnson suggests that Lenin took the concept of dependent nations from bourgeois political economists but that he was guided by materialist reasoning and theoretical analysis. Gary Howe is correct in his view that Marx had not fully developed any systematic analysis of dependent relationships, believing that dependency theory was not based on formulations by Marx. Although Joel Edelstein and Dale Johnson agree that no general theory of dependency has emerged, they believe that the past work on dependency must be used as a foundation for future investigation. Henfrey, Barkin, Chinchilla and Dietz, and Petras all believe that theoretical analysis will profit from new directions, while Weeks insists on a restoration of classical materialist theory in a Marxist tradition.

Does dependency reflect only the needs of competitive capital in the face of monopoly capital in countries where the capitalist mode of production is not dominant? Carlos Johnson answers affirmatively by illustrating his position with a critical analysis of Cardoso and Marini. Howe effectively relates dependency to the failure in Brazil to establish a national alliance of the bourgeoisie and working class to promote autonomous national development. The question is not directly addressed by other contributors, but most, I suspect, would recognize the political implications of class alliances that obscure recognition of class enemies.

What of the significance of dependency for analysis of class and class struggle in Latin America? A decade ago specialists were insisting that theory and investigation incorporate a class analysis. Yet today there remains a dearth of such work. The mode-of-production approach suggests the possibility of empirical study on the class relations of production. Class analysis using other approaches has been suggested. In general, there is agreement that dependency theory has not yet contributed significantly to the study of social classes in Latin America.

Finally, has dependency theory provided any developmental solutions for Latin America? The contributors would answer negatively. Dependency theory served the purpose of questioning old and static formulations, especially in bourgeois thinking, but also in questioning rigid ideas emanating from the Stalinist period and the Communist International's models of underdevelopment and class alliance. The latter models incorporated a unilinear perspective of feudalism and capitalism and called for alliances with the national bourgeoisie. As Munck suggests, even the Communist Party of Mexico recently recognized that dependency theory had confronted these old schema of the Comintern and the Latin American communist parties. It is also clear that dependency theory was conceived as a response to the inadequacies of theories of imperialism in explaining the impact of capitalism on domestic structures of the less developed countries. Most contributors would agree, however, that dependency theory has not provided us with any new theory of imperialism. Nor has it demonstrated any way to solve the problems of capitalist exploitation. Likewise, it seems not to offer any strategy for achieving socialism, and it has not been used to analyze relations of production in the transition to socialism.

In summary, while many contributors acknowledge the fact that questions of dependency stimulated new questions and interesting analyses of Latin America, there is also agreement that past work has suffered from many problems. Those interested in dependency have recognized that no general and unified theory exists and that confusion over terminology has diverted investigation away from central concerns. The criticisms raised in this discussion and elsewhere are numerous. It has been argued that some theories of dependency distort the thought of Marx and Lenin. Idealism and ideology permeate the writing on dependency. Some versions of dependency focus on the needs of competitive capital and thus appear to be supportive of the dominant classes in Latin America. Dependency may divert attention from the impact of imperialist penetration or overlook the importance of precapitalist social formations. Dependency theory may emphasize static categories so that dynamic and dialectical analysis is not possible. Class analysis, for example, is often lacking due to stress on relations of exchange rather than on relations of production.

Given these criticisms, all the contributors suggest that theory and investigation must advance. Some, such as Carlos Johnson and Weeks, urge a return to classical Marxist conceptions of international capital. Others, like Dale Johnson and Edelstein, believe that Marxist formulations do not necessarily lead to adequate analysis of the contemporary world capitalist system; and thus, new concepts and theory building may correct this deficiency. Barkin refers to the need for and approach to the study of the internationalization of capital. Dietz and Chinchilla write on the usefulness of the modes-of-production approach, while Henfrey argues that we must go beyond such analysis toward work on imperialism and class struggle. Petras reinforces this position, while Howe stresses relations of production, and Angotti is concerned about class alliance and political strategy in the struggle against imperialism. It seems clear that the task in the decade ahead necessitates not only familiarity with the classical Marxist texts and theories of imperialism but the development of theory and investigation that benefit from close examination of relations and modes of production, specifically class analysis of social formations that allows attention to state-class relationships and the impact of the internationalization of capital.

2.8

Imperialism and Dependency:
Recent Debates and Old Dead Ends

Ronaldo Munck

An update of the assessment and literature review initiated by Latin American Perspectives *in 1974, the excerpt from this article delves into how Marxism and imperialism relate to dependency.*

> Dependency theory has not died. It still permeates the analysis and theory of the left. . . . That is why the ideological struggle against this theory is not something of the past; it is an urgent task for today. (*Debate*, 1981: 5)

THUS CONCLUDES Thesis 15 of the recent Nineteenth Congress of the Mexican Communist Party. Whether this is representative of the current relation between Marxism and dependency theory and whether an adequate theory of imperialism has superseded the now soundly criticized tenets of the dependency theorists are questions I will try to answer in a review of recent (and not so recent) contributions to the "dependency debate."

Latin American Perspectives opened its pages with a thorough balance sheet of dependency studies by Ronald Chilcote (Chilcote, 1974). This was in reality a synthesis of the dependency literature as the title announced. After careful reconstruction of the main lines of debate, Chilcote pointed to a number of common assumptions "in the hope that they might guide the reader to further under-

First published in *Latin American Perspectives* 30 and 31, vol. 8 (3 and 4), Sage Publications, Inc. Reprinted with permission from the Latin American Perspectives Collective. Selection from 162–163, 166–169, 170–173.

standing, constructive critique, and refinement of dependency theory" (Chilcote, 1974: 21). However, the element of understanding and constructive critique was to be notably absent from some subsequent contributions. Perhaps such guidelines only lead to anodyne, uncontroversial reviews of the literature. Not so, as shown by Kyle Steenland in a later issue when he tackled the thorny question of feudalism and capitalism in Latin America (Steenland, 1975: 49–58) and likewise, Timothy Harding in his introduction on dependency, nationalism, and the state, placed the origins of dependency studies in "the meeting of a sterile and mechanical Marxism and a plainly inadequate bourgeois theory of nationalist development" (Harding, 1976: 4). More recently, in a hard-hitting article, Weeks and Dore (1979) took up the issue of international exchange and the causes of backwardness. At one stage the authors say that "while the discussion to this point has been critical, its result has not been negative; we have not merely sought to point out errors, but to point them out in a way which can carry the analysis forward" (Weeks and Dore, 1979: 78). They then set out an alternative explanation for the "causes of backwardness." The point is that whether we agree or disagree with the content of their analysis the form in which they conduct their critique/supercession is admirable.

Marxism and Dependency

If the Communist Party of Mexico (PCM) can be said to uphold orthodox Marxism, then its recent "official" critique of dependency theory can be taken as representative. Thesis 15 of the recent PCM congress maintains that dependency had a positive role in "breaking with some of the old schemas of the Communist International," but that it now constitutes "an obstacle to the advance of Marxism." Among its negative theoretical effects the following are listed: denying the development of capitalism as a system of social relations of production; denying the existence of a real class enemy, that is, a real, strong bourgeoisie with its own class personality; making imperialism (understood always as the economic, political, and cultural presence of the United States in the continent and not as a phase in the development of capitalism) into the main enemy of the revolution without locating the anti-imperialist struggle in its correct context; seeing the struggle for socialism purely as the development of the forces of production (i.e., economism); exaggerating the specificity of local capitalism to the point of ignoring the operation of the laws which dictate the development of capitalism (*Debate*, 1981: 5). These "deviations" allegedly lead to an anti-imperialism which becomes class-collaboration, underestimation of the class enemy—the bourgeoisie—which is seen as completely subordinated to imperialism, and an inability to analyze the transformations of the working class.

These points are all debatable, and certainly many apply to the crude oversimplified dependency polemics. A communist party is not perhaps the best placed to criticize "anti-imperialism which becomes class-collaboration," but some of the other points are quite sound, notably the neglect of the real power of the local bourgeoisie which comes from so many years of denying the very existence of a national bourgeoisie. . . .

Imperialism and Dependency

It was once widely accepted that dependency studied "the other side" of imperialism as it were. The dogmatic Marxists, however, who have rejected dependency theory, tell us that "it's all in the classics." Thus Raúl Fernández in an analysis of Colombia informs us simply that "the theoretical framework of the essay is the theory of *imperialism* developed by Lenin—imperialism is capitalism in capitalism's advanced or highest stage" (Fernández, 1979: 38). This type of uncritical repetition of eternal truths—à la Little Red Book—may well breed loyal cadres, but it is hardly a substitute for critical (i.e., Marxist) analysis. In fact, the debate around imperialism has resurfaced with intensified vigor in recent years. If Marxists can apply their polemical ardor against dependency theory, they should also critically reexamine the fundamental tenets of the theory of imperialism.

Giovanni Arrighi, well known for his work on Africa, has recently set out to *reconstruct* the theory of imperialism (Arrighi, 1978). He worked on the assumption that "by the end of the sixties, what had once been 'the pride' of Marxism— the theory of imperialism—has become a 'Tower of Babel,' in which not even Marxists knew any longer how to find their way. The truly surprising thing is that even those scholars who were most alert to the changing pattern of international capitalist relations felt obliged to pay a tribute to Lenin where none was due, compounding the confusion" (Arrighi, 1978: 17). The study Arrighi presents is more of a formal and structural reading of the concept of imperialism, rather than a full historical study. Nevertheless, its conclusions are seriously and rigorously derived and merit careful attention. He finds that Hobson's ideotypical structure of imperialism (a prime source for Lenin) is, in fact,

> rigidly circumscribed in time [in its] capacity . . . to order expansionist phenomena synchronically and diachronically. This capacity is zero prior to the second half of the 17th century—that is, before the nation-state began to exercise a decisive influence over the international system; it is maximal for phenomena of the late 19th century, when the nation-state had finally become the basic structure of the international system, while its very application is dubious to times of crisis of the nation-state, such as those in which we seem to live. (Arrighi, 1978: 151)

In conclusion it is anachronistic for us to attempt to ground a theory of contemporary imperialism in *historically determinate* definitions relating to processes and ideologies of the early 1900s.

A different type of venture is undertaken by Anthony Brewer (1980). This is nothing less than an ambitious reappraisal of imperialism from Marx through Luxembourg, Hilferding, Bukharin, and Lenin to Frank, Wallerstein, Rey, Emmanuel, and Amin. Basically, Marx expected the spread of capitalism to lead to full capitalist development everywhere, while Lenin and his contemporaries focused on the rise of monopoly and interimperialist rivalry. More recently, emphasis has shifted to the understanding of *underdevelopment*, where Brewer guides us carefully through the whole range of theories in terms of their logical coherence and their relevance to real problems. The problem with André Gunder Frank, for example, is located in the distance between his grandiose general statements—such as development and underdevelopment being opposite sides of the same coin—and his discussion of particular historical situations. There is a lack of real theory, and Brewer suggests that the Marxist analysis of relations of production can fill that gap. In conclusion, I think this book is an invaluable guide to the literature—its vast scope and explanatory emphasis cannot, however, lead us to the synthesis required today to guide future work. The main problems, however, are identified and that is a magnificent starting point for renewed theoretical clarification. . . .

Without any doubt the most global and challenging critique to the theory of imperialism is Bill Warren's recent posthumous volume (Warren, 1980). Warren's starting point is Karl Marx's view on the historically progressive nature of capitalism and its unprecedented development of the forces of production. Colonialism did not then retard or distort indigenous capitalist development but rather acted as a powerful engine of progressive social change. For Warren, "although introduced into the Third World externally, capitalism has struck deep roots there and developed its own increasingly internal dynamic" (1980: 9). Lenin supported these views on the progressive and dynamic international role of capitalism until his famous pamphlet on "Imperialism: The Highest Stage of Capitalism," which "initiated the ideological process through which the view that capitalism could be an instrument of social advance in precapitalist societies was erased from Marxism" (Warren, 1980: 8). This shift was consolidated at the Sixth Comintern Congress (1928) where "the Marxist analysis of imperialism was sacrificed to the requirements of bourgeois anti-imperialist propaganda and, indirectly, to what were thought to be the security requirements of the encircled Soviet state" (Warren, 1980: 8). On this basis Warren then goes on to criticize the whole conception underlying the post-war analysis of imperialism, particularly the focus from Paul Baran onwards on what he calls "the fiction of underdevelopment."

Bill Warren's critical engagement with the dependency school takes up a whole chapter trying to show it is just nationalist mythology. After setting out what he sees as its main tenet, Warren concludes that "the dependency approach, while not formally excluding alternative answers, has effectively narrowed the intellectual focus of analysis of the dynamics of Latin American society and has foreclosed the posing of critical questions in the name of an irrelevant antithesis between diffusionist (or structural-functionalist) and dependency approaches" (Warren, 1980: 162–163). Dependency theory is seen as static because only the *form* of dependency changes and because it simply *assumes* the continuing validity of the center-periphery paradigm. Dependency theorists usually equate imperialism with the world market and also incorrectly assume that there is a latent suppressed autonomous historical development alternative available. The criticisms are familiar and in some cases and in some ways quite correct. But, as often happens, the critics of dependency theory assume a theoretical/political unity which just does not exist. Warren's reference to the Latin American debate is quite limited and based on secondhand sources; for example, Osvaldo Sunkel and dos Santos are quoted only via Philip O'Brien's critique of dependency (O'Brien, 1975). . . .

According to Ernesto Laclau, "a good example of the theoretical errors to which an ingenuous empiricism leads in social sciences can be found in the now well-known work of Immanuel Wallerstein" (Laclau, 1977: 43–44). This author's wide-ranging articles have recently been collected together (Wallerstein, 1979) and provide us with a useful summary of this perspective. In his introduction Wallerstein restates the classical debate on the rise of capitalism between Paul Sweezy (and Frank) and Maurice Dobb (and Laclau)—again based on the circulation and production emphasis respectively. His conclusion is that "though Dobb and Laclau can both point to texts of Marx that seem clearly to indicate that they are more faithfully following Marx's argument, I believe both Sweezy and Frank better follow the spirit of Marx if not his letter . . ." (Wallerstein, 1979: 9). In support of this, a series of essays trace the historical evolution and structural characteristics of the capitalist world-economy from the sixteenth century to the present.

I think it is important to note that Marx is not unambiguously a "productionist" as the following passage makes clear:

> Whether the commodities are the product of production based on slavery, the product of peasants (Chinese, Indian riots), of a community (Dutch East Indies), of state production (such as existed in earlier epochs of Russian history, based on serfdom) or of half-savage hunting people, etc.—as commodities and money they confront the money and commodities in which industrial capital presents itself. . . . The character of the production process from which they derive is immaterial . . . the circulation process of industrial capital is characterized by the many-sided character of its origins, and the existence of the market as a world market. (Marx, 1978: 189–190)

So, Marx was also a "circulationist" or rather he did not separate the realm of production and circulation counterposing one to the other.

The problems with Wallerstein remain, even more so with the spate of world-system studies generated by his followers. There is an all-encompassing breadth of focus (over space and over time) which tends to dissolve the historical specificity of historical social formations. As a "guide to action"—on, for example, South Africa—they are virtually useless. The basic problem is that the world capitalist economy is the starting point of analysis without any prior *theoretical* construction of the concept (this is where his "empiricism" comes in). The result according to Laclau then is "a merely factual and erudite survey" (Laclau, 1977: 46).

André Gunder Frank's more recent work shows the difficulty of criticizing this author on the basis of classical texts—his work is flexible, progresses, and is eclectic (not in a derogatory sense). His *Dependent Accumulation and Underdevelopment* (1978a) is a brilliant historical sweep through the phases of imperialism from 1500 to 1930. In a companion volume he answers the earlier criticism of his "circulationism" by Laclau and others "by undertaking an analysis of the *mutual* dialectical relations between the changing 'external' (but with respect to the capitalist system still internal) relations of exchange and the transformations of the relations of production 'internal' to each of the major regions of the world at each of the three historical stages of capitalist development on a world scale" (Frank, 1978b: 14). Whether this starting point is sustained in his concrete analysis is, of course, another question. His questionable focus on what he calls "a single worldwide process of capital accumulation" leads him to conclude that the question of internal/external determination is "irrelevant and unanswerable." Nevertheless, he provides a useful analysis of primitive accumulation, and we must be thankful that Frank seems to have outgrown his penchant for the catchy phrase—of which the "development of underdevelopment" was the most notorious—which made him so popular (especially among students) but also made him an easy target for critics. The reservations expressed about Wallerstein's work may, however, apply in part to the new direction taken by Frank.

At the other end of the scale we have the "modes of production" analysis. Here we have the recent collection of essays from *The Journal of Economy and Society* entitled *The Articulation of Modes of Production* (Wolpe, 1980). Though attempting to demonstrate the analytical power of the concept, the essays also reveal a number of as yet unresolved conceptual problems. Most of the articles analyze particular social formations, constituted as they are by a combination of more than one mode of production. The process of *articulation* between these is one of the major focuses. Why it is that precapitalist modes of production tend to be preserved still seems to be explained only in terms of their being "functional" for the continued reproduction of capitalism. This may be so, but one gets an uneasy feeling that these cannot really be independent *modes* of production if their conditions of existence are so inextricably linked up with the expansion of capitalism. That there are noncapitalist *relations* of production, even Frank would not dispute today, but to see the Third World in terms of "combinations" of modes of production is another question. One of the contributors to the Wolpe volume, the French Marxist anthropologist Claude Meillassoux, now has one of his recent books *Maidens, Meal and Money* (Meillassoux, 1981) available in English. This contains a quite brilliant analysis of "imperialism as a mode of reproduction of cheap labor power" which centers on the exploitation of the domestic community in the Third World. Here we find a fruitful meeting point between the studies of imperialism and that growing research field known as the new international labor studies.

The major theoretical text in this area is undoubtedly that of John Taylor (1979), which is an ambitious attempt to go beyond the neo-Marxist paradigm by laying the foundations of a comprehensive modes-of-production approach to the study of the Third World. Taylor's critique of the "sociology of development" treads well-known ground, and he encapsulates this in its "teleological" nature, i.e., that it posits an ideal condition of development which, though non-existent, is potentially realizable. More controversial is his extension of this label to the "sociology of underdevelopment," where he picks up Paul Baran's familiar distinction between actual and potential surplus—i.e., with or without the restrictive and exploitative structures of imperialism. In Taylor's words,

> The major point to be directed at this analysis is that—despite the total divergence of its conclusions from those of the Sociology of Development—it still constitutes a form of explanation in which the contemporary phenomena of an underdeveloped society are defined by being juxtaposed against a potential state, to the achievement of which they do or do not contribute. (Taylor, 1979: 93)

Now, Bill Warren has reminded us that not all anticapitalist ideologies are socialist—they can be utopian or reactionary. Taylor is trying to say that socialism should not have an ethical component at all, which is something different. His Althusserian Marxism, based on the primacy of "theoretical practice," ignores that Marx had a *moral* critique of capitalism too—what else is Baran referring to with his "potential" surplus?

Taylor's construction of a systematic modes-of-production approach is even more questionable. Long pages of Althusserian theoretical practice are matched by far fewer concrete applications of the theory. He accepts Lenin's views on imperialism but tries to translate them into modes-of-production terms. Imperialism restricts the development of capitalism in the Third World, where it might restrict its marketing requirements (or, more broadly, its reproductive requirements), and this restricted and uneven development is "reinforced by the continuing existence of elements of the non-capitalist mode" (Taylor, 1979: 363). These two elements jointly determine the particular pattern of capital accumulation in Third World social formations: urban unemployment, combination of different types of labor, etc. In the end, however, Taylor's elaborate theoretical construction has yet to generate the type of concrete analysis comparable in its depth and scope to that of Cardoso for example. More specifically, we find in Taylor a real retrogression to the old position of the Latin American communist parties when he refers to "the resistance put up against imperialist penetration by the noncapitalist mode (of production)" (Taylor, 1979: 221). He analyzes the Latin American countryside as a semifeudal bastion bravely resisting the encroachments of capitalism. There are two criticisms: (1) modes of production are raised to the level of real "actors" with a life of their own above and independent from social classes, and (2) it misrepresents the symbiotic relation between industrial and agrarian capital in Latin America, albeit with their internal conflicts but never fundamental antagonism.

As I have already intimated, my approach to the world-system and modes-of-production perspectives would be to move toward a synthesis. This was already pointed to in *Latin American Perspectives* (Sternberg, 1974), and a whole volume (Oxaal et al., 1975) was dedicated to pursuing this "marriage." The first remained at the level of pointing out its need, and the second failed to bridge the gap in its various contributions, which tended to adopt just one or the other perspective. Laclau in a postscript to his classical 1971 critique of Frank points also in this direction (Laclau, 1977). The market-focused empiricism of Wallerstein is matched by the theoretical inflation of the concept of mode of production by others, resulting in such confusing categories as "colonial mode of production," which conflates two distinct levels of analysis (mode of production and economic system). Following Laclau, "Marxist thought in Latin America has found considerable difficulty in moving *simultaneously* at the level of *modes of production* and that of *economic systems,* and . . . its most frequent mistakes derive from a unilateral use of one or other of the two levels . . . to perpetuate confusion of the two cannot but lead to the multiplication of pseudo-problems and paradoxes" (Laclau, 1977: 42–50). This still leaves us, however, at the level of a prescriptive statement.

DEBATE FOUR

Introduction

THE CONTROVERSY over how Marxism can help in understanding the failure of capitalist development or of capitalist development's inadequacies was not satisfied by the early debates in *Latin American Perspectives*. During the early 1980s, many left intellectuals in the region began to search for theory that would transcend Marxism and what they proclaimed to be a post-Marxism. The debate that appeared in issue 65 during the spring of 1990 explored the ramifications of the new ideas. The introductory essay by Chilcote (below) identifies the origins, premises, and weaknesses of post-Marxism, while Enrique Dussel offers a critical synthesis of the dependency writers and shows how Marx might have incorporated the dependency idea into his thinking.

2.9

Post-Marxism: The Retreat from Class in Latin America

Ronald H. Chilcote

This piece argues that the roots of a post-Marxism are found in the left discourse and writing of Europe. This influence led to the inclination of left intellectuals in Latin America to cast aside a class analysis in favor of an approach focused on the actual and potential working of political parties and the new social movements.

S INCE ITS INCEPTION, *Latin American Perspectives* has recognized many Marxisms and a Marxist tradition of many contending theories and strategies. More important, the journal represents the view that no single tendency within Marxism should dominate its pages, and that Marxism is not reducible to the conceptualization of class, relations of production, or mode of production, but that all of these concepts are fundamental in understanding the problems of contemporary capitalist society. It is also evident that attention to individual, group, and class interests may be relevant to analysis of struggles that seek political equality, resolution of human needs, and a fair distribution of available resources.

Marxism today, however, is in a period of crisis, provoking a rethinking of its premises and usefulness but also leading some left theorists to search for a new understanding as they move on to a "post-Marxist terrain." This journal issue

First published in *Latin American Perspectives* 65, vol. 17 (2), Sage Publications, Inc. Reprinted with permission from the Latin American Perspectives Collective. Selection from 3–8, 10–13.

explores the implications of this crisis and the turn of some intellectuals away from Marxism in their retreat from analysis of class and class struggle in Latin America. The intent is not only to invite dialogue on this question, but also to challenge the premises of the new thinking. Among questions asked of contributors were: To what extent did Latin American intellectuals exiled in Europe associate with the thought of Gramsci, Poulantzas, Althusser, and others? Did Eurocommunism of the late 1970s influence their thinking? What has been the impact of dictatorship and repression upon the new thinking as discussion moves from rural and urban guerrilla warfare to issues of political culture, pluralist democracy, and reformism? What has been the significance of the split in the Communist movement since the 1960s, especially among currents that sought collaborative political arrangements and alliances with social democratic and liberal currents? What has happened to the political parties as they came to dominate the democratic openings, thereby obscuring the mass popular movements that emerged to challenge the dictatorships? How does a class analysis relate to mass popular movements (feminist, ecological, grassroots, and so on)? What is the situation of the labor movement and its traditional ties to the state (especially in Argentina, Brazil, and Mexico), its struggle for autonomy, and its participation in the electoral process? To what extent have the advances of capitalism worldwide and the reorganization of capital and labor in Latin America had their consequences for the new thinking? Have these changes (including a declining standard of living) undermined the revolutionary commitment of intellectuals tied to the state-financed universities? As regimes moved from dictatorship to democracy, to what extent were state institutions and class forces structurally retained, and what has been the impact on post-Marxist thinking? What is the state of the current search for a "new left" now that some intellectuals see the working class in decline and the traditional left parties in disarray?

The notion of post-Marxism has appeared in recent theoretical literature as the latest of many "post" formulations of an evolution toward a new society. These formulations imply a transition from the contradictions of the bourgeois order, the class struggle, and the dilemmas of capitalism to a newly emerging order devoid of ideology and conflict. Daniel Bell foreshadowed this trend with his advocacy of an "end of ideology" (1960), while his thesis of the "post-industrial society" (1976) envisioned better living standards and a closing of the gap between social classes through mass education, mass production, and more consumption. Other "post" formulations have referred to society as "postbourgeois," "posteconomic," "postcivilized," "postmaterialist," and "postmodern" (see Frankel, 1987, for discussion and criticism of these "post" forms and Jameson, 1984 and 1989, for the view that they are idealistic manifestations in defense of capitalism). However, radical criticisms of these conservative and liberal views have not deterred some left theorists from also moving beyond capitalism. The anticapitalist and utopian socialism of Rudolf Bahro (1984) and André Gorz (1982), for example, provide a basis for their search for a more egalitarian and democratic world. Fred Block (1987) sees the state as comprising less traditional hierarchies, a postindustrial "debureaucratization" dependent on a renewal of citizen participation in the regulation of social life. Samuel Bowles and Herbert Gintis (1986) seek a radical democratic synthesis in their advocacy of postliberalism, and argue that neither liberalism nor Marxism has given priority to democracy. Their postliberalism seeks the expansion of personal rights through traditional forms of representative democracy and industrial liberty while ensuring innovative and democratically accountable economic freedoms. Becker et al. (1987) attempt to move beyond neoimperialist and dependency explanations of capitalist underdevelopment in their conceptualization of postimperialism. They see the coalescing of dominant class elements across national boundaries, the integration of diverse national interests on a new international basis, and the rise of a transnational bourgeoisie as an alternative to a deterministic understanding of imperialism and to dependency orthodoxy. Ernesto Laclau and Chantal Mouffe (1985) move toward a "post-Marxist terrain" in their call for a new politics based on a project of radical democracy (see Chilcote, 1988, for a full discussion of these "post" forms).

Laclau, an Argentine social scientist now residing and teaching in England, is renowned for his attack (1971) on André Gunder Frank's thesis (1966) of capitalist development of underdevelopment in Latin America. He criticized Frank for stressing capitalist relations of exchange and circulation of commodities rather than production as Marx had emphasized in *Capital.* This essential point proved to be an early step in the process of reassessing theories of underdevelopment and dependency in the light of Marxism. (Many of the debates over these questions are found in *Latin American Perspectives,* especially in issues no. 1 [1974], no. 11 [1976], and nos. 30–31 [1981]). In the present period, however, Laclau and Mouffe attempt to move beyond a Marxist analysis in what Ellen Meiksins Wood has characterized as their retreat from a class analysis and declassing of the socialist project. A number of propositions, synthesized from Wood (1986: 3–4), characterize the new direction: Post-Marxism argues that the working class has not evolved into a revolutionary movement; economic class interests are relatively autonomous from ideology and politics; the working class holds no basic position within socialism; a political force may form out of "popular" political and ideological elements, independent from class ties, so that feminist, ecological, peace, and other forces become effective in a changing society; a socialist movement may evolve independent of class; the objectives of socialism transcend class interests; and the struggle for socialism comprises a plurality of resistances to inequality and oppression.

The roots of the post-Marxist thinking may be found in Eurocommunist and Eurosocialist developments of the 1970s and 1980s. Fernando Claudín, a Spanish Marxist, writes (1978) about Eurocommunism in terms of historical conjunctures, the last being the economic crisis of overproduction, recession, and democratic transitions in Southern Europe during the middle 1970s when the international workers' movement failed to move the capitalist crisis to a socialist transition. At the time, the French and Italian Communist parties agreed that while socialism would constitute a higher phase of democracy, small and medium agrarian and industrial producers could participate in the building of socialism; they believed that the democratization of the state must increasingly provide a role for local and regional government, for a plurality of parties, and for freedom and autonomy of trade unions (Claudín, 1978: 65–66). Nicos Poulantzas, a Greek Marxist who lived many years in exile in Paris, applied a class analysis to a structural theory of the state in his comparative study (1976) of the democratic openings made possible by the crisis and fall of the dictatorships in Spain, Portugal, and Greece. In partic- ular, the revolutionary period in Portugal during 1974 and 1975 may have influ- enced him to abandon a Marxist-Leninist position that emphasized dual power so that workers and popular forces who had built their revolutionary base outside the state apparatuses could confront state power; instead these forces might turn to the possibility of a bloodless revolution through penetration and occupation of key state apparatuses. The argument that struggle within the state apparatuses was necessary to disrupt the balance of forces and allow for a socialist transition was expressed in his later work (1978) and may have inspired some left intellectuals in the early 1980s to move beyond structured interpretations and evolve theory within a post-Marxist terrain.

The post-Marxism of Laclau and Mouffe reflects intellectual thinking that has accompanied political discourse on social democracy and democratic socialism within countries where socialist parties have come to power (especially France and Italy, Spain, Portugal, and Greece since the mid-1970s). This discourse has focused on the transition to socialism, the necessity of blocs of left-center political forces to ensure a political majority within a fragmented multiparty setting, popu- lar reforms to mitigate demands of the popular classes (workers and peasants), and tolerance to promote and develop the forces of production in the present capitalist stage. The realities of mainstream politics appear to have obscured the revolutionary rhetoric so that terms like class struggle, working class, dictatorship of the proletariat, and even Marxism itself are dropped from left dialogue.

What distinguishes Marxism from the new thinking is the traditional view that the working class is essential for its revolutionary potential because of its structural position as the class that produces capital. In excising classes from a socialist per- spective, the post-Marxists avoid analysis of the exploitative relations between capital and labor as central to the accumulation and reproduction of capitalism as a mode of production. Further, the emphasis on politics and ideology as autono- mous from economics undermines the attention to political economy which has been of interest to classical and contemporary Marxists. Debate on the nature of the capitalist mode of production no longer appears as important. Consequently, classes and class struggle are displaced by an emphasis on political pluralism, political organizations, and interest groups. Analysis of the state may stress differ- ences between the power bloc and the people while overlooking opposition between capital and labor. There may also be a tendency to focus on a single or a few political institutions; the segmenting of political forces may limit prospects for a societal overview. Political movements attempting to penetrate the mainstream may be isolated; populist strategies designed to challenge the establishment may be diffused and weakened by the separation of particular interests.

Laclau and Mouffe are explicit in their denunciation of Marxism: "it is no longer possible to maintain the conception of subjectivity and classes elaborated by Marxism, nor its vision of the historical course of capitalist development" (1985: 4). Their ideas relate especially to the crisis of left intellectuals. On the one hand, there is the rise and decline of French structuralism once so dominantly represented in the work of Louis Althusser (see especially the useful analysis of Hirsh, 1981). On the other hand, the English experience reflects the moderation of a Marxist position among some intellectuals through such journals as *Marxism Today* (the theoretical journal of British Eurocommunism), *New Socialist*, and *The New Statesman* and their withdrawal from some basic socialist positions. Ralph Miliband (1985) calls them "the new revisionists" and Ellen Meiksins Wood (1986) labels them "the new true socialists." Their ranks include Gareth Steadman Jones of the History Workshop group at Oxford and Paul Hirst and Barry Hindess, who recanted their earlier orthodox interpretation of mode of production. While these intellectuals differ in many respects, they appear to agree that the primacy of organized labor should be repudiated because the working class in capitalist countries has failed to live up to its revolutionary expectations and the model of struggle should now incorporate a multitude of interests emanating from various strata, groups, and social movements.

Historically, the defection of left intellectuals from a Marxist discourse in the United States has been part of a cyclical phenomenon dating to events since the Russian Revolution, the appearance of Communist, Socialist, and Trotskyist groups of intellectuals and the shift of many of them to the right toward social democratic and neoconservative tendencies as they were affected by the Stalinist purges of 1934–1936, the rise of McCarthyism during the early 1950s, and the impact of advanced capitalism. Alexander Bloom (1986), Terry Cooney (1986), and Alan Wald (1987) provide a portrayal of this left and its maverick commitments since the 1930s, while Russell Jacoby (1987) compares a "classical" generation of intellectuals, born at the turn of the century, with a "transitional" generation, born around 1915 to 1920, and then with a generation of the post-1940s which sought refuge in the universities and lost its role as "public intellectuals." Accounts by Gitlin (1987), Isserman (1987), and Miller (1987) do well in delineating the rise and decline of the new left since the late 1960s. . . .

Revisions of Marxist Political Thought

The crisis of Marxist political thought in Latin America dates back a decade. Tomás Vasconi (1990) notes the differences in the rhetoric of the 1970s in which revolution and socialism were stressed to that of the 1980s in which democracy and socialism have become the dominant discourse. He identifies one source of dialogue around the question of democracy as taking place at the 1978 meetings in San José, Costa Rica, of the Consejo Latinoamericano de Ciencias Sociales, and for another he cites a paper by Laclau (1980) on hegemony and popular alternatives in Latin America, presented in a seminar at Morelia, Mexico, during 1980 (this changing discourse is also traced by Lechner [1985a and 1985b] and critiqued by Cueva [1984]).

The roots of the crisis, however, are at least partially attributable to external intellectual influences. Exiles in Europe influenced the substance of the left discourse in Latin America, and it is useful to identify the connections while acknowledging that the debate in Latin America differs from that in Europe just as the debate in England differs from that in France and in Italy or Portugal and Spain (a point emphasized in correspondence from Michael Löwy, Paris, January 27 and May 2, 1987). Eurocommunist developments and the break of the traditional Communist parties from Stalinism provided an opening for a coalition of left forces, most notably in Italy. This also led to splits within the movement, especially in France and Spain. During the 1960s the Sino-Soviet dispute resulted in a serious division within the Partido Comunista Brasileiro (PCB) as well as the Portuguese PCP. In each case the dissident offshoot splintered into a multitude of groups oriented toward a revolutionary outcome influenced by Albanian, Chinese, or Cuban experiences. Within Brazil from 1968 to 1972 many of these groups joined the urban armed struggle but ultimately succumbed to the ruthless and overwhelming repression of police and security forces. Many intellectuals who had associated with these groups fled to Western Europe, where the structuralist influence of Althusser and Poulantzas was dominant in left circles. They also joined a wave of intellectuals inspired by the thought of Antonio Gramsci. Latin Americans exiled in Lisbon, Madrid, and Paris were able to observe the fall of the dictatorships in Southern Europe and contemplate the democratic openings and the pragmatic maneuverings of the Socialist and Communist parties in their pursuit of Marxist theory and practice. Once they returned home, many of them turned to practical politics and the prospects for democracy. In the case of Brazil, for example, before the 1964 military coup Leonel Brizola had followed in a populist-nationalist tradition, but later associated with the Socialist International, especially after his return to Brazil in the early 1980s, when he became governor of the state of Rio de Janeiro.

Periods of Repression and the Impact on Cultural Production and Intellectual Thinking

Prior to the democratic openings, structural Marxism had been assimilated by the left in Latin America (see Harris, 1979, for a useful overview). The influence of Althusser and Poulantzas was visible (see Portantiero, 1974, for an early example and Cardoso, 1982), and the work of Gramsci was popular (Coutinho, 1981). Vasconi believes that Gramsci was consistently Marxist in his thinking, in contrast to the way Portantiero and other Latin Americans used his thought in advocating new directions for socialism. However, leftist parties and labor organizations had also been shaken by systematic repression and internal disorganization. Dialogue began to shift from issues of rural and urban guerrilla warfare to political culture, pluralist democracy, and reformism. At stake were traditional leftist conceptions of the revolution and the need to destroy the bourgeois state, the impossibility of capitalism in the periphery, and the role of popular mobilization and democracy (see, for example, the works by Coutinho, 1979; Kondor, 1980; and Weffort, 1984, along with the essays by Cardoso, Sousa, and Weffort in Stepan, 1989: 299–394).

In his summary of recent debate within the "renovation of the left" in Latin America, Robert Barros (1986) identifies three prominent views. The first sees the reinstitutionalization of democratic forms as only a tactical objective for the working class, a step in facilitating the formation of a revolutionary movement with real participatory, not formal, democracy as its basis. Barros criticizes this "orthodox" tendency because it appears to disguise authoritarian Marxism as democracy with answers to all fundamental questions: "Inevitably, the discourse of 'formal' and 'real' democracy turns out to be a cover for an authoritarian Marxism whose real concepts are objective interests, vanguard party, political revolution, and dictatorship of the proletariat" (1986: 57). A second current envisages democracy without socialism. It disregards traditional left issues such as the concern for capitalism and imperialism and the struggle for equality. Inherent in this view is the hope that formal or representative democracy can lead to a higher form of democracy. Barros criticizes these views for failing to examine objective constraints and strategies that might lead to a different democracy (citing Landi, 1981, and Delich, 1983). A third position, the radical democratic alternative to bourgeois democracy, argues that a political recomposition must move away from traditional left concerns, including a "secularization" of Marxism (Moulian, 1981b), abandonment of predetermined lines of thinking (Portantiero, 1981), and de-emphasis on the role of the working class (Nun, 1981). Gramscian themes of hegemony and national-populism pervade this discourse, which looks to alternative forms of culture, organization, and struggle in the building of a plurality of social opposition against domination and institutionalized hierarchies; the implementation of democratic practices and institutions will lead to the formation of a broad popular-democratic movement (see Flisfisch, 1983, and Moulian, 1983, for reflections on this possibility). Barros believes that these theorists (for example, Aricó, 1980; Nun, 1984; and Portantiero and Ipola, 1981) are not relating to their real situations: "we are left with the contours of a normative conception of democracy, but no attempt to ground possibilities for its realization . . . this position obscures the tension between its

Ronald H. Chilcote

project and fragile bases of postauthoritarian democratic compromises" (1986: 66).

Particularly interesting is the case of Chile, where under the Allende regime socialism was to evolve in a peaceful way, only to be toppled by a military dictatorship, resulting in the repressive aftermath and struggle for a democratic opening in which leftist intellectuals have sought a theory of "socialist renovation." Manuel Antonio Garretón has analyzed this as a process of the left distancing itself from the traditional political model by stripping away the orthodoxy of the Marxist-Leninist tradition so that the economic structure is not determinant in all social transformations, a scientific conception of human political action is abandoned, and a specific class no longer is identified with or finds its expression in a vanguard or party. Furthermore, the conception of socialism need not be deduced from a concrete classical model of socialism, nor must there be an instrumental view of democracy or a reduction of nation-class-party to a particular political action. Garretón argues that the core of Marxism-Leninism is crumbling

> because the very elements of the theory have withered away and lost their internal and logical consistency. This is the product of the material, social, and cultural transformations in contemporary society. The emergence of the tertiary sector of the economy, technological change, the declining importance of the working class in the overall make-up of the labor force, the explosion of demands, and the proliferation of social actors overrunning the world of labor, the growing complexity and heterogeneity of society . . . make it impossible for the socialist project to base itself entirely on one social class. (1989: 21)

DEBATE FOUR

2.10

Marx and the Concept of Dependency

Enrique Dussel
Translated by Aníbal Yáñez

The author argues that the belated publication of the 1844 Manuscripts *(in 1921) and the* Grundrisse *(1932) inspired left intellectuals to seek alternatives to the deterministic thinking. He believes that rather than turn to post-Marxism, we need to return to Marx to examine his categories and theory and practice and that in this manner it is possible to discover how Marx would have assimilated dependency into his own thinking.*

TODAY IT IS FASHIONABLE to consider ourselves in a period of "post-Marxism." I think that especially in Latin America—but also in Europe and the United States—rather than being in a period of "post-Marxism" we are in a time of serious, measured, profound reencounter with Marx *himself.* In the "second century" of Marxism—if one considers the first to be from 1883 to 1983—we will rediscover in Marx a source of scientific thinking that can be used not only for a critique of capitalism but also for a critique of actually existing socialism.

This essay, which aims to re-pose the "dependency issue," asserts that a return to Marx is highly necessary. This work then should be seen as a "practice" or a "method" for trying to interpret the present using the categories slowly elaborated by Marx, especially from 1857 until the end of his life.

First published in *Latin American Perspectives* 65, vol. 17 (2), Sage Publications, Inc. Reprinted with permission from the Latin American Perspectives Collective. Selection from 63–65, 69–73, 74, 77, 92–93, 96.

Marx began *Theories of Surplus-Value* with a thesis that is reproduced here by way of analogy. He wrote that "all economists share the error" (Marx, 1861–63, vol. 1: 40). I would say that many economists, historians, and sociologists share the error of examining dependency not as an international *social relation* and a *transfer of surplus-value* between total national capitals of different organic composition, in the framework of competition in the world order, but through its *particular forms* or merely by means of aspects that are secondary phenomena. They thus confuse the essence with the appearance. Furthermore, they do not elaborate upon the concept, nor do they first construct the necessary categories on an abstract, *logical,* and *essential* plane, but rather they get lost in a chaotic, unscientific, anecdotal history of dependency.

We can state at the outset that frequently in the debate on dependency Marx was notably absent. In some cases, as in the excellent work of Ruy Mauro Marini, the topic of "transfer of surplus-value" was explicitly noted (Marini, 1973: 37), but that transfer became a compensation (that is, a secondary, derivative mechanism based on the essence of dependency: ". . . the central thesis that is defended there, . . . is, that *the foundation* of dependency is the superexploitation of labor" (Marini, 1973: 101).

How can the consequence, or compensation, of the transfer of surplus-value be the *foundation* (the essence) of dependency? A transfer of surplus-value at a fundamental, essential level makes it necessary for dependent capital to superexploit its wage-labor. Superexploitation is a consequence. This mistake, Marx would call it "confusion," is due to there being no prior clear definition of the "concept"—in the sense that Marx gives this notion.

"Theories of Dependency"

This section presents the diverse "theories of dependency" and is intended as a first step in this task, but by no means does it constitute a finished work.

In *Imperialism, the Highest Stage of Capitalism* (1916), Lenin was aware of writing a "popular outline" from a merely economic point of view. J. A. Hobson (1902) also took up imperialism's historical and political aspects but never used the category of surplus-value or, therefore, that of "transfer of surplus-value." There is a reference to "superprofits" (Lenin, 1916: 193)[1] but none to categories such as value of the commodity, cost-price or price of production, market value, or market price, and so forth. The fundamental thesis, a correct one, is that "competition becomes transformed into monopoly" (Lenin, 1916: 205). Put another way, "the old free competition" (Lenin, 1916: 205) gives way to competition at a higher level ("monopoly" with regard to the old competition, but "new" competition between capitals with a greater concentration, both in terms of size as well as organic composition).[2] Lenin writes:

... as a matter of fact the capitalists ... have converted ... railway construction into an instrument for oppressing *a thousand million* people (in the colonies and semi-colonies), that is, more than half the population of the globe that inhabits the *dependent countries*. . . . Capitalism has grown into a world system of colonial oppression ... by a handful of *"advanced" countries*. (Lenin, 1916: 190–91; last two emphases mine)

Not only are the two main groups of countries, those owning colonies, and the colonies themselves, but also the diverse forms of *dependent countries* which, politically, are formally independent, but in fact, are enmeshed in the net of financial and diplomatic *dependence*. . . . An example ... is provided by Argentina. (Lenin, 1916: 263; my emphasis)

Lenin is aware that there is "uneven development" (1916: 241). He sees that after a sufficient level of finance capitalist is reached ("the bank capital of a few very big monopolist banks, merged with the capital of the monopolist associations of industrialists") in the most advanced countries (he gives the examples of Great Britain, the United States, Germany, and Japan) and after the division of the world, there is a transition "to a colonial policy of monopolist possession of the terrritory of the world, which has been completely divided up" (Lenin, 1916: 266). Lenin speaks repeatedly of "dependency"—of the colonies, the semicolonies, and countries formally independent but really dependent, and so on. He knows that the monopolist concentration of capital (in its productive or money form) does not prevent a new type of competition at another level (between the national powers and between conglomerated capitals). What he does not describe is the South-North relationship (referring only to the North-South one: from imperialism *toward* the dependent regions). What kind of transfer of wealth, of value, of surplus-value takes place *from* the dependent countries *toward* the advanced countries? What is the essential structure (at the level of the value of capital in the abstract), and what are the superficial mechanisms (the transformation from value to price in exchange, etc.)? None of this is taken up by Lenin. Therefore, the many authors who sought to criticize or to base the "concept" of dependency on this "popular outline," without returning to Marx *himself*, were not firmly grounded—hence all the confusion, the errors, leaps, and so forth which have occurred.

Rosa Luxemburg, in her chapter on "International Loans" in *The Accumulation of Capital* (1967: 325), also pointed to the tendency of central capital to expand in order to realize its surplus-value (loans, railroad concessions, etc.). She observed that surplus-value is extracted from the periphery, giving as her example German capital in Asian Turkey (Luxemburg, 1967: 343).

To "realize" surplus-value in Germany means first of all that such surplus-value is transferred to the central country. Luxemburg would be even more creative in her enunciation of the "law of the tendency of relative wages to fall" (1951: 100), which is so important for dependency. . . .

Fernanado H. Cardoso and Enzo Faletto wrote a critique of developmental-ism, *Dependency and Development in Latin America* (1970; 1979), in which they concluded that "the relation between economic process, structural conditions, and historical situations makes clear that *theoretical schemes* concerning the for-mation of capitalist society in present-day developed countries *are of little use* in understanding the situation in Latin American countries" (Cardoso and Faletto, 1970: 161; 1979: 172; my emphasis). Exactly the same could be said of the work of these two authors. The weakness is clear. In the entire text, not a single one of the essential categories of Marx's critical political economic discourse is used. The chosen approach is once again historical and lacking in clarity. Chaos is introduced and nothing but chaos can be the outcome.

If we consider the work of Theotônio dos Santos in *La dependencia político-económica de América Latina* (Jaguaribe et al., 1970), and we ask ourselves what categories are used, once again we do not find the essential ones, but we find the reliance upon historical conditions to explain the process of development (in Jaguaribe et al., 1970: 153–154, 174, 180).[3]

Dos Santos's thesis is that historical description comes first; second he defends himself against criticism—false, as we shall see—that dependency is not simply án external factor; third, he places dependency at the level of a "condition" and not of a "determinant" of less developed total national capital as such. For her part, Vania Bambirra, in her defense of the dependency theory, lists the various accusations against the theory as "a neo-Marxist idea; it uses bourgeois analytical categories; the class struggle is absent; it is economist; it does not go beyond the theoretical framework and the problems posed by developmentalism; depen-dency is a nationalist concept . . . ; dependency is viewed as an external phenome-non" (Bambirra, 1978: 34).

However, if we consider the categories used by Bambirra, we can see that she never made use of concepts such as value, surplus-value, transfer of surplus-value, and so on. Her argumentation consisted of categories foreign to those coined by Marx himself (and which I use in this chapter). She shares an extremely important view, however, with other Latin American authors. For her it is a matter of analyzing the situation of dependency:

> Obviously not in the sense of a general theory of the capitalist mode of production, since that *was done by Marx;* nor of a dependent capitalist mode of production, since *that does not exist;* rather, [in the sense] of a study of the dependent capitalist eco-nomic-social formations, that is, an analysis at a lower level of abstraction. . . . In my judgement the theory of dependency should be understood as the creative *appli-cation* of Marxism-Leninism. (Bambirra, 1978: 26)

This is an extremely serious theoretical question for many reasons. In the first place, it is not true that Marx "did" (completed) a "theory" of the capitalist mode of production (in an Althusserian sense or in Marx's own sense?). He only *began* his theory, and it was *unfinished* upon publication of the first of the projected three parts (which represented only 1/72nd of his total project).⁴ To write that indicates a lack of knowledge of Marx's project. Furthermore, the development of the concept and the construction of the necessary categories of the fundamental essence of a dependent, underdeveloped, or peripheral total national capital are perfectly possible, or at least strong arguments must be made to prove them impossible. This would require conceding that the enemies were right in asserting the impossibility of a "theory" of dependency as a development of Marx's own discourse, as yet unfinished at the level of the general concept of capital. Last, it appears that the "study" of historical social formations can never be a theory of dependency: It can only be a phenomenal description in time and in space of the development of the underdeveloped, dependent, peripheral total national capitals. To assign myself the task of "applying" an unfinished theory—such as Marx's—would be to place myself in an unacceptable "scientific and cultural dependency."

We now turn to some authors whose theses come closest to the manner in which Marx dealt with questions. Ruy Mauro Marini studies dependency largely following the approach of authors concerned about "unequal exchange." Marini understands "transfer of surplus-value"⁵ (Marini, 1973: 37), based on his correct use of such categories as organic composition of capitals, differences in values, prices of production and market prices, and so on. Nevertheless, he errs when he confuses a "compensation mechanism" (Marini, 1973: 35) with an essential determinant: "Latin America had to accomplish it through . . . accumulation based on the superexploitation of the worker. In this contradiction lies the *essence* of Latin American dependency" (Marini, 1973: 49). "The central thesis . . . of the *foundation* of dependency is the superexploitation of labor" (Marini, 1973: 101). Actually the essence or foundation of dependency (as Marx would say) is the transfer of surplus-value from a less-developed total national capital to the one that is more developed. It is necessary to compensate for this loss by extracting more surplus-value from living labor in the periphery. Dependent capital hence drives the value of the wage below the value necessary to reproduce the capacity to work—with all the known consequences. At the same time, it intensifies the use of this labor by reducing the time necessary to reproduce the value of the wage, relatively and in new ways. Marini errs, as we said at the start, by confusing the essence with its effect. This was of decisive importance in Latin America since nobody had consistent clarity on the *essence* of dependency. The best proof of this was the 1974 Sociology Congress.

There, Gérard Pierre-Charles, the Haitian intellectual, defined dependency as "the extraction of surplus-value for the benefit of the center" (1979: 47), but like others he did so merely in passing, as if not to give it much importance, and turned to what he believed was essential: "the process of successive approximation and concretion at the level of the dominant mode of production and of the different modes of production prevailing in each national society" (Pierre-

Charles, 1979: 47). He then criticized those who had not gone beyond a "general" (abstract or Latin American) theory. The point was that without having reached some clarity on the *minimal* and *necessary* framework of categories, discussion was to revert to the concrete, to the national. Therefore, *never again* was there an attempt to define the transfer of surplus-value, which was mentioned in passing, without noting that it was a matter of the essence.

Another eminent Latin American sociologist, Agustín Cueva, believes that "national contradictions" (Cueva, 1979: 67) are not of interest to Marxists, who should only be concerned with "class contradictions." Apparently, to analyze the contradictions between nations is characteristic of bourgeois nationalist analysis and contrary to class analysis. He writes that "there is no *theoretical space* in which a Marxist *theory of dependency* can rest. . . . Besides, the theory of dependency presents another problem, which is the nondialectical treatment of the relations between the external and the internal. The all-embracing predominance of the category of *dependence* over *exploitation,* of *nation* over *class*" (Cueva, 1979: 81, 92).

For Cueva there is dependency *or* exploitation, domination of one country over another *or* domination of one class over another. The former excludes the latter for some hypothetical *dependentistas,* but for Cueva, the latter excludes the former. Nevertheless, for Marx, neither one excludes the other, and he says so *explicitly:*

> From the fact that the profit may be *less* than the surplus value . . . it follows that not only individual capitalists but nations too may continuously exchange with one another . . . without gaining equally thereby. One nation may continuously appropriate part of the surplus labour of the other and give nothing in exchange for it, except that here the measure is not as in the exchange between capitalist and worker. (Marx, 1857–1858: 244)[6]

Indeed, and as we shall see, the relationship between capitalist nations is one of *competition* (not one of exploitation, but one of dependency, of extraction of surplus-value by the stronger capital and of transfer by the weaker). But this is not in opposition to the *exploitation* of one class by another, of labor by capital; rather it can be perfectly well articulated alongside it. In this latter case there is no transfer of surplus-value but rather, properly speaking, appropriation of surplus-value. However, the surplus-value appropriated by capital in the vertical capital-labor relationship (exploitation) is the source of the transfer from a weak capital to the stronger on a horizontal level (competition, dependency). In sum, we have a non-Marxist criticism of positions that defend dependency also in a noncritical manner. This is what happens when it is thought that Marx completed the essential theory and that it is only necessary to go to the concrete historical to apply it. To think this is to fail to understand, as we said, the *open* character of Marx's own theory and the need to *continue* it. . . .

In order to understand the "concept" of *dependency in general*, or its *essence* in Marx's sense, it is necessary to develop this concept starting with "competition." It should be stated at the outset that "monopoly" is nothing but the negative moment in the development of the concept of competition; that is, monopoly can be understood from within competition, from its essence, as a "possibility."

I use a strict Marxist method to treat the *abstract* concept of dependency in my section on the "essence" of dependency; in my section on the phenomenon of dependency, in the concrete the question will be much more complex but its development will be based upon the conclusions we may reach not in the *historical* but in the *logical* analysis, just as Marx thought. . . .

Dependency is a moment in the competition of capital. Competition, for its part, is founded on the *possibility* of devaluation and crisis, which are aspects of the very essence of capital (see Dussel, 1988: ch. 10, sect. 4). The workings of competition (and therefore of dependency) are one *real* existing moment of the mere possibility of crisis and devaluation in the spoliated capitals.

Indeed, the movement through which the commodity is transformed into money is inherent to the essence of capital: the realization of capital. The split between commodity and money is founded, in the end, in the contradiction of the commodity, being simultaneously a use-value and an exchange-value. In this original split is contained the *possibility* of competition and of dependency. Or, put another way, dependency would not be possible were it not for the original contradiction between use-value and exchange-value; one capital's extraction of value from another would be impossible (see Kuntz, 1985: 100).

A crisis is a disproportion between two intrinsic and essential terms of capital (for example, between commodity and money; overproduction or underconsumption). It is the devaluation of one of the terms. By the mediation of international competition a crisis becomes apparent and real in the devaluation of the dependent capital with regard to the dominant one. The crisis, in the dependent capital, is not only a possibility but an always-existing *reality*. Its perpetual devaluation in competition marks it as intrinsically contradictory, or as a sphere of capital where contradictions are always really existent. . . .

Capital in general, the concept, is now split in *two*. Here a clarification is in order. There is frequent talk of "less developed nations," "countries," and so on. We should make it clear right now that "nation" and "country" are *concrete* social formations;[7] it would be more correct and strict, however, to speak of "total national capital,"[8] because we are at the abstract level of the concept of *dependency in general*. Because a "total national capital" is dependent upon competition with respect to another more developed capital, the country or nation that contains or is determined by said "total capital" is called the less developed, dependent, and so on, "nation," not vice versa.

In the abstract, then, the concept of dependency is developed through competition among total national capitals—and we are not speaking of states, nor of their *external* national relations, nor of countries—in the *world market*. . . .

Earlier I said that the debate on the "theory of dependency" came to a dead end. The theoretical error that was made was in not having dealt carefully with the abstract essence of the concept of dependency and its fundamental law; this led to a denial of its existence or to forgetting its importance. For the present crises—the international external debt and the need for a revolutionary theory articulated to the praxis of liberation in Central America, the Caribbean, and increasingly in other parts of Latin America—there is no theory to explain them (Marxism just as Marx left it is not sufficient). The contradiction between theory and praxis lies in the following: An international class struggle (capitalist-proletarian) was enunciated as the only possibility, while every attempt at "national" or "popular" liberation was branded as populist. The "question of dependency" would be a bourgeois problem of interest only to peripheral national capitalism; it would not be a Marxist question. Nevertheless, the revolution that will overcome capitalism is not *immediately* a world revolution, nor is it carried out at the level of the factory.

Proletarians liberate themselves from the capitalist class only through *national* revolutions by taking *state power*. Frequently revolutionary vanguard movements have not been only proletarian but also peasant and petty-bourgeois (since Marx or Lenin, through Mao, Agostinho Neto, or *comandante* Borge; one must recall that Fidel Castro and Engels were, strictly speaking, bourgeois, one during his youth and the other throughout his life). The concept of *peripheral dominated "nation"* and of *exploited "people"* (complex political categories at the concrete level of *reproduction*) as a "social bloc of the oppressed" subsumes the (more abstract) category of "class." All of this could have been theoretically grounded had the *concept* of dependency been developed correctly. The process of national and popular liberation is the only way to destroy the mechanisms of constant and increasing *transference of surplus-value* from the less developed total national capital. This assumes overcoming capitalism as such, since the extraction of surplus-value (a living capital-labor relation) is articulated to the transfer of surplus-value in the competition between total national capitals of different levels of development. The *weakness* of peripheral capital (due to its structural transfer of surplus-value) does not mean we can subsume the entire population as a wage-earning class: The marginal *popular* masses play a leading role in the process of change. The popular movement and popular organization become political priorities.

When one speaks of liberation one thinks in terms of a situation of domination. Dependency represents this situation of domination in the world capitalist system. We think that, in the strict sense, the dependency relationship needs two industrial capitals (one in the center and the other in the periphery). Nevertheless, we think that there could be different periods in the *history of dependency* (which is neither Latin American history as a whole nor the histories of each nation alone), consisting of five moments in time. At the *essential* level our starting point is man, and we move toward the ape. Now, *historically,* our starting point is the ape (knowing a priori what man is) and we go toward man. The first moment, which we might call one of monetarist and gradual manufacturing mercantilism (sixteenth and seventeenth centuries) by the center, is that period during which Latin America lives the *prehistory* of dependency in the conquest, extraction of precious metals (money as treasure, Marx would say, or better yet as world money), and other colonial products. There is an extraction of wealth. In certain *obrajes* (workshops), mines, or haciendas there is a wage system, and therefore strictly speaking there is a certain transfer of surplus-value. The product (for example, sugar from sugar mills with slave labor) can even be transformed into a commodity in the central capitalist market and realize a profit.[9]

Notes

1. Lenin also uses the expression "extraordinary profit."

2. Lenin does not relate the greater organic composition to the question of value and price, either, but there are many references to the technological issue.

3. This is as far as the definition of dependency as such goes; in his valuable book *Imperialismo y dependencia,* dos Santos says that "the economy is *conditioned*" (1978: 305). Is it only a "condition"?

4. See what I have written on Marx's *Plans* in my work (1985: sects. 2.4 and 16.4; also 1988: sect. 12.5 and the preface).

5. Marini says "transfer of value" on page 35 and elsewhere in the same work.

6. Cf. Dussel (1985: 371). It seems important to us that in a recent article Cueva says that "it is useful to highlight the fact that through this distinguished group of creators, [Latin American] Marxism became indissolubly fused with the *national* and the *popular*" (Cueva, 1986: 28). "Nation" and "people" are therefore categories to be defined and used.

7. Marx speaks of "less developed countries" (*minder entwikelten Ländern*) (*MEGA,* II, 3: 1161, 31–32; 1861–63 [Spanish edition] II: 498); and of "nation" (1861–63 [Spanish edition] III: 298).

8. Marx frequently uses the expression "the total capital (*Gesamtkapital*) of a nation" (see Marx, 1857–1858b: 227). "If we assume a single capital, or treat the various capitals of a country as one capital (national capital [*Nationalkapital*]) as distinct from that of other countries. . . ." (Marx, 1857–1858b: 52). Marx also speaks of "national wages" (Marx, 1866–1867: chap. 22) or of "the national capital" (Marx, 1857–1858b: 10).

9. The first two volumes of the magnificent work by Immanuel Wallerstein (1979) are an excellent example of this history.

Part III

⊂═══⊷

Capitalist and Socialist Development: Mainstream and Alternative Theory and Practice

IN MY *Theories of Development and Underdevelopment* (Chilcote, 1984), I sifted through various theoretical tendencies to help students sort out the complex array of ideas. I organized these ideas around two thrusts: that advocating reform and change within a capitalist framework and that pushing for revolutionary change in the direction of socialism. The following selections serve as examples of this dichotomy. For instance, we may think of neoliberal and democratic or political development as mainstream approaches and of the internationalization of capital, modes of production, and combined and uneven development as alternative or radical approaches. There might be other ways to organize these conceptual ideas and theoretical approaches. Thus, students should read through the selections in an effort, first, to identify and understand each approach; second, to assess the usefulness of each as a way to understand development in both capitalism and socialism; and, third, to delve into some of the references cited in descriptions of these approaches.

3.1

Neoliberalism

Eduardo Rosenzvaig
Translated by Ronaldo Munck

This article outlines the origins and premises of neoliberalism, emphasizing the influence of the Chicago School upon the creation of a training center at the University of Tucumán, one of Argentina's poorest provinces.

N EOLIBERALISM IS AN ECONOMIC PHILOSOPHY for early peripheral postmodernism. Messianic, authoritarian, and exclusionary, it is mathematical modeling designed in certain academic centers of the advanced world and later in the periphery for the economic conversion of the Third World to a strategy of late colonialism—a structure that makes possible transnational integration, national disintegration, and a veritable reactionary "revolution" in the distribution of national wealth. Technical cadres have been created for the demolition of the welfare and social service structures in the undeveloped countries under the impetus of the third wave of civilization led by late capitalism. The supreme historic moment has come when the few are to concentrate the most through new policies for taxation, finance, income, privatization, wages, and state regimes— the end of an epoch and the spectacular beginning of a colonialism with a cybernetic face, an ontology of inequality.

There was no logic to the creation of a plant or laboratory for neoliberal theory in one of Argentina's most deprived provinces. Indeed, the University of Tucumán functioned entirely independent of that reality—only confirming the suc-

First published in *Latin American Perspectives* 97, vol. 24 (6), Sage Publications, Inc. Reprinted with permission from the Latin American Perspectives Collective.

cess of the conservative project by disappearing in the clouds of metaphysics. From 1960 to 1980 the Faculty of Economic Science's pilot program in economics was based on this reasoning and these interests. Numerous grants from the University of Chicago created a staff rigorously specialized in the new economic model, infecting with its "revolutionary" optimism whole classes of economists that took up the task of diagnosing the death of the sugar industry, in the worst case, or at best assumed an enervating indifference to the problems of the region. Only the statistics department remained immune, an island surrounded by technocratic resentment devoted to the investigation of the socioeconomic problems of the Northwest. The clash between the new theories and social reality had a serious effect on a generation of students: Mario Roberto Santocho, a graduate of this faculty, was to create the Ejército Revolucionario del Pueblo (People's Revolutionary Army—ERP).

The Chicago School had its origins in the erosion of Keynesian orthodoxy at the end of the 1940s. The dominance of the problem of unemployment in Keynes had as a corollary a tendency to minimize the adverse economic consequences of inflation. Monetarism began to emerge as a challenge to the masters, promising an explanation of inflation and a policy for dealing with it. Milton Friedman assumed theoretical leadership of this tendency, and his *Capitalism and Freedom* (1962) became its manifesto. The Chicago School, which had inherited a long tradition in economics of distrust of and disdain for politics, constituted the vanguard of the contemporary process of economic intervention in political thought (Valdés, 1989: 77).

The Chicago School idea of the market incorporated three ideological paradigms: (1) a framework for free individual informed exchange, (2) freedom or a program for free and noncoercive social organization, and (3) a focus on economic science. These represented an echo or a legacy of the classic ideas of Adam Smith and others. Stigler, for example, defined man as an animal that maximizes advantage. Market transactions were seen as voluntary, benefiting one party without prejudicing the other. Individuals pursued their own ends with their own means, and advantage was derived from their capacity to use others as means on the basis of free mutual consent. As a result, the defense of the market, conceived as the defense of freedom, became the principal theme of the normative literature of the Chicago School: if the market functions, then freedom is possible.

Three further prerequisites were private ownership of the means of production, private management of the enterprise, and competitive enterprise. For Friedman this meant free exchange between private enterprises. This did not eliminate the need for government but gave it a role as a forum for determining the rules of the game or as an arbiter interpreting or enforcing the rules once established. The market was thus seen as the mechanism that minimized coercion. As in Adam Smith, the government was the enemy of freedom. For Gary Becker it was preferable to suffer economic monopolies than to suffer their regulation with its political flaws. A key theme in Friedman's ideological production was that government's central task should be facilitating the functioning of the market.

The monetarism of the Chicago School was based on the quantity theory of money, which balanced the economy and ensured the stability of prices that was unfortunately disturbed by the monetary intervention of government. Economics, as the science of the market, stated that if stability was desired, this rational system had to be allowed to operate freely. The economist became priest and seer, and the market society acquired sacredness. The Chicago economists thus became a sort of rational sect, witnesses to the redeeming power of the market system.

Around the same time, the U.S. government began its foreign aid programs— the transfer of economic knowledge to help developing countries improve their quality of life, social organization, and economic growth potential. The University of Chicago received substantial support from the U.S. government on the basis of its commitment to converting the economists of Third World countries. This led, among other things, to agreements between the University of Chicago and the Faculty of Economic Science of the National University of Tucumán and other such faculties in Latin America, including that of the Catholic University of Chile. The Chicago School was not to be on the sidelines during the cold war and the era of counterinsurgency operations in Latin America.

For the Chicago School, the emergence of the Latin American theories of economic development in the 1950s constituted an ideological challenge. At the beginning of the 1950s Raúl Prebisch became the first secretary general of the UN's Economic Commission for Latin America (ECLA), which focused on certain key concepts: a critique of traditional theories of international trade, especially in regard to center/periphery relations, the reasons for industrialization, planning as an imperative of development, adequate forms of international financing to promote development, regional integration, the structural nature of "inflation" in Latin America, the social dimension of development, and the need for structural change. For the Chicago School this program was an affront and even perhaps an act of subversion perhaps not unconnected with concurrent events in Cuba. Ideas such as those of Gunnar Myrdal, for whom the price system in a backward country could hardly present much rationality, greatly upset the new liberals. While Prebisch was drawing attention to the deterioration of the terms of trade, the Chicago School launched an attack on protectionism in Latin America. The U.S. firms needed a theory that would validate their racial right to exist in the face of an incipient industrialization in Latin America that would have to be scientifically condemned to the death camps. The competitiveness of Argentina's SIAM, whose refrigerators displaced General Electric's in South America, is but one example of this challenge.

As for economic aid for the Third World, Friedman believed that it could only have disastrous consequences for the United States, adding that he did not think the world needed a redistribution of wealth. This was the starting point—a political theory of national egotism.

Schultz was the first to identify "human capital" as a category of development in poor countries. His proposal found immediate success, attracting the attention of U.S. organizations concerned with development problems. The notion of higher education as a productive investment reflected, of course, the interests of the private university education system in the United States. "Human capital" became the economic answer to the obstacles to underdevelopment, while elites resistant to change, lack of technology, and poorly organized markets became "noneconomic" factors. The poverty of underdeveloped nations was seen as in no way related to international economic relations; any backwardness was due to "internal characteristics" and the lack of human capital.

One of the theoretical tenets of reformist intellectuals in the 1990s is precisely that the causes of the ills of the Latin American countries are internal. The new realism simply buries U.S. foreign policy, U.S. enterprises and their interests, the CIA, the pressures and blackmail of the cold war, and the foreign debt. This is part of a sclerotic Marxist line of thought that seeks to exculpate Latin American impotence by focusing on the power of "demonic" external forces. Presented as new thinking, this deactivated realism has its source in neoliberal theories. It is possible that the once leftist interested elite itself does not realize that its new "possibilist" philosophical outlook comes from the Chicago School's influence on the academic milieu of the 1970s. Intellectuals submitted to the discipline of capitalist restructuring in the advanced countries and sought external answers to assuage their guilt and excuse their having abdicated the defense of anticapitalist ideas. They advanced the ideas of late capitalism and proclaimed "the end of history" before it happened. This was the end of the reason for existence of the world of the poor. The "real" issue was to have an academic post and the space to publish.

The implantation of the Chicago School ideology in the Economic Science Faculty of the National University of Tucumán points to the roots that a plant develops in different soil. Graduates received grants to study for their doctorates in Chicago and were praised, with or without justification, for their intellectual merits in internal memoranda of U.S. foundations and in confidential reports from the University of Chicago to the National University of Tucumán management. The new economists sent reports to AID designed to encourage its continued support for their research. This relation with AID was based on an increasingly clear affinity with its ideals. For its part, AID demanded from the young economists a "professionalism" that entailed a rejection of any party-political affiliation whatsoever.

The Chicago School thus assembled a unified project for the Latin American countries based on delinking the state from economic enterprise, given that statism had become the basis for dangerously socialist experiments; disarticulating, atomizing, and dominating the various social sectors that would be opposed to privatization; and establishing authoritarian governments as the mechanism for achieving the above and clearing the way for a market democracy. The Chicago model was imposed for the first time in Chile with the Pinochet military coup of 1973. Thus was initiated an extremist ideological adventure, a praxis based on imposing, through a militarized state, an individualist philosophy and a "new man" maximizing opportunity and operating within a free and competitive market. Society was to be transformed according to criteria of economic efficiency. Three years later, in 1976, the same plan was implemented in Argentina. The operation was made possible through the dictatorship of General Jorge Videla and his economy minister, José A. Martínez de Hoz, considered probably the first and most brilliant of the "Chicago Boys." The United States had decided to endorse the coup on the condition that he become minister, that is, indiscriminate repression in Argentina was to serve the purpose of imposing an economic plan based on the theories of the Chicago School. Before the coup, the name of only one potential new cabinet minister was known. The economy minister's second in command—and president of the Central Bank—was Adolfo Díaz, who had been a professor at the National University of Tucumán after a long stay in the United States. Martínez de Hoz's staff included a number of Tucumán professors, among them Valeriano García.

There was a causal link between the massacres carried out by the military dictatorship and the economic plan. The armed forces had experience of government but not as economists. The economic plan was ready for the day of the coup and, as in Chile, had been distributed among the high military command. Here, however, there was no vacillation as there had been in Chile between a "restorationist" project, in which the armed forces would become a classic bridge between two civilian regimes, and a "foundational" project, which implied a revolution, a change in the whole social outlook. The armed forces in Argentina, under the auspices of Chicago, had already chosen the latter. The coup was an association between the military and the Chicago School economists. But the regime had not reckoned on the "adventurers," the opportunist parvenus, and the assassins.

The Argentine model was based on the Chilean one, with liberalization of the market and the price system, an opening of the market to foreign trade and external financial operations, and a dramatic reduction of the role of the state in the economy. Martínez de Hoz became the "star" of the regime, the one to overcome the trauma of the old Argentina. The economic plan entailed a commitment to political authoritarianism as a prerequisite for change, the use of "science" to legitimate the power seized, a reduction in the importance of politics in society, and the declaration of the end of all demagogies. Yet the plan was never fully implemented. For one thing, the armed forces required a strong state as war booty from which to derive multiple benefits, among them the guarantee of formidable external credit for the private companies they were becoming attached to. Subsequently this credit was placed under state control by Domingo

Cavallo as minister of the same military dictatorship. What the economists of the Chicago School had been unable to complete was achieved under the next two civilian administrations, but particularly that of Carlos Menem.

A basic understanding was the need to replace politics with technology and politicians with economists (Valdés, 1989: 30). Another was the reordering of society to deprive it of its base and any possibility of social resistance to the economic plan. That required the atomization, fragmentation, and destruction of cultural, trade union, professional, political, and youth organizations, among others. Individuals would now have to confront alone in the market the problems they had previously faced collectively. This was called "modernization"—a guarantee of individual stability inaugurated by the authoritarian regime.

The preachings of the market economy and the primacy of technicians in public decision making had considerable influence on the leaders of Tucumán's sugar industry, who adopted an attitude of true devotion to the economists, seen as an audacious generation independent of politics and possessed of knowledge of the laws of the market. However, having received the military regime's "political" rather than "scientific" support (abundant credit was granted it during the counterinsurgency war in the region), the industry would suffer the consequences of the economic plan along with the rest of the country. Along with other regional economies, Tucumán would enter an era of deindustrialization and massive layoffs, a crisis that would continue into the mid-1990s.

Alienation under the economic plan of the military and then Menem affected millions of people. Once the disappearances and deaths in one part of society were accepted as necessary costs of the "structural" transformations under way, there followed an internalization of the need for disappearances from the system as an economic cost of its decisive restructuring. Even those who suffered economic disappearance themselves would proclaim during elections this ineluctable and unappealable necessity: after things had gone badly for everyone, perhaps some would do well.

Victor J. Elias of the National University of Tucumán notes in his autobiography (*La Gaceta*, June 6, 1994) that he graduated from the University of Chicago in 1964 and is now an adviser to the World Bank, the Inter-American Development Bank, and the Menem government's Ministry of Economics. Elias sees economic growth as "the most logical way for a society to allow low-income families to achieve more comfortable styles of life"—this while the poor are being driven off the precipice by this very economic reasoning. He declares that he has never engaged in trade union or political affairs "except for voting," but this is an old illusion of the traditional intellectual—thinking of oneself as outside politics simply because one has never occupied a political post, as if one's studies in the United States were not in themselves a form of political commitment. In 1994 three economics professors from Chicago came to Argentina to give courses for the staff of the Ministry of Economics and 80 members of the Fundación Mediterranea handpicked by Cavallo.

INFORMAL SECTOR DEVELOPMENT

3.2

Theoretical Approaches to the Informal Sector

Tamar Diana Wilson

This article focuses on the informal sector or the underground economy, which usually is not taken into account by government economists and statisticians. Yet the informal sector constitutes a large segment of the economy in Latin America. Five theoretical approaches, relevant to the development literature, are identified and briefly discussed in light of the informal sector.

THERE ARE FIVE GENERAL APPROACHES to the informal sector—those associated with modernization theory, dependency theory, neoliberalism, Marxism and neo-Marxism, and worldwide systems theory. Many of these approaches have adopted others' assumptions. The informal sector was first labeled as such by the International Labor Organization (ILO) in 1972. Prior to that names such as the "bazaar economy" and the "traditional economy" were common, reflecting the dualist notions of the modernization paradigm. "Petty commodity production" and "petty commerce" are terms applied to the mode of production of the informal sector, especially by those writing in the Marxist, neo-Marxist, or world-systems traditions. Most of the approaches that have participated in cross-fertilizing debate and dialogue as phenomena observed by researchers working

First published in *Latin American Perspectives* 99, vol. 25 (2), Sage Publications, Inc. Reprinted with permission from the Latin American Perspectives Collective. Selection from 3–10.

within one tradition have been reanalyzed, reinterpreted, and incorporated into other models.

Modernization Theory

Modernization theory identifies the informal sector with "traditional" precapitalist as opposed to "modern" economic organization. The economy is conceived as dual, with the traditional sector having no linkages with the modern one. Those who work in the traditional sector are there mainly because of lack of education or disinclination to accept factory discipline. The traditional sector is also conceptualized as a "peasant system of production" in which a "proto-proletariat" is engaged in self-generated employment (McGee, 1977). It is expected that as economic development progresses, the traditional sector will gradually disappear; the modern sector will take over the production of all goods and services, providing them more cheaply because of higher technology and larger scale (Moser, 1994).

Empirical evidence has disconfirmed these predictions. Not only does the informal sector show no signs of disappearing, but it has maintained its proportion of goods and services produced in Latin American countries from the 1950s to the present (Portes and Benton, 1984; de Oliveira and Roberts, 1994) and has consistently shown signs of expansion during periods of economic crisis. Furthermore, many formal-sector jobs in advanced industrialized countries have been "informalized" (Portes, 1983; Portes and Sassen-Koob, 1987; Sassen, 1990 [1988]), and the informal sector has reappeared in new forms and in new industries such as electronics assembly (Fernández-Kelly and García, 1989; Tiano, 1990) and older industries such as automobile and auto parts manufacturing.

Dependency Theory

Dependency theory attempts to explain the lack of capitalist development in Latin America as due to historical relations of economic dependence between core capitalist countries and peripheral ones. The earliest relations of dependency rested on the export of primary materials from the periphery in exchange for industrial goods. With the introduction of import-substitution programs, consumer goods began to be produced in the periphery; however, the machinery and other infrastructural supports for such light industry still had to be imported, and at a disadvantageous rate of exchange. In the most recent phase of dependency, export-oriented industry has taken center stage, partly in response to the need to repay tremendous national debts (de Oliveira and Roberts, 1994). In Mexico, exports include products manufactured by *maquiladoras,* whether subsidiaries of multinationals whose headquarters are located in the

United States, Japan, or a variety of European countries or subcontracting facilities owned wholly or in part by the indigenous capitalist class. The "marginal pole" of the economy has little to do with the "hegemonic pole," marked by oligopolistic industries and manned by a labor aristocracy (Quijano, 1974). Thus, Castells (1983) contends that cities in Latin America are dependent cities, and the wrongly labeled "marginal" patterns displayed by some of their residents are due to this dependency. Residents cannot control the pace or direction of urban development because of their subjection to the goodwill of the state as well as "to the changing flows of foreign capital" (Castells, 1983: 212).

The initial analyses of the Comisión Económica para América Latina (Economic Commission for Latin America—CEPAL) and the Programa Regional para Empleo en América Latina y el Caribe (Regional Program for Employment in Latin America and the Caribbean—PREALC) grew out of work done by researchers for the International Labor Organization in Africa (Hart, 1973; ILO, 1972). However, the PREALC researchers incorporated insights from dependency theory.

Import-substitution and export-oriented industry are seen as sharing two characteristics: the need to import heavy machinery and high capital/labor ratios in processes of production. Sophisticated machinery replaces the need for an extensive labor force. The result, according to PREALC, is the creation of a surplus labor force with no chance of employment in the formal sector (Pérez Sáinz, 1991; Cartaya, 1987; Tokman, 1987a; 1987b; Mezzera, 1987). This surplus labor force must create employment for itself in order to survive. This self-generated employment, marked by a qualitatively different mode of production from that employed in the formal sector, constitutes the informal sector. The mode of production is marked by low capital/labor ratios, frequent use of unremunerated family labor, low start-up costs, easy entry, low labor productivity, unskilled labor, simple technology (see Pérez Sáinz, 1991: 36; Carbonetto, 1985: 66), and the use of earnings not for capitalist investment but for subsistence (Bennholdt-Thomsen, 1981).

Linkages with the formal sector are conceived as not exploitative. Those employed in informal-sector activities may buy inputs from each other or from the formal sector, exporting personal services in return. The relationship of the informal sector to the formal sector is seen as similar to the relationship between peripheral countries and core countries (Pérez Sáinz, 1991: 21). The informal sector is seen as subordinated to the formal sector in that it exists only in the niches left by the latter (Pérez Sáinz, 1991: 22). In itself it is neither functional nor dysfunctional for the capitalist system. Rather, different occupations within the informal sector have different relationships with the formal sector and are subordinated to it in various ways (Tokman, 1979; Mezzera, 1985). Some informal-sector occupations are relatively autonomous, requiring neither exogenous inputs nor markets; these include the sale of fruits and vegetables purchased directly from small farmers. Others are dependent for inputs, products, or sales on the modern sector of the economy; these may include small manufacturers, whether independent or subcontracted by formal-sector firms, and small commercial establishments that buy from wholesalers (Tokman, 1979: 217–218).

As for the future of the informal sector, the PREALC researchers again stress its heterogeneous character. Some entities, such as small-scale manufacturers, will eventually disappear as more capitalized, modern industry displaces them. Others, such as those offering personal services, will survive, as they have in advanced capitalist countries. Still others, such as vendors and other commercial establishments, will persist longer and will ultimately be replaced by large-scale commercial establishments (Tokman, 1979: 224–225; 1989). The informal sector as a whole also takes on different characteristics according to the country in which it is found and is influenced by prevailing laws (Tokman, 1992).

PREALC policy with regard to the informal sector is to provide credit packages and training in management, accounting, and microenterprise development for informal-sector entrepreneurs (PREALC, 1979: Placencia, 1988: Tokman, 1987a). In recent years, PREALC members have recognized the interlinkages between the formal and the informal sector, although they tend to see them as occurring essentially at the level of product circulation (see, e.g., Mezzera, 1988). Nonetheless, with occasional exceptions (e.g., Tokman, 1992) PREALC continues to focus on microenterprises rather than the informalized labor force, which leads it to exclude domestic workers from its studies despite these workers' "unprotected" working conditions (Mezzera, 1988).

Neoliberalism

Associated with Hernando de Soto (1989), the neoliberal approach considers the informal sector the most dynamic sector of the economy, one notable for its "extralegality." Legal restrictions in the formal sector lead to the formation of microenterprises within the informal sector. Evasion of such regulations is responsible for its dynamism. As in the modernist paradigm, the informal sector is seen in dualist terms, as a separate economy, although populated by emergent capitalists. If given a chance, the informal sector could become the engine of development. It is disadvantaged by the fact that government subsidies tend to go to formal-sector enterprises. Far from being a lumpen proletariat or "marginal mass," informal-sector entrepreneurs are perfect models of petty-bourgeois capitalists, but they can only succeed if misguided and archaic mercantilist state policies are replaced by a truly laissez-faire capitalist environment. No exploitation of the informal sector by the formal is recognized, nor are informalized labor relations related in any way to the profit-making advantages of formal-sector capitalist firms. Labeled as a neoliberal by Cartaya (1987), de Soto is seen as a populist by Pérez Sáinz (1991: 39) and his theory as one of "capitalist populism."

Marxism and Neo-Marxism

As concerns capital-labor relations, Marx (1977) distinguished between "formal" and "real" subsumption of labor to capital. The latter was characterized by full proletarianization; in the former, capital made use of noncapitalist modes of production while leaving the means of production in the hands of the producers and leaving internal labor processes such as self-exploitation and exploitation of unremunerated family labor in place (see Cook and Binford, 1990: 23–24). Instead of the dual-economy framework embraced by the modernization theorists, Marxist approaches visualize the informal sector as a socially and historically determined mode of production subordinated to and subsumed by capitalism.

Nonetheless, the neo-Marxist scholars who first attempted to analyze the existence of what they described as precapitalist economic activities in the growing cities of Latin America explained the persistence of these activities in terms similar to those of modernization theory. They were expected to disappear as modern capitalist enterprise advanced. Meanwhile, they provided subsistence to the "reserve army of labor." The reserve army of labor helped keep wages low; the threat of being replaced inhibited the workers employed in capitalist industry from unionizing or pressing their demands for higher wages. Scholars working within the Marxist framework disagreed among themselves as to whether this reserve army of labor, sometimes labeled the "marginal mass" (Nun, 1969), was dysfunctional and parasitic or functional for capitalism.

A great deal of the literature concerned with structural marginality (Leeds, 1971; Valentine, 1971, 1972) was a Marxist or neo-Marxist response to the "culture-of-poverty" theory associated with Oscar Lewis (1975, 1966), a Marxist offshoot meant to explain the behavior and persistence of the lumpen proletariat. Later still, Marxists and neo-Marxists argued that those in the informal sector were not "marginal" populations at all but rather immiserated masses spawned by the dynamics of capital accumulation (Bennholdt-Thomsen, 1981; Cockcroft, 1986; Perlman, 1976). In contrast to the neoliberals, most recently represented by de Soto (1989), who held that informal-sector enterprises were emerging bourgeois concerns, Cockcroft (1986: 246) pointed out that those in the informal sector were neither part of a marginal mass nor emerging capitalists: "In terms of their overall relations of production these 'self- employed' and 'self-exploited' elements are disguised proletarians whose 'ownership' of a humble workshop or of a *miscelanéa* masks their proletarian incorporation into a larger capitalist structure that appropriates the fruits of their labor."

Gerry (1987: 112) characterizes the neo-Marxist approach to the informal sector as conceiving small entrepreneurs to be petty commodity producers who are actually disguised wage workers exploited through such devices as subcontracting. They benefit the capitalist system both by supplying cheap commodities to the workforce employed in the formal sector and by their continued presence as an industrial reserve army. In the case of supplying goods (or services, as in the case of repair shops) to the formal-sector labor force, whose living wage can thus be reduced, the subsidy provided by those employed in the informal sector to capitalism is indirect, but many commodities produced or services generated in the informal sector represent direct inputs into formal capitalist productive processes.

The neo-Marxist approach is in accord with the PREALC analysis in that the informal sector is constituted by a surplus labor force unabsorbed by the advanced capitalist sector and is subordinated to the formal sector. Neo-Marxists differ from the dependency theorists, however, in that they see this subordination as exploitative but highly beneficial to capitalist enterprise and/or to the capitalist system, national or transnational, as a whole (Bennholdt-Thomsen, 1981; Cockcroft, 1986; Davies, 1979; de Janvry, 1981; Kowarick, 1979; Moser, 1978; Portes, 1983; Portes and Benton, 1984, 1987; Portes and Sassen-Koob, 1987; Portes and Walton, 1981; Safa, 1982). Although this conclusion follows from the logic of dependency theory, for the PREALC scholars who have employed some of the assumptions of this theory in analyzing the informal sector the assumption of links of exploitation consequent on subordination is not one of them. This is in part because they locate the informal sector in the context of dependent development instead of in the context of problems associated with capitalism (Rakowski, 1994).

Although the informal sector is dependent on inputs from the formal sector in many if not most cases, the reverse is also true. This can most clearly be seen in the case of the homeworkers working for piece rates for formal-sector firms or for informal-sector firms that have subcontracting links with such firms (Schmuckler, 1979; Benería and Roldán, 1987; Avelar, 1977; Treviño Sillar, 1988). Such workers have none of the benefits associated with formal-sector work—no social security, no minimum wage or overtime guarantees, and no job security. Such workers are functional for capitalism because of their "cheapness": no socially legislated workers' benefits are extended to them, and they work for lower wages. Because of their "cheapness" these workers produce lower-cost inputs than could be manufactured in the formal sector. Furthermore, the flexibility of such a labor force, which can be hired or not according to production goals, is especially valuable to the formal-sector firms that subcontract part of the process of production to informal workshops.

Garbage pickers and street vendors may also constitute a disguised proletariat. Birkbeck (1978; 1979) has shown how the garbage pickers of Cali, Colombia, sell their cardboard through intermediaries to a multinational paper company. Paid on a piecework basis, the garbage pickers are essentially working for the company but without the benefits enjoyed by the "formal proletariat" employed by that company (see also Wilson, 1994). Street vendors are also functional for capitalist enterprise. They may have only an indirect relationship to ensuring company profits, for example, buying only from wholesalers, or they may work for a commission with one or more companies or suppliers. Finally, they receive credit from while paying interest to the companies or intermediaries whose products they sell (Bromley, 1978b; Möller, 1979).

The indirect subsidy to capitalism results from the fact that workers employed in the formal sector purchase goods and services from the informal economy for less than they would pay for goods and services produced in the capitalist sector; this reduces pressure on the wage (Davies, 1979; Kowarick, 1979; Moser, 1978; Portes and Walton, 1981; Safa, 1982). For example, Portes and Walton (1981: 104) maintain that "the informal sector subsidizes part of the costs of formal capitalist enterprises, enabling them to enforce comparatively low wages on their own labor." The informal sector does this by lowering the actual cost of subsistence below a theoretical cost of subsistence based on the full value of necessities if they had "to be purchased as commodities on the market" (Portes and Walton, 1981: 87–88).

De Janvry, whose work focuses mainly on peasant farmers and semiproletarianization, advances an interesting argument about the "functional dualism" between petty commodity producers both among the peasantry and within the informal sector and the dominant capitalist economy (1981: 34). He argues that Latin American economies are characterized by sectoral and social disarticulation. Under sectoral disarticulation there is external dependence on the import of capital goods and technology: markets for products lie abroad as well. In socially disarticulated economies, formal-sector laborers are only a cost for capital, although they play productive roles as wage laborers; they are seldom consumers of the finished commodities. Workers' subsistence needs are most often provided for by peasant and informal-sector petty commodity producers. Portes and Walton's analysis (1981) can be seen to complement de Janvry's. They show how the informal sector subsidizes the capitalist economy both directly by providing industrial inputs more cheaply than they could be produced under fully proletarian relations of production and indirectly by providing cheaper consumer goods to the urban proletariat, thus reducing pressure for higher wages.

In their policy proposals, neo-Marxists focus on the need for profound structural changes and a more even distribution of income.

3.3

Urbanization and Planning: Inequality and Unsustainability

Thomas Angotti

The author outlines several urban planning strategies, examines planning within the metropolis, and shows possibilities for sustainability that also allow grassroots and left participation.

Urban Planning Strategies

EVER SINCE THE LAWS of the Indies, urban planning strategies have been imported from the North and reinforced the regime of private property. In the postcolonial period they have been based on antiurban and progrowth philosophies, and they have been ecologically destructive.

There is a widespread perception that the large cities of Latin America are unmanageable and unplanned. In fact, however, there has been considerable planning—not just official planning by government agencies but planning by the private sector. Planning is not the exclusive preserve of technocrats who happen to be called planners but the application of human consciousness to the building and preservation of human settlements.

Looking first at regional planning, which addresses national and subnational urban systems, and then at urban planning within metropolitan areas, I will

First published in *Latin American Perspectives* 91, vol. 23 (4), Sage Publications, Inc. Reprinted with permission from the Latin American Perspectives Collective. Selection from 21–31.

attempt to show that these are imported strategies that serve the interests of national and transnational capital.

Regional Planning

Antiurban theory has dominated urban planning in the North since the industrial revolution. It is based on the idea that large, densely developed cities are the source of urban problems. Lipton (1988), for example, explicitly sees urbanization as a cause of underdevelopment. Solutions lie in rural development or in bringing the countryside to the city in the form of low-density suburban living.

The antiurban bias rationalizes attempts to displace the urban poor, limit spending on urban infrastructure, and even stop urbanization. Negrón (1991) notes that the myth that improving the quality of urban life will empty the countryside and bloat the metropolis and the myth of urban "marginality" underlie Venezuelan planning. However, attempts to limit urbanization or urbanize the countryside have been historic failures, and despite limited public investment in "marginal" urban communities, metropolitan areas have flourished.

More serious attempts at regional planning in Latin America were initiated by developmentalist governments committed to the strategy of import substitution. Perhaps the most ambitious effort was undertaken by the government of Juscelino Kubitschek de Oliveira in Brazil, which established a powerful regional development agency for the Northeast and launched the plan for the new capital city of Brasília. A succession of national development plans up to the present has directed significant capital investment outside the two main metropolises of São Paulo and Rio de Janeiro (Guidugli and Barreto, 1986).

Though sometimes motivated by nationalist intentions such as these, regional planning initiatives in Latin America have more often followed strategies imported from the North. They rarely have strong links with national economic policy. As the following discussion shows, without aggressive national planning, regional planning can be little more than a utopian dream of bureaucratic and technocratic elites (see Hopenhayn, 1991). I will consider four problematic regional planning approaches: spatial deconcentration, balanced regional development, strong local government, and growth poles.

Spatial Deconcentration

Planning schemes that narrowly focus on the need to decentralize the urban structure are problematic. Spatially dispersing a highly centralized urban and economic structure has long been seen as a means of promoting national development, eliminating inequalities, stimulating an internal market, eliminating differences between city and countryside, reducing rural dependency, and eliminating urban primacy. Historically it has been promoted as a rationale for declining central government financing in rural areas (see Spalding, 1992: 40–43). Most recently, deconcentration has become a favorite tactic in neoliberal privatization schemes.

The colonial administrations in Latin America tended to be highly centralized. The colonial powers often destroyed popular, democratic, and communal structures so as to enhance the role of their appointed regimes. After independence, most countries adopted the old colonial structures of local government. Centralism was often justified by the lack of resources and the need to strengthen weak national governments. As Roberto Segre (1978) has shown, centralism contributes to the maintenance of ruling-class power as long as national and metropolitan power are in the hands of propertied classes.

As desirable as decentralization may be, decentralization schemes are often narrow and misdirected when viewed as an essentially urban, or spatial, problem. The problem of overcentralization is too often measured by divergence from some ideal geographic notion of even distribution of the population between city and countryside, large and small cities, metropolis and rural areas. However, dispersal of the population does not necessarily affect economic inequalities. Opening up government offices around the country does not necessarily mean the decentralization of political power or resources.

The key to decentralization is economic and political power, not spatial distribution of resources. Even so, central economic planning within the context of independent national development policies provides the best opportunity for a more equitable, decentralized regional planning practice. A greater degree of control over the nation's human and natural resources is a precondition for directing and influencing their location and use. In other words, although it may seem to be a paradox, central planning can provide the best conditions for regional planning. José Carlos Mariátegui (1928), criticizing Peru's decentralization strategies, asserted that the basis for regional empowerment was an alliance of the working class and the peasantry. With a national surplus appropriated for internal use and not for export, such a scenario could indeed strengthen historically forgotten regions. As nations become more urbanized and the size of the peasantry dwindles, this possibility is even more desirable. In many European countries, for example, a political commitment by national governments to preserve productive activities in rural areas has often outweighed the narrow logic of the market. Many nations in which the urban working class has historically wielded greater political power also have more developed and politically powerful rural regions and rural producers.

Balanced Regional Development

A recurrent strategy for regional imbalances favored by the international aid establishment is to promote market activities and infrastructure development, especially road construction, in regions with relatively disadvantaged small and medium-sized settlements (see Rondinelli, 1983). The idea is that capital investments from the center create greater relative economic advantage by helping towns participate in the regional market, thus spurring the growth of small and medium-sized settlements and correcting regional inequalities. Rondinelli and Ruddle (1978) call for the establishment of "urban functions in rural development" so that all settlements above given threshold sizes have urban services that should correspond to settlements of these sizes. Presumably, this strategy would limit pressures for migration from these settlements to the metropolis.

Although such programs can improve the quality of life in less urbanized areas, insofar as they reinforce the local marketplace they reproduce all of the inequalities of that marketplace. The market's tendency is to centralize resources as it develops and to expand and link up with the international market. The roads drain rural areas of population and resources and pull them toward the export-oriented metropolis, and undemocratic centralized power is unaffected by a decentralized government bureaucracy. Indeed, creating urban functions in this economic environment only reinforces the power of urban elites.

This is yet another example of an approach rooted in an abstract ideal theory of geography that equates a particular kind of spatial uniformity with economic equality. It confuses functional and geographical categories. Economic development does not arise from geographical form or "normal" dimensions. A regular size relationship among settlements does not necessarily mean that the economic relations are based on equality.

Local Government

Planning strategies that rely mainly on strengthening local government are among the most problematic. U.S.-supported aid programs are fond of projecting the U.S. experience of local federated government as a model for Latin America. They finance programs to enhance the revenue-generating capacity of local governments and train local administrators. Noting the lack of resources in Latin American nations, they treat local governments as if they were profit-making enterprises whose success must be measured by revenues and fiscal rationale.

But what economic interests do local governments serve? The interests of local elites and property owners, or the interests of workers and tenants? Do the local governments rationalize a central bureaucracy and overcentralized power structure, or do they truly decentralize power? Does strengthening local government mean cutting back national support for local programs as it did in Ronald Reagan's "new federalism"? Local government has traditionally been a means for legitimizing elite political power. David Collier's study of Lima's *barriadas* (1978) is one among many that demonstrate how popular participation at the local level can be used to co-opt potential opposition and reinforce central authority (see also Eckstein, 1982; Herzer and Pirez, 1991).

In Latin America, in contrast to North America, the total economic surplus is usually insufficient to provide adequate resources for municipal planning and regulation. Furthermore, if local governments are part of an unequal development structure, they only reproduce that pattern. Because their powers are geographically limited, they are unable to affect the overall structure of inequality even if they can more equally distribute the minimal surplus available to them within their own boundaries.

Growth Poles

The notion of planning urbanization by establishing industrial growth poles in less developed rural areas has been around since the 1960s, but the idea has rarely been implemented. One of the first and most notable examples of growth poles in Latin America is Ciudad Guayana in Venezuela (Rodwin, 1969). Ciudad Guayana was built, beginning in the 1960s, around a major steel complex in Venezuela's interior. Physically, the city exhibits many features of rationalistic European planning—orderly streets and boulevards, monumental public buildings, and neat suburbs. However, it also has acquired the symptoms of spontaneous growth, mass poverty, and inequality that characterize cities throughout Venezuela (see Friedmann, 1966; Friedmann and Weaver, 1979).

Ciudad Guayana has become more of a traditional company town or enclave than a planned city. The state-financed industries produced a small economic multiplier effect and more unemployment than employment. Air and water pollution are serious problems in the city, and in the region the Guri hydroelectric project created ecological destruction (see García and Kunkel, 1991). Ciudad Guayana was made possible by a relatively short-lived economic boom in the steel industry, and its replication in other new cities is now precluded by the nation's debt crisis. The obsolescence of the industrial technology makes its future questionable.

Growth-pole experiments never took hold elsewhere in Latin America. In Mexico, plans to create a growth pole around the new city of Lázaro Cárdenas had little success. Not surprisingly, the international aid establishment has always been wary of growth poles because they presume an unacceptable level of central economic planning and investment in urban infrastructure and are linked with nationalization of basic industries and import-substitution strategies.

At the theoretical level, growth-pole strategies never adequately dealt with the problem of urban economies of scale. Existing larger settlements probably offer more efficient use of economic resources than completely new cities (see Gilbert and Gugler, 1984: 177–78). Large metropolitan areas have a greater diversity of capital and labor. The metropolis offers many scale economies in the production sphere and in socal and physical infrastructures that are not available in smaller cities.

Planning within the Metropolis

As noted previously, some city planners in Latin America have tried to use planning to assert and consolidate emerging national identities and to establish urban centers as focal points for national development. More frequently, however, city planning has emulated European and North American planning.

The first urban planning regulations, contained in the Laws of the Indies, were products of the Spanish crown. They established rules for the organization of urban space around the central plaza, which became the center of political and economic power. Located on the plaza were the representatives of the crown, the church, and the civic authorities. Urbanization by other colonists around the plaza was regulated, but, significantly, areas occupied by the indigenous masses were unaffected.

After the end of colonial rule, the most influential trend in city planning was European. For example, Mexico City's center was fashioned according to principles of Baroque monumentality. The Paseo de la Reforma was inspired by Georges-Eugène Haussmann's monumental Champs Elysées in Paris. The influence of French planning may also be seen in Buenos Aires, Caracas, and other large cities that introduced monumental boulevards, grand civic architecture, and other Baroque features as part of a strategy to capture control of the city centers from the working class—much as Haussmann had done after the Revolution of 1848.

In the twentieth century, Latin American planners have followed the modernist downtown models of Europe and North America and the laissez-faire approach to real estate development found in North America. The downtown skylines of the major metropolitan areas in Latin America offer stark images of the influence of the Manhattan model, where central real estate values have combined with official urban renewal plans to produce monumental business districts. For example, downtown Caracas is now a collection of giant civic projects such as the Torres de Silencio that dwarf the colonial-era plazas and narrow streets. These megaprojects are connected by a network of highways such as the Autopista del Este that mimic the U.S. interstate highway system. Planned residential areas are few—elite enclaves such as the Country Club neighborhood and public housing ghettos such as 23 de Enero, created during the Marcos Pérez Jiménez dictatorship.

The sprawling low-density suburbs in many Latin American cities, though much more spontaneous and crowded than North American suburbs, are the result of the laissez-faire pattern of development in the urban periphery. Planning is done spontaneously by individuals, associations of property owners, and squatters. It follows an antiurban pattern of dispersed development. In North America, suburban planning follows the parochial interests of exclusionary local governments, supported by regressive fiscal policies and state and federal subsidies. In Latin America, suburban development is just as parochial and chaotic, but the problems are more dramatic because of the absence of adequate resources for basic infrastructure.

Most city planning in Latin America has relied on regulation, not comprehensive planning. Although comprehensive master plans have been completed for most large cities, they have generally been formalistic—emphasizing physical form—and unimplemented. More often than not, they outline approaches to urban planning that require a political will, institutional consensus, and level of social surplus that do not exist.

In theory and practice, most city planning in Latin America has not been sustained by economic development, cultural history, or the natural environment. Perhaps the most damaging consequence of emulating the North American regime of urbanization has been reliance on the private automobile as the main means of transportation. Auto circulation has been favored over more ecologically sustainable transportation modes such as trolleys and subways (see Wright, 1992). Following the lead of North America, many Latin American cities tore up their trolley lines to make room for autos, trucks, and buses. The few cities that now have subways still have horrendous traffic congestion because auto use is still dominant. Intercity freight moves mostly by truck, since the few railroads were built only for individual foreign corporations to extract raw materials from specific locations. Also unsustainable are the urban redevelopment strategies that favor new construction over preservation, subdivision regulations that permit energy-inefficient low-density sprawl, and water and other infrastructure systems that serve low-density areas.

City planning has had no significant impact on the domination of urban development by the real estate market. This is a political choice favored by urban elites, and it is exacerbated by weaknesses in the enforcement of local regulations. Many cities have strict rent, subdivision, and zoning regulations that theoretically govern urban development. However, in the absence of the resources and institutions to implement these regulations, they are ignored or easily violated. Thus, an urban system designed to work with Northern wealth falls apart in Southern poverty. As in the colonial era, the masses remain outside the orbit of planning. At the same time, indigenous forms of planning of human settlements are ignored or overridden by the real estate market.

Self-Help

A strategy frequently promoted by the international aid establishment as a preferred substitute for government-sponsored planning is local self-help. Self-help is basically an acknowledgment that the state will take little or no responsibility for planning and development of working-class neighborhoods (see Burgess, 1982, for a concise critique). The basic strategy of self-help is to finance local groups and organizations that arise spontaneously to deal with miserable urban conditions. Assistance may involve financial aid, construction materials, or technical advice.

The World Bank's Sites and Services program (World Bank, 1974) arose from the self-help strategy, and self-help became a major thrust of the international aid establishment in the 1970s. The best-known model for self-help came out of Peru and the work of John F. C. Turner in Lima *barriadas* (Turner and Fichter, 1972). Turner traced the spontaneous process of upgrading of housing in squatter settlements and compared this with the relative inaction of government. It is perhaps no accident that Turner's theses arose in one of Latin America's poorest countries, where government legitimacy among the poor has traditionally been weak.

Self-help housing programs promoted by the international aid establishment usually involve some form of credit and "cost recovery." This means that housing consumers must have stable incomes in order to qualify for credit, excluding people in the lowest income categories. It means that housing consumers must pay back the banks and international donors for material assistance. This indebtedness in the end winds up promoting private property and a real estate market in which only a weak one existed previously. Mortgage credit, bank involvement, and infrastructure add up to a private real estate market able to house the upper strata but unable to solve the housing needs of the impoverished majority.

This does not mean that self-help cannot be a positive element in development. Self-help actually describes the way in which most metropolises in Latin America have been built—spontaneously and without government assistance (see Hardoy, 1982). Sometimes spontaneous planning can be well organized and sophisticated. For example, in Chile under the Unidad Popular government and in Mexico since the 1970s, local associations for improving the urban environment played key roles nationally as well as locally and have been important forces in pressuring for government financing of urban development (see Castells, 1983: 190–209; Fox, 1989). However, these groups rely on self-help out of necessity, not because they believe it is a preferred national strategy. Indeed, a constant among the strongest and most influential self-help groups is the demand for a stronger government role and a more equitable economic and political system.

The Cuban microbrigade system is an example of how central planning can work together with local initiative. Since 1970, most government-financed construction of housing and local community facilities has been done by microbrigades with volunteer labor organized and backed by local enterprises and government. Microbrigades could not have accomplished as much as they have without government support (Mathey, 1988).

Capital-City Development

Creating a new capital city has long been a popular idea, promising the establishment of a distinct national urban form free of the colonial past. In theory, a new capital can be a national symbol of independence in contrast with the export-oriented colonial seat of power. It can avoid the pitfalls of spontaneous urban development and aid decentralization of historically centrist government functions.

Some countries, such as Chile and Bolivia, have split administrative functions among urban centers. In others, such as Peru and Argentina, there have been recent proposals to move the capital functions to the interior. The Argentine proposal to move the capital to Viedma in 1987 died for lack of political support and funding. The dream of moving Peru's capital to Cuzco, the Mantaro Valley, or somewhere else closer to the indigenous population in the *sierra* has remained a dream since the rebellion of Túpac Amaru.

The most significant planned capital city in Latin America is Brasília. Brasília was planned as a gateway to the development of the interior and a symbol of Brazilian national power. Far from the metropolitan areas of Rio de Janeiro and São Paulo, Brasília was to establish a new pole for urbanization and relieve pressures on the bloated coastal metropolises. Unlike Ciudad Guayana, Brasília was planned primarily as an administrative center, though there were hopes that a more balanced local economy would emerge.

Brasília's monumental civic center symbolizes the Brazilian bourgeoisie on the rise. Its expansive physical layout, rational superblocks, and modern infrastructure contrast with the tangled chaos and spontaneous sprawl of the older cities. However, beyond the planned center, where three-fourths of the population of metropolitan Brasília lives, lies a world of favelas and uncontrolled development unanticipated by the planners. Brasília has in fact become a center for the accumulation of capital and labor in Brazil's interior, even though the coast still dominates the entire country (see Vale, 1992; Shoumatoff, 1987; Holston, 1989; Epstein, 1973).

Brasília's self-conscious design is an example of a universal trend in city planning—physical determinism. Physical forms are presumed to symbolize and promote national pride, civic pride, and economic development. However, when there are no jobs and the buses do not work, one wonders who benefits from the "planned" city center. And without the amenities of the old central plaza, it is often far less gratifying.

Conclusion

Despite its many failures, urban planning can help improve the quality of life in Latin America—if it is part of a progressive, sustainable strategy for economic development. Elements of an emerging progressive approach could be empowerment of the growing network of local community organizations, national, regional, and local planning based on principles of equality, and a "rediscovery" of America's historic, sustainable regimes of urban and rural living.

The large popular community-based movements in almost every Latin American country present new hope for grassroots urban democracy and empowerment. These movements arose spontaneously in response to the lack of government planning in the urban periphery. Women tend to play a leading role and have become politically empowered in community movements. In many countries the movements have evolved into large organizations that negotiate with the state for improved urban services and plan and administer their own urban infrastructure. In many cases they have become significant political forces. In Brazil, for example, urban movements make up a major part of the popular base for the Workers' party, the largest left party in Latin America.

Grassroots urban movements have joined with other forces in the left to win control of local governments in Brazil, Mexico, Venezuela, and Peru, to name only a few countries. This has brought to the fore the contradictory relationship between centralist national governments that reflect the general interests of capital and the historically weak local state. Local government has become one of the main battlegrounds for the political engagement of labor and capital and sectors within each.

To address existing inequalities, urban and regional planning strategies need to be consistent with national strategies that address economic inequalities. They should allocate resources in a balanced way to improve the daily living conditions of both urban and rural populations. Cuba, for example, is the only country in Latin America in which the capital city declined in size relative to secondary cities. This was not the result of any policy to stop urban growth but the consequence of a national policy since 1959 aimed at correcting urban-rural inequalities, shifting productive investments to secondary cities and the countryside, and decentralizing health, education, and other services. As a result, migration to Havana declined (see Susman, 1987). An unforeseen consequence, however, was the deterioration of Havana's housing and urban infrastructure, now exacerbated by Cuba's severe economic crisis.

If Latin America's large metropolitan regions do not have to accumulate poverty they also do not have to be congested and polluted. Sustainable urban transportation modes such as subways, trolleys, and bicycles can help clear the urban air. Some cities, most notably Curitiba and Belo Horizonte in Brazil, have begun to reclaim city streets for nonpolluting transportation modes and pedestrians (see Wright, 1992). However, these are exceptions. Unless economic dependence on oil and auto and the underlying regime of capital accumulation are altered, it is difficult to conceive of an early solution to Latin America's urban environmental problems.

DEMOCRATIC OR POLITICAL
DEVELOPMENT

3.4

Democratization and Class Struggle

Timothy F. Harding and James F. Petras

The authors criticize bourgeois or representative democratic practice in the face of economic crisis in Latin America. They briefly examine revolutionary regimes that have confronted this problem in the struggle to achieve a socialist transition. This selection is part of an introduction to several articles that take issue with a popular mainstream interpretation (O'Donnell, Schmitter, and Whitehead, 1986) of transitions from authoritarian to democratic regimes in Southern Europe and the Southern Cone of Latin America.

D EMOCRACY, DEMOCRATIZATION, and their relationship to class struggle and revolutionary movements have become vital issues since the demise of numerous military governments throughout Latin America. This process began in the mid-1970s and is as yet incomplete since military dictators still rule Chile and Paraguay. A previous issue of *Latin American Perspectives*, "State and Military in Latin America" (1985), published a series of articles analyzing the crises that engendered military regimes in the region and the contradictions that resulted.

Debates on the nature of democratization and the strategies to be followed by the new electoral regimes rage throughout the Latin American political spec-

First published in *Latin American Perspectives* 58, vol. 15 (13), Sage Publications, Inc. Reprinted with permission from the Latin American Perspectives Collective. Selection from 3–6, 14–15.

trum. Thus far in the United States, discussion has been dominated by liberals and partisans of the electoral regimes. This issue of *Latin American Perspectives* broadens the debate and opens the process to a critical analysis.

The U.S. government and much of the political science establishment discuss democratization in terms of the replacement of military regimes with formal electoral democracies. According to this view, for a country to qualify as democratic the property must be preserved, and the country must be kept open to the free operation of international capitalists.

Democratization in the sense of the development of popular democracy essentially implies the achievement of significant political and economic power by the workers, peasants, women, Indians, blacks, and youths who constitute the vast majority. Popular democracy implies the equitable distribution of available goods and services.

The establishment or reestablishment of civilian electoral regimes in Latin America is obviously not the same as the establishment of popular democracies, but since military regimes came to power to safeguard bourgeois rule threatened by the growing power of mass movements and revolutionary organizations, the demise of military governments is a contradictory process.

The transition to civilian elected regimes is both a project of the ruling group and/or U.S. policy and, at the same time, a partial victory of popular mass movements and revolutionary forces. The ruling classes became dissatisfied with military rule when the military were unable to deliver acceptable rates of economic growth and were unable to contain the new upsurge of mass opposition movements (see Su Zhenxing, 1988). At the same time, the left and the mass movements have seized the opportunity to reopen a broader range of struggles aimed at short-run improvements in salaries and services and long-run transformations of the state. The mass struggles that developed in opposition to the military regimes have refused to be contained by the narrow limits of bourgeois electoral rule and the attempt to return to the political manipulation by the reemerging traditional political parties. Throughout Latin America, in countries as diverse as Mexico, Guatemala, and Haiti, these struggles broadened the postmilitary regimes and demanded democracy for workers and peasants (the right to strike and land distribution), improved conditions for the urban poor, recognition of leftist parties, women's rights, the rights of Indians, and so forth.

Economic Crisis and Growing Radicalization

Because the establishment of electoral regimes coincides with the deepening of a catastrophic economic crisis, the "democratic openings" everywhere are precarious. The civilian regimes cannot deal with the crisis and the escalating debt payments without forcing down the real earnings of workers, peasants, and the salaried middle class. Everywhere "restructuring the economy" means deepening the process for which the military was called into power: raising productivity, lowering real wages, and integrating local production with the developed capitalist centers at the expense of national capital.

At the same time, the level of popular mobilization is greater than ever as a result of greater urbanization, higher levels of education, and expansion of media presentations showing levels of consumption in advanced capitalist countries far beyond the reaches of most Latin Americans. This is combined with a more sophisticated level of grassroots organization. Widespread demands for popular democratization now include the rights of urban slum dwellers, women, indigenous peoples, and blacks, and are both broader and more specific than the traditional left focus on mobilizing the proletariat and the peasantry.

Within the context of electoral openings, the people have won greater latitude for struggle than the ruling elites intended. In Haiti and Brazil mass struggle reshaped the constitutions being drafted, and workers demanded that democracy also apply to the working class (the right to strike, control of their unions, etc.). In El Salvador and Guatemala the people took advantage of electoral openings to reorganize and renew urban workers' struggles despite the counterinsurgency intent of the elections in these countries (see Jonas, 1988).

These mass movements have developed independently of left political parties and have tended to remain independent of any party. Peasant and neighborhood movements often insist that no one party be allowed hegemony. The parties may also learn to work together within these movements.

State Continuity and Electoral Transition

Patterns of democratization in Latin America are quite diverse. In most cases this process has involved a continuity at the state level and a limited transition to a civilian elected regime or government. *State* refers to the permanent institution of class rule. The enduring institutions include the army, the police, the judiciary, and the forces that control the economic levers of the accumulation process. *Government* refers to the political officials who occupy the executive and legislative branches of government and who are subject to renewal or removal. *Regime* refers to the form or system of government (electoral, military, bonapartist, etc.).

Since the long-term major policies of a nation are shaped by the composition, orientation, and dominant class of the state, the U.S. government has been willing to accept changes in regime (e.g., military to civilian) in order to preserve the continuity of the state. Elected regimes may try to restructure the state apparatus and class linkages to serve the class interests of workers and peasants. This was the case of the elected regime of Allende in Chile. A period of conflict and instability ensued between the regime and the state, but with U.S. intervention to back the state apparatus, the state overthrew the regime. In Cuba, on the other hand, the revolutionary army became the basis of the new state, and the initial liberal postrevolutionary regime was replaced when it came in conflict with a state linked to mobilized workers and peasants. Thus the U.S. government has been determined to block or destroy political changes that dismantle the existing state if the new state is organized with a socialist or even nationalist project. The United States has been willing to sacrifice dictators such as Marcos and Duvalier if it can thereby preserve the state apparatus, a policy that failed in Cuba and Nicaragua.

To adequately characterize the process of change from military to civilian electoral regimes, it is important to recognize the different levels at which change occurs. In Nicaragua, the revolution uprooted and destroyed the dictatorial state in the course of defeating Somoza's National Guard, opening a process of political, social, and economic democratization. That process includes the development of mass organizations, the establishment of a new constitution, the construction of a new state based on the armed populace, redistribution of property, and the establishment of new priorities for basic services such as health and education so that they serve primarily the needs of workers and peasants.

In the other transitions to civilian regimes, the military controlled and negotiated the process of securing positions of state power for themselves and their supporters. The military, police, and judiciary in most cases have remained in place. The intelligence groups retain control over the means of repression. Moreover, the military have secured guarantees and amnesties from the civilian regimes, thus exonerating themselves for their terrorist behavior (with the exception of a few top military officials in Argentina).

Any characterization of the process of political change must include both the continuities within the state and the changes at the level of regime. It must also consider the civilian regime's capacity for meeting the socioeconomic and political needs of the workers, the urban semiemployed, and peasants, as well as the salaried middle class. . . .

Democracy and the Left

The insistence on democracy by the growing mass movements has had a profound effect on the left parties. They have been pushed toward unity, as shown by the unification of revolutionary forces in El Salvador, the reunification of the Sandinista movement in 1978, and the establishment of Izquierda Unida in Peru. Unification is a central aspect of left politics in Mexico. At the same time, left parties are accepting and encouraging the independence and autonomy of mass organizations (unions, federations of peasant, labor and neighborhood groups, etc.) from the hegemony of any one party. Parties are accepting a democratic principled pluralist struggle within these groupings.

Democracy has also become an issue in the debate between the left and those who have adopted a "post-Marxist" position, which underplays the centrality of class struggle and obscures the class nature of state power through presenting the state as an autonomous bureaucratic actor. This "post-Marxist" position is reminiscent of the liberal pluralist doctrine, which focused on narrow electoral interests, personalities, and party concerns, cut off from the economic and power matrix. . . . But this attack on the left takes the form of a defense of electoral regimes as identical with democracy. Their arguments gained currency in the aftermath of the military defeat of certain revolutionary vanguard groups in South America during the 1970s. In Guatemala, Nicaragua, and El Salvador, where a unification and democratization process took place among left groups engaging in armed struggle, concepts of democracy are closely integrated to revolutionary struggle. This is also the case in Chile and Uruguay, where the left was able to promote a revolutionary conception of democratic socialism. These conceptions of "democracy" have gained hegemony in Argentina, where the 1970s left was dominated by Peronismo. In Brazil and Peru, where mass social movements (neighborhood, Church, trade-union, and peasant groups) have emerged parallel to and independent of the traditional left parties, neoliberal conceptions of democracy are strongly contested by class and quasi-class modes of theorizing.

Another aspect of the democratization debate stems from the opportunities that the postmilitary electoral regimes have opened for participation in national and urban governments by left politicians. In El Salvador, Guatemala, and Honduras, the electoral regimes prohibit the participation of the left because of the imminent danger of revolution, but where the left is allowed to participate, albeit in a context in which monetary resources and media access are the major deciding factors, left parties do win positions (mayor of Lima, Peru; most-voted for senator in Brazil; mayor of Fortaleza, Brazil; provincial governor in Argentina, etc.).

When elected into office in the context of a capitalist economy in crisis, the left is placed in the position of having to solve the problems without the power to change the economic structure. There is a constant tension between electoral emphasis and the need to sustain mass revolutionary organizing.

3.5

Internationalization of Capital

David Barkin

The author moves toward an internationalization-of-capital approach and away from dependency. This allows for analysis of transformation in international settings rather than a departure from the nation-state. The theoretical underpinnings of this approach evolved from the work of the U.S. economist Stephen Hymer and of the French political economist Christian Palloix.

In THIS SHORT ESSAY I shall argue that the "internationalization of capital" is a much more fruitful approach for studying the world economy than "dependency theory." Quite specifically, I suggest that political economy today should not try to explain the backwardness of one part of the world vis-à-vis other parts but rather should explain the dynamics of the emergence of the international capitalist economy. In this context, it is crucial to understand the unequal patterns of development which are characteristic of capitalist development and which leave certain areas and certain classes more impoverished than most. As a framework of analysis, the internationalization of capital obliges us to return to the basic laws of capitalist accumulation, which imply a particular organization of production and the social relations specific to this mode of production.

The internationalization of capital represents a sharp departure from previous

First published in *Latin American Perspectives* 30 and 31, vol. 8 (3 and 4), Sage Publications, Inc. Reprinted with permission from the Latin American Perspectives Collective. Selection from 156–159, 161.

and most current work by political economists on the international economy. Rather than starting from the nation-state as the unit of analysis, this analytical approach presupposes a qualitative change in the nature of the international economy. This transformation is related to the changes in the scale of production and the locus of decision making by those empowered to direct capitalist enterprise. With the emergence of the transnational corporation as the principal organizer of production on a global basis, decisions cease to be made with reference to a single nation. It becomes increasingly clear that the nation, or the nation-state, cannot limit capitalist expansion to its own borders. In the best of circumstances, individual political units might attempt to influence the allocation of investment resources through national policies aimed at increasing the rate of profit or improving the investment climate. But increasingly the dynamics of the world capitalist economy cannot be understood with reference to a single nation or group of nations. Productive decisions are now made on a global scale.

There is another powerful reason for preferring the internationalization of capital as an explanatory theory to understand the world economy and, *particularly*, the plight of the nations of the "Third World." This new approach emphasizes production as its point of departure. Unlike conventional theory and many versions of dependency theory, which pinpoint circulation (or international trade) as the key element to be analyzed, the internationalization of capital insists on examining the determinants of production on a global scale. Therefore, it seems to me, it raises crucial questions about the nature of the new international division of labor which are still not completely resolved. Analytically, we cannot be satisfied with simple positivistic discoveries that there is growing industrial production in former primary producing nations or that there is a new group of intermediate countries producing export products to satisfy basic consumption needs in the wealthiest countries. By starting from production and concentrating on the process of capitalist accumulation, the theory of the internationalization of capital obliges us to look for new categories to use to analyze the dynamics of the reproduction of the world capitalist system. Thus, the descriptive stratification of production into primary, secondary, and tertiary sectors seems less revealing than a breakdown which differentiates those lines of production which contribute to the reproduction of the labor force (means of subsistence or wage goods) and those which are directed toward capital accumulation.

With the focus on production, the internationalization of capital also explains the changing relationships between different parts of the world economy. As capitalism became the dominant mode of production, theoretical debates have arisen over the articulation of "noncapitalist" modes of production to the rest of the system. In Latin America, the discussion of feudal systems seemed of great concern to some dependency theorists. With the framework advocated here, the problem is more neatly addressed by examining the process of moving from the formal to the real subsumption of labor to capital throughout the system (as discussed by Marx in the now famous, but originally unpublished, part seven of volume one of *Capital*, now available as an appendix to the new Vintage edition with an excellent introduction by Ernest Mandel). We can examine the problems of the relationship between peasant and capitalist production by determining if and how surplus value is generated and the ways in which it is appropriated by different segments of the capitalist class. In this way, the complex productive structures within individual countries can be analyzed in terms of their particular contributions to the global process of articulation.

The internationalization of capital does not, however, dismiss the nation-state from the analysis. Many political economists have typically identified the state with the national economy and developed their analyses on the basis of national economies. This focus is specifically adopted by dependency analysts, who often view their objective as explaining the subordination of one country or grouping of countries to another. In this view, a great deal of attention is devoted to the examination of national economic policies with a consequent de-emphasis of trends on a transnational scale. The focus of the internationalization of the capital changes the analysis, placing greater importance on the problem of the relationship between global tendencies and transnational decision makers on the one hand and the individual nation-state on the other. It involves a still incomplete reconstruction of the role and concept of the state. It is incomplete in several senses: (1) clearly at an international level, no real state authority exists, and in spite of well-intentioned efforts to forge such an authority, the efforts have not been successful to date; (2) at the national level, there is a continuing and often ill-understood conflict between national and transnational bourgeoisies, which translates into conflicting policies; (3) the theory itself has not been adequately developed to handle the contradictions created by the changing international economy. In spite of these problems, however, it seems clear that the questions posed about the problems of the role of the state in the accumulation of capital on a global scale now transcend the traditional notion of the nation-state, and new frameworks of analysis must be found. This is an integral part of the approach advocated here and therefore a great advantage of the theory.

The internationalization of capital, in sum, is a relatively new approach to the study of the world economy, to the problem of dynamics of global capitalism and international economic relations. Obviously production still has a geographic specificity, but this approach argues that the logic of allocative decisions is now global even when transnational capital is not involved in a particular activity. That is, even when investment and production decisions are made by national governments or local capitalists, it seems increasingly clear that global economic and political structures strongly influence the individual decision maker. It is possible to state this even more strongly: international markets and economic power structures are increasingly determining the individual decisions made in ever more isolated parts of national economies, even when "noncapitalist" productive groups are involved, such as peasant producers in many Third World economies.

Unfortunately, the body of literature referring to the internationalization of capital is relatively unknown in the United States. Before his untimely death in 1973, Stephen Hymer had begun to do research within the Marxist paradigm on the expansion and integration of the world economy. But recent developments have occurred in France, following preliminary work by people like Christian Palloix. The theory takes as a point of departure the relatively simple proposition that the analysis of the intertwining of the three circuits of capital—money-capital, productive-capital, and commodity-capital—discussed by Marx in the second volume of *Capital,* might be usefully extended to the international economy. A historical examination of the integration of the world market economy reveals the early importance of commercial-capital (in the form of foreign trade), dating back to the very emergence of the capitalist system. The subsequent importance of money-capital was noted most persuasively by Lenin in his influential essay on imperialism. But perhaps the most significant change in recent years has been the expansion of productive-capital on a global scale and the powerful impact of the integration of the various facets of capitalist economic life into an increasingly unified global market.

The theory of the internationalization of capital explains the impact of the growth of the world economy on the productive structure of each of the participating nation-states. Although it also is fundamental for comprehending the dynamics of the global system as a whole and in analyzing tendencies in international trade and investment, in what follows I wish to focus specifically on the impact of the internationalization of capital in altering the particular productive structures of each country. This approach is useful because it also provides a critique of the deterministic analysis of some who focus exclusively on the transnational corporation (TNC) as the motive force behind recent changes in the international economy. In its most simplistic form, these companies are identified as the objective enemy of the people. Their size and international character have conferred upon them a mystique which makes them appear to be uncontrollable. The theory of the internationalization of capital, in contrast, focuses on the laws of expansion of capitalism, laws which Marx analyzed more than a century ago and which are still useful in understanding the dynamics of the societies in which we live. From this perspective, we can understand the behavior of the TNC in the context of the process of the accumulation of capital on a global scale which permits and, at the same time, requires the concentration and centralization of individual capitals. In this context, the TNC is understood as an actor, an important actor, in a process that transcends each actor. . . .

The growing influence of the international economy, however, is not the only determinant of change in capitalist societies. This process creates its own contradictions: growing unemployment, the progressive immiserization of masses of people in the face of material "progress," denationalization, cultural destruction, and the other ills defined in an ample literature of denunciation; these are the phenomena usually focused upon by the *dependentistas*. As an alternative, the analysis provided by the theory of the internationalization of capital also offers alternatives for concrete action. In place of proposals for a code of ethics for corporate behavior or new rules for negotiating with the TNC, the theory suggests that what is necessary is a new strategy for producing the goods which the masses of people need for their own basic survival. This is an approach which can be usefully integrated into popular struggles on a national level. Focusing on changes in the productive apparatus as part of a longer-term political struggle for structural transformations is proving to be a promising result of this new way of analyzing international economic relations.

3.6

Dependency, Modes of Production, and the Class Analysis of Latin America

Colin Henfrey

This selection from a long essay exposes the weaknesses of the work of Frank and turns to a modes-of-production approach which has been popular among anthropologists doing fieldwork mostly in Africa but also in Latin America. This approach allows for study of how a peasant may or may not assimilate into a capitalist economy, and, thus, opens up analysis of whether feudalism, semi-feudalism, or capitalism is a dominant mode of production in the countryside.

FROM A MARXIST STANDPOINT the conspicuous flaw which most exercises Frank's many critics is his conception of capitalism in both its theoretical and historical aspects. To prove his thesis, he defines it in terms of market relations, then applies it indiscriminately to the whole of Latin American history. One might well ask why his revolution was not forthcoming in the sixteenth, let alone in the twentieth century. At first sight the obvious solution is the one Laclau (1977) offers: a more Marxist concept of modes of production in terms of the development of the productive forces, the ownership of the means of production, the mode of appropriation of surplus, and so on; and a recognition that different modes can coexist historically, without this implying their separation (as in the dualist conception) or their identity (as Frank has argued). In practice, though,

First published in *Latin American Perspectives* 30 and 31, vol. 8 (3 and 4), Sage Publications, Inc. Reprinted with permission from the Latin American Perspectives Collective. Selection from 37–42.

if the purpose is that of analyzing class formation, the modes-of-production panacea raises two complex sets of questions. First, how is it to be applied? What notion of the relationship between base and superstructure is entailed? Is it just a historical paradigm or one with reference to the present? What modes of production are at issue apart from the capitalist mode itself? In what sense can different modes coexist in a single accumulation process, and what is their relative significance for relations of production and class formation? And secondly, how sufficient is the concept? Is a social formation to be understood simply in terms of the combination of modes and the interrelations of their various "levels"—the economic, the political, and the ideological? Can we infer from this alone the totality of class relations, including, for example, the nature of the state or the working class in a given instance? Or is more entailed in pinning down the specificities of history?

In all these respects the use of the modes-of-production concept as the heir to dependency has varied, and these variations are closely reflected in the different critiques of Frank's "theoretical" version of it. At the risk of overschematizing, each use is partly a response to a different stage in Frank's progression from his initial problematic (his reified notion of underdevelopment) to his operative concepts (the "capitalist appropriation of surplus from satellite to metropolis," and so on) and finally to his handling of history in terms of such specific matters as the alleged inverse correlation between growth and ties to the world market (Frank, 1971: 35). These differences of critical focus are important because neither of the first two uses of modes-of-production escapes these beginnings, with their distance from substantive issues. The structuralist response to Frank's first step in his underdevelopment problematic has the intrinsic limitations of a substitute "grand theory" of history. The conceptual response to the second one retains much of Frank's economism and his mere labelling of social phenomena. It is only when modes of production analysis is directly addressed to empirical history, or "stage three" of Frank's thinking, that it both orders and investigates data, not least because it no longer attempts a total explanation of them. Instead it affords a framework for looking at specific patterns of class formation without excluding variables, such as the agency of the state, which are not directly given by it. In many ways these distinctions are parallel to those within the dependency perspective between exclusive generalization and more heuristic investigation. Hence this latter use of modes of production is much more open to the issues suggested by Cardoso and Faletto's approach, especially the nature of the state and the specificity of popular movements—in short, the key elements of class struggles, which neither of the first two deployments of modes of production can encompass.

This is not to suggest the discovery of yet another panacea for the Marxist analysis of development. On the contrary, the precedents for taking modes of production as a starting point rather than the object of analysis lie in the pre–Stalinist approaches to capitalist expansion and social formations, without "lines" or labelling or "theoretical practice," by writers like the early Lenin and Trotsky. The future of Marxist analysis in any field, development included, lies primarily in whether it can move on from schematic critiques of the Third International, both ideological and theoretical, to the study of the substantive issues facing contemporary socialist movements: the changing and locally variable nature of capitalist expansion on a world scale; the specificity of the capitalist state and processes of class formation in instances of this expansion into historically varied settings; the handling of political paradigms such as the "permanent revolution" as concrete hypotheses rather than dogmas, as in Gramsci's consideration of its applicability to Italy; the concern with superstructure on the part of Gramsci and Mariátegui; and the sense of class agency and conjuncture which once maintained a continuum between concepts as abstract as modes of production and moments of praxis as political as the writing of the "April Theses." In short, the need is neither for "neo" nor "paleo" but for "neo-classical" Marxism. In concluding, I will therefore examine the trends in both the critical and analytic uses of the modes-of-production concept and their implications for the comparative class analysis of Brazil and Chile.

Mode of Production and Social Formation: The Class Analysis of Latin America

First I will consider Taylor's work, as an instance of the structuralist "grand theory" of history which criticizes Frank's problematic but reproduces its generality. I will then take Laclau's conceptual critique, which, despite its pioneering role, encourages a reductionist use of the concept for labelling local modes of production, and finally I will look at the investigative historical use by Assadourian, Bartra, and Cueva, which seems to me much more suggestive for purposes of class analysis.

While the structuralist analysis is the most recent, it derives a logical priority from its apparent aspiration to provide a total theory of history. It is hardly surprising that its exponents, in their emphasis on the distinction between the theoretical and empirical or "objects of thought" and "real objects" (with the former conceived of as "scientific"), should concern themselves with Frank's first step: his view of dependency as a condition requiring a "theory" of its own, an opinion which he shares with most dependency writers apart from Cardoso and Faletto. Thus for Taylor (1974) Foster-Carter's contention that dependency and related approaches provide a new body of theory appropriate to the realities of underdevelopment is a "sociological fantasy." Its assumption is that the real object of Third World societies produces the theory. On the contrary, Taylor argues from an evidently structuralist viewpoint, theory's scope for dealing with realities depends on its autonomy from them, its scientific universality as Althusserian "theoretical practice." It is precisely this universality which gives Marx's theory of modes of production its scope for dealing with *all* realities, including those of underdevelopment or "peripheral capitalist social formations"— realities which Frank reduces to his single underdevelopment model, for lack of any such key distinction between real objects and objects of knowledge. While this stems from his circulationist concepts like those of surplus appropriation by regions and nations rather than classes, its roots lie deeper in Frank's ill-thought-out "problematic": his basic construct of underdevelopment, which derives from Baran's same circular vision (Taylor, 1979: 71–98). Other structuralist critics have pursued this question of how Frank's "knowledge" is produced. In Leys's view his "underdevelopment theory" is ideologically conceived in emphasizing depredation rather than exploitation and structure, and teleological in being constructed by antithesis with the notional model of autonomous metropolitan development (Leys, 1977). As the fruit of such a misconception, a "theory of underdevelopment" is scientifically "impossible" (Bernstein, 1979: 91). Phillips (1977: 19–20) puts this more practically. Not only is it unable to deal with the questions of major concern to Marxists, like the scope for further capitalist expansion and class formation in Latin America, but its frame of reference, in the presence or absence of a notional autonomous development, prevents it from even asking such questions, since it is not focussed on what *is* occurring.

To dismiss such comments as structuralist abstractions, as does Foster-Carter (1979), evades the issue. There is nothing abstract about arguing that Frank's thinking prevents one from asking questions about Latin American social formations. The question is whether the substitute for it is more directed to substantive enquiry. Taylor certainly maintains this to be his objective in using the modes-of-production concept. He carefully distinguishes his own position from the "formalism" of Hindess and Hirst (1975), who question in principle the possibility of "objects of thought" appropriating "real objects," or of theory as a means of empirical study (Taylor, 1979: 163–171). His concern is precisely with the "contemporary concrete situation in peripheral social formation[s]," in terms of "the *specific* effects of the *different* forms of capitalist penetration experienced by Latin American societies" (Taylor, 1974: 8, 11, italics mine). The results in his book, which rest heavily on a would-be reinterpretation of the Latin American evidence, are therefore a potential test of whether such concrete understanding is afforded by even a non-"formalist" version of the structuralist theory of modes of production.

At its source, this seems somewhat unlikely. The structuralist conception of modes of production (Balibar, 1970) is clearly an advance on the Stalinist notion of their literal existence as linear stages in the one-way historical determination of the superstructure by the base. Instead they are seen by Balibar as essentially theoretical constructs: the thought "dynamics" rather than the literal forms of history, with their ideological and political levels determined only "in the last instance" by the economic. Though this is dominant in the capitalist mode, it determines the dominance of other levels in the forms of surplus appropriation specific to other modes of production—the political in the feudal mode, and so on. Moreover, with this autonomy it follows that each particular level enjoys its own "historical time," or diachronic freedom of movement. Hence any social formation may involve not only distinctive modes of production but the interpenetration of their levels—e.g., the partial reproduction by one mode's ideology, say, of another's particular social relations. If one thinks of such cases as Brazil, with its lasting "patrimonial heritage" from a noncapitalist background, this is obviously a suggestive concept. However, the transition from this mode of thought to such a concrete interpretation of history, as presented in Balibar's seminal statement, is in practice problematical, as the former has such exclusive priority. His whole project of conceptualizing the dynamics of specific modes of production (particularly the capitalist mode) is presented as a self-contained exercise in defining "objects of thought," not applying them. How they relate to actual history is a question which Balibar constantly assigns to a different plane for separate and subsequent consideration. In addition, the notion of the dynamics of each mode of production as self-contained necessarily inhibits the identification of any relationship between them. How then can one "think" the transition from one mode of production to another or, correspondingly, their "articulation," which structuralists identify as the key to Third World social formations?

These problems dog Taylor's sweeping attempt to theorize Latin American history at the "real" level of social formations. Specifically, he sets out to assess the constraints of pre-existing modes of production on the expansion of the capitalist mode and the relationships between them; but given the absence in the structuralist matrix of any effective mediation between modes of production as objects of thought and social formations as real objects, the latter at best are merely reflections of juxtapositions of the former. The sum of the Latin American reality—as distinct from the realities promised by Taylor—is seen as the obstruction of the capitalist relations of twentieth-century imperialism by the persistence of a feudal mode installed by merchant capital in previous phases of expansion.

The problem is not whether this is valid but how much it actually tells us. Its only specificity lies in the contrast with Southeast Asian formations, where a different contradiction arises from merchant capital's interaction and hence imperialism's encounter with the Asiatic, not the feudal mode. However, this by definition imposes a single abstract mold on all Latin America's structural history. No less than Frank's, the picture is one of social formations reduced to, and therefore as homogeneous as, the concepts applied to them (in Taylor's case, the capitalist and feudal modes of production). Hence this conceptual differentiation (in contrast to Frank's mere capitalism) does little to interpret such obvious differences as those between Brazil and Chile. The "Spanish and Portuguese penetration of Latin American social formations" (Taylor, 1979: 188–192) is homogeneously depicted in terms of a predominance of merchant capital and control by a feudal oligarchy, which obstruct the expansion of capitalism into agriculture right down to the present. In the closely examined case of Chile (Taylor, 1979: 261–262), the failure of the structuralist reforms under Frei is just one more expression of this contradiction. There is nothing, despite this subsection's title, "The Class Structure of Third World Social Formations," to suggest why such a specific class force as the Popular Unity should have emerged from this contradiction in the case of Chile. Such factors as might help explain it—the early predominance of industrial capital in the mining sector, for example—are at a level of specificity which tends to elude the structuralist concern with the inner logic of modes of production in overreaction to their previous reduction to "real" as distinct from theoretical objects. Instead of historicized ideas, they become an idealization of history, which is far from providing interpretations of "contemporary concrete situations" (Taylor, 1974: 8). Moreover, even the general relation between the two "modes" involved is uncertain, apart from the notion of capitalism being somehow obstructed by feudalism. Such social formations are described as "transitional"—but to what and how is quite unclear from this account of the contradiction between their component modes of production, since it gives little indication of the forms of their articulation as distinct from their mere coexistence. Hence one gets no impression of a trajectory, let alone of specific trajectories, but only of a single, suspended history. Will the capitalist mode become generalized, and if so, is the current contradiction of anything more than passing importance? Or is it permanently obstructed, and with what political implications? In Taylor's account, there are no mediating concepts like accumulation and class formation between the two worlds of "thought" and "real" objects to help in answering these questions. Class relations and indeed the whole of history appear to be *given* by modes of production. One is reminded of Rancière's critique of this perspective as one in which structure itself is determinant and classes are therefore not merely nonagents but hardly even the ingredients of history in any remotely specific way (Rancière, 1974). Such theoretical practice seems far from pertinent to the politics which Taylor charges both Frank and Foster-Carter with obscuring (Taylor, 1974: 20–21).

Laclau expresses a similar concern with Frank's lack of concrete inferences and his crude political conclusions but attributes them much more directly to his conception of capitalism (Laclau, 1977: 27). Drawing mainly on the Dobb and Sweezy debate on the roles of productive and market forces in the rise of Western capitalism (in Hilton et al., 1976), he observes that Frank's emphasis on the latter as the key to capitalism's expansion is no less historically confusing than Sweezy's. To define the capitalist mode in terms of production for profit and market relations is to take it right back to antiquity, not just sixteenth-century Latin America. Essentially Frank is confusing capitalism with capital—that is, production with exchange—and the homogeneity of a mode of production with the heterogeneity, or various articulated modes, to be found in economic systems.

His urge to show that underdevelopment is linked with capital accumulation by no means demonstrates or depends on the former's being of a capitalist nature. "To affirm the feudal character of relations of production in the agrarian sector does not necessarily involve maintaining a dualist thesis." On the contrary, production for the world market has involved the strengthening of noncapitalist relations in Latin America, as in Eastern Europe's "refeudalization." Even today "peasant proletarianisation . . . is very far from being concluded . . . and semi-feudal conditions are still widely characteristic of the Latin American country-side" (Laclau, 1977: 32). Far from their being mutually exclusive, the interplay between capitalism and feudalism at the periphery, as a source of cheap wage goods and raw materials, has helped counteract the tendency to the former's falling rate of profit.

3.7

Combined and Uneven Development
in Latin America

George Novack

This selection is drawn from a broader debate with David Romagnolo (1975) on the merits of the notion, inherent especially in Trotsky, that development does not occur evenly. The author illustrates with historical examples from Latin America.

DAVID ROMAGNOLO makes two main criticisms of the law of uneven and combined development. First, it supposedly disregards the leading principle of historical materialism that the mode of production determines the nature of a social formation. It thereby bases itself upon the superficial peculiarities, the exceptional features, of historical development instead of its general and fundamental ones. Second, the law of uneven and combined development focuses on exchange rather than productive relations, thus lapsing into the errors of the vulgar bourgeois economists.

Neither contention is factually correct. The law of uneven and combined development proceeds from the premise that the mode of production, constituted by the level of the productive forces and the corresponding relations of production, is the underlying determinant in all social structures and historical processes. Nor does the law subordinate the relations of production to exchange

First published in *Latin American Perspectives* 9, vol. 3 (2), Sage Publications, Inc. Reprinted with permission from the Latin American Perspectives Collective. Selection from 100, 102–104.

relations, although it recognizes that in the generalized commodity relations intrinsic to capitalism exchange relations have far greater importance than in pre-capitalist societies, where the sale and purchase of products is economically marginal.

However, these two elementary Marxist principles only provide the points of departure and serve as guidelines for analyzing historically developed social formations in their full concreteness. With their aid it is necessary to go forward and explain why a particular mode of production manifests itself in such different ways and develops to such disparate degrees under different circumstances. How is it, as Marx pointed out, that "the same economic basis" shows "infinite variations and gradations of appearance"? This can be ascertained, he tells us, "only by analysis of the empirically given circumstances." In this case we must ask: what empirical circumstances account for the variations and gradations of appearance of the modes of production in Latin America after its conquest and colonization? . . .

Rosa Luxemburg stated in *The Accumulation of Capital:* "Capital, impelled to appropriate productive forces for purposes of exploitation, ransacks the whole world; it procures its means of production from all corners of the earth, seizing them, if necessary by force, from all levels of civilization and from all forms of society" (Luxemburg, 1964: 358). Capitalist accumulation in all its stages has depended to one or another extent upon access to means of production and subsistence produced under precapitalist or noncapitalist conditions. In doing so, it annexes precapitalist forms of production as tributaries to its economic operations. Brazilian sugar earlier played the same role in this respect as Southern cotton cultivated by slaves and Russian wheat raised by serfs.

Indeed, the Brazilian plantations, which had a precocious growth as the world's chief exporter of sugar, provide an impressive case of uneven and combined development. Their predominance imposed an extreme lopsidedness upon the economy during the colonial period.

The crop was cultivated and processed by slaves, the most primitive kind of extensive agricultural labor. While the sugar barons directly profited from the surplus labor of their workforce, their type of operation was not the same as the classical slavery based upon a natural economy. It was a commercialized slavery which originated and developed as an offshoot of the capitalist world market.

Although the plantation *(fazenda)* was a self-sustaining, isolated production unit outside the money economy, where the opulent landowning families disported themselves like lords and ladies on the backs of their slaves, it was geared into the vast machinery of commerce. The labor supply came not from the local Indians but, as in the Caribbean, from African traders who dealt in slaves as a commodity.

The sugar mills required a sizeable capital investment. The luxury staple was marketed by monopolistic companies, carried on Portuguese ships alone, sold in Portugal, and exchanged for goods from the mother country. Consequently, unlike the Spanish towns, the few underdeveloped seaboard centers were little more than places for the transshipment of goods.

This symbiosis of slave production with international commerce gave a combined character to the Brazilian economy. It resulted from and embodied the mutual penetration of factors belonging to two different historical species: slavery, which was characteristic of the first stage of class society, and the market and monetary relations that were ushering in its climactic capitalist form.

Of course, once black slavery was established on a large scale (six to eight million slaves were brought into the colony from the late sixteenth to the early nineteenth century), it was actuated by its own internal laws. But this mode of production, beset by a twofold contradiction, had a twin-motored dynamic. Its development was regulated not only by its own momentum but even more by outside conditions and forces. The export economies were not self-determined but shaped and misshaped by the social division of labor bound up with the centralized imperial system and have to be analyzed and appraised in their organic connection with the money economy of the world market.

This linkup was evidenced in the cyclical pattern of Brazilian trade, the "boom and bust" cycles expressed in the rise and decline of the sugar crop and other commodities such as lumber, precious metals, cotton, and later rubber and coffee, which depended upon the fluctuations in foreign demand and the competitive conditions in the world market. The expansion and contraction of these branches of production have been responsible for its one-sided, backward, and dependent development.

The distortions of Latin America's economic and social development under the pressures of the world market and domination by foreign forces is one of the prime peculiarities of its history from which the continent suffers to the present day. The subordinate role clamped upon Latin America as a supplier of raw materials and foodstuffs in the international capitalist division of labor enabled the more advanced metropolitan powers to exploit and rule over its peoples, first under the colonial system and later through the more refined methods of monopoly capitalism.

This unevenness manifested itself, in Latin America as in other parts of the colonialized world, in the emergence and endurance of a broad spectrum of combined forms in which precapitalist relations of one kind or another were fused with capitalist relations. In this way the various precapitalist modes of production were conscripted to serve the demands and interests of the monied men overseas and at home. In the transitional period from the dominance of one mode of production to the maturity of its displacement by another, Romagnolo does not allow for the existence of such mixed modes with contradictory characteristics that give a peculiar twist to the social structure of a country.

Two of the articles in the same issue of *Latin American Perspectives* pinpoint successive stages in the process of combination. The first step whereby institutions of a lower and weaker order were subjected to the influence of a higher and more powerful one is described in the paper by Karen Spalding (1975: 107–121) on the reorganization of social relations in Peru under the Spanish colonial rulers. The *ayllu*, the ancient unit of the Inca community based on kinship, was transmuted when the Andean population was relocated and concentrated into villages controlled by representatives of the Spanish authorities. Although the Indians retained the right of using the land, it became the legal property of the Spanish state.

Here the traditional kinship form of social life with its communal possession was subordinated to the rule of the exploiters and oppressors who exacted tribute from the people. The old communal possession was amalgamated with the new state property in a servile formation under the impulsion of the European exchange economy. Even more brutal was the parcelling out of the Indians to the proprietors of the *encomiendas*, who exacted forced labor from them.

The prevalence of subsequent combined formations is excellently documented by Kyle Steenland in his "Notes on Feudalism and Capitalism in Chile and Latin America" (1975: 49–58). He distinguishes four stages in the economic development of post-conquest Chile: (1) the direct enslavement of the native population; (2) the growth of semifeudal relations of production; (3) the appearance of wage-labor toward the end of the nineteenth century with agriculture remaining semifeudal; (4) the dominance of capitalist relations from the 1930s on. In none of these stages did the Chilean economy have a fully capitalist or a purely precapitalist character. It was, he pointed out, a composite, a singular mixture, of one and the other. While agriculture and mining, the main sectors of production and sources of wealth, were carried on under servile or feudal conditions, these branches of the economy were hooked into commercial capitalist relations that were responsible for their rise or decline, as happened with the Brazilian sugar crop. The precapitalist forms of labor ministered to the needs of the world market dominated by merchant capital.

Steenland poses the problem very clearly when he writes: "One cannot define as capitalist an economy which produces predominantly for the market but in which labor is not free. . . . On the other hand, it is clear that an economy which produces for the market, in which the main goal of the landowners or farmer is commodity exchange, cannot be called feudal" (1975: 52). The solution to this contradictory situation is to acknowledge that Chile during this period was "semifeudal," he says. That is, its economy blended precapitalist productive relations with commodity ties to the local and world market.

3.8

Capitalist Accumulation and
the Marginal Mass Thesis

José Nun

The author returns to his marginal mass thesis of thirty years earlier and focuses on the surplus population and the industrial reserve army of workers in light of recent theory of the social-structures-of-accumulation approach of David Gordon and others, who believe that capitalist accumulation evolves not autonomously but necessarily through social (political and ideological) structures. He illustrates with general reference to the Latin American situation.

M Y OBSERVATION IS THEORETICAL and entails a criticism that applies to my own work on marginality as well. I have mentioned earlier that the classical economists viewed the economy as an autonomous sphere endowed with its own logic. In this sense, Marx also "was a product of his time in perceiving economic logic as aggregating into a coherent—albeit irrational—whole without the need for state action" (Block, 1986: 180). Moreover, in adopting England, "the only country where the capitalist regime of production has fully developed" and the alleged mirror of the future of the rest, as a base for his reflections, Marx (1956, vol. 1: 522) was able to generalize such apparent logic without much trou-

First published in *Latin American Perspectives* 110, vol. 27 (1), Sage Publications, Inc. Reprinted with permission from the Latin American Perspectives Collective. Selection from 17–19, 20–25.

ble, disregarding national differences and other possible determinants of the processes he was studying.

Now, when I chose to place myself explicitly in the same terrain to make a critical revision of the problematic of the relative surplus population and the industrial reserve army, my references to politics and ideology were not strong enough to transcend the productivist economicism of the original phrasing of the issue. And I fear that for various reasons (of which some are probably similar to mine) the same thing is now occurring with the literature on the developed countries to which I have just referred.

Two findings contained in the Organization for Economic Co-operation and Development (OECD) report may be useful to introduce the point I wish to make. The first one concerns the objective stability of today's jobs: "The evidence points to *substantial differences* in tenure, turnover and retention rates *across countries*" (OECD, 1997: 143, my emphasis). The second finding is of a subjective nature and refers to labor insecurity as perceived by the workers: "Insecurity is significantly lower in countries where the unemployment benefit replacement rate is higher, where there is a higher level of collective bargaining coverage, and in countries where collective bargaining is more centralized" (OECD, 1997: 150).

Both these different national performances and the incidence of these diverse normative frameworks help us to enter the field of what Gordon and others have called the "social structures of accumulation" (see, for example, Kotz, 1994). Put very schematically, we have known since Polanyi that the accumulation process is neither autonomous nor possessed of a logic of its own. For that reason, it needs a broad set of social institutions (including political and ideological structures) to be viable. They are called on to ensure the process a certain stability and predictability by regulating capitalist competition in the market as well as conflicts between capital and labor and between different fractions of capital. As is obvious, such regulation will depend on the characteristics and intensity of these conflicts and competition—which is the same thing as saying that it is always embedded in a concrete history and that the solutions implemented will vary with time and place.

The diverse forms the relationships between capital and labor take offer a simple and well-known illustration (Gordon, 1996: 73):

> Compared to most other countries, for example, the United States provides far less employment security—with no statutory provisions for mandatory advance notification of plant shutdowns or mandatory severance pay in case of plant closures— and features one of the lowest proportions of unionized workers and very decentralized bargaining relationships.

This situation brings it closer in various ways to Canada or Britain but clearly distances it from the experience of countries like Germany, Sweden, or Japan.

What I pointed out in relation to the social regime of accumulation can then be applied here as well—that is, that it must be conceived as a matrix of changing configuration within which different accumulation strategies and diverse tactics to implement them are intertwined. As a consequence, capital accumulation always appears as "the contingent result of a dialectic of structures and strategies" (Nun, 1987: 38, quoting Jessop, 1983: 98).

If this is so, any uncontrolled generalization about the end of work becomes immediately suspect. This "contingent result" may or may not lead to a dynamic adaptation between the types of technological innovations that are implemented and the available productive resources. It may or may not protect essential segments of the economy from the effects of globalization. It may or may not lead to fiscal and social policies that foster a progressive redistribution of income, and so on. This is because increases in productivity do not necessarily generate unemployment per se; it all depends, on the one hand, on how they are achieved and, on the other, on whether there exists a global demand that can absorb the consequent growth in production. And this is not a direct effect of technological change but rather the result of the macroeconomic policies that are adopted and, ultimately, of the prevailing power relations and social, political, and ideological context—which means that the employment content of any process of growth is far from being just an economic phenomenon.

The Latin American Case

It is not by chance that the debate on marginality began in Latin America or that it was in this context that the issue of the irrelevance of a substantial proportion of the surplus population, in terms of the reproduction of the capitalist sector that hegemonized an uneven and dependent process of growth, arose as a topic three decades ago. Not even in the best moments of the postwar process of industrialization by import substitution (which varied across countries) were regional levels of unemployment and underemployment ever below 30 percent. At the same time, even where some sui generis forms of the welfare state were implemented, nothing resembling the European salaried society was established.

This does not mean, however, that between 1950 and 1980 the agrarian labor force did not diminish (it went from 55 percent to 32 percent), and with it a proportion of rural poverty, or that there was not in that period a very significant expansion in education at all levels, despite its poor quality and inequitable character, or that the size of the middle and upper urban strata did not increase. However, the general style of development that prevailed (and, I insist, with very different national trajectories) led to a rather discontinuous process of growth that resulted in greater income concentration and ever more serious difficulties in absorbing the available labor force—and this despite a deepening productivity gap with the industrial countries.

The "Lost Decade"

The exhaustion of that stage (perhaps more apparent than real in countries such as Argentina or Brazil), the severe crisis of the external debt, and the mounting pressure of the big transnational interests that were articulated around the Washington Consensus led almost everywhere to drastic changes in the prevailing social regimes of accumulation.

The new watchwords were the reduction of the state (with the privatization of state enterprises and the decrease in public expenditures at the forefront), the achievement of macroeconomic stability through greater fiscal discipline and an all-out fight against inflation, the deregulation of the markets, giving absolute priority to private investment, and an opening of the economies to international trade and finance that was nowhere in the world so abrupt and so intense.

These radical changes were to mark what was to become known as the "lost decade" of the 1980s, during which national per capita income in the region fell by 15 percent while the concentration of wealth grew significantly (except for Colombia, Costa Rica, and Uruguay). According to the Economic Commission for Latin America (ECLA) figures, despite the fact that rural poverty did not increase in this period, the proportion of households below the poverty line moved from 35 percent in 1980 to 37 percent in 1986 and 39 percent in 1990.

Concerning the labor force, in that decade employment contracted in the public sector and nontechnical jobs in the formal urban sector fell, while professional and technical positions increased and jobs in low-productivity sectors tended to increase in relative terms. Employment in formal activities grew at an annual rate of 2.5 percent while the underemployment of urban labor expanded uniformly at a rate of 5 percent annually (Altimir, 1997: 13). That is, marginalization became even more acute.

Inequality and the Marginal Mass

The trend has not been reversed in the 1990s, when supposedly the adjustments were to bear fruit. On the contrary, the regressive changes in the composition of employment have intensified: thus, while the modern/formal sector absorbed 48 percent of the workforce in 1990, in 1996 the proportion dropped to 43 percent. It is not hard to understand why; of every 100 new jobs generated between those years, 85 were in informal activities (self-employed workers, microenterprises, and domestic service), of low quality and income and without any kind of social protection. At the same time, since employment declined in the large and medium-sized industrial firms, 9 out of 10 new jobs were created in the services sector, and in turn, 90 percent of these jobs were informal.

In such a context, my previous observation that social marginalization is far more important than unemployment acquires much wider significance. Latin

America's rate of open unemployment oscillates around 8 percent. At first sight, then, it is lower than the average rate of the European Union countries. However, it is extremely high when one realizes that in contrast to their European counterparts almost all of the unemployed in Latin America lack both insurance and benefits. Also, over half of the employed persons in the cities of the region today are unregistered, poorly paid, unstable, lacking in social protection, and without any real prospect of improvement in their work situation. In addition, the reforms that were introduced into the modern/formal sector in the name of flexibilization have lowered the costs of labor by laying off permanent workers and expanding the number of those working without contracts or on a temporary basis—that is, by increasing the precariousness of employment in the modern/formal sector itself.

Accompanied as it was by a huge concentration of income among the wealthiest 20 percent of the population, this process has had an obvious outcome: "in Latin America, inequality is now greater than before the outbreak of the debt crisis" (UNCTAD, 1997: 133). What is more, at present there is no indication that this inequality—which is the highest in the world—will be corrected in the foreseeable future (UNCTAD, 1997: 148).

And this, the question of inequality, was always at the heart of our considerations on the marginal mass and on the increasing segmentation of the labor markets and the activities directly or indirectly related to them. Regarding how open unemployment in Latin America will evolve in the coming years, Heilbroner's (1995) forecast for the industrial countries is in part also appropriate here: it will be very inadequate and erratic but not necessarily much worse than it is now, barring unexpected but not improbable events. Instead, if nothing changes, the perspective is that the quality of most jobs will continue to deteriorate seriously and there will be a further regression in income distribution. And that, in a globalized world, will surely end up negatively affecting the very process of capital accumulation, given the lack of incentives, the insufficiency of domestic markets and savings, and the way in which the process has come to depend on foreign investment.

To set in motion a different strategy, one fostering equitable and sustainable economic growth, would demand, among other things, active policies to promote national savings, to develop scientific and technological capabilities, to educate and train the labor force, to enact progressive fiscal reform, to redistribute income in favor of the less advantaged, to incorporate the excluded, and so on. In other words, it would entail profound transformations in the social regimes of accumulation now in force. It is easy, for example, to agree with Altimir (1997: 27) that the acceleration of growth and the increase in equity require a state that complements the market signals and specifically coordinates macroeconomic management, institutional reforms, the development of factors markets, and microeconomic measures to that end. However, this means transforming the now dominant alliances and escaping from the "there is no alternative" straitjacket. In other words, the great subjects are, as always, politics and power relations.

Thirty Years Later

When I first presented the marginal mass thesis, I had three main objectives in mind. First, I wanted to emphasize the structural relation between the processes of capitalist accumulation that prevailed in Latin America and the phenomena of poverty and social inequality, in contrast with the tendency then in vogue to lay the blame on the shoulders of the victims themselves (e.g., programs of popular promotion and the culture-of-poverty literature). Second, I wished to single out the heterogeneity and growing fragmentation of the Latin American occupational structure and its important consequences for the formation of social identities. Thus, it was by no means insignificant that Marx's view of the relative surplus population had been dominated by the floating modality, since that led him to suppose that most workers would at some time or other in their lives have the experience of factory work that he considered so essential in terms of the shaping of their solidarities and antagonisms. My third aim was to call attention to the way in which the need to afunctionalize the population surpluses conditioned system integration and gave rise, for example, to dualization and segregation mechanisms that were far less remnants of a still traditional past than expressions of an already modern present.

Whereas all this occurred during a time when the dominant ideologies in Latin America included the issue of income distribution on their Keynesian-inspired agendas and gave state action a central role in this matter, the situation has deteriorated notoriously nowadays, as witnessed by the data I have presented here. On the one hand, globalization has very much worsened the phenomena that I have mentioned. On the other, the neoliberal currents now in vogue not only reject Keynes but take for granted the neoclassical abandonment of the classical economists' concern for income distribution: the market will provide and do it far better the smaller the government is and the less interference there is from trade unions and popular organizations.

Nevertheless, there is certainly a major difference in the context with which my analyses of thirty years ago were concerned; since the 1980s, political regimes of representative democracy of various kinds have been established in Latin America. What, then, is the link between these regimes and both the marginalization processes in progress and the poor future that can be conjectured for good-quality wage work in the region?

I have pointed out elsewhere the strong Schumpeterian stamp that the Latin American political literature has acquired as dictatorships have tumbled and the way in which that literature has inverted a relationship that had been an almost undisputed point of agreement in the postwar years among theorists of modernization: first economic and social development and then political democracy (cf. Nun, 1991). With this it fell into a rather obvious contradiction: it extracted the procedural definition of democracy from Schumpeter without the conditions he imposed on his own definition, beginning with the far-from-irrelevant fact that it was explicitly restricted to the case of the modern industrial countries.

To use terms that T. H. Marshall made popular from the end of the 1940s on, all the emphasis has thus been placed on the political dimension of citizenship while the civil dimension has been taken for granted and the attention given to the social dimension has been almost exclusively rhetorical. Some of the consequences are right before our eyes.

In the first place, the Latin American population is far from fully enjoying civil rights, as is apparent almost everywhere in the crisis and political subordination of the justice system, the widespread privatization and feudalization of legal apparatuses, the openly discriminatory practices of most security forces, the recurrent attempts to curb freedom of the press and freedom of association, the absence of punishment for corruption practices, and so on.

Then, if even in well-established democracies the contractualist individualism of the civil dimension of citizenship has always been in open or latent conflict with the collective solidarity by which its social dimension is inspired, in Latin America (with few exceptions) the clear class bias of the former and the extreme weakness of the latter have deepened and widened the distinction advanced by Marshall between full citizens, semifull citizens, and noncitizens.

Ever since Rousseau, Jefferson, or Tocqueville we have known that democracy requires the participation of persons endowed with moral autonomy, without which neither deliberation nor conscious and responsible choices and decisions are possible. In turn, such moral autonomy demands a reasonable degree of economic independence and security, and that is why the farmer played such a central role in those writers' analyses. Many years later, the stable worker of the salaried society was to replace the farmer as the subject of a citizenship that was not only civil and political but social as well.

This is precisely what is not happening in Latin America today for substantial sectors of the population. Unlike the postwar democratic transitions in West Germany, Austria, and Italy, first, and in Greeee, Portugal, and Spain several years later, here the increase in poverty and inequality and the lack of appropriate networks of social protection are leading to the consolidation of exclusive representative democracies with a minority of full citizens, which is the same as saying that present political regimes are scarcely democratic and scarcely representative.

Given these general conditions, few signs of a progressive and all-embracing reform of the situation can be detected for now. This does not necessarily mean that an explosion of social protest is on the immediate agenda, since we have long since learned that not even social protest is always an abundant or accessible resource for the disadvantaged—especially when they are largely redundant. Localized conflicts, particularly those of a defensive nature, will doubtless continue to multiply. What is more likely, however, is that perverse forms of social integration will keep developing in the shape of clientelism, criminality, illegal trade, proliferation of ghettos and marginal populations, persistence of brutal forms of exploitation, and so on.

To sum up, if the closely related problems of the surplus population and income distribution are not placed squarely in the center of the most pressing Latin American economic, social, and political debate, neither the one nor the other will be solved as just a side effect of other processes, and the gloomy future of wage work will then cast an ominous shadow on every aspect of social life.

3.9

Imperialism and Marginality
in Latin America

Aníbal Quijano
Translated by Peggy Westwell

This selection reflects the earlier debates on marginality to which Nun refers in his essay and is included here to capture the dimensions of the debate.

What Is the Problem of "Marginality"?

O NE OF THE PROBLEMS that has been dealt with at greatest length in the social research on Latin America during the past decade is that of "marginality." The ideas and images that have been circulated under this heading are so contradictory and vague, especially because of their frequent misuse in the press and in the most banal political jargon, that José Nun (1969a) is completely justified in saying that "marginality is one of those commonly used concepts of which one can ask, and from which one can derive, almost anything one wishes." For this reason, it is not easy to remove the rubble and clearly establish the limits of this research field in the difficult process of being correctly defined. However, after ten years of debate and concrete research carried out by many of the leading investigators of various theoretical positions from Latin America and other

First published in *Latin American Perspectives* 37 and 38, vol. 10 (2 and 3), Sage Publications, Inc. Reprinted with permission from the Latin American Perspectives Collective.

countries, enough information has accumulated to make it possible to assert that a discussion of "marginality" today refers to a well-defined problem:

What happens to the relative surplus population produced by the movement of capital, according to historically necessary laws, and what are the conditions and mechanisms involved in producing it, when capitalist accumulation is characterized by the full predominance of monopoly capital and by the maturation of the internationalization of capital under the control of its monopolistic centers; when this internationalization involves the articulation within a system of different accumulation modalities—both the most developed forms of intensive accumulation, characterized by the predominance of technical production over human labor, and sectors in which primitive forms of extensive accumulation still link capital and *precapital* under the hegemony of the former; when, simultaneously and contradictorily, capital is becoming an increasingly integrated international circuit but the preexisting national circuits are still intact and the formation of such circuits is still under way?

Marx clearly demonstrated that the movement of capital necessarily and permanently produces a tendency to exclude from the productive apparatus part of the labor force that has arisen under its domination and that this inactive labor force contracts and expands according to the phases of contraction or expansion in capital's cycles. He also demonstrated that, as the spiral of capitalist accumulation develops, the centralization of capital and growth in the organic and technical composition of capital tend to increase the inactive part of the labor force. This inactive labor force is, therefore, a surplus population relative to the needs of capitalist accumulation. Since the expansion of the productive apparatus is founded upon its existence, this labor force is "a condition of existence of the capitalist mode of production. It forms a disposable industrial reserve army, that belongs to capital quite as absolutely as if the latter had bred it at its own cost" (Marx, 1974a: 632). Marx also discovered that "the general movements of wages are exclusively regulated by the expansion and contraction of the industrial reserve army, and these again correspond to the periodic changes of the industrial cycle" (Marx, 1974a: 637). Thus the labor market is based on the existence of a relative surplus population.

In this way, Marx established a specific area of research within the field of problems related to capital: that of the relations between the movement of capitalist accumulation and that of the structure of the working-class population and, in particular, that of the relative surplus population or "industrial reserve army." This is precisely the area of research within which the debates on and investigations of "marginality" take place.

What Is the Place of the Term "Marginality" Here?

The difficulties caused by the use of the term "marginality" in research in this field have been amply demonstrated. They arise from its eminently ideological origin, which has been demonstrated in numerous studies. It is this origin that permits the extreme ambiguity and recognized capacity for confusion in its use, which have survived all efforts to clarify its conceptual content. If, in spite of these difficulties, the word continues to be used to refer to a problem which falls within the province of scientific investigation, this is no accident. Since Marx's time we have known that an ideological construct is no mere fantasy without any basis in reality but instead a partially or totally false way of referring to that reality. It is an inescapable indication that, in this particular area of research, there is something in present-day capitalism that is particularly visible in Latin America and that does not seem to fit the existing categories or, alternatively, that those categories have not been appropriately employed in research.

One might think that, once the laws and mechanism that govern the relations between capital accumulation and relative surplus population had been discovered by Marx, the categories formulated at that time would suffice to explain what is occurring in this regard within contemporary capitalism and, furthermore, that the use of the term "marginality" could only serve to confuse the issue. The problem is, however, that, ever since Marx made these scientific discoveries, capital has continued to change and develop according to the general laws he identified, assuming forms that did not exist in his time; in this way, new concrete modalities are established that express his general laws.

Since Marx, a number of these specific problem areas have been investigated and given a theoretical basis, resulting in basic contributions such as those of Hilferding, Bukharin, Luxemburg, and Lenin on monopoly capital and the emergence of capitalist imperialism and the more recent studies of the internationalization of capital, transnational corporations, and the new relationship between the state and capital. In contrast, specific research on the changes in the structure of the working-class population as a whole and on the problem of the relative surplus population within the context of the new conditions of present-day capitalist accumulation has scarcely begun, although there have been important contributions such as that of Harry Braverman (1974). It is important, therefore, to undertake new specific investigations, within the context of today's capitalism, of the relative surplus population that Marx described in the context of premonopoly and preimperialist capitalism. It is important to recognize, however, that, just as has happened in other research fields, it will probably be necessary to formulate new categories to refer to new phenomena and to reformulate existing concepts from the ideological quagmire.

In the present state of our knowledge of contemporary capitalism, it is undeniable that it shows a growing incapacity to absorb or reabsorb cyclically an increasingly large part of the inactive labor force while at the same time it produces an ever larger relative surplus population. This tendency affects the capitalist system at all levels, but its most extreme expression is to be found in underdeveloped areas in social formations dominated by imperialist monopoly capital.

Taken as a whole, and especially from the perspective of the emergence of an international circuit of accumulation, at present, capital is creating a growing mass of relative surplus population on a global scale, and a decreasing proportion of this population is being absorbed or reabsorbed into the global productive apparatus during the expansive phases of the accumulation cycle. This means that the relative surplus population tends to expand continuously. This situation contrasts with that of the premonopoly period and particularly that prior to the formation of an international circuit of accumulation, when its contractions and expansions according to corresponding phases of the industrial cycle might be proportionately equal.

To the degree that this situation implies the inevitable impoverishment of the excess labor force, poverty within the capitalist system is growing and worsening just as Marx foresaw. Considering the capitalist system as a whole, never before have the poverty stricken masses been so numerous or the misery so great for so many—and this is true despite all the efforts of the apologists for capital to maintain the contrary in their attempt to ignore the existence of an integrated capitalist system under the imperialist domination of monopoly capital, preferring to see capitalism, before the present crisis, only within the borders of certain countries that are the headquarters of monopoly capital. . . .

Marx uses the term "consolidated" here to refer to that part of the relative surplus population which, in the course of the development of the established tendencies, is destined to fall victim to a situation of constant surplus with regard to the needs of capitalist accumulation. In the Latin American debate, this is the part of the relative surplus population that has been called "marginal." Obviously, Marx did not include the "consolidated" modality of the relative surplus population in his list because this modality did not yet exist. It was instead a modality likely to occur only in the future, since in premonopoly capitalism the conditions existed for the almost total absorption of the inactive labor force during expansive phases, as indeed they did even under monopoly capitalism before it became internationalized and the technical means of production came to dominate completely the human labor force in the most developed sectors.

Therefore, it is possible to conclude tentatively that, although it was anticipated, "marginality" is a new modality of the relative surplus population; this does not cast doubt on the existence of the earlier modalities, for it is a modality which covers that sector which, in present-day capitalism (1983), is never absorbed during expansive phases and which Marx called "consolidated." Is there anything to be gained by replacing "marginality" with this term? Only the future development of debate and research will tell.

It must be stressed, however, that it is no accident that the use of the term "marginality" has caused so much confusion, even permitting "dualist" interpretations of some of my own texts (Singer, 1973) in spite of my explicit declarations to the contrary. As Lander (1975) correctly indicates, the term has "a connotation which exactly reflects a dualist conception of capitalist development in Latin America." Its birth in an ideological field of Latin American thought dominated by developmentalist and modernizationist positions seems to have severely limited the possibility of its purification and conceptual rescue within the theory of social classes, since its connotations inevitably tend to make us forget that the phenomenon to which it refers, far from being "marginal" to capitalism and the essential dialectic of its movement, is a basic and necessary part of its present-day existence and a product of the ironclad laws which govern its development. And there is no doubt, from this point of view, that, in spite of our explicit intentions, the term's ideological overtones have crept into our research and conclusions.

If, in spite of this fact, the term continues to be used, even with the incorporation of the clarifications in its conceptual content presented here, confusion can be avoided only if we do not lose sight of the fact that "marginality" is, in the words of Murmis (1969), *central to* and a constitutive part *of* the current process of exploitation and capitalist accumulation and absolutely excludes any form of dualism.

LATE CAPITALISM

3.10

Late Capitalism and Cultural Production

Tânia Pellegrini

With attention to Brazil during the 1970s and 1980s, this analysis examines cultural production in an era of late capitalism and focuses on the problem of culture as merchandise and the impact of fragmentation and globalization on intellectuals and their cultural output. Of particular concern is how censorship and control under the dictatorship affected cultural production and in the ensuing period how the commercial system brought changes to cultural production.

IN THE CONTEXT OF WORLD capitalist development, culture is affected by the economic implications of what, even in Brazil, we now call postmodernity or rather, by the emergence of a new type of social life and a new economic order also known as the postindustrial society, the consumer society, late capitalism, "savage capitalism," and so on.

Fredric Jameson (1991: 35) considers late capitalism (the term he prefers) the purest form of capital that has so far appeared, "a prodigious expansion of capital into areas not previously commercialized," and the latest of the three successive ages of capitalism—market capitalism, monopolist or imperialist capitalism, and now, multinational or late capitalism. Although each of these in turn has represented a dialectic expansion over its predecessor, this last stage is characterized by an incredible technological leap (in electronics, information, nuclear energy)—the "third industrial revolution"—and is managing to eliminate, at the

First published in *Latin American Perspectives* 113, vol. 27 (1), Sage Publications, Inc. Reprinted with permission from the Latin American Perspectives Collective. Selection from 124–128, 140–141.

center of the developed world, the enclaves of every precapitalist organization. However, in discussing Brazil, the specific nature of the formative movements of our economy and society must be emphasized. Our obvious position on the periphery means that these factors work in a different way, in time and in their dynamics. This has clear consequences for our own cultural coordinates, which cannot simply reproduce here those of the outside world (however great may be the hegemony of the center—or centers, as students of globalization aver).

Despite Brazil's having become part of a "global cultural community" that, thanks to the power of the media, practically ignores national boundaries, we cannot overlook the coexistence here of poverty and technological sophistication, backwardness and progress, and regional disparities. As Roberto Schwarz (1987) has stressed, these incongruities have been from the very beginning an important determinant of our culture.

To the coexistence of temporal incongruities (elements at different stages of development, on different time scales, sharing the same present) is added another incongruity, also perceived by Schwarz, that is more spatial—that of "ideas out of place." Analyzing the European liberalism introduced into Brazil during the slavery period, Schwarz (1977) considers it "out of place" in that it is inconsistent with the country's social and political reality. In this respect he emphasizes the gap between intention and achievement, the oddity of ideas imported into Brazil before the country had developed the socioeconomic forces that had created them in Europe, thus underlining, once again, the incongruities of Brazilian society.

These twin concepts (of temporal and spatial incongruities) are but the two faces of the same coin: the idea that Brazilian cultural life has always been determined by the attempt to harmonize the backwardness of Brazil with the progress attained abroad, symbolizing the wish to appear advanced while lacking the necessary material conditions. The history of our literature has, as always, much to teach us about this.

Brazil's insertion into late capitalism, albeit on its periphery, at first created the illusion that these incongruities would finally cease to exist as, thanks to the media, identical ideas began to circulate universally and almost contemporaneously in a process of synchronization never before achieved. But this synchronization of ideas did not eliminate the reality of either our economic and social backwardness in relation to the so-called First World or our regional disparities, although it sought to neutralize both these factors through a homogenizing discourse. The many aspects of this situation have long been familiar. What has changed is the medium: the electronic discourse is now much more powerful.

Speaking generally, we can say that the period since 1964 has also been one of important changes in the way in which Brazilian culture is organized commercially. This has been especially so since the political opening (*abertura*) of 1979 has revealed the existence of a wholly new structure in place and in constant expansion.

162 *Tânia Pellegrini*

We can therefore divide our topic in this article into two periods. The first is that of the military governments of the 1960s and 1970s. The whole of the decade of the 1980s constitutes its working out: where we close this second period is only a question of method, since the transformations are still going on.

Regarding the 1970s in particular, the development of the market for cultural goods coincided with the raising of the standard of living of the middle classes (provided by the climate of the Brazilian economic miracle). This development also bore the ideological burden implied by the censorship that, for better or worse, represented the type of direction the state sought to confer on Brazilian culture. Indeed, the censorship became a sort of emblem of the epoch through which one might interpret the country's entire cultural output much as one interprets a secret code, accessible only to its initiates.

The censorship did not, however, function in a uniform way, and therefore its effects were not uniform but selective, hindering some types of cultural orientation while stimulating others. Thus, individual texts (plays, songs, literary works, motion pictures) were censored but not the general production of these genres, which grew and solidified, supported by the interest of a public that was itself increasing during this period.

Also, the imposition of the censorship had several phases. The regime imposed by the coup of 1964 tried without initial success to limit artistic creation, which flourished among an intelligentsia concerned with its social aspects and ideologically oriented to the left. The mechanisms of cultural control were initially used only as an attempt to build solid bases for the regime that had just achieved power. A degree of flexibility still existed, with many contradictions in the way in which the policy was implemented. The real blow in the cultural field was struck in December 1968, by Institutional Act 5.

When Brazil began to suffer the first crises resulting from the breakdown of the so-called Brazilian miracle, the state, besides trying to recover the ground lost in its decreasing popularity among the general population, the middle classes, and businessmen, implemented the Geisel administration's policy of "relaxation" and of increasing investment in culture. In 1975 it began to intervene directly, creating a national culture policy. This policy was quite contradictory, since it sought to stimulate culture by means of subsidies at the same time as it was repressing it through censorship. It reinforced the need for culture to be organized through business methods, in which professionalization and the conquest of the market were crucial points.

Cultural production is becoming more and more a trade, reigniting discussions on the extent to which it can be immune to financial influences. In the felicitous and oft-quoted words of Hollanda and Gonçalves (1980: 35), "the fact is that the state, even if it was motivated only by short-term tactics, was the great Maecenas of Brazilian culture in the 1970s, both in its ideological flexibility and in its underwriting of the precarious material basis of cultural production in Brazil."

Asking whether censorship had a determining impact on the cultural output of this period is appropriate, because it was clearly a constituent element, but this only scratches the surface of a much deeper question. What has in fact been going on since 1964 is the gradual adaptation of the Brazilian cultural product to the requirements of the national and international marketplace.

The great transformation of the cultural process during these years endowed it with certain specific features. One, it seems, was a new sort of jingoism based on the idea that (at last!), despite the censorship, our cultural industry had attained its "majority" and we were entering into "global modernity" (Ortiz 1994)—a feeling, superficially well founded, that we had at last caught up with the rest of the world.

If the circumstances of the 1970s were propitious in creating conditions for putting a new structure in place, the 1980s saw its large-scale implementation, with all its consequences. The political and cultural prospect of the late 1970s raised many new questions posed by the new conditions of production, that is, by the consolidation of the market for cultural goods and by the role, implicit or explicit, of the state as Maecenas. Such questions concerned above all the appropriate relationship between intellectuals and the government, expressed in the discussions about "co-optation." This term, much used at the time, referred to those intellectuals and producers of culture who had opted for a "neutral" cultural stance, socially aseptic, and sought "intimacy in the government's shadow": that is, they were no longer discussing the bases of authority of the regime under whose shadow they were free to cultivate this "intimacy" (Coutinho, 1979). In return, the state, at its pleasure, rained on them scholarships, jobs, financial aid, and help with publishing. The "undeserving" others had unemployment and the censorship to fight as obstacles to the circulation of their work, whether artistic or theoretical.

While this matter of co-optation was being discussed, other alternative forms of cultural production appeared, such as "marginal poetry" and experimental groups in the theater and cinema, all still seeking to create ways to get their work out that would bypass the already firmly established cultural marketplace and the centers of power.

During the 1980s, all this yielded to the implacable logic of the market system and the dynamic of the media. The word "co-optation" ceased to be politically correct and fell into disuse (but without disappearing in practice). Marginal poetry found a powerful publisher, expanded its readership, and (in the words of one of its practitioners) "put on formal dress." Experimental drama groups gradually died out or were taken over by television.

Already under the Figueiredo administration (1979–1985), the pattern of the government's relations with culture seems to be established on solid bases. With some doors now open, intellectuals and producers of culture could feel that they had more space—except that the extent of this space was already being determined by the outlines of the culture industry, the decisive factor being the symbi-

osis of the media and the market. A new "international popular" aesthetic, based
on a proliferation of images through television—the aesthetic of the spectacle—
was becoming widespread. This was breaking down boundaries, attenuating
nuances, and completely erasing the distinction between what is culture and
what is the market.

The problem of culture as merchandise is not new, and we must be careful in
discussing its ambiguities. What was new, in this period, *was the marriage
between media and market,* which introduced a lack of differentiation that had
not previously been possible. The use of the electronic image established connections and stimulated perceptions that had hardly even been thought of before.
On a more immediate level, the products sold on the market (whether soap,
records, deodorant, or even the revered "book") become, among other things,
the real content of the image transmitted by television; they are broadcast in the
middle of programs, in the plots of soap operas, and are so built into what we
view that sometimes it is not very clear what is a commercial and what is not.
But this is all part of the advertiser's strategy. The time is long gone when it was
thought that literature, for example, had irretrievably lost its aura with the arrival
of the feuilleton (the novel serialized in the nineteenth-century newspaper).

The characteristic of the decade of the 1980s, therefore, was that features
already present in the previous era had developed to the degree that there was,
in the new context, a different type of emphasis on the international dimension
of culture (an attitude contrary to the constant emphasis on its national dimension). This was in fact, under the new conditions, nothing less than the legitimation of the media. It is now a question of Brazil's catching up by being immersed
in a supposedly universal and electronically unified world, in which all differences are abolished, what Schwarz (1987: 33) calls "the new terms of oppression
and cultural exploitation."

All the elements I have just sketched translate into formal features in cultural
products in changes of style that function as detectors of ongoing economic and
social changes. These emergent features now coexist with the residual features of
older types of cultural products characteristic of earlier ages, with the result that
different solutions are always around, evidence of the contradictions that exist in
society. There are innumerable examples of these in movies, music, literature,
and television itself. . . .

As in all of the West, Brazilian modernity is also tied to the transformation of
the cities into poles of industrial development, although, of course, in accordance
with the time on our own clock. During the period we have been discussing, our
great conurbations centers—as they always were of cultural effervescence—
expanded alarmingly, creating a gradual but profound modification in spaces
and ways of living because of unchecked and unplanned growth, the creation of
shantytowns along their peripheries, increase in marginality and violence, and
deterioration of the quality of life.

This increase in size and population determined lifestyle in the great cities of

Brazil. At the same time, the influence they exerted was no longer the slow and gradual affair it had been before the growth of the media but was transmitted equally and simultaneously to every corner of the country—a global influence. Cities today, throughout the world, are the powerful agents of the dominant, technically most advanced economies, whose products are transmitted as universal values.

That the development of cities should give rise to important cultural transformations and new structures of feeling that are superimposed on former patterns is no new phenomenon; it was already pronounced in the nineteenth century—one has only to reread Baudelaire and Benjamin's perceptions in respect of his work, not to mention the prolific Brazilian *modernista* writers of the 1920s on the same theme. But besides the revival of the urban perspective as the subject of writers' works, what changes from era to era and has great importance is the specific place of artists and intellectuals as producers in the ever-changing cultural milieu of the great urban centers.

The period under study is, as we have seen, witnessing in Brazil a radical change in the position of artists or intellectuals within the productive process. They no longer have offices and desks in some government department but have had to move to the office of some production or broadcasting company. Now that culture has been totally adapted to the circulation of capital, businesses, generally located in the great cities of southeastern Brazil, are reorganizing their use of "personnel," seeking greater productivity, while they try to make the product they sell fit the "taste" of the consumer. This new approach requires a definitive and irreversible professionalization of the artist or writer.

To sum up (if indeed one can talk of summation in this era in which fragmentation and globalization combine in an insatiable dynamic), culture, as a good produced and consumed in the conditions, many of them radically new, that are specific to contemporary Brazil, clearly bears the marks of the changes that I have sought to explain, built into the very forms of each product. That is to say, the profound transformations effected in the modes of production, reproduction, and cultural reception and in a technical ambience full of images that change according to the dizzying rhythm of the market are certainly imprinted in the themes, the structure, and the composition of all cultural and artistic manifestations. It is therefore up to the student to analyze and interpret these manifestations with a view to understanding the world we live in a little better and, if possible, trying to improve it.

3.11

Dependency and World System Theory

James F. Petras

This critique takes issue with both dependency theory and the world systems theory that emanated from the earlier dependency work. The idea of world system emerges from the work on Southern Europe of the French historian Fernand Braudel and the ensuing ideas in the writings and thought of the sociologist Immanuel Wallerstein.

W ORLD SYSTEM THEORY (so designated by one of its major practitioners, Immanuel Wallerstein [1975]) is derived from the intellectual heritage found in the critique of the developmentalist perspective of liberal political economy. This critique was articulated in the work of Paul Baran (1957), A. G. Frank (1967, 1969a), Theotônio dos Santos (1971), and other dependency theorists (for a recent review and effort to defend the dependency perspective, see Cardoso, 1977). Recently, dependency has achieved a new status in the attention given to the "unequal exchange" theses of Arghiri Emmanuel (1972), Samir Amin's discussion (1974) of the "accumulation of world capital," and Immanuel Wallerstein's historical interpretation (1974; 1976) of the rise of a "single capitalist world economy."

The basic framework of a world systems theorist is strikingly elementary. The problematic to be explained is the fact that there exist different stages or levels of national development within what appears to be a unified global economy. The key to explaining this phenomenon, it is argued, is to specify the different

First published in *Latin American Perspectives* 30 and 31, vol. 8 (3 and 4), Sage Publications, Inc. Reprinted with permission from the Latin American Perspectives Collective. Selection from 148–151.

political and economic roles which a state or geographic area plays within the overall system. This notion gives rise to the basic categories of analysis: core, semiperiphery and periphery; core and periphery; metropole and satellite.

The real innovation of the world systems approach lies in the choice of the primary unit of analysis—the capitalist world economy. All phenomena are to be explained in terms of their consequence for both the whole of the system and its parts. It is asserted that the internal class contradictions and political struggles of a particular state, like Rhodesia for example, can be explained as "efforts to alter or preserve a position within the world economy which is to the advantage or disadvantage of particular groups located within a particular state" (Wallerstein, 1975: 16).

What is important to notice is the direction of generalization in world systems theory, for that is the key to understanding the approach. Specific events within the world system are to be explained in terms of the demands of the system as a whole. Actors are acting not for their immediate concrete interests but because the system dictates that they act. As Wallerstein (1975: 26) has put it: "Where then in this picture do the forces of change, the movements of liberation, come in? They come in precisely as not totally coherent pressures of groups which arise out of the structural contradictions of the capitalist world economy" (Wallerstein, 1975: 16).

The central theme of the world systems approach is the proposition that core regions exploit peripheral regions through various mechanisms of unequal exchange. Superficially, this idea of unequal exchange seems similar to the focus by structuralists on unequal economic transactions. In fact, the world systems conceptualization is distinguished by an effort to ground unequal exchange in a labor theory of value. This labor theory of value forms the basis of an attempt to explain how surplus value extracted from the working class of the periphery is transferred to core regions. It is further hypothesized that the transfer of value from one region of the world capitalist economy to another is a form of primary accumulation that is necessary to the maintenance of monopoly forms of capitalism in the core. As a means of extracting surplus, unequal exchange is not only different from the extended reproduction of capital that is characteristic of the core, but it is the principal contradiction of the modern capitalist world.

The economic arguments purporting to demonstrate the functioning of unequal exchange are most fully developed by Emmanuel. He begins by critiquing Ricardo's theory of international trade for being based on unrealistic assumptions. According to Emmanuel, it is statistically more accurate to assume that capital is mobile and labor is immobile on the international market. With this revised set of assumptions, it is possible to demonstrate a tendency for profits to become equalized internationally while wages remain different. Emmanuel then claims that it is these two tendencies which explain the deterioration in the terms of trade of peripheral regions which are emphasized by structuralists. In this analysis, the wage differential between core and periphery is the independent variable that accounts for the phenomenon of unequal exchange. Amin and Wallerstein agree with Emmanuel regarding the centrality of wages, but they also draw attention to other differences between core capitalism and peripheral capitalism.

Given this analysis of world capitalism, the salient question for radical praxis becomes, "What can regions of peripheral capitalism do in order to mitigate or eliminate the effects of unequal exchange?" Assuming that a sudden raising of the level of wages in the periphery to that prevailing in the core is impossible, the logical tactic is to develop means for preventing the movement abroad of the surplus value extracted from workers in the periphery. Emmanuel argues that since somebody has to benefit from these low wages, and since it is desired that foreign consumers not be the beneficiaries, it is best that the benefits accrue to national capitalists. He proposes taxes on exports and diversification of production as two mechanisms for accomplishing this goal. It is assumed that this excess surplus will be used for development purposes.

An Evaluation of World Systems Approaches

To conceptualize the issues of the Third World in terms of dependency or as part of a world system is to lose sight of the most decisive processes of class formation and social relations which beget change and the particular configurations of social forces which emerge on a world scale.

It is not the world system that begets change in social relations, but rather social forces that emerge and extend their activities that produce the world market. The transformations wrought within societies by their insertion in the world market must be seen as an ongoing reciprocal relationship: between the forces and relations of production within a social formation and those that operate through the world market. From the perspective of international political economy, a comprehensive analytical framework must focus on the structural variations and transformations within the capitalist mode of production and the state capacities for exercising hegemony, both within a social formation and on a global basis.

The principal features which characterize capitalist development have varied considerably over time: the process of primitive accumulation, the growth of commercial capital, the expansion and growth of industrial and later financial capital have their own laws of development, generating their own class structures and appropriate state organization. The class and state variations within core countries are determinants of their relative position in the world capitalist system. Among the capitalist countries (core), the variations in imperial state organization, development of the productive forces, and homogenization of the social formation (absence of precapitalist social formation) affect the relative competitive position of each in terms of establishing areas of hegemony. The differential in class formation contained within each core society is, in turn, essential to understanding the types of class alliances within a social formation and between capitalist countries. Finally, the crystallization of class forces—the degree of polarization within a social formation, outcome of the combined developments of productive forces, external expansion, and internal polarization—determines the level and scope of class conflict, which itself feeds into and influences the worldwide position of a given capitalist class.

The metaphor of a metropole/satellite relation eliminates the most essential factors that account for the specific relations and processes that shape historical development. The focus on the external relationships between social systems leads to an incapacity to differentiate the different moments of capital development, the specific configuration of types of capitals, the particular class relationships and conflicts engendered between capital and labor. This, in turn, leads to overly abstract sets of assertions: the core exploits the periphery through unequal exchange or the metropole appropriates surplus. Vague enough, to be sure, but not only is the core constantly changing in its internal organization of capital—shifts from merchant to industrial to financial—but the relationships of capitals within the core are in unstable competition; moreover, the social relations of production themselves are changing, creating new sets of demands and crises.

The long-term cycles of capital expansion and contraction on a world scale, the particular forms they take—wars, colonialism, imperialism, etc.—are reflections of the unstable relationships between competing and expanding capitals within the core and the crises (depression or stagnation) which are engendered. The notion of core and periphery, especially in the work of Amin, sets up a set of fixed exploitative relations that leaves unexamined the internal crises that disrupt the operations of expansion and what he describes as surplus appropriation.

Moreover, the general crises of core capital have engendered, in specific but recurring instances, class conflicts and shifts in the axis of state power. Changes of class forces alter the boundaries for the continued reproduction of capital—decisively affecting the global position of the ruling class, i.e., its capacity to appropriate surplus. The indefiniteness of systems analysis before the historic confrontation of classes and the absence of any notion of how the class struggle interacts with the actions of the ruling class—specifically related with its movement in the international arena—substantially weaken the theory's capacity to explain societal change. The conception of the world system remains a static description of national features abstracted from the class realities which produce it.

From the other side of the metaphor, the imposition of satellite status is not a uniform or completed process: the persistence of precapitalist classes and institutions within the restructured peripheral society inserted in the world system suggest a whole complex of social forces that conflict or collaborate in the subordination of peripheral society.

The heterogeneity of precapitalist social formations and the particular ways in which imperialist forces interlock makes notions of dependency and periphery rather vacuous. The internal variations in class development are largely a product of the interface of the original organization of production and the particular moment of imperialist domination. The social relations of production that emerge from and shape the further development of the subordinated peripheral society cannot be encapsulated in any vague and amorphous notion of "under-development."

The pivotal unit which facilitates core subordination of peripheral society is the existence within the latter of collaborator classes whose function is to organize the state and economy in accordance with the core definitions of the international division of labor. The creation of an international political economic order based on the inequalities of nations is rooted in the existence of an expanding center of capitalism and a set of classes within the periphery whose own expansion and position is enhanced in the process. The insertion of particular social formations within the world capitalist market and division of labor is largely the product of classes which combine a double role—exploit within the society and exchange outside the society. This dual process leads to the expansion of production relations and antagonistic class relations within peripheral society, growing exchange relations, and competition with the core.

3.12

Globalization and Globalism in Latin America and the Caribbean

Richard L. Harris

The following is drawn from an introduction to an issue on globalization and global-ism and is especially helpful in its review and synthesis of essential issues and ques-tions. It also identifies the parameters of debate and moves beyond polemics to assess some of the serious work that envisages globalization as a new trend in develop-mental theory and a new phase in the evolution of capitalism. A distinction between globalization and globalism is also offered.

THE CONTEMPORARY LITERATURE and ideological debates on "globalization" involve a highly contested, complex, and multidimensional discourse on the nature of the present world order, its historical antecedents, underlying causative forces, and future evolution. The concept of globalization itself tends to be used, both uncritically and critically, to focus attention on the dynamic inter-relation-ships between international, regional, national, and local affairs in all the major domains of human concern—including economics, science, technology, politics, religion, culture, communications, transportation, education, health, and ecol-ogy. The rapidly expanding international body of literature and the increasingly more intense ideological debates on this subject reveal a wide array of different perspectives. They also reveal a great deal of confusion and profound disagree-

First published in *Latin American Perspectives* 127, vol. 29 (6), Sage Publications, Inc. Reprinted with permission from the Latin American Perspectives Collective. Selection from 5–10.

ment, particularly with regard to the following concerns (Held et al., 1999: 10–28):

- The definition and application of key concepts such as "globalization" and "globalism"
- The causation associated with the various contending conceptualizations of globalization
- The historical periodization associated with globalization
- The effects or impacts of what are variously considered to be globalization and globalism
- The future evolution or trajectory of what are regarded as globalization and globalism
- The possible alternatives to globalization and globalism

The concept of "globalization" tends to be used in a highly multivalent manner to describe contemporary social reality. It is generally employed as a meta-concept for comprehending and explaining a diverse variety of complex and inter-related processes, structures, forces, agents and effects. Those who use the concept in this manner generally try to view these phenomena from a historical, multi-level, interdisciplinary and/or holistic perspective. Most theorizing and empirical research on globalization tends to be organized around five key issues or questions (Guillén, 2001: 235): is globalization really taking place, is it producing convergence and integration, is it undermining the authority of nation-states, does globalization characterize the present era of human history, if so how does the present era of "globality" differ from the previous era of modernity, and is globalization producing a global culture, a global economy, a global political system, and so on?

Generally speaking, globalization is regarded as a global process of increasing cross-border flows of products, services, capital, people, information, and culture (Held et al., 1999: 16). Many observers call attention to the effects this global phenomenon is having on our sense of time and space. For example, Anthony Giddens (1990) believes globalization has created a decoupling or "distanciation" between space and time, while Roland Robertson (1992: 8) argues that globalization "refers both to the compression of the world and the intensification of consciousness of the world as a whole." Manuel Castells (1996: 92) stresses the informational aspects of globalization and characterizes the global economy that has emerged as "an economy with the capacity to work as a unit in real time on a planetary scale." In a similar vein, Martin Albrow (1997: 88) defines globalization as the "diffusion of practices, values and technology that have an influence on people's lives worldwide."

The Brazilian social scientist Octavio Ianni contends that the complex and multidimensional nature of the phenomena associated with the use of this concept have challenged the theoretical and analytical capabilities of the contemporary social sciences. According to Ianni:

> The originality and complexity of globalization, in conjunction with its distinct aspects, challenge the social scientist to mobilize the suggestions and conquests of diverse sciences. Globalization tends to be seen as a vast process that is not only politico-economic, but also socio-cultural, and that includes demographic, ecological, gender, religious, linguistic and other problems. Even when the investigation privileges a determined sphere of analysis, one is continuously challenged to take into account other aspects of reality, without which an economic, political, sociological, ecological, or any other kind of analysis results in abstractions that lack realism, consistency and verisimilitude [i.e., probability]. (Ianni, 1998)

Added to this challenge is the fact that since the 1990s, globalization has become a "buzzword" that is used frequently in the mass media, in political propaganda, and in intellectual circles.

Globalization is the focal point of the increasingly intense ideological and political conflicts that have been ignited by the "anti-globalization protests" that have taken place in various countries, starting with the first of these protests at the summit meeting of the World Trade Organization (WTO) held in Seattle at the end of 1999. In intellectual circles, globalization has become "the primary attractor of books, articles, and heated debate" in much the same way "as postmodernism was the most fashionable and debated topic of the 1980s" (Kellner, 2002). Thus, there is a great deal of "hype" about globalization, it is an increasingly popular subject of intellectual inquiry, and it has become the focal point of intense ideological and political conflict at both the international and national levels.

The discourse on globalization in recent years has been increasingly heated between those, on the one hand, who employ the concept as the label for what they consider, in a positive sense, to be an unfolding process of global economic, political, and cultural integration that is bringing about the progressive integration of humanity; and those, on the other hand, who use the concept to describe, in critical terms, what they perceive to be a largely unjust and inequitable process of transnational corporate expansionism that involves both the increasing exploitation of a large proportion of humanity and the increasing despoliation of the biosphere of the planet.

Globalism

The term "globalism" has also been employed in a multivalent and contested manner, generally in close association with the concept of globalization. It has generally been used to describe the values, ideas, and beliefs (i.e., the ideology) of those who believe in and who seek to promote the global economic, political, and cultural integration of humanity. More often than not, it is used to describe the ideology of those who seek to advance the global integration of humanity through "free markets" and "free trade" as well as the global application of new information, communications, and transportation technologies. On the other hand, it has been used to describe the values, ideas, and beliefs of those who hold a holistic worldview founded on the fundamental belief that "we share one fragile planet the survival of which requires mutual respect and careful treatment of the earth and of all its people" (Ritchie, 1996).

In the latter sense, the ideology of globalism is most often connected with a critical conceptualization of contemporary globalization. In this usage, it describes the ideology of those who see the multidimensional globalization process as a process of global integration dominated by large transnational corporations and intergovernmental institutions. These organizational structures are perceived to be both inherently undemocratic and destructive of the planet's natural environment. This definition of globalism is revealed in the following quote from an essay written by Mark Ritchie:

> While globalism incorporates the idea of the Global Commons to describe the ozone layer, oceans, and genetic diversity, globalization is the acquisition and exploitation of these resources by giant corporations beyond the reach of democratic processes. While globalism implies a respect for diversity, globalization demands the standardization or homogenization of almost everything and everybody. . . . true globalism is the only weapon we still have for tackling the level of economic, ecological, and social dislocation caused by unbridled globalization and the resulting political violence of war and the personal violence related to crime, racism, and xenophobia. (Ritchie, 1996)

In yet another sense, the concept of globalism has also been used to characterize the perspective of those who believe the present era of globalization has created a new historical epoch of "globality" (as opposed to modernity or postmodernity) in which transnational or global agents are undermining the political and economic sovereignty of the nation-state. Some even see this process resulting in a single global economic, cultural, and political system. Those who hold these kinds of views have been characterized as "globalists" (Sklair, 2000: 1).

William Robinson's analysis of the globalization of capitalism and the incorporation of Latin America into the global capitalist system provides a good example of this type of perspective. Robinson contends "globalisation represents a shift from the nation state to a new transnational phase of capitalism" (Robinson, 1998/99: 111). He argues that "the globalisation of production and the global integration of national and regional economies" are responsible for "a fundamental economic, social political, and cultural-ideological restructuring in every country and every region," and as a result globalization "has profoundly changed the terrain on which social struggle" is taking place in Latin America

(Robinson, 1998/99: 111). According to Robinson, the dislocations and conflicts associated with globalization have given rise to a system of "polyarchy" (Robinson, 1996) in most of the Latin American countries. In this system of elite domination, transnational capital is hegemonic and the majority of the population "is confined to choosing among competing elites in tightly controlled electoral processes" (Robinson, 1998/99: 120).

Latin American social scientists such as Octavio Ianni and Aníbal Quijano also hold perspectives that can be described as globalist, since they emphasize the growing importance of the transnational or global agents involved in the globalization process and discuss the challenges this process and these agents pose to the sovereignty of nation-states, nationalities, peoples, and tribal collectives. For example, Ianni conceptualizes "globalism" as a new "logic" and an "historical category" that comprehends all "the relations, processes and structures of domination and appropriation that are developing on a worldwide scale."

> Alongside concepts such as 'mercantilism', 'colonialism' and 'imperialism', as well as 'nationalism' and 'tribalism', the world is witnessing the emergence of 'globalism', as a new and embracing historical category and logic. Globalism comprehends the relations, processes and structures of domination and appropriation that are developing on a worldwide scale. All social realities, from the individual to the collectivities of peoples, tribes, nations and nationalities, as well as transnational corporations, multilateral organizations, political parties, unions, social movements, currents of public opinion, religious organizations, intellectual activity, and others, are being influenced by the movement and configuration of globalism, and they are in turn influencing it. They are articulations, integrations, tensions and contradictions that affect each and all organizations and institutions, the most diverse social realities, to such an extent that globalism appears more or less to decisively determine the manner in which individuals and collectivities move around in the new map of the world. (Ianni, 1998)

Peruvian scholar Aníbal Quijano has identified what he calls a "genuine world imperial bloc" that is hegemonic on a worldwide basis and that consists of the most powerful nation-states (i.e., the Group of 7, plus Russia in a more subordinate role) combined with intergovernmental entities such as NATO, the International Monetary Fund (IMF), the World Bank, the Inter-American Development Bank (IDB), and the "great global corporations" (Quijano, 2000: 9). He believes these institutions constitute a de facto kind of global government.

As Quijano sees it, "globalization consists of the concentration of world public authority, strictly speaking the re-privatization of the control of collective authority, that is providing the basis for the deepening and acceleration of the basic tendencies of capitalism" (Quijano, 2000: 13). He considers globalization to be a "global counter-revolutionary process" that despite its false image of being an inevitable and "natural phenomenon" is in fact the "result of a vast and prolonged conflict for the control of power." In this conflict, "the forces that represent colonialism and capitalism have been victorious," but are increasingly encountering resistance from those who have been conquered and who are suffering the consequences of their oppression and exploitation (Quijano, 2000: 14).

Quijano argues that "what is in dispute is not the integration of the world," rather it is "the capitalist, counter-revolutionary and predatory character of the world power that is globalizing it." He believes this form of world domination and global integration needs to be replaced with the "democratic integration of the world."

> The democratic integration of the world is one of the most illustrious and persistent dreams of our species. What we are dealing with, therefore, is not impeding the integration of the world, rather, on the contrary, it is permitting its most complete development, to liberate it from the systemic conflict and perverse violence caused by the present tendencies of capitalism, so that the diversity of the species stops being an argument for the inequality of society, and the population of the planet integrates itself into a world of relations between peoples of diverse identities who are social equals and free individuals. (Quijano, 2000: 21)

One of the consequences he sees resulting from the present process of capitalist globalization and the exercise of imperial domination is the erosion of the "the local processes of the nation-state in the periphery." Quijano believes this erosion of the nation-state is associated with the emergence of fundamentalist tendencies around the world and "the reproduction of local forms of pre-modern authoritarianism, the hierarchicalization of society and the limitation of individualization" (Quijano, 2000: 22).

3.13

A Theoretical Understanding
of Globalization

Claudio Katz

The writer argues that Marx and Engels anticipated the present process of globalization and that the ensuing theories of imperialism offer a more useful explanation of world capitalist accumulation.

THE COMMUNIST MANIFESTO anticipated the present process of globalization, and the subsequent theory of imperialism provides a more direct theoretical foundation for understanding it than the theories associated with Keynesianism, which approach economic problems in purely national terms. This article emphasizes the relationship between the incipient globalization of the productive process and the laws of capitalist development, questioning the apologetic neoliberal view of globalization. It links the transformation of the division of the labor process, new forms of investment, mergers, and technological changes to an increase in the internationalization of production and underscores how this process contributes to increasing exploitation, unemployment, and poverty. It points to the difficulty of analyzing globalization from a purely commercial or financial perspective. In addition, it examines the problems associated not only with a dogmatic denial of the new phenomenon but also with characterizing it exclusively in political terms. It concludes by emphasizing the continuing rele-

First published in *Latin American Perspectives* 121, vol. 28 (6), Sage Publications, Inc. Reprinted with permission from the Latin American Perspectives Collective. Selection from 5, 7–15.

vance of the *Manifesto* for the construction of a socialist project based on the politics of working-class internationalism.

The paragraphs of the *Communist Manifesto* devoted to the worldwide expansion of capitalism continue to impress commentators on the text. Marx and Engels's (1967) 1848 descriptions of the creation of a world market, economic cosmopolitanism, the universal extension of commercial rules, and the destruction of tariff barriers have a surprisingly contemporary ring to them. The *Manifesto* anticipated the international character of accumulation with the same insight as *Capital* presaged the cyclical crises of capitalism. On many levels, these two texts have a deeper correspondence with our present economic reality than with that of the nineteenth century. . . .

Imperialism

The immediate antecedents of the current discussion of globalization are found in the theory of imperialism formulated in the early twentieth century by Lenin, Luxemburg, Bukharin, and Trotsky. Their analysis sought an interpretation of the great transformation that occurred when monopoly replaced free-trade capitalism. This change was based on an important advancement in the internationalization of the economy, especially on the commercial and financial level, as well as on the development of the first forms of direct investment. The four theorists postulated convergent characterizations of a single phenomenon but highlighted different and controversial aspects of the new stage.

For Lenin (1973), the international expansion of capital implied the parasitic predominance of financial capital along with the creation of monopolies that stifled free trade. For Luxemburg (1968), what was important was the core nations' reaction to underconsumption—exporting their unsold surplus to the periphery. She believed that the collapse of these compensatory peripheral markets led to a point in the crises of profitability where there would be a characteristic decline. Bukharin (1971), in contrast, saw a new type of contradiction emerging under capitalism as a result of the conflict between the persistence of national forms of appropriating profit and increasing economic internationalization. He emphasized that the monopolistic groups that globalized their networks of supplies, production, and commercialization tended to coalesce around increasingly protectionist states. He believed that this process produced not only the "internationalization" of capital but also its "nationalization."

Trotsky's (1972) initial analysis underscored that the primary consequence of the creation of a unified world market was a widening of the gulf between the developed and the underdeveloped countries. He asserted that this polarization drastically reduced the peripheral countries' opportunity for replicating the accelerated industrial development of the central powers.

With the construction of a world capitalist system, Trotsky concluded, it was impossible to isolate a triumphant revolution's socioeconomic development from international conditions, and this is why he considered the attempt to "construct socialism in one country" utopian (Trotsky, 1969). He understood that the new imperialist stage demanded a revision of the strategy and project of socialism on a world scale.

These four interpretations represent the theoretical foundations for an analysis of globalization because from different angles they characterize the transformations that capital penetration introduces into all corners of the world. To assess these contributions, however, it is necessary to separate their circumstantial elements from their essential components. A lasting contribution of Lenin's theory is the proposal of a transformation from free competition to a rivalry between monopolies as opposed to the idea that finance capital will subjugate industrial capital. The growing need for markets of the imperialist powers and their recourse to the oppression of the underdeveloped nations is the most valuable aspect of Luxemburg's work and not her vision of a crisis exclusively derived from the "collapse of the noncapitalist regions."

The contradiction between the internationalization of the productive forces and the persistence of national boundaries effectively constitutes the core explanation for the great worldwide economic and military conflicts, but the forms of these conflicts have substantially changed since Bukharin's time. Trotsky's view of the growing polarization between oppressed and oppressor nations has survived, and so has his focus on the unfeasibility of any socialist project that is conceived in purely national terms. This process does not imply a prolonged stagnation of the productive forces, as was believed in the 1930s, but rather its opposite. What has emerged is the increasing difficulty of reconciling the intensification of production and of productivity with the spread of markets and the expansion of profits. By separating the central elements of an analysis of imperialism from the characteristics it assumed during the interwar period one can arrive at the essential theoretical core that permits us to advance a contemporary interpretation of globalization.

Keynesianism

During the postwar period, analyzing capitalism in solely national terms once again predominated. This focus represented the continuity of the protectionist course initiated in the 1930s and, especially, the primacy of interventionist economic policies in the major nations. Keynesianism, which nurtured this trend, approaches global economic problems (trade, fluctuations, investment flows, etc.) as an extension or derivation of a national focus. Neither macroeconomic categories nor fiscal and monetary policies are conceived outside of this framework.

The limitations of this focus for an understanding of globalization are obvious, especially because the world market is interpreted as a simple beneficiary of the "growing interdependence between nations" and not as a new site for global accumulation. The inadequacy of the Keynesian criteria for analyzing globalization is apparent also in the various schools, such as that of regulation (Boyer, 1997), that have sought to reconcile the tradition of Keynes with that of Marx. For example, the concepts "rule of accumulation" and "mode of accumulation" are restricted, by definition, to the national sphere, and the same is true of "Fordism," "Taylorism," and "post-Fordism." The classic opposition between the "Austrian model" and the "Anglo-Saxon neoliberal model" also place strategic national rivalries at the center of their analysis, overlooking the new conditioned reality of globalization.

This same difficulty also underlies the Stalinist proposal of reaching socialism through the "competition between two systems." In the same way as Keynesianism, this approach characterized the world economy as a meeting between distinct forms of accumulation struggling for supremacy. It failed to understand that the twentieth-century internationalization of the economy was not an amalgam of different national characteristics but a major new referential axis for every nation. Ignoring this reality made it possible to believe, mistakenly, that socialism could be constructed within the confines of a region, coexisting with capitalism or conquering it by the "successes achieved by the socialist bloc."

Globalization

During the 1970s and 1980s the analysis of globalization was undertaken by studies that tried to update the theory of imperialism, incorporating the new role of corporations now designated "transnational firms." Michalet's work especially served to identify the appearance of a new type of firm that by strategically developing a single internationalized management can profit from national differences in productivity and salaries (Michalet, 1976). These corporations obtain extraordinary profits by constructing a homogeneous sphere within the fractured geographical environment in which their principal firms and branches operate. They are corporations that maintain their privileged links with their national states and headquarters but adopt the world market as the reference point for their activities by establishing an unprecedented internal circulation of capital, labor, inputs, and technology.

These corporations have created a new international division of labor based on the principle of maximum extraction and realization of surplus value around themselves. They have introduced both increased uniformity and increased differentiation into the process of accumulation. On one hand, competition obliges them to increase the international distribution of their products, processes, innovations, and forms of management. On the other hand, to maintain their huge profits they must preserve the great international differences between productivity and salaries. The study of transnational firms based on new empirical data gathered by the United Nations Center for Transnational Corporations and proceeding from innovative theoretical reinterpretations, for example, of the "product cycle" generated the field of Marxist investigations of globalization. To a great extent, the most recent analyses of globalization have distorted or denied the significance of these investigations.

The abrupt rise of the term "globalization" signified the sanctification of an idea that refers not to a specific type of economic internationalization under capitalism but to a postindustrialist stage. It is assumed that in the era of "global communication" and "global marketing" industrial capitalism is being replaced by an "information society" in which property loses all significance and is replaced by information. In this view, the dynamics of the new "social actors" bury the class struggle, the nation-state loses its importance, and the market is transformed into the undeniable master of all human actions. The purely apologetic character of this approach is obvious, beginning with the elimination from the analysis of the very idea of globalization. Its most widely accepted ideas do not go beyond a rudimentary embellishment of "deregulation," privatization, or the "free market."

In a critical analysis, it is necessary to avoid the neoliberal superstitions that characterize the modern period. For example, authors like Sivanandan (1997) correctly question "social exclusion," the "marginalization" of the peripheral nations, or the "increase of inequalities," but erroneously accept the idea of a "transnationalization of the bourgeoisie." With this approach, globalization is identified with the emergence of a new capitalist class that is predominant and cohesive on a worldwide scale.

Advocates of this idea overlook the fact that with internationalization competitive pressure between firms increases, and so does the need to resort to the state for support to prevail in this struggle. They forget that the state structure is not weakened but reorganized on a geographical level and functionally restructured for its struggle for global hegemony.

The Internationalization of Production

The most significant characteristic of globalization in the past decades is the movement toward the internationalization of the productive process. Here is where the central differences between the current transformations and those of the first decades of the twentieth century lie. This transformation is related to the crisis of capitalism and its reorganization since the 1970s. Along with overproduction, the decline of long-term profitability, and the disjunction between production and consumption that contributed to the current crisis, there has been a restructuring of the main branches of industry in the core nations. A cen-

tral component of this new environment is an increase in the internationalization of production.

This increase can be measured by observing the great multiplication of foreign
investments directly managed by the 600 firms that control a third of the world's
gross domestic product. Through subcontracting, "joint ventures," and aid contracts, these firms have expanded their control over all the international linkages
of the manufacturing process and the sale of goods and services. This is not a
strategy for supplying themselves with primary products or capturing markets
through the establishment of branches but the initiation of what Andreff (1996)
calls the "international decomposition of the production process," with each
branch specializing in an operation that contributes to the global strategy of the
company. It is for this reason that they generally place their high-quality activities
in the developed countries and those of "Taylorist" type in underdeveloped ones.

Since the 1980s, the new international rivalry on the production level has
caused a spectacular wave of mergers that have required reduction of costs and
an increase in productivity. It has also produced an increase in the centralization
of capital (in no important sector are there more than ten huge competitors
operating), the formation of complexes that integrate services to industry's
requirements, and the proliferation of agreements between firms to ensure the
distribution of the various goods. The substitution of the label "Made in such-
and-such a country" with "Made by such-and-such a company" symbolizes this
transformation. The "global factory" and the "global product" are not yet the
norm, but this is the central tendency of capitalism today.

An important theoretical implication of this process is the potential transformation in the determination of prices under the law of value. A significant portion of the production undertaken in the internal space of these internationalized
firms is based on the "transfer price" administered by managers who are to some
extent independent of market instability. Thus, a fracture emerges in the classical
process of the determination of average profit and the costs of production based
on national prices and currency, contributing to a regional structuring of new
monetary standards and policies regarding subsidies and tariffs.

At the same time, the internationalization of production is responsible for the
dynamic acceleration of innovation in the field of information technologies. It
simultaneously constitutes a great stimulus to the ongoing technological revolution and is the determinant of its major contradictions (developed in Katz, 1998).
On this point, two major ideas in the *Manifesto* have special relevance: the characterization of the bourgeoisie as a class that "cannot exist without constantly
revolutionizing the means of production" and the appearance of an "epidemic
of overproduction" as a consequence of this idiosyncrasy. Both phenomena are
evident today. Under capitalism, the multiplication of new goods and forms of
production is indissolubly linked to the production of surpluses in relation to
the purchasing capacity of the population. It is for this reason that poverty,
unemployment, and exploitation are increasing alongside the internationaliza-

tion of the productive process. Latin America is one of the regions most affected by this transformation.

Finance and Commerce

Some writers focus on "financial globalization" and link it with the emergence of a new "financier mode of production," emphasizing that the disproportionate expansion of credit increasingly disassociates the financial processes from the "real economy." They maintain that financial capital subordinates industrial activities and that investment flows are fictitious, concealing operations that are purely speculative. This approach fails to recognize the methodological importance of arranging the analysis of the productive sphere hierarchically and privileging the study of the laws that operate there. The fruitful discussion that has recently emerged concerning this question (Husson, 1997; Chesnais, 1994; 1998) has been the background of the debates surrounding the "decline of U.S. imperialism" (Brenner, 1995; Malloy, 1995). On the specific level of globalization, the exclusive focus on finance tends to divorce the analysis of the "global banks" from the strategic constitution of "global firms."

Without a doubt, the expansion of the unproductive parasitism of financiers enriched by playing the stock market or raiding indebted countries is a fundamental reality of the present crisis. In condemning this pillaging, however, we should seek to understand the capitalist logic underlying it, and to do this we should focus on the productive sphere. All the major changes in financial globalization registered in the past few years are connected to its industrial determinant. This dependency is visible even in the description of the financial transformations that, for example, Philon (1997) observes. The banking intermediary is bypassed by a direct issuing of bonds by companies, thereby circumventing the need to acquire credit for investment purposes. The increasing deregulation of banking is facilitating this type of self-financing, while the liberalization of operations—eliminating their previous segmentation by type of activity—aims to facilitate fusion and the formation of financial industrial holdings. It is evident that the issuing of credit independent of real economic transactions exacerbates the crisis, along with the capitalist demand to halt recession and aid bankrupt firms. The dynamics of accumulation orders the entire process and limits any margin of independence achieved by finance. Furthermore, it coexists with an inverse trend of a stricter adaptation of financial movement to the industrial demands of each participating company.

A similar neglect of the centrality of the production process appears in approaches to globalization that emphasize the progressive formation of a "world economy" resulting from the successive phases of "commercial globalization" (Adda, 1996). One loses sight of the fact that the increase in international transactions in contrast to production has occurred through the adaptation of commercial legislation (primarily liberalization by the General Agreement on Tariffs and Trade and the subsequent creation of the World Trade Organization and of regional markets without internal tariffs) to the demands of the internationalization of the productive process. The epicenter of this process is the movement of inputs and goods within the same corporations, and this requires a detailed study of the changes occurring in these firms' organization of production. The "world economy" approach has a tendency to assume that there is a continuity between the "first commercial globalization" of the sixteenth century and contemporary developments, making it difficult to perceive the specificity of today's internationalization of production.

Dogmas and Subjectivism

Some analysts go so far as to question the very existence of globalization. They maintain that internal markets continue to predominate in relation to exports, that protectionism persists as a habitual practice, that the level of the internationalization of production is less than what is usually believed, and that capitalism's cosmopolitanism is not new but is characteristic of the history of this social order. These ideas contain many allusions to the regulation school concerning the continuing "pull of the national space" in the contemporary period.

The data that they present in favor of these arguments are very useful in refuting the caricature of globalization created by neoliberal apologists. In opposing the image of a "completely new global world," the dogma of the invariability of capitalism is not very promising, especially if one remembers that the *Manifesto* clarifies the particularly dynamic and changing character. . . .

Workers without a Country

Economic internationalization creates very favorable objective conditions for bringing the political actions of the world's workers together in a common program. When the *Manifesto* asserts that "workers are without a country" and for this reason they "act above any national differences," it is expressing a principle that has enormous relevance today. The same pressure that requires the bourgeoisie to equip itself on a worldwide scale with political instruments, forms of management, and methods of coercion contributes to the need for workers to organize their struggles and defend their rights on an international level. But what is a reality for the dominant class is scarcely considered a necessity for the dominated class. For a long time, corporations have been converting international (International Monetary Fund, United Nations, World Bank, World Trade Organization, and others) and regional (European Union, North American Free Trade Association, Association of South East Asian Nations, and others) organizations into "committees to administer their affairs"—the central characteristic that the *Manifesto* attributes to the modern state. Corporations are even discussing how to design a "multilateral investment accord" that will have constitutional powers to guarantee capitalist investments, property, and profits when confronted by any popular challenge in any corner of the world. In relation to the international spread of the bourgeoisie's forms of domination, the level of organization and actual consciousness of the worker is obviously very low. This political backwardness of the exploited is not new (and is the result of a combination of political-historical factors whose analysis is beyond the scope of this article), but it has become a crucial question. All of the objective conditions exist for the globalization of the economy to serve as a point of departure for action to achieve the workers' just demands. A response on the same level as that on which the corporations operate would produce impressive results, and therefore the major problem is how to advance workers' political power through the organization of labor unions on an international scale. This structure must transcend the segmentation of professions, qualifications, nationality, race, ethnicity, and gender that is promoted and exacerbated by the dominant classes. In the age of "just in time" and "productive flexibility adjusted to demand," workers have increasing capacity to assert their demands through coordinated international actions, as current struggles for workers' rights in Europe and Latin America have begun to show.

The *Manifesto*'s call for the workers of the world to unite is its most contemporary aspect. It is a message that is not limited to the circumstances of 1848 but responds to the oppressiveness of capitalism in every period and every country. Internationalism is the pillar for a revival of the socialist project of emancipation.

Note

This article was first written in November 1998. For a further treatment of globalization see also Claudio Katz's "Desequilibrios y antagonismos de la mundialización" in *Realidad Económica* no. 178, February–March 2001, Buenos Aires.

Part IV

⊂══⟨⟩⟩⟩

The Question of Transitions:
Capitalist and Socialist

THE DEBATES THROUGHOUT this volume allude to the historical transitions that have affected much of the world. The transition from feudalism or semifeudalism to capitalism and efforts to describe the process and consequences of this transition were at the heart of concerns in Latin America about development and underdevelopment. Traditional understanding explained backwardness and underdevelopment in the region as consequences of semifeudal conditions in the countryside. The new interpretations that appeared in the 1960s and 1970s (and that to some extent continue to influence thinking today) rejected the old ideas and attributed backwardness and underdevelopment to the consequences of capitalism itself. A theory of imperialism could be utilized in either approach, in the former as a means of explaining the impact of external conditions upon countries and in the latter as a way of analyzing the internal class structure and its consequences.

For all the pretensions to envisage or implement socialism in Latin America, it has not been clear what constitutes a real transition from capitalism to socialism. The selections below attempt to delineate a theoretical model and way to conceive such a process.

4.1

The Transition to Socialism
in Latin America

Richard L. Harris

The selection from this significant synthesis on the socialist transition emphasizes early and recent attempts to outline a model and offers a summary assessment of the Latin American experience. The interested reader is encouraged to read this full article.

THIS ESSAY EXAMINES the extent to which Marxist thought on the transition to socialism is relevant to the contemporary reality of Latin America. It provides a general overview of the more important issues dealt with in the expanding Marxist literature on this subject, and it relates these issues to contemporary cases of socialist transition in Latin America and the Caribbean.

At the beginning of this century, most Marxists assumed that the transition from capitalism to socialism would initially take place in the advanced capitalist societies of western Europe and North America and not in the underdeveloped countries of Asia, Africa, and Latin America. However, it is precisely in these underdeveloped areas that socialist revolutions have occurred throughout this century. This has forced contemporary Marxists to reevaluate the original body of thought on the transition to socialism and to develop a new theory and practice that takes into account the problems of constructing socialism in underdeveloped capitalist societies.

The Relevance of Early Marxist Thought

Marx and Engels theorized in general terms about the transition between capitalism and communism (Marx and Engels, 1972: 331). They reasoned that between

First published in *Latin American Perspectives* 56, vol. 15 (1), Sage Publications, Inc. Reprinted with permission from the Latin American Perspectives Collective. Selection from 7–18, 46–49.

capitalist and communist society, there would be "the period of the revolutionary transformation of the one into the other" (1972: 331). They also contended
that the social order during this period would be "a communist society, not as it
has *developed* on its own foundations, but on the contrary, as it has *emerged* from
capitalist society" (1972: 323). They referred to this transitional social order
between capitalism and communism as the "inferior stage of communism" and
frequently as "socialism."

It was in the *Manifesto of the Communist Party* that Marx and Engels first set
forth their general ideas on how capitalism would come to an end and how communism would come into being. As the following quote indicates, they believed
the first step would involve the seizure of state power by the proletariat, which
would thus become the new ruling class.

> The first step in the revolution by the working class is to raise the proletariat to the
> position of ruling class, to win the battle of democracy. The proletariat will use its
> political supremacy to wrest, by degrees, all capital from the bourgeoisie, to central-
> ize all instruments of production in the hands of the State, i.e., of the proletariat
> organized as the ruling class; and to increase the total of productive forces as rapidly
> as possible. (Marx and Engels, 1972: 52)

This basic conception of the first steps involved in the establishment of socialism
has influenced revolutionary thought and practice ever since it was first introduced in 1848.

Believing that the victorious proletariat would most likely take similar measures in different countries to initiate the process of socialist construction, Marx
and Engels reasoned that the following list of measures would probably be "generally applicable."

> (1) Abolition of property in land. . . . (2) A heavy progressive or graduated tax. (3)
> Abolition of all rights of inheritance. (4) Confiscation of the property of all emi-
> grants and rebels. (5) Centralization of credit in the hands of the State, by means of
> a national bank. . . . (6) Centralization of the means of communication and trans-
> port in the hands of the State. (7) Extension of factories and instruments of produc-
> tion owned by the State. . . . (8) Equal liability of all to labor. Establishment of
> industrial armies, especially for agriculture. (9) Combination of agriculture with
> manufacturing industries; gradual abolition of the distinction between town and
> country by a more equitable distribution of the population over the country. (10)
> Free education for all children in public schools. (Marx and Engels, 1972: 52–53)

This list of measures gives a fairly clear idea of what Marx and Engels thought
would be the initial program of a proletarian regime that had seized power in an
advanced capitalist society.

Most of these measures were adopted by the new Soviet state in the first years
of the Russian Revolution and, to a greater or lesser extent, by most revolution-

ary regimes committed to the construction of socialism in underdeveloped Third World societies since then. For example, during the first five years of the revolutionary regime in Cuba, substantial progress was made in each of the areas listed above (see Boorstein, 1968; Pierre-Charles, 1976; Rodríguez, 1978).

Lenin was the first Marxist theorist and political leader to confront the problem of applying Marxist thought to the construction of socialism in concrete historical conditions. Moreover, he had to do this in an underdeveloped capitalist society (Russia). In essence, he took Marx and Engels's basic concepts and incorporated them into a new conceptualization of the transition to socialism that could be applied to a "backward country" (Harnecker, 1986: 128–129). Lenin based this conceptualization on the premise that the immediate and direct construction of socialism was *not* possible in a backward society such as Russia. The underdeveloped nature of the economy and the low cultural development of the masses, he contended, made it necessary to depend initially upon a combination of capitalist relations of production and centralized state control of the economy in order to develop the country's forces of production rapidly. He referred to this combination of capitalism and statization as "state-monopoly capitalism," and argued that this was necessary in order to achieve "a complete material preparation for socialism" in Russia (Lenin, 1976: 445).

This idea of a "preliminary transition" or initial stage of preparation before beginning the actual construction of socialism has been adopted by most contemporary revolutionary regimes in underdeveloped societies. However, there appears to be considerable variation between regimes in terms of the time allotted for this period of preparation. In the case of Cuba, this period appears to have taken place during the first four years of the revolutionary regime. Thus Cuba's President Oswaldo Dorticos stated in January 1963 that "these first four years constitute the stage during which the conditions for the construction of socialism have been created in our country" (quoted in Pierre-Charles, 1976: 173).

In the case of revolutionary Nicaragua, the Sandinistas believe that the conditions prevailing in their country preclude an immediate transition to socialism and necessitate a prolonged period of preparation. This is revealed in the following statement made in 1983 by Comandante Jaime Wheelock, Nicaragua's Minister of Agricultural Development and Agrarian Reform:

> Now, for a series of reasons, many of them political, and others having to do with hunger and desperation, certain peoples have made a revolution in the worst conditions of social development. . . . This is our case. Even though we have socialist principles, we cannot effect the transformation of our society by socializing all the means of production. This would not lead to socialism, rather the contrary, it could lead to the destruction and disarticulation of our society. What we seek is the articulation of a project in which the most strategic and most developed sectors of the economy constitute a spearhead, and the organization of a social project in which

associational forms of labor will predominate, although in a rudimentary form. (Wheelock, 1983: 101–102)

According to the Sandinistas, it is not feasible to undertake a sweeping socialization of their underdeveloped economy. Therefore, they are committed for the foreseeable future to developing a "mixed economy" based on both private and state capitalism. How and when this will evolve into a socialist economy is an open question (Harris and Vilas, 1985: 227–230; Vilas, 1986: 263–269).

Lenin believed strongly that dictatorship and coercion were necessary during the transition from capitalism to socialism because of both the continuing resistance of the bourgeoisie and the external/internal wars that socialist revolutions generate (Lenin, 1976: 421). Recent history has shown, in the case of Latin America and the Caribbean, that the resistance of the bourgeoisie and counterrevolutionary wars are, indeed, conditions that must be confronted by revolutionary regimes in this part of the world. However, it is a matter of continuing debate whether a dictatorship must be established in order to deal with these conditions. We shall return to this debate later in this essay.

It is important to note here that Lenin's ideas on the transition to socialism were challenged at the time they were first formulated by Marxists in the Soviet Union and in western Europe, notably by Karl Kautsky and Rosa Luxemburg (e.g., see Luxemburg, 1971, 1972; Stephens, 1986: 53–69). They differed with Lenin over such important issues as the pace of the transition process, the use of coercion in the process, the nature of the class struggle during this period, whether a dictatorial form of government was necessary, the importance of establishing political democracy in the transition, and the role of the revolutionary party during the transition period.

For example, Kautsky argued that the transition from capitalism to socialism in the more advanced capitalist countries could and should take place in a democratic manner following the electoral victory of a mass-based socialist party. He thought that this parliamentary road to socialism would quickly lead to a revolutionary break with capitalism and the rapid construction of socialism within one or two decades (Stephens, 1986: 57). Kautsky contended that this could take place with a minimum of coercion and under the direction of a democratic regime committed to a socialist program of reforms.

This idea of a peaceful, parliamentary road to socialism became the perspective of social democratic parties throughout western Europe and elsewhere following the Second International. In the recent history of Latin America, this was, of course, an important aspect of the strategy of the Popular Unity (UP) government of Salvador Allende, whose attempt at a peaceful, democratic transition to socialism in Chile was brought to a tragic end by the military coup in 1973.

Lenin totally disagreed with the idea of a parliamentary road to socialism espoused by Kautsky and the other theoreticians of the Second International. He criticized them for abandoning Marx's fundamental notion that the proletariat could not seize power by simply assuming control of the old state apparatus, and he reminded them that Marx had argued that the proletariat would have to smash this apparatus and replace it with a new one (Lenin, 1976: 345). This debate between Lenin and Kautsky over the parliamentary road to socialism continues to have great relevance for the left in Latin America and the Caribbean. The demise of the Popular Unity regime in Chile appears to provide evidence in support of Lenin's position in the debate with Kautsky. Further support could be derived from the overthrow of Cheddi Jagan's government in Guyana and the failure of Manley's government in Jamaica (see Manley, 1982; Mars, 1984: 83–110). However, in the case of the Allende regime in Chile, there are those who argue convincingly that it was not the choice of a democratic road to socialism, but the way this strategy was carried out in Chile, that was at fault (see Bitar, 1979).

Rosa Luxemburg, like Lenin, rejected Kautsky's and the Second International's conception of the parliamentary road to socialism, but she disagreed with Lenin on the need for a dictatorship during the transition to socialism. Luxemburg's basic position was that the working class needed a mass-based, democratic party that would overthrow the existing capitalist order through mobilizing the masses in a revolutionary general strike.

Luxemburg argued that, following the overthrow of the capitalist state, civil liberties and popular democratic forms of organization would have to be instituted in order to ensure that the working class remained in control of the process of constructing socialism.

> Without general elections, without unrestricted freedom of the press and assembly, without a free struggle of opinion, life dies out in every public institution . . . only the bureaucracy remains as the active element . . . socialist democracy is not something that begins only in the promised land after the foundations of socialist economy are created . . . it begins at the very moment of the seizure of power by the socialist party. It is the same thing as the dictatorship of the proletariat. . . . But this dictatorship must be the work of the class, and not a little leading minority in the name of the class—that is, it must proceed step by step out of the active participation of the masses; it must be under their direct influence; subjected to the control of complete public activity. (Luxemburg, 1972: 247–249)

As this quote reveals, Luxemburg's conception of the transition to socialism rested upon the fundamental notion that the construction of socialism must be a mass-based, democratic process of revolutionary social transformation.

It is important to recognize that the differences between Lenin, Luxemburg, and Kautsky appear to have been, to a considerable degree, the product of the different social contexts in which they operated (Stephens, 1986: 62). Lenin's perspective was obviously influenced by the objective realities of carrying out a revolution in a war-torn, largely agrarian and autocratic society, whereas Kautsky was influenced by the fact that Germany, at the time of his writings, had become a major industrial power with the largest legal working-class party in Europe. Luxemburg, on the other hand, was an activist in the revolutionary movements of Germany, Poland, and Russia. As a result, she was exposed to the varying conditions and various currents of leftist thought and practice in these three societies. This clearly had an important influence on her thinking and helps to explain her distinctive perspective.

No General Theory of the Transition to Socialism

In the past three to four decades, many Marxists seem to have concluded that a general theory of the transition to socialism—that is, a theory that applies to all societies that undertake such a course of development—is not possible. For example, Marta Harnecker, a Chilean Marxist scholar who now lives in Cuba, has written the following: "because the historical transition depends upon the concrete form of the class struggle in each country, no general theory of transition can exist" (1986: 128). She further contends that "each transition is materially different, therefore, conceptually different." As a result, Harnecker claims that it is up to the revolutionary vanguard in each country to elaborate a *particular* strategy for the transition in their country that depends upon the characteristics of that country's class struggle.

The problems involved in applying Marxist thought on this subject to the conditions prevailing in revolutionary societies today have been addressed at length by French Marxist scholar Charles Bettelheim, particularly in his book *The Transition to Socialist Economy* (1978). In this important study, he argues that the application of Marxism to concrete situations should not be confused with the practice of applying abstract models to a specific social reality, so common in the bourgeois social sciences, since this approach always fails to account for important "accidental conditions" or "external factors" that fall outside the model. Instead, Bettelheim argues that Marxism involves considering "every reality as a structured whole which has to be analyzed as such" (1978: 148). This means that the analysis of a particular transitional society must take into account the totality of concrete, historical conditions that exist in that society.

Bettelheim uses Marxist theory and analysis to demonstrate that there are different forms of societal transition in existence today in the Third World, and that one should not be confused by the use of the label "socialist" in cases that do not involve a genuine transition to socialism. According to Bettelheim, only societies undergoing a "radical form of transition" from the capitalist mode of production to the "socialist mode of production" are engaged in a genuine transition to socialism. He contends that this kind of transition requires "the passing of *state power* to the working class, or a coalition of formerly exploited classes within which the working class plays a dominant role" (1978: 21). Without this preliminary condition, the transition to socialism is not possible.

According to Bettelheim, a genuine transition to socialism also requires certain political and ideological conditions and a conjuncture of internal and international contradicitons that enable a society to do without the further development of capitalism and "pass directly to the building of socialism" (1978: 21). As examples of genuine socialist transitions, he cites China, Cuba, and Vietnam. If we use Bettelheim's conception, then neither Chile during the UP government nor Jamaica under Manley qualifies as a case of socialist transition. In both cases, state power did *not* pass into the hands of the working class or a coalition of exploited classes, and there was an absence of a conjuncture of internal and international contradictions that would have enabled these societies to do without further capitalist development and to pass directly to the construction of socialism.

Bettelheim (1978: 12–13) warns against confusing societies that are engaged in a genuine socialist transition with Third World countries that are involved in what he refers to as a more limited "postcolonial transition." In the latter case, the previous structures of domination are not abolished but merely modified, or there is an unstable situation of "momentary equilibrium between the social classes confronting each other" (1978: 22). Quite often, the postcolonial regimes in these countries use terms such as "Islamic Socialism," "Buddhist Socialism," or "African Socialism" to describe themselves (e.g., see Babu, 1981). These labels, as the Yugoslav Marxist scholar Branko Horvat has noted, are frequently little more than "a proxy" for ideological notions based upon nationalism and a commitment to rapid economic growth (Horvat, 1982: 963).

Samir Amin holds a somewhat similar perspective on this question (see Amin, 1980, 1981, 1985). He argues that national liberation struggles in the Third World can serve as the "primary force" for a socialist transition, but, more often than not, he contends that they produce a postcolonial regime based upon either some form of neocolonial capitalism or a pseudosocialist "state mode of production" (Amin, 1980: 189–202). According to Amin (1980: 252), the struggle for national liberation gives rise to a socialist transition only if it involves "an uninterrupted revolution by stages," if it is led by the peasant and worker masses and results in a classless socialist society.

Counterposed to this perspective is the contemporary Soviet conception of "the noncapitalist way," which is based upon the fundamental assumption that a direct transition to socialism is not possible in most contemporary underdeveloped societies. Therefore, it is assumed that these societies must go through a stage of "noncapitalist development" before they begin the transition to socialism (Brutents, 1983). According to the Soviet perspective, this path of development involves the nationalization of the holdings of the large bourgeoisie and feudal landlords, restriction of the activity of foreign capital, state control of the commanding heights of the economy, the development of state planning, the strengthening of the government apparatus with cadres loyal to the people, the pursuit of an anti-imperialist foreign policy, and so forth (Brezhnev, 1981: 7).

The Soviets assign the designation "socialist orientation" to Third World states that are involved in a "noncapitalist" path of development. Some states that fall into this category are Afghanistan, Algeria, Angola, Burma, Ethiopia, Mozambique, South Yemen, and Syria. Grenada was also assigned this designation during the period of the People's Revolutionary Government (Pryor, 1986: 238–239).

However, with regard to Nicaragua, the Soviets appear to have been reluctant to use this designation, preferring instead to characterize the country as being "on the road of democracy and social progress" (Edelman, 1987: 39). This reluctance seems to be due to the heterodox nature of the Sandinista revolution, the country's geopolitical position, and Soviet concern about the possibility that Nicaragua's revolutionary process could be rolled back by the United States (1987: 40–41). Nevertheless, Soviet military and economic assistance has been crucial to the survival of Nicaragua's revolutionary regime.

Having reviewed these different conceptions of the transition to socialism, it is clear that there is no commonly agreed-upon theory of the transition to socialism. Moreover, the arguments of contemporary Marxists such as Harnecker and Bettelheim are quite convincing that a universal or general theory of the transition to socialism is not possible. Nevertheless, it does seem possible and useful to make some generalizations about this important subject. Figure 4.1–1 provides a list of generalizations about the transition to socialism that are based upon what Harnecker calls the "general principles" of socialism that can be derived from Marxist thought and practice (Harnecker, 1986: 120–121).

These principles represent a set of basic generalizations about the nature of the transition to socialism that can be applied to contemporary conditions in Latin America and elsewhere. They offer a basic framework that can be used in developing a specific strategy of socialist transition in any country and for assessing the progress of societies that are already involved in a process of socialist transformation.

Dictatorship and Democracy

In his *Critique of the Gotha Program*, Marx asserted that "the revolutionary dictatorship of the proletariat" would be the form taken by the state during the transition between capitalism and communism (Marx and Engels, 1972: 331). He was reluctant to give a blueprint for the exact form of this state, but in his 1871 address to the First International on the "Civil War in France" (1972: 274–313), Marx praised the Paris Commune as the harbinger of the form of "working-class government" that would likely be created by the proletariat once they had seized power and smashed the bourgeois state.

The main characteristics of the Paris Commune that Marx praised were (1)

Figure 4.1-1. General Framework for the Transition to Socialism

---

1. The precondition for initiating the construction of socialism is a revolution at the political level, involving:
   a. the seizure of political power by a revolutionary bloc of popular forces in which the proletariat is a central element;
   b. the destruction of the bourgeois state apparatus;
   c. the establishment of a revolutionary regime that functions as a democracy for the popular masses and as a dictatorship for those that resist the measures taken by the regime;
   d. an alliance between the proletariat and the entire working population;
   e. the support of the socialist countries;
   f. solidarity with the revolutionary processes of other countries.
2. There must be a revolution in the relations of production, involving:
   a. the elimination of private property in large industry and agriculture;
   b. work for everyone;
   c. economic planning that ensures a harmonious and intensive development of the forces of production and the satisfaction of the population's basic needs;
   d. pay according to the type of work performed and the elimination of any other sources of income;
   e. worker participation in the control of production at the level of both the unit of production and the societal level.
3. There must be an ideological/cultural revolution, involving:
   a. a struggle against the remnants of bourgeois ideology;
   b. popular education and technological training for the working population;
   c. the combining of study with productive work.

---

the abolition of the standing army and its replacement by the armed populace, organized into a militia, (2) the disestablishment and disendowment of all churches as proprietary bodies, (3) direct election of all public servants, including administrative personnel, magistrates, and judges, (4) universal suffrage, (5) the combination of legislative and executive functions in the hands of the communal council, the members of which were elected on a ward basis for short and revocable terms of office, (6) the immediate recall of elected delegates to the communal council by the citizenry when dissatisfied with their actions, (7) local self-government within a federation of urban and rural communes, (8) workers' wages for all public servants, and (9) free education, divorced of religious teachings, for all.

Until the Russian Revolution, most Marxists agreed that what Marx and Engels had in mind when they spoke of the dictatorship of the proletariat was a regime that would be dictatorial toward the old ruling class and its allies but genuinely democratic in terms of the formerly exploited classes (Sweezy, 1980: 116). This perspective was also shared by Lenin, as evidenced in his work *The State and Revolution:*

Democracy for the vast majority of the people, and suppression by force, that is, exclusion from democracy, of the exploiters and oppressors of the people—this is the change democracy undergoes during the transition from capitalism to communism. (Lenin, 1976: 327)

This perspective is still shared by many Marxists today. Thus Orlando Núñez Soto, one of revolutionary Nicaragua's most outstanding social scientists, has recently written that the revolutionary state in a transitional society must be "a combined form of dictatorship and democracy: intransigent towards those who oppose or endanger the proletarian project, but democratic in implementing that project" (Núñez, 1986: 247).

However, the early Marxist conception of the transitional state was not realized in the Russian Revolution. The new Soviet state that emerged was far more authoritarian and centralized than that imagined by the early Marxists. Objective conditions, such as the backwardness of the economy, the civil war, foreign intervention, the unfamiliarity of the masses with democracy, and the general state of economic chaos in Russia, forced the new regime to take exceptional measures (Harnecker, 1986: 116). According to Trotsky and his followers, these objective conditions, particularly the underdeveloped nature of the forces of production, made it impossible to establish a genuine workers' democracy in Russia and gave rise to a deformed bureaucratic regime (Mandel, 1978; Trotsky, 1972).

Many contemporary Marxists reject the Trotskyist thesis that the Soviet Union has been stalled in the transition process by the bureaucratic deformation of the Soviet state. Instead, they argue that a new type of statist society has developed in the Soviet Union, unlike anything foreseen by Marx, Engels, and Lenin (see Amin, 1980: 207–210; Bartra, 1982: 140–142; Sweezy, 1980: 137–138; Horvat, 1982: 43–56).

Branko Horvat, for example, claims that the Soviet Union and other statist societies are not involved in a transition to socialism; rather, they are a new kind of society that is characterized by a self-reproducing centralized, authoritarian state, which "has swallowed the entire society" (1982: 48). He contends that this type of state is incompatible with socialism, because "political domination must be eliminated just as any other form of domination" in the transition to socialism (1982: 56).

Roger Bartra, a prominent Mexican Marxist, believes that one of the main causes of the contemporary crisis of Marxism is the failure of Marxists to explain the existence of the kind of authoritarian statist society that has developed in the Soviet Union (Bartra, 1982: 124). Like Horvat, he concludes that a genuine transition to socialism cannot be effected in the USSR or anywhere else unless there is a thoroughgoing democratization of both political and social life. . . .

Conclusion

The preceding presentation has been concerned with demonstrating the extent to which Marxist thought on the transition to socialism has been and continues to be relevant to the reality of countries involved in the construction of socialism within the Latin American and Caribbean region. The generalizations that can be drawn from this tentative effort are at best knowledgeable reflections and informed comments, rather than defensible affirmations and firm conclusions. With this qualification clearly in mind, we offer the following final considerations.

First, although classical Marxist theory does not specifically address the problems of constructing socialism in contemporary Latin America and the Caribbean, it does appear to be invaluable as a fundamental conceptual framework for understanding the basic nature of the transition to socialism in this part of the world. This is due in part to the fact that the revolutionaries who have undertaken socialist transformations in Latin America and the Caribbean have been greatly influenced by Marxist thought. But it is also because the basic concepts developed by Marx and Engels on this question can be applied to a much wider range of social contexts than they themselves imagined.

This does not mean that classical Marxist theory can be applied in an inflexible and dogmatic fashion to the reality of the contemporary societies of Latin America and the Caribbean. Lenin clearly rejected the mechanistic and dogmatic application of Marxist thought. In fact, his success in applying Marxism to the Russian Revolution seems to have stemmed from the "elastic relationship" that he established between his use of Marxist theory and his revolutionary practice (Cerroni, 1973: 110). The leaders of the Chinese, Cuban, Vietnamese, Nicaraguan, and Salvadoran revolutions appear to have used Marxist thought in the same manner. Thus it is clear that the construction of socialism in Latin America and the Caribbean requires the flexible adaptation of Marxist thought to the particular social conditions of the region.

Second, most of the main questions and points discussed in previous Marxist debates clearly seem to be relevant to understanding the problems and conditions of contemporary societies involved in the transition to socialism in Latin America and the Caribbean, especially on issues such as the nature of the revolutionary state, dictatorship versus democracy, bureaucratism, the pace of the transition process, the relationship of the vanguard to the masses, class alliances, the expropriation of large capital, the socialization of agriculture, the continuance of commodity relations during the transition, central planning versus local initiative, workers' control, the role of ideology and popular education in the development of a new revolutionary culture, the emancipation of women, and so forth. The earlier debates on these questions provide a valuable frame of reference for understanding and dealing with contemporary conditions.

Third, when Marxist thought is combined with an adequate understanding of the experiences of countries that have undertaken the construction of socialism, it is an invaluable weapon in the arsenal of revolutionaries seeking to construct a socialist order in their particular historical context. However, this body of thought needs to be constantly developed and updated so that it does not lag behind contemporary efforts to build socialism. There is a rich literature on the revolutionary experiences of the many societies that have undertaken the construction of socialism in recent decades, but there does not appear to be enough effort devoted to synthesizing these experiences and updating Marxist thought on the transition to socialism. Dogmatic and empiricist tendencies in contemporary Marxist circles may be partially responsible for this lack of effort. But I suspect it stems mostly from the shortage of Marxist intellectuals interested and involved in the type of synthesizing and updating work that is needed.

The experience accumulated in the construction of socialism within Latin America and the Caribbean offers valuable contributions to the development of Marxist thought on the following issues: (1) the role of multiclass alliances, mass-based movements, and armed vanguards in the revolutionary seizure of political power and the construction of socialism, (2) the necessity of destroying the bourgeois state apparatus (particularly the armed forces) before undertaking the construction of socialism, (3) the difficulties encountered in consolidating a socialist or national democratic revolution in the face of counterrevolutionary resistance and imperialist aggression, (4) the pace at which the major means of production should be socialized in underdeveloped and export-dependent economies, (5) the problems associated with incorporating small peasant producers into the revolutionary process through land distribution and cooperativization, (6) the need for democratization at all levels of society in order to combat bureaucratism and statist tendencies, (7) the importance of ideological struggle and cultural transformation in the process of revolutionary transformation (especially with regard to issues of gender, race, ethnicity, and religion), and (8) the role that assistance from existing socialist, Third World, and European social democratic governments can play in the revolutionary consolidation and the economic transformation of transitional underdeveloped societies.

Finally, the Latin American and Caribbean experience clearly seems to confirm the proposition that there are no universal models for Marxist revolutionaries to follow in constructing socialism. The founders of Marxism introduced a conceptual framework for interpreting the complex, changing reality of *each* capitalist society. They had no intention of producing a static, theoretical model that could be applied to all societies under all historical circumstances. Armed with this understanding of Marxist analysis and an appreciation of the "lessons" of other revolutionary experiences, revolutionaries in Latin America and the Caribbean can successfully devise an appropriate strategy for the socialist transformation of their particular social realities. Carlos Rafael Rodríguez is correct in stating that the "variety of contemporary roads to socialism . . . reflects the enormous influence of socialism on the social life of our times" (Rodríguez, 1978: 14). However, if this rich variety of experiences ("roads" to socialism) is reduced to a model or models that others are supposed to follow, we run the risk of closing off new roads to socialism in the future.

4.2

Authoritarianism and Democracy in the Transition to Socialism

James F. Petras and Frank T. Fitzgerald

This essay explores the roles of extent authoritarianism and democratic participation in the experience of failed socialist regimes in Latin America.

E VERY REGIME INTENT on effecting a transition to socialism inevitably confronts the necessity to utilize both authoritarian and democratic measures. On the one hand, recent historical experiences provide ample evidence that neither local bourgeois and imperial interests nor their military and police protectors can be expected to peacefully allow themselves to be divested of privileges. Regimes that shy from utilizing authoritarian measures against such opponents can expect to find their transitions aborted, often in the most bloody fashion. On the other hand, any transition to socialism worthy of the name must entail an extension of popular democratic control over state and society and of the democratic freedoms of speech, assembly, and petition. A regime that fails to extend democracy may enhance its chances for survival, but does so, typically, at the cost of compromising the democratic essence of its socialist project.

These issues of authoritarianism and democracy in the transition to socialism are mystified by two opposing, yet equally demagogic, perspectives. One sacrifices the need for democratic practice in the name of security. Typically, the regime unduly expands its definition of political enemies, and unduly extends the measures designed to deal with the exceptional circumstances of direct and serious threat to its survival. In short, the emergency and the measures put in

First published in *Latin American Perspectives* 56, vol. 15 (1), Sage Publications, Inc. Reprinted with permission from the Latin American Perspectives Collective. Selection from 93–96, 99–108.

place to deal with it become the norm. Democracy is judged an expendable luxury, impugned as a lower form of political practice, or redefined to include authoritarian centralized rule. The other perspective rejects the use of necessary authoritarian measures in the name of democracy. Typically the regime unduly narrows the way in which it defines its enemies, and fails to deal decisively with the very real threats to its survival. Failing to specify appropriate political, military, and social policies for sustaining itself in the face of opposition, the regime often naively expects enemies to abide by the democratic rules of the game. As necessary authoritarian measures are shunned, democracy is often ahistorically judged appropriate for all times and places.

Clearly, these issues of authoritarianism and democracy cannot be—and, in the past, largely have not been—discussed independently of political and social context. Eighteenth-century revolutionary democrats, as well as nineteenth- and twentieth-century anticolonialists, liberal democrats, and socialists, have at one time or another supported varying degrees of democracy and authoritarianism according to the context. It is sheer demagoguery devoid of historical substance, then, to wave the flag of democracy, as some writers do, in every place and point in history, particularly in periods of large-scale, long-term change from one social system to another, when invasion by an imperial military power is imminent. On the other hand, it is a perversion of democracy to extend and institutionalize authoritarian practices beyond the context that evoked them and to claim that the new autocratic polity constitutes a higher form of governance.

In discussing these issues of authoritarianism and democracy, it is necessary to distinguish two distinct but interrelated phases in the transition to socialism: (1) *establishing the foundation* of the new social system and (2) *building the participatory institutions* for the normal, long-term operation of the system. Each of these phases defines the extent to which authoritarian or democratic practices are necessary or inappropriate. In moving from one phase to the other, a process of *conversion* must take place. If the tasks of each phase are accomplished and the process of conversion is successful, a securely founded, democratic socialist society can be created. But, as everyone knows, the success of the process is not guaranteed. The transition to socialism can go awry in many ways and at many points.

We analyze both of these phases of the transition to socialism and their interconnections. Our analysis will be based on, but by no means limited in relevance to, key recent Latin American experiences in Chile, Jamaica, Cuba, and Nicaragua. The first section will focus on the need for authoritarian practices in establishing the foundation of the new society. The second section will focus on the need for democratic practices in building participatory institutions. The third section will attempt to draw out the implications of our argument for recent debates on authoritarianism and democracy.

Establishing the Foundation for Socialism:
The Authoritarian Imperative

Establishing the foundation for socialism requires organizing and mobilizing the beneficiaries of the new society and displacing its adversaries. The latter, made up most immediately by local bourgeois and imperial interests and their military and police protectors, have never given up their privileges without resistance. Building the foundation of the new society, then, necessarily entails profound social and political polarization, intense conflict, and frequent resort to force. Neither the forces threatened with large-scale, long-term displacement nor the regime and its supporters share a common set of values or interests that allows their differences to be resolved in an electoral, parliamentary framework.

Concretely, the necessity for authoritarian practices in the foundation-establishing phase can perhaps best be observed in their absence. In Chile between 1970 and 1973, Salvador Allende and his Unidad Popular (UP) government pursued a policy of realizing socialist reforms through the electoral, parliamentary system; and, in Jamaica between 1972 and 1980, Michael Manley and his People's National Party (PNP) attempted to construct "democratic socialism" through existing state institutions. Both governments made consequential efforts to redistribute wealth, income, and political power. Both nationalized or placed significant limits on the prerogatives of domestic and international capital. Both extended new benefits and legal protections to workers and peasants, while creating or emboldening popular mass organizations, which began to play an active role in workplace and community decision making. Internationally, both turned to the nonaligned movement and took leadership in the struggle for a new international economic order. Both, unfortunately, failed to take authoritarian measures sufficient to defend themselves, and both failed to establish the foundation of a new socialist society.

In the absence of decisive authoritarian measures, opposition forces violated the norms and procedures of the legal system, engaging in extralegal violence and illegal economic transactions (Smirnow 1979: 100–156; Manley 1982: 169–174; Kaufman 1985: 187–191). Capitalists, bankers, and merchants held back on investments, illegally sent money abroad, hoarded goods, and speculated on the black market to undermine the economy. This was followed by propaganda directed at the populace blaming the economic problems on the regime's incompetence. Worse still, with their imperial backers, they funded, organized, and encouraged a host of antiregime activities, including violent paramilitary attacks on loyal civilians. The terrorists were aided and abetted by opposition politicians, who not only opposed the regime in parliament but openly encouraged antiregime activity in the streets, in the military, and among civil servants. In addition, in both countries military and police remained subject to imperial influence and funding, and most senior civil servants retained ties with their patrons among the foreign and domestic rich and were well-placed and ideologically oriented to block effective implementation of many of the regime's programs. In the end, with political violence beyond control and the economies of both countries in shambles, their transitions were blocked. In Chile, Allende and tens of thousands of his supporters were subjected to a bloodbath at the hands of the military, a coup initially supported by the Christian Democrats and other supposedly democratic parties (Sobel, 1974: 145). In Jamaica, Manley and his associates were overwhelmed by the Jamaica Labor Party (JLP) in the 1980 election.

But were there alternatives? Did either regime have the political wherewithal to take the authoritarian measures necessary to block the opposition? The answer is yes. . . .

In both Jamaica and Chile, socialists failed to recognize the gravity of the challenge to their democratic mandate. They failed to assert their authority by strengthening democrats and purging rightists in the military and civil service to ensure order, by assuming executive power and temporarily recessing or reforming parliament in order to pass essential legislation, and by institutionalizing and providing resources to workplace and community organizations to implement programs. Both regimes banked on an alliance with the "middle class," and restrained themselves in the hope of cementing such an alliance. They continued the politics of democratic pluralism, even after the bourgeoisie and its allies had declared violent class war. By not restricting the political participation of those who would, and eventually did, destroy it and by not expanding the participation of those who were its primary defenders, the Chilean and Jamaican socialists undermined the transition to socialism.

It is ironic that some left-liberal commentators argue that Allende and Manley went too far and too fast and that they should have sacrificed major sectors of their programs in order to continue in office. This ignores the fact that the compromises they did make only emboldened the opposition and the fact that the initial reforms engendered tremendous energy and support from increasingly class-conscious and organized workers, peasants, and poor. The opposition could not be stopped with compromises, and supporters could not be denied basic changes necessary to improve their everyday life. Once the popular social movements experienced their newly won political power, they had to be either institutionalized or repressed by force.

The real problem was that changes in civil society were not accompanied by structural changes in the state. The question of the rate or scope of socioeconomic change was less important than the need for a coordinated shift in the organization of state power. In fact, greater changes in state power would have allowed for a more measured tempo in social transformation.

This proposition can best be illustrated by examining the contemporary Nicaraguan experience. There, after eight years of revolutionary power, a mixed economy and a plural democracy still operate (in 1988). Nicaragua differs from Chile and Jamaica in that the Sandinistas have transformed the state and empowered mass organizations. As a result, they have effectively limited economic sabotage by private capitalists and destabilizing efforts by opposition forces. As in Chile and Jamaica, the Nicaraguan socialists have attempted to maintain an alliance with the "middle class," but only on terms consistent with the new social foundation, only so long as middle-class behavior conforms to what the Sandinistas call "the logic of the majority" (Brundenius 1985: 21). Private capitalists who do not produce run the risk of expropriation, and, although a wide range of political opposition is accommodated within the political framework laid down by the revolutionary regime, the Sandinistas have not failed to use authoritarian measures, from censorship to arrest, against serious attacks against the regime (Gilbert 1985: 169–177). As a result, much of the opposition not willing to function within the legal framework has been displaced to places like Miami or to *contra* bases in neighboring countries. The revolutionary regime is thus still under threat, but the decisiveness of the Sandinistas in dealing with the illegal acts of the opposition inside the country has so far enabled them to transform civil society in a relatively gradual and orderly fashion.

Although the foundation of the new society is not fully secured in Nicaragua, it has been for many years now in Cuba. That process too required authoritarian measures, emanating from a transformed state and allied mass organizations (Morley 1980: 387–424; Fitzgerald 1985: 94–96). Even more so than in Nicaragua, the Cuban oppositionists who relied on violent and illegal activities departed, not infrequently subordinating themselves to U.S. intelligence agencies. The economy was rapidly nationalized and the benefits distributed to the masses. As we shall see in the next section, the Cuban revolutionaries overstepped some critical boundaries in the process of establishing the new basis of rulership, but they did secure the foundation of the new society, an accomplishment that would not have been possible without resort to exceptional measures.

Conversion to Participatory Institutions:
The Democratic Imperative

Although some restrictions are imperative in the early phase of the transition to socialism, in the process of establishing the foundation for the transition to socialism, it is essential that *political boundaries* be delineated and respected. Clear boundaries must be established between those political and social forces that defend the old regime and those that back the new, between those that cooperate with foreign intervention and those that defend the nation against such aggression. These boundaries serve the functions of restricting the participation of those who would destroy the new regime and of encouraging the participation of those who accept the new regime but who may differ on policies, institutional practices, and procedures. These boundaries are crucial for the conversion to participatory institutions that are fully democratic. Without clear boundaries, the tendency is to lump together democratic critics and enemies of democracy and to fail to recognize that, in establishing the foundation, but especially after it has been securely established, the interests and opinions of democratic socialists will differ in a variety of matters.

For the same reason, temporal boundaries must also be established and respected. These make clear that the necessary politically restrictive measures are time-limited in nature. For the democratic regime under military or political attack, authoritarian practices are the order of the day and must remain in force so long as survival is in question. But the fact that these are exceptional measures—to be jettisoned as soon as the new foundation is secured and the emergency ended—must be openly stated. Authoritarian practices must be defined as reflecting a specific, exceptional situation. Authoritarian necessities must not be turned into virtues and built into the basic conception of socialism. These conditions are necessary to prepare the groundwork for conversion to full democratic participation and rulership immediately upon the ending of the emergency.

It is precisely with this process of conversion that twentieth-century socialist revolutionaries have had the most difficulty. One of the differences between the American Revolution and contemporary socialist revolutions is not over the initial period of authoritarianism, which all of them share, but over the establishment of boundaries and the process of conversion. The American revolutionary leadership, for example, more or less delineated the political elements (empire loyalists) to be excluded from effective participation (to be sure, many nonloyalists, including women, blacks, Indians, immigrants, etc., were also excluded) and recognized the temporal limits of its repressive measures. Upon the new foundation (an independent republican nation-state based on private property), political participation to debate and discuss policies was granted. In contrast, contemporary socialist regimes typically operate with elastic boundaries.

Cuba, at least up to 1970, offers a good example. Even after the decisive defeat of internal counterrevolutionary forces and the defeat of the counterrevolutionary returnees at the Bay of Pigs, and even after the guarantee of no further invasions wrenched from U.S. imperialism in resolving the missile crisis, the revolutionary leadership kept Cuba on an emergency footing and maintained a high level of centralized and authoritarian control (Fitzgerald 1985: 112–124). As the 1960s progressed, restrictions were maintained. Channels, such as political and scholarly journals through which socialists could debate issues such as forms of representation, strategies of economic development, market, and plan, were unduly controlled. Politicomilitary defense organizations, such as the Committees for the Defense of the Revolution and the Revolutionary Armed Forces, which were allied to the government and directed from the top, took over increasing responsibility for mobilizing the population and economic resources, while potentially participatory organizations, such as the trade unions, withered away (Bengelsdorf 1985: 164–213; Fuller 1985: 435–438; Pérez-Stable 1985: 149–156). The Party was unified and interlocked with the state. Centrally directed politicomilitary organizations, instead of representative or democratic participatory organizations, inhabited political and economic spheres. The relationship between leaders and followers was defined in authoritarian-mobilizational terms, rather than in terms of democratic debate.

The revolutionary leadership failed to establish temporal boundaries and projected authoritarian practices, initially invoked to establish and secure the foundation of the new society, as the norm rather than the exception. They expanded political boundaries and introduced the politics of amalgamation: dissent and debate were conflated with the (previous) military activities of the (already defeated) counterrevolution. Those who did not agree with how or why they were being mobilized were often treated as enemies whose continued existence justified continued authoritarianism. Ideologically, the revolutionary leadership violated the language of politics and invoked the imagery of permanent war. Further, it legitimated elastic boundaries with reified conceptions of the revolutionary classes and their social interests. Different and competing revolutionary classes, strata, and groups, and their specific immediate interests were obscured by conceptions of *The* Working Class and *The* Peasantry and their Historic Interests. Reified and teleological notions served to justify *monolithism*—the opposite of democratic *pluralism*.

Many have used and abused the term pluralism in discussing the issues of democracy and socialism. Pluralism refers to the existence of a variety of competing interests, ideas, and policies among a variety of political forces seeking to influence decision-making structures. Liberals and conservatives, however, associate pluralism with a specific set of socioeconomic interests in a given social order and with a particular distribution of political power. They define the minimal conditions for "pluralist politics" by the presence of capitalist property-owning groups that defend property interests, profits, and so forth, by private control of the media, and by political structures subject to the influence of unequally distributed economic resources.

Unfortunately, many socialists agree with this view and commit two opposing types of errors. On the one hand, some socialists accept the liberal-conservative conception of political pluralism, and permit property-owning groups and their allies to dominate strategic positions within the economy, state, and society, positions they can exploit to destroy democracy. In both Chile and Jamaica, socialists attempted to elicit the cooperation of private capitalists in their economic development plans. The capitalists responded by massively transferring capital out of the country, running down plant and equipment, and working in tandem with international capital and the U.S. imperial state to destabilize and erode the popular base of the democratic-socialist regime. Subsequent to the downfall of the regime, the liberal and conservative "defenders" of pluralist democracy supported a military dictatorship in Chile and an authoritarian parliamentary regime in Jamaica. On the other hand, some socialists reject the idea of pluralism altogether. By failing to distinguish between the ideologically loaded liberal-conservative conception of pluralism and a notion that recognizes a plurality of interests within a collectivist society, these socialists contribute to the installation of a monolithic political regime.

A more adequate conception of pluralism is evidenced in the efforts of Nicaragua's Sandinistas to fashion a political framework for socialist transition. The Sandinistas have transformed the state apparatus, initiated a dynamic public and cooperative sector, and encouraged the rapid growth of autonomous and semiautonomous mass organizations. They have designed and implemented an electoral system that accommodates a broad range of competing political parties, some to their right and some to their left (Latin American Studies Association, 1985). Moreover, the top Sandinista leadership did not arrogate to itself task of codifying the foundation of the new society in a new constitution. Constituent as well as legislative powers were granted to the National Assembly, where the Sandinista majority debates and negotiates with representatives of all other political parties (Instituto Histórico Centroamericano 1985).

The Sandinistas have defined the political boundaries and have allowed and encouraged wide-ranging democratic participation within these boundaries. They have also clearly delineated and openly stated the temporal boundaries of authoritarian practices. In a characteristic statement about La Prensa, the opposition newspaper that was ultimately shut down, censor Nelba Blandon, for example, has said that "when the danger to Nicaragua from armed attacks by ex-Somoza guardsmen disappears, La Prensa would again be allowed to commit the sin of publishing lies" (Nichols 1985: 193). Depending on how the U.S.-contra war against Nicaragua proceeds, the Sandinistas may have to widen or be able to narrow the range for authoritarian measures. But what was notable (in 1988 was that, even in this period of military defense, democratic civilian organizations were debating issues and programs and were infusing the processes of establishing the foundation of the new society and building participatory institutions with a democratic pluralist ethos.

In the 1960s, this was not done in Cuba. By 1970, however, it became clear to the Cuban leadership that the system had to be reformed, that a conversion to more participatory institutions had to be achieved. This realization was induced by growing popular discontent, which manifested itself in heightened absenteeism and lessened productive effort and by a variety of deepening economic problems (Fitzgerald 1985: 120–124). Yet the direction and extent of change was largely determined by the revolutionary leadership, which had already accommodated itself to centralized practices. The conversion to participatory institutions has been substantial, but it is important to underline the extent to which restrictive practices continue. The conversion to democratic practices remains incomplete.

Perhaps the best example of participatory measures was the structure and functioning of the Organos de Poder Popular (OPP) (Bengelsdorf 1985: 225–327; Fitzgerald 1985: 302–310), which are elected assemblies that have been in existence at the national, provincial, and municipal levels since 1976–1977. The OPP provide the population with a formal structure through which criticism can be voiced and solutions proposed to economic and social problems. This is especially the case at the municipal level, where OPP delegates are responsible for the administration of local social service and economic units. Also at this level, OPP delegates are subject to direct popular nomination, election, and recall, all of which doubtless help to keep them responsive to local popular concerns.

Yet, at the higher levels of the OPP structure, where the responsibilities become greater in importance and scope, the extent of democracy diminishes. The provincial and national OPP assemblies, for example, are elected not directly by the population but by the municipal delegates. Moreover, officially constituted "nominating committees," not the population itself, nominate the candidates for the higher positions. These nominating committees are made up of representatives of state- and Party-allied mass organizations, under the chairpersonship of a representative of the Party. These committees must nominate 25 percent more candidates than the available vacancies, and the municipal delegates may reject the lists of nominees in whole or in part (González Mendoza 1986). Nevertheless, this structure gives the Party a great deal of control over who is elected to higher OPP positions (Fitzgerald 1985: 303–307).

Although Party members do not necessarily predominate at the municipal level, they do at the provincial and especially at the national level. This predominance of Party members at the higher levels of OPP is clearly a major mechanism for Party control of OPP decisions. Party members in OPP positions remain under Party discipline and are duty-bound to attempt to persuade non-Party delegates to follow the Party line. If this does not work, matters are to be taken through the Party structure all the way up to the National Assembly, if necessary, where compliance with the Party line is assured (Castro 1974). Thus the big decisions and the power to control lesser decisions taken at lower levels remain in the hands of the Party, that is, of the top revolutionary leadership.

The conversion to participatory institutions is also inhibited in ways the leadership never intended. Currently, the Cuban politicoadministrative apparatus is occupied by a considerable number of individuals who rose to and were socialized to their positions of responsibility before the authoritarian-mobilization system was reformed. By habit, and for other reasons that we cannot go into here (Fitzgerald, 1985: 354–370, 390–412), such individuals are, according to the former head of the Central Planning Agency, "impregnated with the old centralizing and in many cases bureaucratic habits" (Pérez 1979: 14). Such individuals have difficulty adapting to the participation envisaged by the revolutionary leadership. The conversion to democratic participatory institutions in Cuba is thus inhibited by the authoritarian ethos implanted in the 1960s.

While noting the continuing restrictions that operate in Cuba—a legacy of the real and continuing military threats and actual attacks launched from Washington, D.C.—the important point is the historical direction that the revolution is taking: its movement away from a decision-making system informed by an authoritarian ethos toward structures that have been opened up to truly mass participation. Moreover, the social foundation of the regime has effectively operated to allocate the benefits of economic growth in a very egalitarian fashion (Brundenius 1981: 102–151). The social foundation has democratized the benefits of the revolution. Yet full democratic political participation remains to be realized.

Although, for purposes of analytic clarity, we have distinguished the foundation-establishing and the institution-building phases of the socialist transition, these phases, in fact, interpenetrate one another. If clear political and temporal boundaries are not instituted in the foundation-establishing phase, then authoritarian practices threaten to carry over into the institution-building phase, become identified with the basic notion of socialism, and block the development of a democratic socialist pluralism. On the other hand, if the authoritarian imperative of the foundation-establishing phase is not recognized or acted upon, then the very chance to build democratic participatory institutions upon a socialist foundation will be jeopardized. In this regard, the Nicaraguan practice of combining national defense and pluralism, building participatory institutions, and operating with a realistic understanding of state power, presents a major breakthrough in conceptualizing the transition to socialism.

Conclusions

The basic theoretical error of the Allende and Manley regimes that translated into practical disaster was the idea that "democracy is a good in itself." This rather vacuous phrase translates into the notion that the procedures and institutions of a parliamentary electoral system operate independently of class relations, class conflict, and imperial penetration. By assuming that shared values of political democracy override partisan class interests, these regimes provided space for the right wing to recruit coup-makers within the military, while preventing democratic military forces from acting . . . politically; they negotiated compromises with the bourgeoisie, which utilized concessions to make new demands and transformed tactical negotiations into transitional demands oriented toward a strategic rupture with the existing democratic socialist regime. The right had no illusions about democracy being a "good in itself." It was good insofar as it safeguarded their basic interests, but it was to be discarded or disrupted when it eroded their prerogatives. The tragic mistake of the Manley and Allende regimes, which sought to radically reform society without transforming the state, is being repeated today by a group of democratic theorists who abjure social reform in the name of a "realistic democracy." "Realists," such as O'Donnell (1986) and his coauthors, tacitly recognize the impotence of political regimes constrained by the military and the international bankers, yet loudly proclaim the preeminent "democratic" virtue of these compromised and weakened regimes.

The transition to socialism raises several basic issues concerning the relationship between political power and class relations, more particularly between state, regime, and class conflict. Many contemporary democratic practitioners in Latin America have reverted back to a 1940s political version of democracy, emphasizing legalistic and formalistic criteria rather than examining the historical process and class and institutional relations that constrain the operation of elections, presidents, and parliaments. These democrats operate within the boundaries established by the military, the international banks, and the local bureaucratic and propertied elites, and they formulate policies that "manage" conflicts, social pacts to contain class conflict, and political formulas that subordinate social movements to elite negotiations and bargaining (Petras 1986).

The deep structural affinity between these democratic theorists and practitioners and the Reagan administration is located in their unacknowledged acceptance of bourgeois hegemony as the precondition for contemporary "resurgent democracies." The fundamental absence of any analysis of the class relations that underpin these electoral regimes undermines the theoretical and practical utility of these arid conceptions of democratic transition. In contrast, the Reagan administration understands perfectly well that class and property relations are central in defining its view toward political regimes. Hence the administration is able to support "death-squad democracies" in Guatemala, El Salvador, and Honduras, as well as state terrorist regimes in countries like Chile, and civilian regimes based on the traditional military and international banks in Argentina, Uruguay, and Brazil. By factoring out imperial and class ties, these democrats contribute to the ideological obfuscation engendered by the Reagan administration, which has become quite adept at using formalistic electoral formulas to defend propertied, military, and imperialist interests.

The significant issues are those concerned with the profound connection that exists between class relations and political power, the deep structural linkages that define the scope and depth of political and social transformation (Wood 1986). Regimes that wish to succeed in transforming social relations must transform the state or end up reproducing the existing pattern of social relations. The notion of "state autonomy," which has been extended to include what its proponents call "state-centered" approaches, divorces the state from the matrix of class relations and contributes to "classless" conceptions of politics, as can be seen in the recent work of Laclau and Mouffe (1985). Such theorists fail to recognize that state "autonomy" has not prevented bourgeois class power from destroying "autonomous" states and instituting very nonautonomous bourgeois dictatorships.

The difference between the Cuban and Nicaraguan revolutions and the demise of the Allende and Manley regimes is rooted in the theoretical issue of the relationship between class and state. The Nicaraguans have reorganized the state and created the social and military organization to sustain a pluralist regime. The United States and the local bourgeoisie reject the *state and class basis* upon which the pluralistic party-electoral system functions. They want to have their own army—the contras—and their political organizations in control of the civil bureaucracy in order to create their version of a pluralistic bourgeois democracy. Debates over socialism and democracy in the period of transition have as their primary focus precisely this problem: the necessity to transform the existing state apparatus in order to achieve durable and consequential socioeconomic reforms and to institutionalize a popular democratic political system.

Mass Participation and the Transition to Socialism: A Critique of Petras and Fitzgerald

Keith A. Haynes

The Fitzgerald and Petras essay "Authoritarianism and Democracy in the Transition to Socialism" is a significant contribution to the debate about democracy and its relevance to socialist struggle. The authors raise useful questions and offer perceptive insights. However, I am convinced that their conceptualization of the issue is flawed. The following essay examines these flaws and emphasizes the critical role of mass participation in securing a transition to socialism that respects its democratic traditions.

Briefly, Petras and Fitzgerald argue that (1) democracy is the essence of any "worthy" socialist project and (2) that "authoritarian measures" are nonetheless necessary in order to defend a socialist transition against "local bourgeois and imperial interests or their military and police protectors." Perhaps anticipating their libertarian critics, they quickly caution against sacrificing "the need for democratic practice in the name of security." Socialist transitions, the authors tell us, require a delicate balance of authoritarian and democratic practices. . . .

According to the elite/mass conceptualization of revolutionary societies, elite officeholders monopolize the policy-making process and impose their decisions on an otherwise passive and excluded citizenry. Those who subscribe to this view typically assume that the regime's ideas and actions alone determine how the society will function. Although one of the authors has elsewhere correctly criti-

First published in *Latin American Perspectives* 56, vol. 15 (1), Sage Publications, Inc. Reprinted with permission from the Latin American Perspectives Collective. Selection from 112–113, 115–121.

cized this view in the specific case of Cuba (Fitzgerald 1988), it is clear that successful implementation of their model for a democratic socialist transition depends almost exclusively upon the wisdom, courage, and self-discipline of an enlightened vanguard. Notwithstanding the authors' strategic use of the passive voice to avoid direct allocation of social responsibility for these important decisions, the only reasonable inference is that the regime's leaders must decide the appropriate mix of "democratic and authoritarian measures." It seems to me that the authors' conception of a democratic socialist transition places too great a burden on these leaders to make wise choices; in the vernacular, it puts the fox in charge of the chicken coop. This vision underestimates the critical importance of mass participation in the revolutionary process as perhaps the most effective guarantor of a socialist transition that respects its democratic traditions. . . .

Note the supreme irony here and the essential flaw of the Petras and Fitzgerald analytical framework. In both case studies, the authors criticize as insufficiently authoritarian or excessively democratic those governments that abandoned the popular will in order to appease a numerically small, but politically and economically powerful, minority. Of course, in each instance, the leaders justified their actions by claiming that "the people" were not ready for such "drastic" change. Notwithstanding these justifications, it is nonetheless strange that Petras and Fitzgerald should describe these policies as "democratic"; analysts generally concede that an authoritarian regime is one that monopolizes public policy making, excludes the vast majority of citizens from participation, and makes policies contrary to their expressed interests or desires. This certainly describes the policies of an Anastasio Somoza or a Rafael Trujillo, but, in many respects, it also suits Allende and Manley; their behavior could only be labeled democratic if one adopts Madison's classic bourgeois formulation of a properly constituted republic: political pluralism that still guarantees the right of propertied minorities to rule in open defiance of the will of a propertyless majority. But this implicit embrace of the Madisonian vision (without properly appreciating Madison's analysis) directly contradicts the authors' critique of the socioeconomic limits of bourgeois democracy.

Thus democracy, in the Fitzgerald and Petras model, becomes instantly associated solely with preservation of pluralistic political competition, while authoritarianism is identified with asserting latent and overt authority. The pitfalls of this approach become evident again in the authors' discussion of Nicaragua's embryonic experiment in democratic socialism. Here, they praise the Sandinista leadership because it has "not shied away from authoritarian measures, from censorship to arrest." While this certainly conforms to the authors' appeal for a combination of democratic and authoritarian measures to achieve a socialist transition, it clearly does not take seriously the Sandinistas' own defense of their policies as essentially democratic, since they represent the "logic of the majority." Why? . . .

A more plausible explanation of Fitzgerald and Petras's reluctance to take seriously the Sandinistas' claims of democracy is their implicit assumption that a tutelary vanguard is critical to a successful socialist transition. But the Sandinistas apparently could afford to have believed in democracy as the essence of their transition to socialism precisely because they drew their political strength directly from the popular majority that stands to benefit most from the revolution's programs (Walker 1982; Black 1981; Harris and Vilas 1985; Weber 1981; Ruchwarger 1987). . . .

This dialectical relationship between governmental leadership and mass organizations committed to autonomous participation in public policy formation explains the FSLN's success at establishing "political boundaries" that make possible the "conversion to participatory institutions that are fully democratic." It also explains, at least in part, the difficulties that the Cubans have encountered in their attempt to create a truly democratic socialism. As the product of a "foco" strategy that emphasized the critical role of a tutelary vanguard, the new revolutionary regime was not much inclined toward autonomous mass participation in the process of revolutionary reconstruction. As the authors' case study makes clear, the revolutionary regime in Cuba initially consistently undermined independent "participatory organizations, such as the trade unions." In the case of Nicaragua, the Fitzgerald and Petras notion of political boundaries and conversion, which appears in their formulation to be abstract and dependent upon "wise" leaders, actually flows from the Sandinista understanding of the democratic essence of their movement for socialism (Castaneda 1980). This understanding, in turn, appears to derive from their experiences in the revolution, experiences that convinced them that a conventional tutelary vanguard was unnecessary in Nicaragua; in fact, many quickly discovered that a majority of the Nicaraguan people were far more ready than the FSLN vanguard had previously supposed to oppose the Somoza dictatorship and build an autonomous democratic socialism. . . .

But this connection between popular democratic participation in revolutionary struggle and the establishment of "political boundaries" that constrain and guide revolutionary regimes is common to many revolutions that produce democratic outcomes (Moore 1967). Socialist revolutionaries ignore the lessons of these past experiences only at their peril. In the North American Revolution, for example, popular participation established the "political boundaries" and guided "the process of conversion"—those two stages identified by Fitzgerald and Petras as essential to facilitating the transition to democracy. Despite their horror at widespread confiscation of loyalist properties, revolutionary leaders like John Adams and Gouverneur Morris tolerated these practices because they were the product of mass participation. Similarly, Thomas Jefferson endorsed attacks on loyalists' civil liberties (Levy 1963). The massive participation of "common people," not the revolution's conservative leadership, radicalized the revolutionary movement and ensured its commitment to building democratic institutions (Ferguson 1979: 225–228).

Socialist revolutionaries in the twentieth century have had "difficulty with political boundaries and the process of conversion," largely because they have frequently embraced a sectarian view that the majority of the people were not ready for the transition to socialism; consequently, they, as the revolutionary vanguard, have decided to lead the people along, even against their will. Where the revolution is successful, the inevitable consequence is socialist centralism and elimination or retardation of socialist democracy; more often, however, such sectarian policies have derailed the revolutionary socialist transition, as the authors' case studies of Chile and Jamaica demonstrate.

Essentially, then, my problem with the Fitzgerald and Petras thesis is that it reduces the process of socialist transition to a struggle between authoritarianism and democracy where both appear as instruments for achieving socialism; in their view, a successful transition requires a mix of both instruments and an enlightened vanguard to determine the appropriate proportions. But if, as the authors contend, popular democracy (i.e., rule of the proletarian majority) is the essence of socialism, it can be consolidated and nurtured only if the majority of citizens actively participate in representative institutions that actually make public policy. It does not require authoritarian measures; it merely requires popular power. . . .

But the far more interesting question is this: why do Fitzgerald and Petras place democratic socialists in the equally uncomfortable position of defending the necessity of "authoritarian" measures to protect a socialist transition? This is all the more incomprehensible when we consider that socialists need not inhabit the same box as the Reaganites. That is, democratic socialists can preserve their intellectual honesty, defend majority rule, and promote popular participation in policy making precisely because we are not constrained to defend the property rights of a minority against the social, political, and economic demands of a propertyless majority. Democratic socialists are free to defend the "logic of the majority" as the only way of creating an ethically meaningful democracy. If it is intellectually dishonest for corporate capitalists, their political representatives, and theorists to defend the rhetoric of democracy and the reality of authoritarianism, it is equally dishonest and downright foolhardy for socialists to do the same.

In fact, democratic socialists cannot offer a convincing, spirited, and principled defense of "the democratic commitments and accomplishments of the Sandinistas" or any other democratic socialist revolution if we are bound to the Petras and Fitzgerald thesis that accepts an ahistorical definition of democracy and thus requires support for "authoritarian practices as well." What we must do is shift the terms of the debate to ask the elemental question of what democracy really means; we must, as the authors correctly argue, place democracy in the context of class relations and the struggle for political power.

But this means we cannot embrace, as do Fitzgerald and Petras, the post-Madison liberal view that equates democracy with pluralism. Does democracy mean government of, by, and for the majority of propertyless people with due respect for the civil rights of the propertied minority? Or does it mean government of, by, and for the minority of propertied citizens with due respect for the civil rights of the proletarian majority? If it means the former, then any action undertaken and supported by a popular majority—including a wide range of activities from execution of tyrants to temporary restrictions on the public press—is democratic, even if it may seem unfair or immoral to the propertied minority. Cast in this light, the confiscation of Somocista and contra property, the imposition of universal conscription, and the war-time censorship of *La Prensa* in Nicaragua appear to be democratic, not authoritarian, measures.

I agree with Fitzgerald and Petras that the Reagan administration was intellectually dishonest in defending as democratic those regimes that clearly neither represented nor actively involved the majority of their citizens in policy decision making. But it is a theoretical and tactical error for socialists who correctly criticize the narrowness of this definition to employ it nonetheless in their evaluations of, and prescriptions for, democratic socialist transitions. Perhaps we should criticize the sectarianism of the previous Manley government and the Allende regime, which moved them to surrender their democratic mandates only to embrace positions that were manifestly unpopular with a majority of their constituents, but we should not criticize them for failure to employ authoritarian measures. Likewise, we should not praise the Sandinistas for employing authoritarian practices; we should applaud their commitment to democracy, to upholding the "logic of the majority"even and especially when it collides with the class prerogatives of a numerical minority. Those who need to support authoritarian measures are corporate capitalists and their political representatives. Democratic socialists should rally to the cause of democracy as both the essence of socialism and the most effective means of securing a socialist transition that respects this historical legacy.

Confusion about the Transition to Socialism: A Rejoinder to Haynes

Frank T. Fitzgerald and James F. Petras

Theoretical Problems

In criticizing the way we join together terms such as *democratic* and *authoritarian* to describe the selfsame regime, Haynes chides us for not having fully absorbed the political theory of James Madison. His explicit choice of a bourgeois political thinker, and his implicit choice of the tradition of bourgeois political thought, as the sole standard for the proper use of such terms, however silly, is no accident; he seems totally unaware of any other tradition of political thought with which our usage of such terms may be consistent. Specifically, he appears unaware of the Marxist tradition.

By no means to cite them as authorities for our argument, but simply to illustrate to Haynes that another theoretical tradition exists wherein our use of terms is by no means "strange," as he calls it, let us quote some prominent Marxists. And let Haynes take note that, in each of the following instances, these Marxists are describing aspects of what they consider to be socialist democracy or the historical preconditions for its achievement. First, let us quote Engels (1959: 485) on revolution, Engels who even uses the forbidden term.

> A revolution is certainly the most *authoritarian* thing there is; it is the act whereby one part of the population imposes its will upon the other part . . . [emphasis added].

Second, let us quote Lenin (1975: 39) on proletarian "dictatorship," for in contemporary parlance, this is certainly a term that has a connotative resemblance to "authoritarianism," and that, therefore, Haynes likely finds "strange" when used to describe the requisites of socialist democracy.

> The indispensable characteristic, the necessary condition of [the] dictatorship [of the proletariat] is the *forcible* suppression of the exploiters as a class, and, consequently, the *infringement* of "pure democracy," i.e., of equality and freedom, in regard to that *class*.

Third, on the chance that Haynes judges this last as the distorted ravings of one of the "tutelary vanguardists" he so readily finds on the left, we quote one

First published in *Latin American Perspectives* 56, vol. 15 (1), Sage Publications, Inc. Reprinted with permission from The Latin American Perspectives Collective. Selection from 127–132.

of Lenin's critics and an eloquent defender of socialist democracy, Rosa Luxemburg (in Waters 1970: 394):

> Yes, dictatorship! But this dictatorship consists in the *manner of applying democracy*, not in its *elimination*; in energetic, resolute attacks upon the well-entrenched rights and economic relationships of bourgeois society, without which a socialist transformation cannot be accomplished.

Fourth, Haynes should be aware that the phrase "dictatorship of the proletariat" was spawned by Marx himself, who also launched the tradition of political analysis within which it is hardly "strange" to describe socialist democracy as either authoritarian (in relation to opposition classes) or insufficiently authoritarian (in relation to those same classes). The irony here, of course, is that Haynes believes that underlying any such "strange" conjunction of *terms is* "a very basic *liberal* assumption" (emphasis added).

Haynes's ignorance of the Marxist tradition, unfortunately, has consequences far beyond any terminological issue. He approaches political realities with concepts that have the character of abstract essences that lack a solid class grounding. But this is not just a conceptual problem. It is a profoundly theoretical one. For it prevents him not only from understanding the theoretical propositions we put forward, but from formulating any insightful theory of his own.

Haynes castigates us for putting forth an "elite/mass" theory of socialist transition. He explains that our model, which requires that decisions about the appropriate mix of authoritarian and democratic measures be taken in each phase of the transition, "places too great a burden on . . . leaders to make wise choices." The reason this troubles him, as he tells us "in the vernacular," is that "it puts the fox in charge of the chicken coop."

Haynes consistently associates revolutionary leaders—and us—with the Blanquist notion of an "enlightened" or "tutelary vanguard." So, we must ask: How are leaders like "foxes" (and masses like "chickens")? His implicit but definite answer is that leaders qua leaders, that is, in their abstract essences, are clever and wily creatures who think the masses ("chickens") need tutelage and enlightenment, and who are, thereby, likely to make decisions that run counter to the interests or desires of the masses ("chickens"). If Haynes were simply underlining the need for leaders to be responsive and accountable to their mass supporters, there would be nothing objectionable here. But, through most of his critique, he puts this sort of claptrap forth as serious political analysis of revolutionary leadership.

The easiest way to see that Haynes is dealing in abstract essences is to ask what is missing from his evaluation of revolutionary leaders. The first thing that is missing, of course, is any class analysis. Leaders, revolutionary or otherwise, should be evaluated not on the basis of what an analyst thinks they are in essence but on the basis of how they act toward and respond to various concrete class forces. It is this type of analysis that we presented in our text, where we quickly sketched the relationships between various leaderships and their class environments. We showed, for example, that the Allende and Manley leaderships failed to sufficiently support their mass bases, not because, as Haynes would have it, these leaderships were essentially foxlike "tutelary vanguardists," but because they feared the radicalism of their mass bases. Both leaderships constrained their mass bases out of a desire to play by the parliamentary "rules of the game" and to conciliate upper- and middle-class forces.

The second point that is missing from Haynes's approach is any notion of the positive functions, as opposed to the abstract, foxlike essences, of leaders. For Haynes, leaders cannot be trusted—it is usually as simple as that. But this ignores that leaders can unify or stifle the unification of the often inchoate or contradictory strivings of the masses. They can call forth a mass mandate and then either energetically carry it out or subvert it. They can allocate organizational (or regime) resources in a variety of directions, take initiatives that invigorate mass organization, take initiatives that stifle opponents—and they can do many other things besides. Haynes might study Peter Winn's (1986) book on the Yarur textile workers under the Popular Unity government to understand that Allende was no "tutelary vanguardist" and that his assumption of the presidency was critical for mobilizing the Chilean mass movement. Of course, leaders can perform their functions well or ill. But this, again, has nothing to do with their abstract essence qua leaders. It has to do with their relationships to concrete class forces.

In his discussion of the Sandinista leadership, Haynes does for a moment break out of his mental world of abstract essences. He treats these leaders as relatively concrete entities who, out of real experiences, have gained an appreciation of the need for genuine mass participation. But one caveat: even here, Haynes one-sidedly stresses the way in which the Sandinista leaders have been "guided and limited by, mass participation." He remains mum on the positive functions of the Sandinista leaders. Is he presuming that, with the undoubted popular mandate that they enjoy, the Sandinista leadership checks every decision with the masses or their immediate representatives? If so, and admittedly what he says is too general to know for sure, it would betray an extreme lack of appreciation of the need for leaders to lead on the basis of the mandate given to them, especially in times of heightened class struggle and external aggression but in formal political times as well. Perhaps, despite his words, he does not see the need for a "dialectical relationship" between leaders and their mass base. Perhaps he sees no positive role at all for revolutionary leaders.

Early on in his critique, Haynes points out that, although we argue that decisions must be made about the appropriate mix of authoritarian and democratic measures to be taken in each phase of the transition, we never say specifically when and by whom these decisions should be made. He is right, at least to the extent that we never do say when and by whom at the level of *specificity* he demands. And he does, indeed, get very demanding and very specific: "How does the regime know its hegemony is firmly established?" "Who—that is, what individuals, functional or political interest groups, movements, and/or social classes—are the actors who must stage this drama?" "Who makes these very critical decisions?" But since he fails to comprehend the method, and thereby the limits, of class analysis, he has no way of understanding why we never give specific answers to his specific questions.

It is not, as he supposes, because we are "tutelary vanguardists" who assume that "the regime's leaders must decide." It is because no general theory of class struggle can be formulated to answer these specific questions a priori. The specific answers to these specific questions depend on the peculiarities of each concrete situation. They are questions of political judgment, judgment that should be informed with a concrete analysis of the class conjuncture, but judgment just the same. And when we say judgment, we are not putting the responsibility solely on leaders. In any democratic socialist movement, every participant must be involved as fully as possible in making such judgments. By demanding a *general* theory to answer such *specific* questions for all times and places, Haynes, once again, displays his ignorance of the Marxist theoretical tradition of concrete class analysis.

He thinks that, where we failed to answer such questions, he succeeds. In discussing the Sandinista revolution, he suggests that "mass participation" is the answer to such questions, that the masses in "dialectical relationship" to their leaders should decide when and in what mix authoritarian (which, of course, they are not to be called) and democratic measures should be taken. But is this the type of *general* answer he was demanding that we give to his very *specific* questions? If so, he could have easily found it on and between the lines throughout our text, where we often referred to the need for mass mobilization and organization and for leaders who respond to their supporters. The tragicomedy here is that Haynes, in repeating a generality we have already made, believes he is offering something new and profound, and he thinks that he is specifically answering the specific questions that we, for the above good reason and with full knowledge, addressed in only a general way.

Finally, without showing any awareness of what we consider our text's important distinction between liberal-conservative versus socialist definitions of pluralism, Haynes accuses us of "equat[ing] democracy with pluralism." In attempting to fix up our "flaw," he falls, also unawares, into theoretical confusion. He offers this formal definition of democracy: "government of, by, and for the majority of propertyless people with due respect for the civil rights of the propertied minority." As surprised as he might be, we can accept Haynes's definition as, however, a definition of socialist democracy rather than of democracy per se, at least up to the "with due respect" clause. But, if we take his definition literally and in full, the "with due respect" clause effectively defines out of existence the very possibility of a socialist transition. For, as we argued in our text, the regime that would establish the foundation for socialism must typically take—excuse us, but we must say—authoritarian measures to limit or deny the "civil rights" (for the meaning of which see Walker, 1980: 225), such as the freedoms of speech, press, assembly, and movement, of those opponents who support armed resistance and foreign intervention and who call for amnesty for torturers and mass murderers.

But, in the same paragraph in which he formally defines democracy, Haynes agrees with us that the transition to socialism requires measures to limit or deny the civil (and property) rights of opponents. However, because these measures are supported by the majority, he does not want to call them "authoritarian." Instead, he wants to call them "democratic," although they are excluded by his own formal definition of democracy. We fear that by playing with words rather than engaging in serious analysis and debate, Haynes ultimately lands himself in a muddle.

Part V

Case Studies in Capitalist Development: Impact and Consequences

THE CASE STUDIES FOLLOWING illustrate popular resistance to capitalist development in Latin America. They help to understand the practical, human consequences of capitalist projects, plans, and enterprise. These in turn can be used to evaluate various theoretical approaches to development itself.

These essays illustrate, first, resistance to U.S. colonialism and imperialism as described by Michael González-Cruz and, second, traditional responses, as in the case of struggling workers in urban areas depicted by Ricardo Antunes and Ronaldo Munck and of the mobilization of peasants and the landless in rural areas analyzed by James Petras. New social movements also have mobilized to pressure for local needs and changes.

5.1

Rural Responses to Neoliberal Strategy

James F. Petras

With the rise of neoliberal regimes throughout Latin America, the author examines the popular grassroots responses of peasants, guerrilla movements, and massive mobilization in the countryside, suggesting that traditional forms of resistance are being supplanted by new social movements.

Contrasting Strategies

N EOLIBERAL POLITICAL REGIMES have had a strategic advantage in relation to their adversaries in the popular movements: they have a vision of a coherent, global change involving reorganization of the state, the economy, the class structure, and the values of individuals. They also have an image of "a New Person" and do not focus merely on economic changes to increase profits in the present conjuncture. In sum, they have adopted a world-historical structural approach in the elaboration of their policies.

Their strategy involves taking control of the state and shifting state resources to the local propertied groups and multinational corporations, increasing exports to finance external debt payments, reducing wages to allow for the concentration of capital, and destroying or controlling labor unions and undermining labor legislation to strengthen the power of capitalists in the workplace. Their social

First published in *Latin American Perspectives* 92, vol. 24 (1), Sage Publications, Inc. Reprinted with permission from the Latin American Perspectives Collective. Selection from 85–91.

policy is to increase state expenditures (subsidies, loans, financing, socialization of financial losses) for the wealthy and lower their taxes. Their cultural policy emphasizes individual outlooks over collective ones, private problems over social ones, clientelistic relations over solidarity, and mass spectacles over community-organized cultural events. They seek class cohesion at the top, fragmentation in the middle, atomization at the bottom.

The global strategy of the neoliberals has depended on two types of tactics. The first is to attack workers sector by sector or even industry by industry. Sequential privatization—first the petroleum industry, then communications, transportation, etc.—mobilizes all of the state's power against a single sector isolated from others. Defeating one sector sets the stage (and provides an example) for moving on to other sectors, leading eventually to the privatization of all state enterprises and utilities. The second is to combine repressive and even violent activity against an organized sector of the working class with appeals to the unorganized sectors. For example, the Cardoso government in Brazil attacks the petroleum workers as "privileged" and promises to provide low-cost consumer services and to use the income from privatization to finance social services in other sectors of the workforce. In fact, the attack on one sector of the working class is accompanied by further attacks on others, thus perpetuating and deepening class inequalities as newly privatized enterprises enrich a handful of private monopoly buyers.

Faced with the neoliberal attack, in the recent past most popular movements have engaged in sector-by-sector resistance: prolonged strikes, mobilizations, and confrontations between the affected sector and the neoliberal state. And practically every time the popular movements lose in this uneven struggle.

Accompanying these popular struggles are appeals for solidarity that elicit limited support from militant sectors: one-day stoppages, financial contributions, symbolic declarations. The material bonds that could change the correlation of forces in the struggle are absent. Each working-class sector refuses to risk pay or job loss to generalize the strike. Each sector acts as if the state action were directed only against a single group of workers and enterprises instead of the whole class and economy.

While the neoliberals rely on politicizing the state in every instance—drawing the army, the judiciary, and public administration into the battle to impose the neoliberal agenda—the popular movements look exclusively to "civil society," and the neoliberal regime backed by the state and the ruling class is more than a match for them.

The Neoliberal Policy Cycle and Popular Responses

Neoliberalism, like previous politico-economic regimes, is a historical phenomenon that contains contradictions. It has various phases: beginning, consolidation, and decline. Obviously, "free-market" capitalism is not the culmination of history as some of its more enthusiastic apologists are prone to argue. At each stage, neoliberal policies have met popular resistance, although the highest levels of opposition tend to occur at the beginning, when the initial policies are imposed, and at the end, when the deep structural contradictions manifest themselves.

The origins of free-market capitalism lie in the blood and gore of the military dictatorships of the 1970s. It was only after a massive attack on the working-class trade unions, urban civic associations, and peasant organizations that the neoliberal policies could be implemented. Popular resistance was aimed not only at the dictatorships but at the socioeconomic policies that they pursued: in Uruguay a prolonged general strike in the early 1970s, in Chile resistance in the factories and shantytowns, in Argentina the illegal strikes in factories and transport sectors, and in Bolivia the miners' general strikes were defeated by force and violence. Neoliberalism did not establish its ascendancy because of the "failure" of the left or because of the economic superiority of the market but because of the effectiveness of military force.

In the subsequent period of implementation of the neoliberal agenda there were strikes in practically every sector affected by neoliberal policies; privatization of ports, telephones, airlines, mines, and factories frequently confronted strikes or popular resistance. As I have said, these sectoral actions were defeated by the neoliberal regimes because of their political and social isolation.

In the more recent period a new and more powerful wave of opposition has arisen in the context of the decline of neoliberalism. This opposition has taken various forms, from electoral campaigns to guerrilla warfare, but what distinguishes it is that it is taking place when neoliberalism no longer has the economic resources, political reserves, or social support of the earlier periods. In the first instance, the prolonged process of privatization has deprived the neoliberal regimes of a potential source of income, valuable assets to attract overseas loans. Secondly, the open economy has undermined the productive forces of the country, increased trade imbalances, and caused the regime to pursue speculative investments to balance external accounts.

In the social sphere, the unending series of "adjustments," each implemented with the promise that it was the "final one" before takeoff into First World prosperity, has eroded the credibility of the neoliberal regimes among the popular and middle classes. It is clear that the adjustments simply provide short-term resources while depressing markets and weakening the capacity to produce, thus creating a new cycle of debt, balance-of-payments crises, and capital flight. The erosion of confidence in the middle and working class is accompanied by downward social mobility for key supporters of the neoliberal model—not only the poor and public employees but sectors of the professional and business class who are badly hit by dollar-indexed debts and devalued earning. In its declining phase, pivotal sectors of the middle class, the trade union bureaucracy, and even sectors of the military and the church hierarchy part company with the neoliberal regime. In the political sphere, the neoliberal regimes increasingly rely on military force to impose their policies or retain power, thus calling their legitimacy into question.

Recent political history illustrates the increasingly heterogeneous opposition to neoliberalism in decline: the prolonged general strike of the workers and peasants in Bolivia, the guerrilla movements in Chiapas, the massive mobilization of 400,000 workers and middle-class in Mexico City, the urban popular and military uprising in Caracas, Venezuela, the industrial and public employee revolts in provinces of Argentina, the growing peasant movements and the general strike in Paraguay, and the continued land occupations and strikes in the major cities in Brazil.

Since the defeat of the center-left electoral coalitions, popular opposition has increasingly assumed extraparliamentary forms of struggle; the limits of electoral policies in an authoritarian setting have become clear. Mass movements outside of the control of the pragmatic left have assumed increasing importance, in the first instance as a defensive strategy against the deepening of the privatization strategy but in a deeper sense linked to new forms of production; the land occupations and peasant co-ops of Brazil and Paraguay and the coca farmers in Bolivia are linked to cooperative forms of production and allied with urban working-class organizations. The electoral losses of the center-left do not result in demobilization because the social movements are not disciplined or controlled by the pragmatic politicians. As evidenced in the recent strikes in Bolivia and elsewhere, there is a tendency to extend solidarity beyond particular sectors affected by neoliberal policies: to extend the resistance beyond sectoral protests into a "general struggle." The movement toward the occupation of "state property" and the creation of dual power evidenced in Chiapas and other regions in Mexico offers a glimpse into revolutionary processes that seek to accumulate forces and political spaces for sustained struggle. The efforts in Brazil by the Landless Workers' Movement to unify diverse rural segments and concentrate on large-scale land occupation near urban centers are part of a new strategy to consolidate a multiclass popular alliance capable of opening divisions in civil society and the state.

As the neoliberals increasingly politicize the state, a similar process is likely to occur on the left, causing fissures in the state apparatus. Venezuela's nationalist-military revolt is one indication. The resort to military violence—as in the case of Cardoso's use of the military to break the petroleum workers' strike—is an indication of the regimes' weakness in civil society—their inability to mediate social forces. More important, the illusion of a peaceful transition to neoliberalism in Brazil is now open to question. The strategy of the left must be to pose the question of a socialist alternative to neoliberalism as the only "global alternative" available. The basic issue is how to move from massive, militant defensive struggles within capitalism to a transformation of the entire system. The answer is in large part to be found in the *subjectivity* of the popular classes.

Subjectivity and Liberation

For too long the left has defined revolution in economic terms: economic crises, poverty, exploitation. The problem is that these economic conditions have been abundantly present in the 1980s and 1990s and there has been no revolutionary upsurge. At the same time the neoliberal right has devoted extensive attention to capturing the minds of the people adversely affected by its policies. In developing an alternative approach it is useful to examine the basic neoliberal arguments as a point of departure. Essentially the defense of neoliberalism revolves around four strategies: (1) globalism (the idea that "global imperatives" require neoliberal policies if the country is to compete, secure loans and investments, etc.), (2) the absence of alternatives, (3) local projects, and (4) poverty pockets. The neoliberals argue that the only alternative (communism) has collapsed and therefore neoliberalism is the only realistic approach in a global marketplace. As part of their strategy for dismantling the welfare state and public enterprises, they advocate private local "self-help" projects that allow them to channel state resources from social expenditures to the private oligopolies. Given the highly visible increase in mass poverty, neoliberals disconnect the social problem from its systemic roots and attempt to identify poverty with individual ethics—"work" or "entrepreneurial spirit."

Each of these arguments is deeply flawed. The focus on global imperatives overlooks the crucial fact that it was national class interests and state policies linked to multinational banks and corporations that reoriented the economy toward neoliberal policies. Participation in the world market need not be associated with the class/state configurations associated with neoliberalism. For example, even within the framework of capitalism, the Asian and Scandinavian versions of "protected" and "social-welfare" capitalism are based on export-oriented development. Their global integration was determined by the internal correlation of social forces rather than by external market imperatives.

The argument that there are no alternatives to neoliberalism is false. Both the national-statist capitalism of Asia and the welfare capitalism of Scandinavia are alternatives. Moreover, and more significant, the growing socialization of production on a world scale (the global social division of labor) and the increasing degree of central planning by the global multinationals makes the objective basis for social ownership and planning a more reasonable and feasible "next step." The increasing dependence of capital on state intervention, subsidies, and expenditures to promote capitalist growth is the basic argument against local projects by nongovernmental organizations (NGOs). The problems of the working class—education, employment, health—are not being dealt with by local NGO charity programs. The problems are political and require struggle to change the *nature* of the neoliberals' state intervention. The "statism" of neoliberalism needs to be reversed. Finally, the social problems of poverty and underemployment are long-term and large-scale and affect a broad array of social forces. Given their social nature, they require social rather than psycho-personal explanations.

The question of changing the subjective responses of the exploited majorities revolves around four foci of struggle: ideological, cultural, consciousness, and ethics. The ideological level requires a clear definition of the social character of work and unemployment and their contradictory relationship to private ownership. Socialism or social ownership (in its self-managed form) is necessary to bring social needs into congruence with social production and distribution.

At the cultural level, we must revive the critical view of contemporary conditions, exposing the link between private discontent and social power and the infringement of the macroeconomic world on personal intimacy, comparing the music of the street with spectacles performed by touring millionaires at the price of a Third World worker's weekly/monthly salary, and encouraging the production of theater/films that confront the contradictions of individualism and cultural imperialism, consumerism, and poverty. Cultural struggle must start on the personal, everyday level of universal themes of love, death, and personal desires and move to the socially specific world in which we live.

Consciousness can be learned from experience, reading, and winning. It can be transformed only in the context of sustained everyday solidarity. Consciousness must be transformed about the individual in community, class, family, and friendships and how these social mediations define the conditions and ethics of everyday existence. Consciousness is about choices: to move up with the bosses or to link up with the workers. It is both "voluntary" and determined. It can never be imposed or forced. It is, in the final analysis, the product of "self-understanding" and the realization that becoming class-conscious is a better way of living with oneself and with friends, lovers, family, and neighbors.

Socialism is not the "unfolding of history." There are too many choices to make at every turn. These choices are based on material interests, but these material interests involve not only commodities but personal and social relations. How one pursues material or class interests—whether through political corruption or through social solidarity—is an ethical question.

The collective decisions of workers in Tierra del Fuego and Oruro, the decisions of landless rural workers in Brazil and Paraguay to occupy a factory, a municipal building, or a piece of land are not only about material necessities but also an affirmation of their self-worth, dignity, and capacity to govern themselves, to become full human beings and share friendship and intimate relationships without the constant threat of abuse, hunger, and fear. The subjective factor today is the great terrain of struggle: the economic and social conditions for the overthrow of neoliberalism are being created every day in every country, workplace, and neighborhood. What is necessary is the steady creation of a new social consciousness, culture, and ethics to convert those conditions into the basis for a social transformation.

5.2

Workers' Resistance to Structural Adjustment and the Social Pact in Latin America

Ronaldo Munck

The author briefly reviews the impact of structural adjustment on workers, discusses the implications of the social pact, and looks for a way out of their crisis.

WORKERS IN LATIN AMERICA are today confronted by a process of structural adjustment that goes beyond the economic arena to affect the very fabric of social relations. In the "democratic decade" that began with the elections of 1982 in Argentina, there have been various attempts to develop a social pact *(concertación social)* in the region. In this article I seek to clarify the complex interplay between workers, structural adjustment, and the prospects for a social pact. Whereas each of these aspects is usually dealt with separately (workers as passive victims of structural adjustment and workers as possible protagonists of a social pact) I propose to discuss both together within the broader context of the transition to democracy in the region. After examining the objective constraints of structural adjustment and the ambiguity of the social pact, I will explore the possibility of alternative scenarios. In particular, the so-called new social movements are often seen as providing alternative strategies to the traditional corporatist orientations of labor organizations. To anticipate my conclu-

First published in *Latin American Perspectives* 82, vol. 21 (3), Sage Publications, Inc. Reprinted with permission from the Latin American Perspectives Collective. Selection from 90–96.

sions, I do not believe in a simple "social movement unionism" alternative if it fails to confront the reality of structural adjustment and the objective need for the type of democratic compromise implicit in the incipient movement in some countries toward *concertación social.* Practical examples are drawn from the Southern Cone, but the implications of this analysis are, I believe, of broader relevance.

Labor and the Crisis

A new "Washington consensus" now dominates Latin American economic policies. The watchwords are privatization and deregulation; the main targets are protectionism, restrictions on foreign investment, and the state sector. As John Williamson sums it up, "Structural adjustment, then, aims at the replacement of a traditional statist system by a market system" (1990: 402). This entails opening up the Latin American economies to the world market, ensuring "fiscal discipline," greater respect for "property rights," and supply-side measures that create the right conditions for "entrepreneurship" rather than speculation to flourish. There is, in brief, a wholesale redefinition of the appropriate development model for Latin America or, in other words, of the prevailing regime of accumulation. There is considerable evidence that this process of structural adjustment, in its external and internal aspects, has proceeded beyond the point of no return. Even among its supporters, however, there is a recognition that the stages of this adjustment have not flowed smoothly. Thus, Rüdiger Dornbusch makes the damning admission that "Washington has failed to recognize that stabilization and supply-side economics are not enough. Even today the IMF [International Monetary Fund] has no research available on how to proceed from stabilization to growth" (1990: 324). In spite of the growing consensus on the nature of the problems, the much-promised return to prosperity after the "lost decade" of the 1980s seems as far away as ever.

Workers have generally been the main bearers of the social debt of structural adjustment. A restructured labor market and the deregulation of labor relations established the context for this process. In the course of the 1980s, the minimum wage in Latin America declined by a quarter, and average earnings in the informal sector fell by 42 percent (PREALC, 1991: 35). The participation of labor incomes in the region's gross domestic product declined from 44 percent to 38 percent. Structural adjustment has led, furthermore, to increasing heterogeneity in terms of opportunities and income and the implementation of "flexibility" policies to increase labor productivity. This has led to decreased stability of employment, replacement of full-time by temporary employment, and an increase in subcontracting. "The region faces the decade of the 1990s in conditions of marked inequity and social differentiation" (PREALC, 1991: 39). The prospects are for continued expansion of the informal sector, which will probably not be matched by an increase in wages in the so-called modern sector consequent on capitalist restructuring and a projected increase in productivity. This scenario calls objectively, I would argue, for a minimal degree of social negotiation and compromise to alleviate its effects. As Ian Roxborough puts it, "Class compromise is inevitable; the point is to make sure that the terms of the compromise are as favourable to the working class as possible" (1992: 37).

The response by workers' collective organizations, primarily the trade unions, to the process of structural adjustment has been, perhaps inevitably, defensive and reactive. Faced with uncertainty we all tend to fall back on received wisdom and react by trying to protect what we have. The trade unions feel "cornered" (*arrinconamiento* is a term much used by labor leaders) by the crisis and argue that today their maximum aspiration is simply to maintain minimal rights and conditions. They feel, on the whole, that faced with the failure of the old model they have no option but to go along with change. An Argentine trade union leader thus complains of how "trade unionism is pressured from all sides, overcome and surpassed, things pass over us" (Quijano, 1991: 30). That this is not an isolated expression of despondency should be clear from the sorry fate of the once proud Bolivian mineworkers' union, bastion of a classical confrontationist trade unionism in Latin America. Already battered by the military regimes, the trade unions now face an even more threatening economic transformation and exclusionary order. Having lost much of their socioeconomic weight, they can now choose either to support or to oppose governments, but they do not seem able to offer (credible) alternatives. In the face of structural adjustment, individual trade unions fall back on defensive struggles in pursuit of the sectoral interests of their members. Outside the ranks of organized workers, in the so-called informal sector the crisis is even more profound. The possibility of the trade unions' broadening their appeal to include the wider aspirations of the working population has not as yet materialized, with the partial exception of the Workers' party in Brazil.

The stages of structural adjustment are, theoretically, (1) a halt to inflation, (2) state reform and deregulation, and (3) increased investment leading to sustained economic growth. As I have noted above, this third stage has largely failed to materialize. There has been some success in terms of stabilization, and the state sector no longer holds the dominant position it had achieved in the postwar economic model. Deregulation and privatization have robbed the state of the central role it held in the previous model but left it incapable of articulating a replacement. This has led Adolfo Canitrot to call for "a reconstitution for the capitalist bourgeoisie of the mechanisms of accumulation" (Canitrot, 1988: 18, my translation). The alternative for Latin America (and Argentina in particular), according to this argument, is stagnation and decline. Because of the previous model of accumulation, labor had developed the social weight and system of alliances to block transformation at least in part (cf. Waisman, 1987). Canitrot is thus implicitly calling for labor to lift its veto, encourage state reform, and help create stable conditions for an outward-oriented accumulation model. Labor cannot realistically be accused of the type of short-term speculative attitude characteristic of Argentina's capitalists, but the proposition is a valid one. We can certainly agree that labor cannot benefit in the long term from a rearguard action against a now superseded model of capitalist accumulation centered around the state sector and oriented toward a protected internal market.

It would be wrong to view structural adjustment as an economic policy alone. In fact it signals a significant capitalist restructuring with profound ramifications throughout the society. There is an absence of a clear-cut hegemonic capitalist sector as competition intensifies. Social structures are more heterogeneous than ever as the destabilizing effects of adjustment make themselves felt. Social and political identities are labile, and the "representation" of social interests suffers a practical as well as a theoretical challenge. These effects of structural adjustment will continue until a new, more stable system of accumulation and mode of regulation are generated. In the meantime, as Eugenio Tironi and Ricardo Lagos note, the various social actors (including workers) "can hardly be expected to rearticulate themselves within a context of economic crisis, reorganization of the systems of production and regulation, and institutional and political change" (1991: 44). Old strategies, alliances, and aspirations seem to evaporate as social classes and factions within them jockey for position while the old socioeconomic edifices crumble. It is, indeed, one of those situations that Gramsci referred to in which the old has died but the new has not yet been born. In the political arena this leaves the new democratic regimes in the awkward, perhaps impossible position of having to reconcile the socioeconomic transformations of structural adjustment with the reconstruction of democratic institutions and processes.

Labor and the Social Pact

One of the main features of the "new democracies" in Latin America has been the rhetoric if not the reality of the social pact. Edgardo Boeninger, the organizer of a 1984 conference in Chile on the issue (and now a key actor in the post-Pinochet period), writes of how "democracy cannot be consolidated and will find it difficult to survive in Chile if confrontation prevails over *concertación*" (Boeninger, 1985: 5, my translation). This process has taken the form of explicit political pacts during the transition to democracy and a reprise of the social democratic type of social pact afterwards. Against the previous zero-sum conception of politics, the proponents of the social pact envisage a situation in which all can benefit or at least all may suffer equally. Mario dos Santos writes that "*concertación* implies somehow making different interests compatible, but perhaps much more important is the intersubjective dimension of collective creation and legitimacy created by this process" (dos Santos, 1985: 13, my translation). This pact entails recognition of the socioeconomic reality that establishes its context while seeking, to varying degrees, its progressive reform. Its significance will depend on the conjuncture in which it is introduced and the relationship of social forces that prevails. Thus a social pact may indeed lead to a degree of change within a stable framework or, alternatively, become a displaced discourse of domination in which the rhetoric of conciliation and compromise simply masks the desire of one party to make another (usually the workers) accept the status quo ante.

In practice, the balance sheet of this process has been mixed (see CLACSO, 1986). In Brazil the Central Unica dos Trabalhadores (Workers' Central—CUT) agreed in 1990 to participate in the Forum Nacional de Negociação alongside employer and government representatives. According to one sympathetic commentator, the internal union debates on this process "demonstrated a very high degree of depoliticization and confusion" (Central Unica dos Trabalhadores, 1991: 3). Whatever the union weaknesses, the government seemed more intent on creating "national understanding" and a consensus agenda than genuinely dealing with workers' grievances. Throughout the democratization process and the successive calls for a social pact to deal with the economic crisis, it was workers' struggles for a living wage that were portrayed as threats to democracy and trade unions that were being asked to do most of the compromising. In Argentina, given the severity of the military era and its precipitate fall, one could have expected a social pact to have a chance. However, the various parties concerned had different conceptions of what it would entail (see Ducatenzeiler, 1992). For the government it was a way of compensating for the weakness of its social base. For employers it was a way of subordinating the unions to a rationalization project and of influencing the government. Most trade unionists came to oppose it for its failure to prevent factory closures and wage reductions as the economic crisis deepened. At best, a limited nonaggression pact was achieved between the various social and political actors that allowed for a level of dialogue even if a mythical social consensus was never really feasible. When the new democracies of Argentina and Brazil came to apply their heterodox stabilization projects (the Austral and Cruzado plans) the time for a social pact had clearly passed. The language of economic warfare accorded ill with the democratic discourse of citizenship and coexistence.

In Uruguay and in particular in Chile, the experience has been considerably more positive. In both countries there were explicit political pacts preceding democratization, making a social contract a logical follow-up. In Uruguay, the Concertación Nacional Programática of 1984 brought together representatives not only of trade unions, empoyers, and the government but also of various sectors of civil society. The ensuing accord in industrial relations did not preclude conflict but did ensure an unprecedented era of trade union freedoms. Oscar Groba of the Plenario Intersindical de Trabajadores-Convención Nacional de Trabajadores concluded that "this experience showed that participating in the dialogue while maintaining independence and defending our own project was

better than isolated resistance. . . . At no point did negotiation mean the demobilization of the union movement in regard to other questions" (Central Unica dos
Trabalhadores, 1991: 15, my translation). In Chile the trade unions are currently
seeking to redefine their strategic role in society after the difficult Pinochet years.
At present there is a tension (even division) between those advocating decisive
intervention in the political arena through the mechanisms of *concertación* and
those who seek to address the postponed demands of workers through social
mobilization. Thus Manuel Giménez of the CUT leadership argues that the
accord was useful "in establishing the terms of reference for what we might discuss with employers and the government while maintaining our autonomy"
(Central Unica dos Trabalhadores, 1991: 5, my translation). Specific examples
would be the reform of Pinochet's labor laws, the reestablishment of trade union
freedoms, and the increase in employment stability. Trade union membership in
Chile increased by 38 percent between 1989 and 1991, and less than 10 percent
of collective bargaining resulted in strike action. This would seem to indicate
some success for the accord, but other CUT leaders, such as Cerro Aguirre, still
maintain that trade union restraint is due to political manipulation, that the
socialist ideal still lives, and that trade unions should "maintain the class alternative of ending the exploitation of man by man" (Central Unica dos Trabalhadores, 1991: 8).

A provisional conclusion would be that *concertación* does at least allow for the
possibility that trade union struggles can become less dependent than in the past
on the vagaries of economic cycles. Furthermore, even the weaker experiences of
concertación seem to develop a framework in which social demands during a
period of economic crisis do not inevitably lead to a crisis for democracy, and
avoiding a crisis of governability may be of benefit to more than just the dominant classes. In this regard, Argentina presents both negative and positive lessons;
we should recall the negative role of the trade unions in creating the conditions
for the military coup against the democratic Illía government in 1966 (see
Munck, Falcón, and Galitelli, 1987).

It would be wrong to attempt a simplistic balance sheet of *concertación* as
either good or bad for labor. Debate on this issue can very easily become polarized between those who view *concertación* as a democratic panacea for labor and
those who see it simply as a way of containing and demobilizing the labor movement. Labor movements with an all-or-nothing attitude toward negotiation are
likely to lose heavily. Bolivia might stand as a warning here. Yet we cannot ignore
the historical gains that have been made through confrontation and (dare one
say it?) class struggle. *Concertación* often seems to be opposed to confrontation
in a simplistic either/or model that has the weaknesses of all such binary opposi-
tions. In fact we can recall a strategy of trade unions in Argentina since the 1960s
that consisted of simultaneous confrontation and negotiation (or, more pithily,
golpear y negociar). Eraldo Crea has also argued persuasively in relation to Chile
that "social struggles and *concertación* are not mutually exclusive alternatives but

must be integrated in a unified strategy" (Central Unica dos Trabalhadores, 1991: 27 my translation). A realistic appraisal of the need for class compromise certainly does not preclude a social mobilization that can strengthen labor's position in and extend the limits of the present institution of *concertación*.

In a broad overview of labor in the "post-Fordist" era, John Mathews has recently argued that "the role of social contracts, indeed the necessity for them in providing a framework for a process of transformation, is now firmly on the labour movement's agenda" (1989: 37). A first reaction would be to question the relevance of Swedish tripartite industrial relations to Bolivia. Nor can we expect a sudden outbreak of consensus politics in Argentina. Yet the attractions of what Streeck and Schmitter (1985) have called the "associative model of a social order" for Latin America seem obvious. In Argentina, trade unions are widely viewed by social and political scientists as "corporations" on a par with the armed forces. Unions are seen, quite simply, as antithetical to the consolidation of parliamentary democracy and a threat to its legitimacy. Yet, in a model of associative democracy with trade unions as participants in tripartite structures (with the state and employers' associations as the other "social partners"), stable poitical arrangements and a degree of social equity can, theoretically, be achieved. The project of *concertación* is, of course, ambiguous and inevitably contains a dynamic of co-optation, but it also presents at least the possibility of overcoming sectionalism, corporatism, and the inevitable political impotence that flows from them. At present it appears that *concertación* is a better bet (if available) than a retreat into sectionalism or, indeed, Roxborough's somewhat grim scenario of wholesale retreat.

5.3

Trade Unionism and Struggles

Ricardo Antunes

Translated by Laurence Hallewell

*This chapter looks at the impact of capitalist technology on labor and its organiza-
tion and demonstrates that the transformation of labor everywhere has negatively
affected the worker. Especially affected has been the new unionism during the 1990s
as government applied neoliberal policies of deregulation and privatization. In place
of the traditional unions, new grassroots movements of resistance have appeared.*

I T WAS APPARENT BY THE END of the 1970s, in the countries where capitalism
was most advanced, that it was undergoing a structural crisis, one entailing
profound changes in the world of work, how it fitted into the structure of production, and how it was represented on the trade-union level and politically. To
try to overcome its crisis, capital looked for new responses. So profound were
the consequent changes in capitalist labor and production processes that one
could fairly say that the working class was experiencing its most acute crisis of
this century, one that did not merely concern its material conditions but had
implications for its fundamental character.

The period has been one of great technological leaps forward. Automation and
robotics have invaded the universe of manufacturing to become a factor of growing importance in capitalist work relations and production. We are undergoing,
in the area of production, a range of experiences of varying degrees of severity
and potential for development. Fordism-Taylorism is no longer the only system

First published in *Latin American Perspectives* 115, vol. 27 (6), Sage Publications, Inc.
Reprinted with permission from the Latin American Perspectives Collective. Selection
from 9–21.

of production. Other methods are now being added or have even sometimes replaced it, as the Japanese experience illustrates. New work patterns have emerged in which the stopwatch and the assembly line have been replaced by flexible production, new ways of furthering productivity, and new ways of adapting production to the logic of the market. Attempts are being made to break down the manufacturing process. New patterns of managing the workforce are being introduced, of which quality control circles are the visible expression not only in the Japanese situation but also in several other countries of advanced capitalism and of the industrialized Third World. In a number of regions, Toyotaism has filtered into the Taylor-Ford model or even replaced it (Amin, 1966; Harvey, 1992; Gounet, 1991; Clarke, 1991; Coriat, 1992a; 1992b; Murray, 1983).

The transformation of production is having an acute impact on workers' rights. Instead of being regulated, such rights are being made flexible in order to give capital the means to adapt to this new phase. Historic rights and victories won by labor are being replaced and eliminated from the world of production. Taylor-type despotism is being replaced by (or mixed with, according to the intensity of the change) the manipulation of labor through the appropriation by capital of the worker's knowledge and know-how. This is manipulation of the factory taken to the extreme, and it brings with it advanced forms of alienation of labor.

These transformations (achieved or being introduced, to a greater or lesser extent, depending on the differing economic, social, political, cultural, and so on, conditions in the various countries affected) penetrate deep into the traditional manufacturing workforce, bringing with them fundamental changes in the very nature of work. It is plain that the crisis also intensely affects the universe of consciousness—the very nature of labor and its forms of representation. The trade unions are confused and are playing an increasingly defensive game. They are giving up the class-based unionism of the 1960s and 1970s for an acceptance of the nonconfrontational trade unionism of participation negotiation, and partnership that in general acquiesces in the rules of capital, questioning only specific aspects of the resulting situation. They are abandoning their search for emancipation, the struggle for socialism, and the liberation of the human race, adopting an equally uncritical acceptance of "social democracy" or, what is even more perverse, shaping its policies in terms of the agenda and ideology of neoliberalism. The completely defensive posture of the unions in the face of the wave of privatization is an example of what I am talking about. The defeat of Eastern Europe and the overthrow of Stalinism—what the media have dubbed "the end of socialism"—have increased this defensive attitude of the unions linked to the traditional left, unable to see that the end of Eastern Europe is not the end of socialism but just the end of an attempt to build a society that did not manage to go beyond capital (to use the expression of István Mészáros [1995]). The unions—and the political parties too—are steadfastly going about institution building and getting farther and farther away from independent class-based movements. They are distancing themselves from the struggle for the social control of production and submitting to participation in the existing order. They operate according to values determined by the social behavior of the market and of capital. The world of work does not find—as a dominant principle—in its organs of union and political representation any inclination to struggle against capitalism. The various forms of independent class resistance are impeded by the absence of unions with any desire to go beyond capitalism.

This situation, whose more acute problems I only sketch here, has critical repercussions on the world of work. What will be the more obvious consequences of these changes? Is the working class disappearing, as many people are suggesting? The answer is more complex, and in this article I seek only to indicate some tendencies that are present in today's world of work: (1) decrease in the "stable," manual, industrial workforce typical of the Taylor-Ford model and the phase of the vertical integration of industrial production; (2) a sharp increase in the new proletariat—in the innumerable forms of underproletariatization or insecure employment that result from the worldwide growth of part-time, temporary, subcontracted, and outsourced employment; (3) a significant increase in female employment within the working class on a global scale, due principally to the growth in temporary, subcontracted, outsourced, and part-time work; (4) an enormous growth in low-paid work, especially in the "service sector," which, after having grown on a large scale, is now also experiencing levels of technological unemployment; (5) the exclusion of young workers and of "older" workers as defined by capital (i.e., those over 40) from the labor market of the developed countries; (6) greater exploitation and overexploitation of labor, with brutalizing use of immigrant labor, and an increase in the levels of child labor under criminally inhuman conditions in many parts of Asia, Latin America, and elsewhere; (7) an explosive development of structural unemployment, which, together with insecure employment, affects about 1 billion workers, about one-third of the world's workforce; and (8) an expansion of what Marx (1994) called combined social work, in which workers from different parts of the world participate in production and services. This, obviously, tends not to eliminate the working class but instead to make it more complex, enlarge it, and use it in an increasingly diversified and precarious way. In this way, the working class is becoming ever more fragmented, more heterogeneous, and more complex.

In other words, as various countries of advanced Western capitalism have been reducing the number of full-time jobs, they have been simultaneously increasing the number of forms of subprotelarianization by expanding the ranks of part-time, insecure, and temporary workers. According to Helena Hirata, 20 percent of the women in Japan in 1980 worked part-time without any security of employment. "Whereas the official statistics counted 2,560,000 women working part-time in 1980, three years later the Tokyo journal *Economisto* estimated the total of part-time women workers at 5 million" (Hirata, 1986). A significant part of the increase in the subproletarianized workforce is female. Of the part-time jobs created in France between 1982 and 1988, more than 80 percent were filled by women (Bihr, 1991: 89). Female labor has greatly increased in the most diverse countries and makes up approximately 40 percent of the total world workforce.

A significant proportion of the working class in countries of Western Europe such as France, England, and Germany is now out of work or dependent on temporary or part-time work, an indication of the great changes that have been taking place in the advanced capitalist countries. This proportion has reached almost 50 percent of the total workforce. At the same time there has been an intense increase in employment in the service sector. The United Kingdom, the United States, and other countries have seen their service sectors grow enormously to a point where they are absorbing about 70 percent of the workforce, counterbalancing the retraction experienced in their manufacturing sectors (Beynon, 1995; Wood, 1997). These data show, on one hand, a sharp reduction of the "stable" industrial proletariat in the countries of advanced capitalism, whether as a result of the general recession or as a result of automation, robotics, and the many types of flexibilization. On the other hand, there is also a clear expansion of a new proletariat in both manufacturing and services, one that is more intensely exploited and deprived of any job security.

Besides the other changes in the production and labor process, the introduction of automation and robotics has other important consequences. Parallel to the quantitative reduction in the traditional workforce there is a qualitative change in the nature of the work itself. Reducing the variable dimension of capital as a result of the growth of its constant dimension—in other words, replacing live work with dead work—tends to make it possible to convert the worker into a supervisor and regulator of the production process, in accordance with Marx's formulation in the *Grundrisse*. However, Marx himself pointed out that this could not be fully effective under capitalism, simply because, in the logic of a society producing consumer goods, capital can diminish live work but never eliminate it (Marx, 1974). Thus, under capitalism, even under the impact of technology one cannot expect the end of labor as a measure of value. We can expect instead a qualitative change, caused, on one hand, by an increase in the amount of more skilled labor, of multifunctional work, and of work with information technology and, on the other hand, by an intensification of the forms of exploitation of labor in the new proletariat and in the manufacturing and service industry subproletariat not only in dependent countries but in the very heart of the system.

A steadily increasing capacity for what Marx called combined social work becomes the real agent of the whole work process, which makes it totally irrelevant whether this or that worker's function is closer to or farther from direct manual work (Marx, 1994: 443–44).

At the same time, trends in the world of work vary from field to field and from sector to sector, quite apart from differences between regions or countries. There has been a loss of demand for skilled labor in some fields, a reduction in the skills required in others (such as mining or the automotive industry), and a need for new skills, such as the coordinating jobs in the operating cabins of blast furnaces and those for the repair and maintenance of highly automated installations in the automobile industry (Lojkine, 1990; 1995).

It is apparent that to argue that work or the working class will disappear under the existing mode of capitalist production is to make an enormous mistake, because two-thirds of the workforce live in the Third World, where the tendencies we have been talking about have their own particular rhythm. It is a profound mistake to restrict one's analysis to Germany or France and make generalizations based on those countries about the end of work or the working class without taking into account what is going on in countries like India, China, Brazil, Mexico, South Korea, and Russia. It is worth adding that the thesis of the end of the working class, even when limited to the developed world, is without any basis in either analysis or empiricism.

The automated Japanese factory Fujitsu Fanuc illustrates what is happening in a country that has been on the cutting edge of the technological process in recent decades. There more than 400 robots manufacture other robots, 24 hours a day, while the 400 or so workers work a normal day. With traditional methods, about 4,000 workers would be needed for the same output. About 8 robots break down in an average month, and the workers' task consists, basically, in taking precautions to avoid such breakdowns and repairing the robots that are affected. The firm has another 1,700 persons employed in research, administration, and marketing (data extracted by Gorz, 1990: 28). These data show that even here there is no elimination of work.

Quite apart from this, the elimination of labor and the generalization of this tendency under contemporary capitalism—including the enormous number of workers in the Third World—would suppose the destruction of the market economy itself by making it impossible to integrate the process of capital accumulation. Being neither consumers nor wage earners, robots cannot participate in the market. The very survival of the capitalist economy would be compromised, to say nothing of the many other explosive social and political consequences of such a situation (Mandel, 1986: 16–17). It is a mistake, then, to anticipate the end of work as long as the capitalist consumer society endures or—and this is fundamental—the elimination of the class that lives from labor as long as the basic pillars of the capitalist mode of production exist. The essential elimination of paid work as a fetish and a form of alienation and a creation of a "free association of workers" is indissolubly linked to the need to eliminate capital in all its forms. This should not, however, impede a careful study of today's working class and the changes in it that I have just mentioned.

Responses to Changes in the World of Work

Trade unionism cannot remain immune to these far-reaching and complex challenges. Its overriding tendency has been to go overwhelmingly onto the defensive, often without any project or vision for a society going beyond capital. One example of this crisis can be seen in the significant decline in rates of union membership over the past decade (or longer) in the United States, Japan, France, Italy, Germany, Holland, Switzerland, and the United Kingdom, among other countries (Visser, 1993; McIlroy, 1997; Antunes, 1995b). The increasing gap between workers in secure employment (to whom the unions have historically catered) and those lacking such job security greatly reduces the power of the unions, which have proved unable to bring the latter into membership. This critical situation began to affect unionism in the advanced countries first and more recently has emerged in the subordinate countries as well, especially those like Brazil that have a relevant manufacturing sector.

When we reflect on the transformations that the world of work and trade unionism have been undergoing in the central countries and on their repercussions in Brazil, it is clear that we must adapt our responses. Our starting point is an economic, social, political, and cultural context that has both the universal features of a globalized and worldwide capitalism and a number of features that are specific to it. Not every element of the situation affects the whole world equally, and one cannot uncritically assume that what happens in the center and what happens in the subordinate countries will necessarily be identical.

Brazilian capitalism, particularly the pattern of industrial accumulation that developed in the mid-1950s and has intensified since the 1964 military coup, is structured toward two markets. One front is geared toward the production of durable consumer goods, such as automobiles and domestic electrical appliances for a limited and selective internal market composed of the dominant classes and a significant fraction of the middle classes. The other front is geared toward exporting not only primary products but also manufactured consumer goods. The incremental decline in Brazilian workers' wages has made possible levels of accumulation that have proved a strong attraction for monopoly capital. Thus the capitalist expansion of manufacturing has sustained itself through the over-exploitation of labor made possible by low wages combined with a long and arduous working day in an industrial sector that is significantly large for a developing country. This pattern of accumulation has developed with great strength, especially in the 1950s, 1960s, and 1970s.

During the 1980s this process began to undergo its first modifications. Although the pattern of accumulation and its "economic model" remain basically the same, there have been organizational and technological changes in the processes of production and provision of services, although obviously at a much slower rate than that experienced by the central countries. While capital's restructuring of production is already well advanced in the central capitalist countries, Brazil still lags behind in this process.

Since 1990, with the rise of President Fernando Collor and then Finance Minister and subsequently President Fernando Henrique Cardoso, this process has been greatly accelerated as countless items of the neoliberal prescription have been implemented. The downsizing of firms, entailing an enormous compression of the workforce, has been combined with changes in technological processes. Flexibilization, deregulation, and the new forms of managing the workforce are intensifying, resulting in a combination of Brazil's still dominant Fordism with new processes of production and the so-called Toyotaism of the Japanese model (see Gorender, 1997; Antunes, 1997; Jinkings, 1995; Teixeira and Oliveira, 1996; Faria, 1996; Ramalho and Martins, 1994; and Hirata, 1993).

What capitalist production really needs is a combination of a skilled workforce trained to operate microelectronic equipment and an established pattern of very low wages and the means to avoid conceding job security—in short, overexploitation of labor, combining the extraction of relative surplus value with the expansion of the forms of extraction of absolute surplus value, that is, technological advance along with a faster pace of work and a longer working day.

The restructuring of capital on a world scale is in fact redefining Brazil's position in relation to the international division of labor and to its (re)integration into capital's global system of production at a time when nonproductive finance capital is suffering from hypertrophy and strongly affecting the forms of this integration and redefinition (see Chesnais, 1966). Certainly, the conjunction of these more universal experiences with the economic, social, and political conditions characteristic of Brazil has had a serious impact on its labor and union movement.

During the 1980s, before the accentuation of these more general tendencies, the workers' social movement and Brazil's new trade unionism were particularly active and effective. There were an enormous number of strikes, involving a wide range of occupations—industrial workers (especially those in heavy industry), rural laborers, civil servants, and various middle-level wage earners—in a vast movement characterized by the existence of general strikes within particular trades (like that of bank workers in 1995), strikes in which workplaces were occupied (like that of the General Motors factory in São Jose de Campos in 1985 and that of the National Steelworks in Volta Redonda in 1989), countless strikes of entire firms, and even the outbreak ot nationwide general strikes like that of March 1989, which involved about 35 million workers, making it the largest and most wide-ranging general strike Brazil has ever had. In 1987, for instance, there were 2,259 strikes, and in 1988 some 63 million days' work were lost (see Antunes, 1994: 24–37; Gracciolli, 1997).

There was an impressive growth of trade-union membership among middle-level wage earners in the service sector (bank workers, teachers, physicians, civil servants) during this period, and these workers were organized into unions of significant size. Already by the end of the 1980s the number of unions in Brazil had reached 9,833, and by the mid-1990s this had become 15,972, including urban and rural unions, management, and workers. There were 10,779 urban unions alone. There was an impressive growth in the number of workers' unions, not only of those linked to the industrial working class but also among middle-

level employees, contributing together to a large increase in the level of unioniza-
tion in Brazil. In 1996 there were 1,335 unions of civil servants, 461 unions connected with the so-called liberal professions, and 572 unions of the self-employed
(Brazil, Ministry of Labor, 1996, quoted in *O Estado de São Paulo,* September 8,
1996).

The growth of rural unions that began in the 1970s continued, permitting an
organizational restructuring of agricultural workers. In 1996 there were 5,196
rural unions, of which 3,098 were of laborers. This rural unionism developed
with a strong presence of left-wing Catholicism, which has subsequently made
possible the birth of the Movimiento dos Trabalhadores Sem-Terra (Landless
Peasants' Movement—MST).

Trade-union confederations emerged. The Central Unica dos Trabalhadores
(Sole Confederation of Unions of Workers—CUT), for example, founded in
1983, was inspired by the desire for a class-based unionism autonomous and
independent of the state and heir to the social and workers' struggles of earlier
decades, especially those of the 1970s. This has resulted in the confluence of the
new unionism, born within the union structure of that period (of which the Sin-
dicato dos Metalúrgios de São Bernardo—Metalworkers' [mostly automotive]
Union of São Bernardo—is an example), and the movement of opposition
unions, which act outside the official government-sponsored union structure
and oppose both government control and the verticality of official unionism (for
example, the Movimiento de Oposição Metalúrgico de São Paulo [Movement of
Opposition Metalworkers of São Paulo—MOSP] and the Oposição Metalúrgia
de Campinas [Campinas' Opposition Metalworkers]).

There was an attempt, albeit a limited one, at organizing in the workplace to
remedy the chronic weakness of Brazil's trade-union movement, creating countless factory councils and other forms of workplace organizations. Examples
include the trade-union factory councils of the ABC industrial area (the municipalities of São Andrés, São Bernardo dos Campos, and São Caetano—Greater
São Paulo's industrial belt), such as that in the Ford works, linked to the Metalworkers' Union of São Bernardo, and the independent councils under the influence of the MOSP.

Another significant advance in the struggle for union freedom and independence from the state was the opposition to the automatic salary deduction levied
by the government to finance the official unions, with their top-down administration, federal structure, and marked vestiges of corporatism of the 1930s, that
have functioned as instruments of the state for subordinating and controlling the
unions.

All this and other factors meant that, throughout the 1980s, the picture in
Brazil could be regarded as clearly favoring the new unionism and the workers'
social movement, which were then headed in a direction quite contrary to that
already being followed in various advanced capitalist countries. But by the last

years of that decade, economic, political, and ideological currents began to appear that would pull Brazilian trade unionism into the wave of regression.

Changes in the process of production and the restructuring of firms, often as a response to economic recession, started a process whereby large groups of workers lost their jobs while the remaining workforce had to give up security of employment and accept harsher working conditions. What happened in the automotive industry is a good example. Whereas there had been about 200,000 factory workers employed in the ABC area in 1987, by 1996 this number was down to 120,000, and downsizing has greatly increased since. In Campinas, another important industrial area of the state of São Paulo, there were about 70,000 industrial workers in 1989, and by 1996 this number had been reduced to about 40,000. The cutback in bank staff as banks have adjusted and technology has advanced has also been significant. In 1989 there had been about 800,000 bank workers. By 1996 this number had been cut to 570,000, and since then the rate of job cuts has been increasing.

Proposals for deregulation, flexibilization, and faster privatization and deindustrialization have received a strong push under the Collor and Cardoso administrations, as both these presidents have applied and pursued what has been basically a policy of neoliberal cuts. In parallel with the reduction in the industrial working class there has been a growth in the subproletariat, those doing outsourced work, and the underemployed—an increase in various forms of insecure employment. For example, 54 percent of employed women have jobs not covered by the social security laws (cited by L. Lavinas in *Veja*, February 26, 1997).

This new reality has weakened the new unionism and made it more defensive. On one hand, it has found itself up against the emergence of a neoliberal unionism, representing the new right, of which the Força Sindical, a trade-union federation created in 1991, is the best example. On the other hand, it has been faced with a change within the CUT, inspired by Articulação Sindical, taking it closer and closer to the model of European social-democratic unionism and therefore farther away from its combative origin and social struggle. This is making it far more difficult for the CUT to make the qualitative shift from resistance to the loftier goal of working out alternative economic proposals in opposition to the present pattern of capitalist development giving priority to the entire working class. For this, the CUT's greatest challenge is to recover its former combative posture, with a critical and anticapitalist perspective of clearly socialist dimensions to resist not only the avalanche of capital and the ideology of neoliberalism but also social democratic accommodation, which, despite the crisis it is undergoing in the developed countries, has been greatly strengthening its political and ideological ties with the Brazilian trade-union movement. Social-democratic unionism increasingly attempts to present itself as the only possible alternative in the fight against neoliberalism, but its lack of an anticapitalist viewpoint in either politics or ideology draws it ever closer to the neoliberal agenda.

All these factors have aggravated the critical state of Brazilian trade unionism in the 1990s. The new right wing of unionism is represented by the Força Sindical, with its strong political and ideological commitment to the preservation of order, in tune with the design of globalized capital, for which Brazil's role is that of a country assembling goods designed elsewhere, with no technology or scientific capability of its own, wholly dependent on external resources. In the CUT a stance of distancing itself from socialist and anticapitalist conceptions is beginning to gain strength among some of the top leadership in the name of an accommodation within the established order. The cult of negotiation, of "sectoral chambers" (joint management-worker councils for specific industries), of capital and labor collaborating with a view to developing "partnership" is offered as a breath of fresh air, oxygenated with the ideology and practice of a social democracy that is even managing to adapt to the institutionalized, bureaucratized, and hierarchical structure that has characterized Brazilian official unions since the 1930s.

The results of this policy have not been at all encouraging. The more one participates in the existing order, the less one can manage to preserve the interests of the world of work. The sectoral chambers, for example, part of the much-vaunted program of Articulação Sindical and conceived as a pattern for restructuring manufacturing industry and increasing employment, were tried out in a number of cases only to end in total failure, with an enormous loss of jobs. This is not to mention the ideological and political significance of accepting such a program: the São Bernardo Automotive Workers' Union was led to agree to and support a lower tax rate for the automobile manufacturers as a way of dynamizing the industry and thereby saving jobs. The participation of the CUT, through its newly dominant nucleus, the Articulação Sindical, in the so-called reform of social insurance (in reality, a process of dismantling social security rights in Brazil) during the Cardoso administration is another expression of the ambiguity of this attitude in union affairs and politics. Besides agreeing to an increase in the length of employment needed to acquire pension rights (in a country where 38 percent of children younger than 14 are already employed in production, typically in orange groves, sugar plantations, coal mines, etc.), this attitude has had the effect of undermining the workers' social movement, as well as those on the left of the CUT who had been preparing and organizing active resistance and opposition to Cardoso and his social security "reform."

The difficulties are also enormous in what is acknowledged as the socialist and anticapitalist party within the CUT, but some significant cases are worth noting. The Campinas Opposition Metalworkers, for example, have always been against participating in sectoral chambers, negotiating with the government, or entering into pacts with it. This is an important union, established in one of Brazil's major industrial centers, and is structured as a grassroots, class-based, socialist social and union movement. Within the CUT it puts its weight behind the opposition to the social-democratic leanings of the CUT leadership. Within Brazilian unionism as a whole, it is active in promoting a more clearly grassroots and socialist approach (see Possan, 1997).

In the same way, a significant effort is being made in the direction of unifying and articulating socialist and anticapitalist sectors within the CUT in a more effective manner, especially through the Alternativa Sindical Socialista (Socialist Union Alternative—AAS), the Movimento por una Tenência Socialista (Movement for a Socialist Tendency—MTS) and, in a more limited manner, the Corrente Sindical Classista (Class-based Union Current—CSC). At the CUT's 1997 national congress, there was an increase in these sectors of the left, which had benefited from the new context of social struggles, especially that of the MST. At the beginning of 1997, a year after the barbarous massacre of many landless workers in Pará, the MST was responsible for the most important act of opposition by ordinary people to the Cardoso administration. Marches were organized throughout Brazil against government policy and in favor of land reform. These passed through innumerable cities to converge on the capital, Brasília, where the government was forced to receive them in the midst of an overpowering social and political mass demonstration.

This new situation now makes it possible to envisage the resumption of social actions in Brazil at a level perhaps more intense than that experienced in the 1980s. To achieve this, however, we need a clear picture of recent Brazilian trade unionism. What path will the new unionism, born in the late 1970s and early 1980s, take? Will it negotiate within the established order, as Articulação Sindical has proposed? Will it try to work out an emergency program to manage the crisis of capital through the sectoral chambers or by emphasizing negotiated participation, "partnership" with capital with a view to "growth," "development," "increase of productivity," "broadening the export market," "incentives to attract foreign investment," and so on—all points clearly in tune with and ideologically subordinate to capital? Alternatively, will the more left-wing sectors of unionism get together with social movements and socialist political parties to work out an alternative policy directed against the established order, with clear anticapitalist objectives? The greater challenge faced by the left-wing sectors of the CUT, linked to social struggles such as those of the MST and many other grassroots experiences of the workers, will be that of taking steps to work out an alternative economic program, formulated from the viewpoint of the workers and capable of responding to the immediate demands of the world of work but having as its ultimate goal the organization of a society based on socialist values and real freedom. This means drawing up a project of social organization that will begin with the elimination of the overexploitation of work that is a characteristic of Brazilian industrial capitalism, whose minimum wage is set at a level of penury, despite the strength and importance of the country's productive sector. This project must, in its basic provisions, begin the dismantling of the pattern of capitalist accumulation that prevails in Brazil through a set of measures that will cease to tolerate an economic globalization and integration imposed by the logic of capital that is destructive for the workers. The project must include far-reaching and radical land reform that takes into consideration the various collective interests of workers and the landless. It will have to stimulate and raise the level of technology use in Brazil but on a solid base, using cutting-edge science and technology developed in our own country and directed toward remedying the enormous inequalities and meeting the needs of the working class. It will even have to control and forcefully restrain the monopolies, the hegemony of finance capital, and the various forms of expansion and speculation of money capital, besides encouraging forms of production directed toward the social needs of the workers—toward the production of socially useful things. The collective farms and settlements organized by the MST provide examples.

A project of this nature, sketched only briefly here, will be the result of combining social experiments at the grass roots with collective reflections. It will be able to create the conditions necessary for its subsequent elaboration, by then already endowed with a universalizing sense, clearly socialist, in an area that will necessarily overflow the boundaries of Brazil. This will happen because the experiences of the so-called socialism in a single country have shown themselves to have entirely failed. The challenge is to look toward a society that will go beyond capital but provide an immediate response to the barbarism that devastates the daily lives of those who live from their work. In other words, the project must seek the essential link between immediate concerns and clearly anticapitalist strategic action, having as its ultimate goal a social organization based on socialist and liberating values.

5.4

The Colonial and Imperialist Experience

Michael González-Cruz

Published on the centennial of the 1898 invasion of Puerto Rico by U.S. troops in a successful intervention to overthrow Spanish colonial rule, this article reflects the long tradition of nationalist and anti-imperialist resistance to the presence of the United States.

It is fitting that *LAP* publish an article on Puerto Rico this year (1998). Just over 100 years ago, on July 25, 1898, U.S. troops invaded and soon captured the Spanish colony. The Peace of Paris (December 1898) formally awarded Puerto Rico to the United States. No Puerto Rican (or Cuban, or Filipino, or Guamese, and so on) sat at the negotiating table, nor was any consulted, and this boded ill for the future. The following article briefly traces the history of Puerto Rican anticolonial resistance, revealing a long tradition of nationalist and anti-imperialist struggle. Space limitations, however, mean that important topics get shelved. This article does not examine, for example, the massive emigration to the United States starting in the 1920s and 1930s. Traditional historiography explains this exodus in purely economic terms (the spread of large landholdings, the Depression, etc.), but many came because colonial authorities drove them out. Others felt that they could better resist in exile. Still others, like Jesús Colón, the Marxist and American Labor party activist, became politicized in the United States. Nor does the article mention the fifteen prisoners of war and political prisoners now serving long sentences in U.S. jails. These men and women (some held in solitary confinement) were punished

First published in *Latin American Perspectives* 102, vol. 25 (5), Sage Publications, Inc. Reprinted with permission from the Latin American Perspectives Collective. Selection from 7–11, 15–16, 18–19, 22–23.

for defending their homeland against an illegally constituted government. The solidarity movement to free these patriots constitutes an integral part of the tradition of resistance that González-Cruz so amply documents.

—Hobart A. Spalding Jr.

T HE SPANISH-AMERICAN WAR, more appropriately, the Spanish Cuban-American-Philippine-Puerto-Rican War—was a product of both U.S. expansionism and the decadence of the Spanish empire. The U.S. ruling class had occupied the continent from east to west, including the southwestern area once under Mexican rule, and had been developing a colonial agenda since it first took land from the Native Americans. At that point its strategy for economic growth revolved around the globalization of an export economy and tariff protection of the internal market. Over the past hundred years, this ruling class has consolidated its political and economic power through direct colonization of other nations and through the use of extraterritorial laws that, together with other measures, have promoted a modernization model in the so-called developing countries. Puerto Rico has borne the brunt of the hegemonic agenda of the United States in terms of colonization, modernization, and neoliberalism. This article examines these processes at work and shows how they have shaped the island's current political situation.

Spain handed Puerto Rico over to the United States as spoils of war and to liquidate its war debts. The island's autonomous government was abolished and a military regime established. To this day, the political, economic, and cultural impact of the occupation and subsequent "annexation" of Puerto Rico as an unincorporated territory remains subject to controversy and debate. This article focuses on the consequences and impact of this annexation. It examines how resistance, repression, and modernization have come together in the formation of the state, pointing out how they systematically prevented the consolidation of a nation-state and substituted a colonial state for the initial occupying military regime. It documents the ways in which U.S. imperialism operated to colonize Puerto Rico and looks at how a local ruling class or elite was developed to administer the colonial state. It pays special attention to the role of the opposition as a trigger for class struggle and a motive force for the project of establishing a nation-state.

Invasion and Occupation:
The So-called Sovereignty Transfer

Before 1898, the Puerto Rican people had already rebelled against the decadent Spanish crown, first at Lares (in 1868) and then at Yauco (in 1897). In addition to these attempts to escape Spanish rule, various members of the local elite supported the idea that the island should have greater independence and more civil liberties. As a result of these efforts, the first autonomous government in Puerto Rico was established in March 1898, but it lasted only until the U.S. military forces occupied the island on July 25 of that year.

Several political and military factors made it possible for the United States to colonize the island. First, it was familiar with the area because of its commercial relationships with Spaniards and Creoles there, and this allowed it to recruit informants and infiltrate spies. Second, separatist sentiment was widespread, and some members of the intelligentsia admired the United States for its republican form of government. Third, the Spanish crown had responded to the threat of war in June 1898 by putting an end to all the individual liberties granted by the Charter of Autonomy (Negroni, 1992: 320). The leaders of the invasion tailored their expansionist plans to the requirements of those who favored autonomy, whose political platform revolved around reforms that represented the interests of the local elites (Corretjer, 1977: 32). General Nelson Miles, the commander of the invading force, promised in the official occupation proclamation to overthrow the Spanish authorities and guarantee individual freedom for the inhabitants. Once the island had been occupied by more than 15,000 U.S. troops, however, the structures of autonomous government were replaced. When General John R. Brooke became the first military governor, he did away with the insular parliament and with the provincial delegation (Trías-Monge, 1997: 30). The occupation and recolonization of the island did not improve basic rights such as health or labor conditions but rather reinforced the barriers that increased social inequalities among the population.

The New Order and Resistance

The establishment of the military government provoked immediate resistance. The new regime had suggested that it would bring justice to the island, but it failed to develop Puerto Rican public institutions democratically. In spite of the fact that the invasion was aimed at driving out the Spaniards, they were the only ones who received U.S. citizenship; it was not until 1917 that the Jones Act made Puerto Ricans U.S. citizens (Fernós, 1996: 92). Moreover, U.S. troops protected the Spanish landowners against attacks by members of secret societies originally dedicated to the achievement of independence from Spain (locally known as *tiznados* for the soot with which they blackened their faces for night raids). Now in rebellion against both their former colonizers and the new military government, the *tiznados*, armed with machetes, torches, and a few firearms and spread out in the mountains, were one of the first guerrilla groups in the Puerto Rican nation. They moved rapidly over terrain favorable to them, lightly armed so that they could attack and then retreat. They financed their activities by expropriating food, money, and other commodities from the landowners. The military government considered them seditious because it feared that their rebellious behavior might become general. The government of the occupation felt threatened by this irregular war. The state entered into crisis, and the propertied class was left without its instruments of political control (Picó, 1995: 43).

The campaign of repression aimed at breaking up the "seditious groups" was extended throughout the island, and the landowners were disarmed to keep the rebels from acquiring their weapons—at the same time ensuring that the landowners lacked the means to revolt. This made the landowners completely dependent upon the invading troops for their safety. In Hatillo, in the northern part of the island, the authorities arrested nineteen men and children on charges of being partisans of the seditious groups. As proof of their offenses, the authorities pointed only to the possession of a machete—the principal tool and defensive weapon carried routinely by most Puerto Ricans—by one of the accused (Picó, 1998). The defendants were acquitted.

The Creole press and some journalists resisted at a different level. The new military government, in addition to pursuing anyone who seemed opposed to it, devoted itself to repressing the media critical of the invasion and occupation. When the newspaper *Bomba* pointed to the vandalism committed by U.S. troops, it was shut down, and the author of the article, Izcoa Díaz, was incarcerated (Paralitici, 1997: 238). Other journalists were systematically pursued, fined, and arrested for reporting on the behavior of the troops of the occupation. Thus, the new colonial regime sought to consolidate its military and economic authority by repressing any activity that might destabilize it or threaten its economic interests.

Two other levels of resistance have not yet been widely documented. One instance of conflict and urban resistance occurred in the capital, San Juan, where the communities of El Labertino, Salsipuedes, and Venecia were uprooted and relocated by force to establish U.S. naval facilities there. The Puerto Rican historian Fernando Picó describes the way in which power at the municipal level was distributed at the time. One of the tasks of the U.S. military was to reestablish municipal government throughout the island, and this direct intervention in the local structures of power was designed to place political leaders in favor of annexation in these local governments. Professionals, merchants, and landowners educated abroad dominated positions in municipal government. The military took advantage of the political differences that existed within the landowning, mercantile, and professional classes, which prevented these sectors of society from uniting in opposition to the regime. Many of these local politicians simply shifted their loyalties from the Spanish crown to the military government. The government's strategy was to recognize the municipalities under the supervision of the military authorities in each district. In Aguadilla, however, the local U.S. commander assumed the post of mayor and personally appointed the members of the municipal board (Picó, 1998: 35–44). In other municipalities the military maintained a separation of powers but retained authority over a wide range of public affairs.

Concerned with maintaining a stable landowning group and public order, the military regime had serious problems in doing so. For example, in the municipalities of Utuado and Yauco direct confrontations took place between local police and U.S. troops (Picó, 1998: 97). In Utuado, the mayor welcomed the *tiznados* and they continued their march toward the mountains undisturbed; when the commander of the U.S. troops heard this news, he responded that they were "bandits who were terrorizing the local population" (Hernández Cruz, 1992: 31). In addition, some mayors confronted the military on issues such as the grazing of animals, prisons, sanitation, and health care. The military government manipulated the most influential strata in the municipalities to keep itself in power. As Eugenio María de Hostos pointed out, the North American military regime substituted itself for the absolutist Spanish tradition, despite President McKinley's assertion that annexing the Philippines, Puerto Rico, and Cuba would be a crime (Henríquez Ureña, 1988: 537). The military campaign, the occupation, and the reconstruction of the municipal governments became the basis for the extension of colonial control.

The establishment of the military regime assured the North American governing class of political stability in its newly annexed territory, not yet incorporated into the union. U.S. military and commercial interests were protected by the new colonial power structures; the military structures would shape the colonial state.

This period, which some researchers have called "the transfer of sovereignty," is marked by class conflict, violence, and the loss of even the most elementary civil rights. Five measures stand out in this process: (1) militarization, (2) control over the means of communication, (3) defense of the privileged classes, (4) repression of political movements critical of or opposed to the regime, and (5) the establishment of new local government structures. . . .

Development and Industrialization

In Puerto Rico industrialization and the establishment of public service agencies were parallel projects. This populist project for national industrialization began with the Industrial Incentive Act of 1954, which instituted three programs that changed the island's infrastructure: the establishment of import-substitution industries, Operation Bootstrap, an aggressive program of incentives for North American entrepreneurs to invest in the island, and the 500 Acres Law, which redistributed land across the island. This model, designed to exploit cheap labor, export the island's production, and provide a market for consumer goods from the United States, further deepened Puerto Rico's dependency (Pantojas-García, 1990: 68–69).

The encouragement of local production by means of import-substitution industrialization lasted only about six years, because the private sector proved very critical of it (Dietz, 1993: 183), but it influenced the development of the economy by serving as a training ground for local entrepreneurs. Later, under Operation Bootstrap, the Government Development Bank allocated the majority of incentives to North American capitalists, whose greatest contribution to the economy was the generation of employment; the goods produced were exported to the United States, and the corporate profits were not reinvested in other sectors of the local economy. From 1940 to 1970 the Partido Popular Democrático (PPD) consolidated its reformist agenda by promoting industrialization, implanting a model of capital imports and the export of processer goods. This model changed the political-economic structures of the country and opened the way for the establishment of various subsidiaries of U.S. transnational corporations (Pantojas-García, 1990: 102).

The expansion of industry hastened the transformation of and incorporation of new actors into the working class; for example, thousands of women joined the workforce in manufacturing and petrochemicals (Ríos, 1993: 97). The intensification of the export model caused a movement of people to the periphery of urban centers. The government became the largest provider of services such as education, housing, and health, and this was an integral part of the modernization plans for the island. Operation Bootstrap caused the migration of rural proletarians to urban areas in search of housing close to job centers and the public services located in those areas (Cotto, 1993: 120). At the beginning of the 1960s, the social changes and conflicts induced by industrialization were already apparent, among them an upsurge in the workers' movement, land invasions, and the struggle to protect the environment. By the late 1960s communities had begun to organize to defend their rights to housing, health, and a clean environment. . . .

Civil Society's Response

The workers' movement has reemerged to criticize and oppose government policies that do not benefit the working class. Puerto Rican labor unions along with diverse religious, community, and political organizations have mounted a broad movement against the privatization of public services. The Federación Universitaira Pro-Independencia, among other entities, has extended its scope of activity into almost all the areas of public education in the country and is even organizing the Federación Estudiantil Pro-Independencia in secondary education. FUPI has taken a strong position in favor of public education, displayed militant solidarity with local labor organizations, and demonstrated against the privatization of public services.

The sectors most affected by privatization have been housing, health, telecommunications, and most recently the educational system, including the University of Puerto Rico. Thousands of people have marched against the expansion of the U.S. military presence and the sale of the telephone company and other public services. The government has penalized those within its reach. In spring 1998 Governor Roselló presented legislation to reduce the university's budget by

US$40 million in an obvious reprisal for its opposition to his agenda. He also proposed the elimination of important environmental controls. He has approved new labor legislation that has been denounced as highly restrictive by progressive labor leaders *(Claridad,* May 1–7, 1998), and he has continued to use military force in housing projects under the guise of fighting crime.

The PNP came to power by default. In the election of 1990, a majority favored a change in administration that would improve health standards and employment opportunities for the working class. The vote favoring the PNP was, in reality, a vote against the PPD government. The PPD lost two important votes after 1990: a referendum to amend the constitution and the status plebiscite of 1993 referred to earlier. It has not proposed a new model that will generate employment or increase the purchasing power of the working class. Because of the uncertainty of the status question, the proannexationist government has steered the island toward a neoliberal model in which statehood would not generate additional costs for the United States. This model would create a dismantled welfare state ready for privatization. The PNP majority, for example, has voted for flex time and to repeal environmental laws among other measures that conform to a neoliberal model.

In spite of reprisals and threats, some sectors of civil society still maintain a strong opposition to the neoliberal regime. For instance, the Ejército Popular Boricua (Puerto Rican People's Army) sabotaged the superaqueduct that delivers water to San Juan, a project that the population had massively rejected for health and environmental reasons, and declared this the first popular action against privatization (Torres Negrón, 1998; Martínez, 1998). Once again violence has surfaced as a result of the political and economic crisis of Puerto Rican society. . . .

Civil Society: Possibilities and Alternatives

As a result of the PNP's failures, social movements have reemerged to pose an alternative to neoliberalism. Among the organizations that stand out in the labor movement are Federación de Maestros de Puerto Rico (Puerto Rican Federation of Teachers—FMPR), the Unión de Trabajadores de la Industria Eléctrica y Riego (Union of the Electrical and Irrigation Industry Workers—UTIER), and certain other independent unions. Also participating in the movement are religious congregations (the Catholic church in Caguas, the Presbyterian church in the southwestern part of the island), student organizations, and the environmentalist movement at the national and local levels.

Some factions exist within the electoral parties that have the potential to become a part of a political opposition to the PNP. For example, in the 1990s, the autonomist sector of the PPD openly challenged the conservative wing of the party, but it has not taken a stand against either neoliberalism or the annexationist plans of the party. The PIP considers itself a social democratic party dedicated to social justice, protection of the environment, and the interests of the working class. It has confined itself, however, mostly to parliamentary tactics and no longer displays the militancy of the 1970s. PIP representatives in the Puerto Rican House and Senate do, however, monitor the government and its neoliberal policies. The PIP congressional delegation has traditionally been a part of the party's leadership, and in elections they usually get about 250,000 votes. The PIP's candidate for governor, however, receives far fewer votes. The party has firmly maintained its position as the parliamentary opposition and has backed legislation in favor of labor and the environment, but it has not managed to develop a program favoring alliances that would allow it to grow beyond the survival level. The PIP's participation in civil society is vital for defending the gains made by the working-class and social movements.

The annexationist government is negotiating the repeal of the constitutional guarantees protecting the health and the environment of the less privileged classes (Law no. 9). A majority of PNP House members are trying to pass legislation to create a kind of "fast-track" approval that would eliminate environmental impact studies for projects that might affect local communities and the ecosystems in which they live. The environmental movement has become one of the popular responses most critical of the development policies of the colonial state and the U.S. government. The neoliberal thrust of the annexationist government openly attacks the interests of the communities and groups working to protect health and environment at the local and national levels. The ecology movement has learned from the experiences of the working-class movement, from the new struggle for independence, and from civil and religious organizations. The PNP is attempting to take away from civil society its opportunity to participate in public policy debates.

Conclusion

The annexation of Puerto Rico as an unincorporated territory of the United States resulted in a colonial state that fostered U.S. control over public affairs and the development of a dependent economy. The commonwealth allowed some space for the formation of a collective national identity expressed in cultural terms and through the growth of a working-class movement and civil society. Popular resistance has existed since the occupation. Its change over time into anti-imperialist demonstrations and actions, both reformist and nationalist, clearly indicates that the annexation of Puerto Rico is not a fait accompli. The presence of political actors opposed to statehood, capitalist developmentalism, and neoliberalism will be the motive forces for social change. The pillars of a democratic and popular state will most likely be found in the social movements and in the traditions of the independence movement. With the emergence of the new independence movement it has become clear that it is impossible to achieve full sovereignty without establishing more equitable relations among all sectors of the population.

PUERTO RICO

5.5

The Weakness of the Bourgeoisie
in the National Revolution

Manuel Maldonado-Denis

This essay explores consequences for Puerto Rico of U.S. imperialism, which inter-feres with the development of a national bourgeoisie and its prospects for breaking with dependent capitalism and achieving independence.

CONTRARY TO THE REST of the Latin American republics, Puerto Rico is a nation under direct control by U.S. imperialism. This alone explains in a large part the character of Puerto Rican nationalism as a historical phenomenon: it has been and is a movement whose immediate goal is political independence, a goal reached by other Latin American countries a century ago. Latin American nationalism manifests itself in areas such as the recovery of national wealth from imperialist interests, the struggle against imperialist penetration in education and culture, the effort to improve the conditions that cause unequal exchange and uneven development, and so on. It could be argued that what is being sought through these efforts is economic independence—which is sought by Puerto Rican nationalism—but the question of political independence is definitely something which is not in the immediate agenda of Latin American nationalism as it confronts U.S. imperialism. Consequently, it should be evident that the mechanisms of which Latin American countries in general have availed them-

First published in *Latin American Perspectives* 10, vol. 3 (3), Sage Publications, Inc. Reprinted with permission from the Latin American Perspectives Collective. Selection from 42–44.

selves against imperialism, e.g., a policy of import substitution, are not real options for Puerto Rican nationalists even in the unheard-of case that they could exercise any influence within the colonial government.

Insofar as the Puerto Rican nationalist movements have been historically directed by a petty-bourgeois sector and the middle class, they share the common ground of *class basis* with Latin American nationalism in general; even the great populist Latin American movements have in fact been headed by analogous class elements. In the rest of Latin America, the same vacillation on the part of the petty bourgeoisie has been noted when the incorporation of the working class into the revolutionary process of the nationalist struggle has become an issue. As in the case of Puerto Rico, the very class composition of Latin American nationalism, as well as the nature of the nationalist ideology, has held back a popular movement which could advance toward the supersession of nationalism and the social class which is its material substratum.

One thing is clear in our case: the history and development of Puerto Rican society in the twentieth century seriously endangers the capacity and will of the local bourgeoisie to act as an agent of revolutionary change in our country. First, the economic development of Puerto Rico under the aegis of dependent capitalism has served to bring about what Professor Quintero Rivera has accurately named an "anti-national" class whose interests as an intermediate bourgeoisie coincide with those of the metropolitan bourgeoisie. Secondly, we must take into account considerable sectors of the middle class whose interests are directly or indirectly linked to the imperialist presence in Puerto Rico. The whole processes of strengthening the bonds of cultural, ideological, economic, political, and military dependency have unquestionably reinforced the social forces whose goal is the annexation of Puerto Rico to the United States as a state of the union. In Puerto Rico today there is not a national, let alone a nationalist bourgeoisie. In a country where 80 percent of the industrial enterprises belong to stockholders from the metropolis, it can be said that, at most, the Puerto Rican bourgeoisie struggles to survive in economic sectors such as cement, beer, construction, and so forth. And, if nationalism is, historically and socially, an ideology that characterizes the bourgeoisie, then we must explain the weakness of Puerto Rican nationalism as the undeniable product of the weakness of our bourgeoisie as a social class. To put it yet another way, the Puerto Rican bourgeoisie has demonstrated an incapability to carry out to completion its historical task of national liberation as has indeed taken place in the rest of Latin America.

The classic colonial character of Puerto Rican history makes nationalism a collective kind of sentiment which is extremely difficult to eradicate. But the problem lies in the fact that such a nationalism can only become a genuine force not through the class which has used it historically but among the Puerto Rican working class, the only social class capable of synthesizing the national and the social struggles. Marx himself warned on one occasion, "Though not in substance, yet in form, the struggle of the proletariat with the bourgeoisie is at first a national struggle. The proletariat of each country must, of course, first of all settle matters with its own bourgeoisies" (1970: 45). Also, "Since the proletariat must first of all acquire political supremacy, must rise to be the leading class of the nation, must constitute itself *the* nation, it is, so far, itself national, though not in the bourgeois sense of the word" (1970: 55).

Of necessity, this implies that it is the Puerto Rican proletariat which ought to lead the process of emancipation toward national liberation and socialism, in alliance with the nationalist petty bourgeoisie and all those sectors and strata which respond to an anti-imperialist political call. From this point of view, traditional Puerto Rican nationalism can be an important force in the processes of breaking the ties of secular economic dependency of our people, but without losing sight that this is only a "moment" in the struggle for a social revolution and not the culmination of a petty-bourgeois-directed project.

Lastly, after the Second World War imperialism utilized Borinquen as "the showcase" where the virtues of free enterprise could be displayed for the edification of other Latin American countries. Puerto Rico became for Latin America, in terms of "democracy," what Berlin was for Western Europe. Within this context, the program known as Fomento was put into effect on the following bases: tax exemptions for North American enterprises; provision of a network of infrastructural works for the benefit of investors, a cheap and abundant labor force, a "favorable investment climate" or "political stability," and so forth. The present crisis of world capitalism has shown the fragility of the showcase: economic growth on the island not only has stagnated, but it is now *retrogressing.* The colonial administration is facing a crisis comparable only to that of the 1930s with over 40 percent unemployed and underemployed and the tremendous growth of a marginalized mass which is barely maintained on the basis of food subsidies from the U.S. government. In this situation, the Puerto Rican proletariat is moving into position for the playing of its historical role.

"The proletarians are not gods," exclaimed Marx on one occasion. This phrase may be of more consequence in Puerto Rico than in any other Latin American country at present. In today's world, the proletariat is a world proletariat in the same manner that the bourgeoisie has become an international class. Nevertheless, the immediate struggle of the proletariat is given, of necessity, at the national level. As such, the working class has two options: to become protagonists of a process that will radically transform those structures which produce and reproduce exploitation nationally and internationally or to become a puppet in the hands of the petty bourgeoisie in its reformist projects. If the Puerto Rican proletariat chooses the first alternative, it will be embracing proletarian internationalism as well, thus transcending, eventually, the bourgeois conceptions of nation and nationalism.

5.6

The Barzón Debtors' Movement

Heather Williams

This is a fascinating account of a new social movement of landed farmers who were dissatisfied with worsening conditions and who organized against corruption and the accumulation of wealth that accounted for disparities in Mexico. It is but one example of local and national resistance against financial globalization of capital.

THIS ARTICLE PROFILES the rise of a debtors' movement known as the Barzón. For five years members of this movement blocked highways, occupied banks, flooded the courts with lawsuits, protested in Congress, and introduced antibank legislation at state and national levels, claiming that collusion among government officials, corrupt judges, and banking elites had caused the general bank failure of 1995–1996. This movement, which expanded from a few thousand farmers to half a million debtors from urban and rural sectors in the first half of 1995, captured headlines in the national press and received international attention for its raucous but peaceful protests and its radical critique of Mexico's economic policies. Beyond protest, the Barzón also pushed the limits of the PRI-dominated government, challenging presidential and central bank policies in the courts and in the national legislature.

The Barzón movement merits attention for many reasons. Social movement scholars have outlined its use of public theater (Chávez, 1996), its deep roots in the agrarian sector (Rodríguez Gómez and Torres, 1994), its migration from

First published in *Latin American Perspectives* 119, vol. 28 (4), Sage Publications, Inc. Reprinted with permission from the Latin American Perspectives Collective. Selection from 32–38, 45–48.

street protest to courts to legislative activism to direct action again (Charnas, 1999). In this discussion, I concentrate on the movement's ability to direct the anger of normally conservative middle-class urban actors and commercial farmers in a surprisingly left-leaning direction. Although the movement crucially stopped short of an analysis of the economy that addressed the crisis of wage labor, it popularized a nationalist economic discourse in which Barzonistas declared that they, as "producers" in the national economy, were being undermined by the activities of "speculators" in the global economy. In this reckoning, producers would include farmers, merchants, service providers, and small to medium-sized manufacturers: speculators would include bankers, loan sharks, financiers, stockbrokers, foreign investors, and multinational corporations. Subjects' "class" identity, in this rendering, is defined not by their relation to the means of production but by their relation to domestic and global financial markets.

Since 1995, the Barzón—at one point probably half a million strong—has tapered off to close to nothing in activity and membership. I argue that crisis alone does not account for the coalescence of this particular movement and macroeconomic recovery does not fully explain its demise. Instead, personal crises of debtors combined with an already well-developed critical narrative of political economy gave force to this movement. Contradictions in the movement and external support afforded its enemies in the banks made it a difficult organization to sustain. People often went to the Barzón out of a need for asset protection and/or representation but became radicalized through the indignation created by its compelling explanation for their hardship. Leaders of the Barzón—specifically that branch of it that was founded in the north-central state of Zacatecas[1] among grain farmers—echoed and added to a long-standing condemnation by leftist scholars and left-party activists of the economic policies pursued by Presidents Miguel de la Madrid and Carlos Salinas de Gortari since the early 1980s. Such critics had accurately pointed out that Mexico's "economic modernization" (as fiscal retrenchment, trade opening, and privatization together were labeled by their architects in government) had pushed significant portions of the population backward into a misery not seen for some decades. Even before the currency crisis of 1994, when the Mexican economy was said to be booming, over 60 percent of small and micro-sized enterprises were in financial trouble (Gómez Salgado, 1994). Also by the early 1990s, farmers throughout the country were in serious trouble. An overvalued peso, artificially buoyed by short-term debt instruments, had rendered Mexican grains and produce uncompetitive on national and international markets. With unit prices below the cost of production and farm credit prices liberalized, even wealthy farmers with good land were unable to compete with imports from the United States and Asia. The stage was set for a widespread political backlash against economic policy makers in Mexico City.

Notably, Barzón leaders went beyond charging the nation's private banks with fraud and duplicity. The Barzón, in fact, operated on a more radical set of premises that questioned many currently accepted practices of modern private banking of the sort originally developed in Europe and later the United States. In so doing, its leaders criticized and deconstructed what architects of the prevailing market order have sought to portray as natural and above criticism. They questioned, for example, the legality and prudence of floating interest rates. They further asserted that compound interest rates (interest charged on interest) were unconstitutional. Finally, they demanded that the state guarantee new lines of credit and force banks to forgo interest on overdue debt, calling for the government to intervene in capital markets on behalf of small and midsized consumers and businesspeople. Their demands—backed up by substantive accusations of bank corruption and of collusion among government, banks, and ruling party—shook up Mexican elites and foreign brokers, who had expected to see massive profits generated in a deregulated private banking sector.

I set forth two general arguments explaining the Barzón's initial surge and gradual ebb. First, I contend that the movement's criticisms of Mexico's economic policies—echoing what the left had long been saying—provided a parsimonious explanation for what had happened during the crisis and who was to blame. The crisis of 1994, as well as the measures President Ernesto Zedillo took to restore the faith of international markets in Mexico, confirmed predictions made years before by the left-wing critics of the 1980s and 1990s. As José Luis Calva (1993: 9, my translation), for example, had written presciently in 1993:

> The Mexican economy remains vulnerable to a financial crisis worse than what occurred in 1982 not only because of the magnitude of our external debts but also because of the volatility of foreign portfolio investment, which we did not have at the beginning of the last decade. In addition, neoliberal programs of structural adjustment and stabilization have deepened the fragmentation and inequality in manufacturing and production. They have reduced the ratio of savings to investment; and they have subordinated the needs of productive enterprises to financial accumulation and speculation.

Zedillo's monetarist fix for Mexico's financial crisis not only caused a lot of suffering but in fact exacerbated an ongoing crisis of legitimacy for the ruling party, the PRI, seemingly confirming what the opposition had argued. In the case of Mexico, measures that might have been taken to meet social demands for relief from generalized household and business insolvency were proscribed by the multilateral financial institutions and foreign governments lending Mexico funds to cover its short-term debts, as well as by the private-sector market actors making decisions about whether to reenter Mexican markets. As a result, President Zedillo's stonewalling of social demands—interpreted by outside authorities as "doing what had to be done"—provided a political lag time in which great numbers of people began to protest government policies and to develop short-term means of protecting themselves against lender repossessions of their property. The Barzón provided people with a means of doing both while articulating a broader political critique of financial liberalization and free trade. My second point bears on the issue of debt as a political unifier. I argue that while this debtors' movement successfully recruited across class and industrial sectors, its particular character and ideology—both nationalist and center-left—contained contradictions that would limit its ability to deepen and institutionalize its ties with leftist groups representing working-class, peasant, and popular sectors. Its ability to unite grievances across classes and industrial sectors made it hard to dismantle at the height of its powers but difficult to sustain as external forces eroded the sources of its leverage.

Devaluation, Domestic Crisis, and Civic Response

Officially, the cross-class, cross-sectoral organization that burst out of the Mexican north and west in the depression of 1995 is called the Civil Association Representing the National Union of Agricultural and Livestock Producers, Businesspeople, Industrialists, and Service Providers. It is a title that few ever used, however. This group, best known for its large numbers, its trademark banners with green tractors, and its public demonstrations that ranged from raucous street theater to rousing and cheerful occupations of public squares and buildings to stalwart collective defenses against bank repossessors who come for properties whose owners are in default, was known by press and the public as the Barzón. Taken from a perversely funny folk song about a hacienda peon who must borrow from his boss to pay for an ox yoke (the *barzón*) that has ripped apart, the organization's name recalls the song's winding tale of woe about the peasant, who sinks deeper and deeper into debt as interest on his loan rises faster than he can pay it off and he ends up, for the sake of the ox yoke, a slave for life.

The song is more than a story of one man's bad luck. It is instead a popular complaint, barely softened by humor, about an unjust system of debt peonage in which hacienda lords backed up by the state keep the poor unfree through usury. In the spring and summer of 1995 the Barzón movement, as a mass organized complaint of so many debt-slaves (as some also called themselves), came to serve as a clearinghouse for political objection to a neoliberal economic regime.

Although it had begun as a regional movement almost two years before in Jalisco, the Barzón really emerged as a national force in Mexico as the country slogged through month after month of economic depression in 1995. Unleashed by a disastrous currency crash in December 1994, this depression heaped new hardship on a population still recovering from the economic convulsions of the 1980s. As the nation's economy contracted by about 7 percent in 12 months' time, 1 million workers joined the unemployment rolls, 20,000 businesses filed for bankruptcy, and aggregate buying power declined by 37 percent (Banco de

México, cited in *La Jornada*, December 18, 1995) as inflation surged and government-controlled wages stagnated.

Taking as great a toll on domestic economic dynamism as the devaluation itself were the measures taken to massage macroeconomic indicators and reassure panicked investors holding government bonds. A U.S.$50 billion bailout package pieced together from U.S. loans and loan guarantees plus loans from the International Monetary Fund (IMF) and the World Bank was conditioned on anti-inflationary monetary policy and renewed promises of fiscal cutbacks and more aggressive revenue collection (DePalma, 1995).

This in turn constricted the amount of cash at the disposal of consumers and businesses. Value-added tax rose from 10 percent to 15 percent, while public subsidies were scaled back and transportation prices doubled. Salaries were effectively capped by official accords signed by peak associations of labor and business. In addition, businesses in crisis were given legal leeway to furlough workers or pay them half-time, further dampening buying power in tens of thousands of households.

Domestic manufacturing and retail sectors went into a tailspin. Describing this phenomenon in interviews and casual conversation, pushcart merchants and factory owners alike described the times in remarkably similar terms. "Es que no hay circulante [It's that there's no money]," several told me independently. For market farmers and businessmen, the worst of it was that falling sales were accompanied by a rise in the price of production capital and a termination of production subsidies. Interest rates tripled in the early months of 1995, reaching 90 and 100 percent and more. A U.S.$500 business loan became a U.S.$1,000 liability in a year's time and then U.S.$1,500 if the client did not pay on time. The way interest accumulated under these conditions sent even merchants fortunate enough to maintain their sales into bankruptcy.

Consumer Desperation and Movement Response

It was in this widening sea of rapid decapitalization that the Barzón movement expanded from a primarily rural constituency of indebted farmers to a vast legion of mostly urban consumers and businessmen. Many hundreds of thousands of people who borrowed in 1993 and 1994 with expectations of fairly stable interest rates and dynamic national growth rates realized that they stood to lose their businesses and houses within months. As an organizer said to me, gesturing at several hundred Barzón members who had gathered at a weekly meeting in Culiacan, Sinaloa, "Do you see these people? Ninety percent of them come to us when they realize they're going to have their houses or cars or businesses repossessed." Though numbers are hard to come by, the movement itself saw its membership expand by degrees of magnitude in the panicked months after the December devaluations, rising from somewhere around 60,000 to 500,000 by

July 1995. At any rate, its numbers and persistence quickly made it one of the largest nonparty civil organizations to emerge in Mexico in this century.

In campaigns of recruitment and mobilization, Barzón activists focused on consumer debt, identifying it as a scourge visited upon the masses by unscrupulous men. Reversing the normal shame internalized by individual debtors who find that they cannot meet their obligations with the bank, organizers of the Barzón assured members and potential members of the organization that their debt was not legitimate but a great scam perpetrated by the handful of billionaires and foreign brokers who controlled the greatest part of the country's capital. At assemblies all over the nation, leaders emphasized the structural nature of each individual's insolvency, telling people simply, "Your debt is unpayable." The Barzón movement's public critique echoed popular suspicions circulating since the currency crash: first, it identified the primary culprit of the devaluation crisis as ex-President Carlos Salinas de Gortari, maintaining that he had robbed national reserves and bought controlling shares of former state-owned industries under assumed names; and second, it condemned the emergency policy measures taken by Salinas's successor, Ernesto Zedillo, as a palliative for bankers and foreign portfolio investors produced at the cost of domestic enterprise, the poor, and the middle classes. The Barzón fingered speculative investment, tight monetary policy, lack of democracy, and predatory banks as the culprits behind the economic crash. Calling for a radical departure from national policy and international trade agendas, leaders proposed a platform of national economic recovery whose planks closely matched principles of Keynesian demand management—a policy paradigm frowned upon by the technocratic elites now dominating economic policy in the developing world.

Given their nonconformity with the rules and expectations of domestic financial elites and foreign trade officials, it is not surprising that the movement's demands evoked little more than shrugs from banks and the federal government until the organization began appearing daily in the national papers in the spring of 1995. It was almost inevitable that the government, committed in treaty and ideology to a development path that included market liberalization and fiscal austerity, would reject debtors' petitions for mass debt restructuring and lower interest rates. When government ministers, the president, and the banks' central leadership finally did begin to respond to the Barzón movement in mid-1995, they did so almost invariably in dismissive tones. Whenever possible, state and bank elites at high levels avoided speaking of the group by name, instead referring obliquely to the movement as "groups of people who don't want to pay their debts" or the "culture of nonpayment." While from the banks' and finance ministers' point of view the Barzón's demands were completely out of conformity with the rules and expectations of the prevailing system of finance and fiscal administration, they were forced in some manner to acknowledge the movement in large part because of the potential damage that it and other debtors' groups might cause by declaring that they would not pay any of their debts to the banks.

The banks, meanwhile, already endangered by some 160 billion pesos in nonrecoverable consumer debt by late 1995, could not afford to provoke even more radical actions by debtors. . . .

Potential and Limits of the Barzón Movement

What began as a local movement of landed farmers dissatisfied with worsening production conditions ended as a conduit of mass backlash against the official corruption and concentration of wealth that had accompanied Mexico's neoliberal transformation. For a time the Barzón movement upended the rules of normal finance, forcing private and public banks to restructure loans and to desist from repossessing land, equipment, houses, and businesses. Through multifaceted local campaigns that included direct action, legislative pressure, press conferences, and legal activism, the movement was able to provide members with protection from the banks while also pressing a public agenda for a variety of policy reforms. As I have argued here, however, crisis itself does not explain why a movement of debtors would emerge as a powerful protest force, nor does it explain the particular strategies and organizational forms that materialized. Other debtors' organizations formed in 1994 and 1995, for example, such as the National Association of Debtors and the National Association of Debtors Anonymous, remained small, local, and largely ineffective when they were not acting in conjunction with the Barzón.

Notably, the movement that exploded in 1995 and 1996 declined in numbers and strength in the following three years. This was attributed to a number of factors. First, because of the pressure exercised by the organization, many people were able to restructure their debts. While many continued working with the organization, others returned full-time to businesses and farms. Second, legal channels narrowed sharply. The basis of many thousands of legal injunctions issued from 1995 to 1998 had been a claim that charging interest over interest violated the 1917 Constitution. After a 1998 Supreme Court decision ruling compound interest legal, many lower courts refused to hear debtors' cases.

The success of direct action in relieving some members of debts and the failure of court action in eliminating the basis of the others' debts explains some but not all of the movement's trajectory. The strategies that enabled the movement to maintain protest also imposed lasting contradictions on the organization. Five years after my initial research on the Barzón in the state of Zacatecas was conducted in 1994 and 1995, in a return visit to the region in 1999, the strains inherent in its various means of mobilizing and maintaining protest were apparent. On the one hand, the leaders of the Barzón had emerged over time as national opposition figures. On the other hand, the cells of local activism had dissipated in Barzón strongholds in the central part of the state.

Decline had much to do with conflicting visions of the organization and the inherent tension between aggressive direct actions by the base membership and leaders' new official roles as members of the government, where legitimate activism meant playing by prescribed rules of order. In Zacatecas, informants pointed out that participation in the organization declined markedly after the 1997 decision to launch leaders as candidates for national office. Despite leaders' arguments that reviving farms and businesses was contingent on reaching universal policy reforms, many members saw the decision as an autocratic back-room deal that betrayed earlier commitments to organizational independence. Debtors—many of whom had refused to restructure debts under official programs at the urging of Barzón leaders—now faced imminent repossessions and lawsuits by lenders. Such debtors saw the exit of leaders to Mexico City as an abdication of local responsibilities.

In the final account the Barzón's greatest influence on the future of civil politics will be its imaginative non-violent tactics and inclusive protest narratives. The movement pioneered new forms of protest and expanded the use of older ones. Indeed, it has created many movement "joiners" and political activists among normally noncommittal middle-class people. The mutualist forms of aid seen in brigade-type protests that protect individual debtors from banks and police, for example, echo the actions of the tenacious neighborhood movements that sprang up after the 1985 earthquake that leveled portions of Mexico City (Monsiváis, 1987). Those actions and occupations of the sort that the Barzón movement has carried out with machinery and large crowds (formerly common on rural highways but not in urban centers of power) have gained it the reputation of a new but not alien sort of social movement in Mexico. In training leaders and organizers, it heightened awareness of rights people had under the law with respect to police and public institutions. In establishing new networks linking private citizens to the press and to one another, it taught a great many people how to organize collective action and how to use a combination of direct action, the vote, and the courts to protect their interests against extremely powerful opponents. Relatively few of the rank-and-file Barzón members I interviewed, for example, reported previous experience in political organizations. Many, however, reported that, despite the pressures of their debts, they felt renewed and exhilarated by the experience of organizing and talking about politics and that they would participate in political action in the future. Many also felt that the Barzón represented a "family" of sorts. The Barzón also altered the profile of people expected to be leaders, as substantial numbers of women took leadership roles in the organization. National leaders included Liliana Flores of Monterrey and Monica Soto of Sonora. At state and local levels, women also participated in large numbers, particularly in urban sectors.

The Barzón movement, like the Mexican crisis itself, may be an indicator of things to come in an era of financial globalization. Its explosive growth suggests that crises born of volatility in global markets combined with well-developed critiques of free-market policies may contribute to new forms of collective action and protest. During economic downturns, state officials who are constrained by external market factors from addressing distributive demands from domestic groups in crisis may find their bedrock constituencies dissolving beneath their feet. Lines of affinity and opposition among social classes and sectors may disappear and emerge again in unlikely combinations. When crises abate, social movements may persist as political actors with novel forms of protest and social mobilization. These new forms of protest and participation may be the most important aspect of economic crisis because they indicate much about the terms upon which citizens in Mexico will engage in public affairs in the twenty-first century.

During the hellish eighteen months following the peso devaluation, the Barzón movement displayed an almost Carnavalesque set of role inversions and unlikely coalition partners. It was a moment when businessmen declared their solidarity with workers against the interests of external investors and when urban retailers marched in protests alongside corn farmers, housewives, and taxi drivers. As an emergency mobilization put together by a mass of people who had been brutally and unexpectedly driven into bankruptcy, the movement did not have indefinite power to detain bank repossessions and force government officials to intervene in markets on behalf of debtors. However, the memory of the movement's raucous public theater and irreverent mobilization may continue to pose something of a liability for neoliberal policy making in the form of a now-popular idea that the distribution of capital and the terms of its use are negotiable by civil society.

Note

1. It is important to note that what is known to the Mexican and foreign media as the Barzón movement actually encompasses two separate organizations that have been somewhat at odds with one another since the fall of 1994. The original Barzón organization of farmers that came to the attention of the Mexican public when it occupied the central plaza in Guadalajara, Jalisco, in the summer of 1993 was headed by Maximiano Barbosa. The Barzón organization profiled here, sometimes known as the new Barzón, arose in the state of Zacatecas and was headed through the period profiled in this article by Juan José Quirino Salas and Alfonso Ramírez Cuellar.

5.7

Planned Development and Women's Power

Cathy A. Rakowski

This study looks at the relative power of women in patriarchal capitalist society in two industries in Venezuela and how planned opportunities led to fewer possibilities for women than men.

D IVERSE FACTORS INFLUENCE women's and men's relative power—defined as control over one's own choices and influence over others—in patriarchal capitalist societies. The most commonly cited factors are directly economic—control over the means of production, surplus production, and income. Other factors include physical force and coercion, political influence, the privilege that accrues to membership in certain social categories (including race, ethnicity, and location), access to social goods (education, health care, housing), and the socially constructed sexual division of labor, gender ideology, and gender relations (Blumberg, 1984; Chafetz, 1991; Eisenstein, 1979; Mackintosh, 1981). For women, economic dependence on men combines with domestic burdens imposed by the sexual division of labor and gender ideology to maintain men's superior power at both the macro level (institutions, laws, customs) and the micro level (household, community) (Blumberg, 1984; Chafetz, 1991: 80–81). Typically, these factors and the resulting power differences between women and men tend to be incorporated in and reproduced by development plans and interventions (Elson, 1992; Mies, 1986; Jaquette, 1990; Papanek, 1990; Tinker, 1990).

First published in *Latin American Perspectives* 85, vol. 22 (2), Sage Publications, Inc. Reprinted with permission from the Latin American Perspectives Collective. Selection from 51–58.

This article considers the potential for women's relative power in Venezuela. It compares the different gendered inpacts of two planned state industries—a steel complex and a forestry concern, both managed by the Corporación Venezolana de Guayana (Venezuelan Guayana Corporation—CVG), a regional development corporation. Both industries were designated the cornerstones of regional development programs and were—at the time of the studies—the most important sources of employment in their respective areas. Ciudad Guayana's steel mill was the cornerstone of a large industrial complex in a new planned city (about 650,000 inhabitants by 1990) and benefited for over thirty years from high levels of state investment and integrated planning (economic, urban, social programs).[1] The other industry—half a million hectares of commercial forest in southern Monagas and Anzoátegui states and related logging and sawmills—is spread across a sparsely populated rural zone, was controlled by three separate state agencies until 1987, received low levels of state investment, and limited itself to corporate planning. Its center of operations was located near Chaguaramas, a town in Monagas State with no more than 2,000 inhabitants in 1990. The two cases were studied at different points in time—1979–1981 for the steel mill and Ciudad Guayana and 1989–1992 for forestry and Chaguaramas. These were peak years of employment for both industries.

This article argues that (1) the industrial complex and Ciudad Guayana have been characterized by a division of labor by sex and a planned structure of opportunities (access to social goods) that promoted female economic dependence and depressed the potential for women's relative power, while (2) forestry and Chaguaramas are characterized by a division of labor by sex and a structure of (mostly unplanned) opportunities that are supportive of female economic independence and increase the potential for women's relative power. Evidence supporting the differential potential for women's relative power is provided by data on employment and income generation, the domestic division of labor and household structure, development plans and policies, rules governing access to social goods such as housing, and macroeconomic and institutional-legal changes between 1981 and 1989. Finally, the relative importance of economic versus noneconomic factors in women's reported decision-making power and independence from male control is assessed.

Theoretical Framework

Blumberg's (1984) general theory of gender stratification holds that in capitalist patriarchal societies relative male/female *economic* power is the most important of all power variables. Economic power is conceptualized in terms of degrees of control over key economic/productive resources—income, land, technology, and other means of production—and surplus production (for the market) generates greater power than subsistence production. Other power variables include education, wage differentials, and occupational stratification. Noneconomic variables are also important and can operate to discount or exaggerate the relative power normally associated with economic factors. For instance, Chafetz argues that definitional power—the ability to impose values, norms, standards of judgment, and situation definitions on others—can play a critical role in inequality and legitimate coercion and bribery to bring into line individuals who deviate from socially assigned statuses and roles (Chafetz, 1991: 80–81). Of particular importance are role definitions that assign production to men and reproduction to women (Mackintosh, 1981; Papanek, 1990). Under capitalism, definitional power accrues to those who have economic power; under patriarchy, it accrues to men. Therefore, men who control key economic resources should have greater relative power than women with similar resources.

Some power variables operate primarily at the micro levels of household and community, others at the macro level. Together they form a "nested" system in which relative power and status "may vary at least somewhat independently of each level . . . [with] more micro levels . . . encompassed within larger also interlinked, macrostructures" (Blumberg, 1984: 48). Change may enter at any level, and a group's relative power and status may improve in one area and deteriorate in another, but control over surplus is more important than control over subsistence, and macro-level factors have greater impact than micro-level factors and may compensate for the lack of key economic resources.

I propose that under certain conditions (e.g., economic crisis), noneconomic power variables may *outweigh* or *counterbalance* control over productive resources as determinants of women's relative power and status or may act as preconditions for access to some productive resources. Likely noneconomic variables could include women's leadership roles, legislative reform, demographic change, and cultural-ideological change (Benería and Feldman, 1992; Development Alternatives with Woman for a New Era [DAWN/MUDAR], 1990; Blumberg, 1991). However, the lower a group's relative economic power, the more likely it is to be oppressed physically, politically, and ideologically (Blumberg, 1984: 75; Chafetz, 1991).

The relative importance of different power variables can be measured through their relation to women's and men's relative autonomy in decision making, particularly in the household and community. Women's relative power should be expressed in their fertility decisions and other life choices such as marriage, divorce, and migration, household budgeting, self-esteem, and struggles over conditions of employment and community quality of life. It may also be reflected in incidents of male violence as men resist women's decision-making autonomy and their own displacement as breadwinners/household heads.

Background: Gender and Economy in Venezuela

Venezuela is a petroleum-producing nation of approximately 20 million people located on the northern coast of South America. It presents an interesting context for a study of women's relative power. Like most Latin American nations, it inherited from Spain a legacy of highly centralized, authoritarian administration, male dominance and a norm of male sexual exploits, and Catholicism, with its reification of motherhood and self-sacrifice. Since independence, middle- and upper-income groups' ideals of male authority and female domesticity have been consecrated in custom and in law. At the same time, they have been contradicted by real patterns of widespread serial monogamy, significant numbers of female-headed households, low self-esteem, sexual violence, and high rates of illegitimacy and paternal abandonment (Montero, 1983; 1990; Barroso, 1991).

Venezuela is interesting also because of the way in which democratization and planning post-1958 have become intertwined with gender and class ideology to influence the content of national and regional plans for promoting economic and social development. Centrist, populist, and paternalistic democratic governments have assumed the role of technocratic coordinator and investor to promote economic growth and diversification. Prior to 1983 (after economic crisis set in) the state also assumed the role of defender of social welfare and distributor of oil wealth to improve the quality of life of lower-income groups (Naím and Piñango, 1984; Lander and Rangel, 1970; Rodwin et al., 1969). Thus, planning is both an ideology (justifying selective investment choices) and a technocratic exercise dominated by economists and technicians. Planners' and politicians' values and notions of appropriate social organization (including stereotypes of women and the poor) have been incorporated into plans (Rakowski, 1989; Peattie, 1981). Only recently have plans shown greater sensitivity to issues of gender, grassroots initiatives, and multiculturalism (Oficina Central de Coordinación y Planeamiento [CORDIPLAN], 1990).

Petroleum has been an important factor in maintaining democracy and financing planning since 1958. The petroleum boom of the 1970s led to rapid urbanization and expansion of education, health care, and employment (Karl, 1987; Mommer, 1986; McCoy, 1986–1987). In particular, women's share of education and employment rose rapidly (Valecillos, 1983). By 1990–1991 women were about 32 percent of the national labor force (40 percent in Caracas), their educational levels differed little from those of men, and they were the majority of college graduates in all professions except veterinary science and engineering (Pulido, 1990; OCEI, 1992). However, occupational segregation remained important; women were concentrated in public employment, especially social services, and in office work, commerce, and personal services. The decline in petroleum revenues post-1978 and the recession of the 1980s had greater negative impacts on women and children than on men (Márquez, 1990; Cartaya and García, 1988; Bethencourt, 1988).

Finally, Venezuela is an interesting case because since 1975 so-called women's issues have gained increasing importance in the political arena and the public eye, resulting in a series of legal reforms since 1982 and support programs for women.[2]

Traditionally, Venezuela's family and gender ideologies legitimated a gendered division of labor and rights in the family (male head and breadwinner, female wife, mother, and homemaker subject to male authority and control). These ideologies have their roots in the Spanish colonial era and influenced development planning and implementation (Rakowski, 1991; Montero, 1983).

Until July 1982, Venezuelan law defined "family" as a stable husband-wife-child unit. Married women—classified as legal minors under the tutelage of husbands—were charged with obeying their husbands and supporting their decisions on children and home (Montero, 1983). Men established the conjugal domicile, managed community property, and granted or denied women the right to enter into contracts and employment. Since men represented the family legally, there were no requirements that both a husband's and a wife's name appear on property titles or bank accounts.[3] Male infidelity (except for outright abandonment and concubinage) could not be used as a cause for divorce, while suspicion of female infidelity was admissible. There were no readily enforceable legal obligations for men to recognize or support children born out of wedlock, and women in consensual (nonlegalized, common-law) relationships had no rights to property or support. The lack of fit between ideology and reality is evidenced by registry and census data showing that, at least since the turn of the century, over half of all children have been born out of wedlock and consensual unions comprise between 30 and 50 percent of all urban unions, often more in rural areas.

The UN's International Women's Decade (1975–1985) and women's increasing visibility in education, employment, politics, labor unions, neighborhood associations, and social movements legitimized attention to women as a group. This contributed to and was reinforced by the sudden increase in the 1980s in the number of women appointed to ministerial posts and higher courts and to alliances across women's groups to promote debate and resolve issues of particular interest to women, including legal equality in the family, job security, equal pay, protective labor legislation, and child care. Venezuelan women's professional associations—especially those of lawyers, journalists, artists, and physicians—also gained strength in this period, and feminist groups proliferated.

Since the reform of the civil code in 1982 this situation has changed. Now women and men are legal adults with equal rights and responsibilities. Married couples manage community property together, establish a domicile through mutual consent, and share legal repesentation of children. Women are free to enter into contracts and employment at will. All children have the right to know and be supported by their fathers and to share in paternal and maternal inheritance. Women in consensual unions for five or more years have the same rights as legal wives (including a share of property), and the law recognizes women's economic contribution to the family through domestic work as well as paid employment. Government and privately sponsored campaigns have sought to "democratize"[4] the family, although programs for poor families and children (e.g., student subsidies) target mothers as recipients of assistance for children. These changes provided the impetus for other legal, administrative, and cultural reforms, including a shift from chapters on "women's issues" in the sixth and seventh national plans to the "gendering" of all chapters and topics in the eighth national plan (CORDIPLAN, 1990).

In sum, the 1970s, a period of economic expansion and prosperity, and the 1980s, a period of debt crisis and impoverishment, were marked by dramatic change in critical macro-level factors that affect gender ideology in general and gender relations at the macro and the micro level.

Planning began in 1959 with the establishment of CORDIPLAN, the national planning agency designated to coordinate planning and investment efforts at the national, regional, and local levels. The Corporación Venezolana de Guayana (CVG) was created in 1960 as a regional development corporation charged with exploiting the natural resources of the vast and sparsely populated region south of the Orinoco River. The CVG's primary objective was the progressive industrialization of natural resources (minerals and hydroelectric potential) as the key to the diversification and decentralization of Venezuela's petroleum-dependent economy (CVG, 1963: 3; Rodwin et al., 1969). To do so, it created an industrial complex and a planned city and coordinated the economic and social activities of other public agencies and the private sector. Although the CVG developed three related plans, one economic, one urban, and one for developing human resources, planning tended to be a technical enterprise controlled by economists (Izaguirre, 1977: 12–13; Peattie, 1981; Rakowski, 1985; 1989; CVG, 1974; 1979). Inputs by sociologists and anthropologists were limited. As a result, social development was subordinated to economic objectives, and social objectives tended to be based on the beliefs and class and gender ideologies of professionals (engineers, planners, managers) and politicians. The CVG's most important industrial projects (out of over 80) are an iron-ore/steel complex, a bauxite-aluminum complex, a series of hydroelectric dams, and a commercial forestry project (with high-tech sawmills and export-oriented multinational wood-processing industries).

In the 1960s and 1970s the CVG assigned women roles in development that were consistent with the gender ideologies of the time. They were to be the wives-mothers-homemakers whose domestic work would replenish the daily strength of male workers. Thus, the "integration of women in development" (also referred to as "the development of women") was defined primarily as the improvement of women's homemaking abilities (Rakowski, 1989). As part of its social plan, the CVG attempted to reinforce the patriarchal nuclear-family ideal (male head and breadwinner, female homemaker) by creating a structure of opportunities and benefits that encouraged female economic dependence and male authority in Ciudad Guayana. Policies and programs included deliberate exclusion of women from nontraditional jobs in industry and construction (the highest-paying jobs); special orientation sessions with the wives, mothers, sisters, and daughters of industrial workers to impress upon them the importance of a peaceful, orderly home environment to male psychological and physical well-being; educational programs to improve homemaking skills; financial incentives for workers to legalize consensual unions and paternity; public housing and credit programs limited to male workers with spouses; and exclusion of women from technical training programs through the late 1970s (Rakowski, 1985; 1989; CVG-Sidor, 1973). Planners expected a resulting patriarchal nuclear family to be the mechanism for promoting proper work attitudes and habits, job stability, and a greater sense of responsibility on the part of modern male industrial workers.

Since 1979, I have studied the CVG, planning, the division of labor between men and women in Ciudad Guayana, nearby rural communities, and selected industries—particularly steel and forestry (subsidiaries of the CVG). The study summarized below focused on the gendered impacts of steel and forestry during their respective boom periods and—in the case of steel—as industry entered a recession. The difference in time frame is important, since for steel it is the period preceding reform of the civil code while for forestry it is well after the reform. In both cases, industries faced persistent financial crises, currency deval-uations, and declining petroleum revenues and were just beginning to experience political pressures to downsize and privatize. . . .

In general, the comparison of the two cases suggests differences in attitude and social-cultural factors as well as in economic opportunities that favor greater relative power for women in the forestry zone. Women were far more likely in 1990 to assume that domestic responsibilities and income generation were com-patible and expected of women. Although both settings were zones of in-migra-tion at the time of the studies, male employment in forestry included a greater proportion of contractual or seasonal activities than did that in Ciudad Guayana. Therefore, although in both settings consensual unions constituted 40–43 per-cent of working-class and low-income unions, the risk of instability or of "sea-sonal" spouses was higher in the forestry zone.[5] Thus, family and relationship factors contributed to women's relative independence.

The relationship among the macro/micro level and economic, social, and definitional variables associated with women's relative power is complex and conditional. Therefore, caution should be exercised in generalizing from the Venezuelan cases. In the cases discussed, the significance of economic variables (such as well-paid and stable employment and type of economic base) for pre-dicting women's decision-making power became clear only when considered in conjunction with social and demographic variables such as migration (changing sex ratios, family structure), the policy environment (broad versus specialized authority of the CVG, legal refom, rules governing social programs), and defini-tional variables (women's roles as mothers and rural leaders, for instance). These cases also revealed the potential for change to be highly selective across different types of variables. In the case of definitional variables, this was clear when women leaders reaffirmed the value of motherhood but expanded it to include women's employment or when the term *head of household* was applied to women who stayed home as well as to breadwinners. Selectivity was present, as well, in changing economic variables such as occupational stratification (stratification in forestry did not mean wage gaps between men and women as it had in steel) or when the demand for home-based enterprises made housing a productive resource. Finally, the Venezuelan cases suggest that noneconomic macro-level variables (such as legal rights and access to housing and to social services) may establish preconditions for women's empowerment in the household and in society. But the importance of these variables is likely to vary according to whether and how they are translated into concrete programs and policies relevant to women's needs and whether women have adequate economic opportunities to meet their needs.

Notes

1. The CVG's programs accounted for approximately 20 percent of all state investment funds from 1963 to 1983 and no less than 10 percent through 1990.

2. Private and public social programs include women's centers with rape and legal counseling, family planning, and training, among others. These programs are found only in large cities.

3. One result was that women often found during divorce proceedings that husbands had already disposed of community property. In other cases, men who had abandoned their families sold the home out from under them or had them forcibly removed. Some men also established a new legal residence without the wife's knowledge, subsequently divorcing her for abandonment.

4. The reform of the civil code was promoted not as a demand for equal rights for women but as necessary to guarantee democracy in Venezuela. The principal author of the reform, Yolanda Poleo de Báez, told me during a 1991 interview that this strategy was the only way to generate widespread support for the reform. As a result, the themes of the reform campaign were "Democracy begins at home" and "How will a child learn to defend democracy if raised in a dictatorship?"

5. It was not uncommon for women respondents to be able to answer few questions about the men they named as their spouses, persons who spent no more than two to four months a year living with them and maintained other housholds elsewhere.

Part VI

⟨══⟩⋈⟩

Case Studies in Socialist Development: Obstacles and Contradictions

THE ATTEMPTS TO TRANSFORM CAPITALISM and bring about socialism in Cuba and Nicaragua have captured the attention of scholars and practitioners everywhere, so it is appropriate to include the selections below, which delve into the problems, struggles, successes, and failures of the experiments in both countries.

The Cuban Revolution came to power in 1959, the Nicaraguan Revolution two decades later. In Cuba, considerable attention was devoted to providing for human needs through a reorganization of agriculture and expansion of the economy beyond sugar production. Participatory democracy was a concern early on, but was difficult to implement in the face of a U.S. embargo and counterrevolutionary activities. These problems and the prospects for democracy in Cuba are analyzed in the essays by Haroldo Dilla Alfonso and Joel Edelstein. In Nicaragua, an initial concern was with elections and representative and popular forms of democracy, but U.S. support of counterrevolutionaries led to disruption of the economy and political instability, until the Sandinistas eventually were defeated in national elections. These developments are analyzed by David Broad, Doug Brown, and David Ruccio.

6.1

Between Utopia and the World Market

Haroldo Dilla Alfonso
Translated by John F. Uggen

This stimulating analysis considers the internal obstacles and contradictions in Cuban development and delves into the implications of integration into the world market and the U.S. embargo on Cuba. These issues are relevant in consideration of socialist development.

I T IS A COMMONPLACE in contemporary Cuban society that the current crisis can be resolved only through daring measures that take into account the various sectors of Cuban social life. Opinions begin to diverge, however, when the discussion touches on exactly what type of action should be undertaken and what weight should be given to economic as opposed to political factors in the policy mix.

A first look would emphasize the economic character of the present crisis (1994), and therefore economic factors assume a privileged role in the debate, with access to technology, markets, and capital becoming if not a sufficient at least a cardinal premise for the survival of socialism. There would be little doubt of the correctness of this position if it were not for the subordinate role played by political factors with respect to the critical need for new rules in the organization and interaction of the various actors in the economy. Following this line of reasoning, Cuba would require both modernization and liberalization, with systematic decentralization of authority, a clearer definition of institutional pro-

First published in *Latin American Perspectives* 83, vol. 21 (4), Sage Publications, Inc. Reprinted with permission from the Latin American Perspectives Collective.

files and roles, more economic autonomy, and the opening of local opportunities for negotiation between economic and social interest groups.

Viewed from another angle, modernization, though clearly indispensable, is insufficient and even counterproductive unless it is accompanied by greater opportunity for popular participation and control—most important because a formalization of the political system in these terms in combination with an economic policy subordinate to the demands of the world market is constantly teetering on the brink of a restoration of capitalism and is far from efficient with respect to the socialist goal of human self-realization in its fullest sense. From the perspective that I will develop here, the basic premise of which is the necessity of salvaging and developing Cuba's patriotic commitment to socialism, politics is the chief protagonist. Every development project has its cost and depends to a great degree for its viability on the forging of a national consensus on the desirability of its objectives through public policies with regard to the acceptance or transformation of values, norms, and beliefs and the creation of a scenario with which the ordinary Cuban citizen can identify.

The Cuban revolutionary program has from the beginning enjoyed a popular consensus that is intimately linked to Cuba's autonomy. During the 1960s, political consensus was supported by the capacity of the revolutionary project to protect the organic values of popular political culture (among them ethics as the governing force of political action, anti-imperialist nationalism, and egalitarianism) through the gradual redistribution of wealth and power in a dynamic relation between the young revolutionary leadership and the popular masses. The 1970s set the stage for the reinterpretation of values and the rearticulation of the political consensus regarding the basis for Cuba's incorporation into the Soviet submarket on favorable terms and the implementation of a model of extensive growth (Carranza, 1992). This permitted not only a considerable increase in levels of personal and social consumption but also an institutionalization whose pivot was the model of paternalistic participation-legitimation (Dilla, 1992).

The first cracks in this model—and also in the scheme of participation legitimation—appeared when external supports began to deteriorate in 1986. It was at this critical juncture that the process of "rectification"—a program containing positive changes but postponing any systematic attention to the economy and the economic adjustments called for by the growing crisis—was initiated. The rectification had insufficient time and even less opportunity to become effective, and its proposals were swiftly buried by the crisis. In 1990 economic growth declined by 3.6 percent, and in the following year it plummeted another 25 percent. Experts estimate that in 1992—when the country functioned at only one-third of the purchasing power it had had in 1989—economic growth declined another 10 percent, and 1993 was predicted to be even worse. To even the most casual observer it was apparent that the internal economy was barely able to provide for its own reproduction. Consequently, at the close of 1990 an emergency program was put into effect that has since become known as the "special period."

The special period was primarily designed to guarantee national survival under extremely difficult internal conditions in an international environment that was severely hostile and characterized by persistent North American aggressiveness against Cuban socialism (Bill Clinton years, 1990s). The battle cry—"Resist!"— that has dominated public discourse roughly reflects the gravity of the situation. There remains little room to imagine any other option. The present dilemma is, as a consequence, how to do so without letting short-term measures mortgage the future of a socialist Cuba.

The Price of Economic Integration into the World Market

The Cuban economy, along with those of the rest of the Third World, is facing what has come to be called "the export challenge," and along with these other economies it must meet this challenge by entering and competing in the international marketplace and, in particular, by developing a dynamic export sector. At the same time, a successful response to this challenge inevitably involves other measures directed at internal growth, higher levels of productivity, the incorporation of scientific and technological advances, and the building of a national consensus to guarantee the sustainability of the project.

The conditions under which Cuba must confront this challenge, however, are disadvantageous and extremely contradictory. In the international arena, the Cuban economy has been wrenched from what had for three decades been its protected markets (1961–1991), and without any other external supports it is facing a world market that is not only extremely competitive and exclusive in economic terms but also politically conditioned by the obsessive hostility of North America. Internally this means a costly process of technological reconversion involving the adoption of "hard" technology and a vast reorganization of the relations between economic actors in the production, distribution, and consumption process—a process that will inevitably have profound political and social consequences. It would not be possible, with the knowledge available, to present a complete analysis of the contradictory transformations that are being produced and will continue to be produced in Cuban society. It is possible, nevertheless, to examine closely some of the more visible manifestations, particularly the new articulations in the processes of production, distribution, and consumption and their impact on the popular sectors, on the redistribution of social power, and on ideological questions.

The designers of Cuba's economic strategy have taken into account the uncommon obstacles that separate Cuba from the world market. Succinctly, it is based on measures such as import substitution and in particular the attainment of substantial self-sufficiency in food, the creation of dynamic new export products, the development of leading-edge technologies, and the capture of finance and technology through incentives for foreign investment (Carranza, 1992).

Because of these measures, various constitutional amendments, both legal and operational, have been implemented to open up opportunities for foreign investment and facilitate the response of Cuban economic institutions. In this latter regard, steps have been taken to decentralize the decision-making process and to extend market mechanisms, particularly in areas linked to the external sector. However, none of these measures has involved the proposal of a system of direction and economic planning—such systematic organization has officially been considered impossible since the onset of the crisis—and there is little doubt that any such proposal will need to transcend the time period in which it is conceived and its originally intended scope.

The more dynamic areas of the economy controlled either totally or partially by foreign investors or even under state ownership must adjust to the new rules of the game dictated by the market. This will require substantial change in the organization of production, distribution, and consumption. By the same token, since any economy is a system of communicating components, this change will have repercussions on the rest of the national economy, which will either be forced to succumb or to pursue competitive efficiency on the world level and as a consequence to adopt the same technological and organizational models as those of the mixed and private economies.

A major and more significant impact, one that implies significant alterations in the nature and relations of the economic factors of production, is on the productive matrix itself. This is the case in part because the transformations that the entrepreneurial sector must undergo and that state administrators must adapt to as the number of foreign investors increases augment their power (mainly because of their relations with the world capitalist market) but also rob them of the paternalistic protection of the central government.[1] Moreover, because these transformations are manifested at the intraenterprise level by the emergence of a scenario lacking the no less paternalistic labor legislation of the 1980s that was a component of the labor consensus, they cannot help but create a new contradiction—not necessarily between capital and labor (which can be mediated by the socialist state) but in relation to the socialist state itself, which requires high levels of accumulation and conducts its activities in terms of technological dictates and production incentives that demand the intensive use of labor. A scenario of this nature inevitably means the transfer of power in favor of business elites and the obsolescence of many of the mechanisms, practices, and opportunities for participation that characterized the previous paternalistic mode. As a consequence there is clearly a need for a process of adjustment and institution building capable not only of absorbing the emerging contradictions but also of providing the labor sectors with new mechanisms of power, action, and negotiation in accordance with the new reality.

This contradictory projection has not been absent from the various projects of enterprise "improvement" that have been developing in the country, for example, the renovation projects that have been implemented in some of the military industries explicitly informed by a systematic evaluation of the experiences and models of the developed economies of Western Europe and Japan. Their innovative elements are apparent, for example, in the more intensive use of technology and labor, in the introduction of a more flexible system of organization of work, and in production incentives and efficiency (Casas Regueira et al., 1990).

The proposal of a "participation by objectives" model is certainly an improvement on previous practices, which were marked by bureaucratic formalism and paternalism, but the question remains whether the rebuilding of a labor consensus based on satisfactory wages and participatory opportunities marked by criteria of technical rationality will be sufficient, given the transfer of ever-increasing power to the business sectors (state or foreign private), without losing sight of strategic socialist goals. If this course is chosen, it may be possible to persuade Cuban workers to sing a hymn to business enterprise every morning with sincere enthusiasm, but by no means will this lead to the building of a participatory democracy in which each individual is an effective participant in the most important decision-making processes (for a more thorough discussion of this topic, see Dilla, 1992).[2]

Another of the contradictory obstacles that arise from this situation is related to employment. The achievement of full employment was a political and social victory of the revolutionary program and a basic component of the political consensus. In the absence of a sufficiently dynamic economy, however, full employment can be achieved only at the price of the extension of underemployment or disguised unemployment and in the long run seriously threatens productive efficiency. According to a well-documented study by García (1990: 29–38), around 1987 each Cuban worker linked to direct production worked for himself and for four other persons within a framework of low productivity and a system that guaranteed social services and subsidized consumption for all citizens. This situation is becoming increasingly incompatible with the new modalities of accumulation and economic reproduction. On the one hand, economic restructuring demands readjustment of existing patterns of employment and the elimination of excess workers, whether through internal rationalization of the businesses themselves or through the simplification of large bureaucratic organizations performing functions that have become irrelevant under the new conditions. On the other hand, the state is losing its capacity to create new employment opportunities and to satisfy the demands of new entrants into the labor market. And even though rates of unemployment remain low—largely because of the assistance policies of the state—this poses a challenge that was totally unknown in Cuban society for three decades of revolutionary life: unemployment has increased and will continue to increase to the point of becoming structural both economically and socially.

The consequences are predictable. In the first place, a partial reversal of the sociopolitical gains achieved in the previous decades can be expected. This means that measures will need to be aimed at preventing poverty and the marginalization of the affected population, but more important is its probable selective effect on the most vulnerable sectors, especially young people just entering the workforce and women. Cuban women have played a very active role in the production process and in the service sector, and in some of the more strategic sectors, such as health and education, they hold the majority of positions. At the same time, many of the strongholds of female employment—bureaucratic and secretarial positions—are precisely the ones that will most likely be affected in any rationalization of the workforce. Women will also be more affected by the increasing difficulty of the reproduction of daily life. It is no coincidence that, according to some academic estimates, the female component of unemployment has grown from 53 percent in 1985 to 60 percent in 1990. Although the most serious effects of unemployment can be softened by political commitment to social justice via subsidies or other economic and social programs such as those proposed at the Fourth Congress of the Communist Party of Cuba (PCC, 1991), this is a problematic option from the standpoint of economic rationality and is consequently limited in scope unless accompanied by measures aimed at stimulating employment and by private initiatives that, without affecting fundamental socialist principles, fulfill social goals.

This last consideration takes us directly to the sensitive topic of the informal sector of the Cuban economy, a sector of production and services outside the official economic sphere and therefore difficult to measure and to control. This sector has had a history as erratic as official policy itself. The years immediately after 1959 were receptive to small producing or commercial enterprises, but since 1968 policy has varied radically. Within the framework of a period officially known as the "utopian," it aimed at eliminating the material remnants of capitalism and advancing toward communism. Except for small agricultural producers, who had commercial relations only with the state, and a few cooperatives of motor vehicle owners, all of the small and medium private sector was taken over by the state. It was not until the introduction of the SDPE in the 1970s that steps were taken to permit private enterprise in some service and production activities by self-employed persons and the establishment of a direct relationship between small agricultural producers and consumers through the creation of the "peasant free market." This opening was closed a decade later during the period of rectification, with the peasant free market being included on the list of "commercial excesses" that needed to be corrected. The Fourth Party Congress, on its own, retraced its previous steps and, in conjunction with a pledge to respect the existence of cooperative and individual property in the agricultural and ranching sectors (though not with respect to the peasant free market), declared itself in favor of regulating self-employment activities, especially in the minor service sector and in "others which may develop, thereby assuring that they offer their services to society within the limits and conveniences which the circumstances of the special period impose and according to the requirements for the construction of socialism" (PCC, 1991: 66, my translation).

Of course, the Congress's declaration regarding the informal sector was a response specifically to its dramatic growth in direct relation to the extreme disparity between a very restricted supply of goods and services and greatly increased demand. The value of the production of this informal sector and of the underground economy on which it is based is very difficult to calculate, but tentative estimates have suggested a monetary figure similar to that of the formal sector and regularly involving somewhat more than a half a million persons. This situation is the source of numerous problems. Above all, the informal sector and the underground economy that serves as its base of support should not be idealized. In a certain sense this market satisfies a classic demand of orthodox monetarism in the Third World by placing a depreciated workforce in contact with a speculative and dollarized market of consumer goods and services. A large part of this underground economy is nurtured by illicit activities of various kinds and serves not simply as a mechanism of income redistribution but also as a mechanism for its concentration in the hands of a group of intermediaries and speculators who thus enjoy a highly predatory type of original accumulation. Any kind of political opening toward the informal sector will entail considerable risks in areas such as the use of the more highly trained elements of the labor force and the distribution of income. It is scarcely necessary to point out the global—including ideological—impact of this situation on Cuban society and the political implications of the growth and consolidation of a segment of the population that is economically independent and organically linked to the rules of the marketplace.

For these reasons, the informal sector—which has become a structural feature of the society as well—requires a type of policy that is not limited to the traditional oscillation between repression and tolerance. What is envisioned is a strategy that will both integrate the informal sector through resource allocation, prices, credit, and other controls (including repression when agreed-upon societal norms are transgressed) and fully realize its potential social function with regard to the creation of employment and the satisfaction of the basic necessities of daily life for all citizens.

The expansion and inevitable acceptance of the informal market as a component of the Cuban economy is only one facet of the restructuring of the politics of consumption. As we have seen, one of the most pressing immediate problems is excess liquidity resulting from the imbalance between increased demand and restricted supply. A project of economic takeoff can succeed only if it has previously managed to reduce liquidity to manageable limits. Numerous mechanisms can be employed to this end, but in the long run they are reduced to affecting either supply or demand. Beyond the shadow of a doubt, sustained increase in supply is the most attractive and advantageous route in political and social terms, but it is also the least likely in the midst of a crisis like the one that currently affects the national economy. Consequently, the only recourse is reducing demand, which means a real subversion not only of traditional patterns of consumption but also of the ideological premises that have sustained them.

A cardinal principle of the politics of consumption ever since the 1960s has been the maintenance of very low prices for the basic basket of necessities. Since the subsequent 1970s this has been combined with a market of excess supply but controlled retail prices. Prices adjusted to the interaction of supply and demand were found only in particular areas such as the previously mentioned peasant free market and the informal sector, and here to a very moderate degree. This meant very heavy subsidies that created budgetary and internal financial deficits.

No even-handed evaluation could overlook the virtues of such policies, which, in combination with the extension of health, education, and social welfare programs, protected Cuban society from the extremes of poverty and social marginalization. But at the same time, long-term subsidization on this scale is not sustainable, and economic takeoff requires its modification. Leaving to one side the ethical-ideological implications of this, one must not forget that Cuban wages are very low (precisely one of the attractions for foreign investment, given the monetary exchange rates currently in force), and consequently a considerable part of the population (according to extraofficial estimates close to 80 percent having a monthly per capita income of less than 125 pesos) is vulnerable to any economic adjustment based on a more active role of prices, even if implemented gradually and with compensatory mechanisms.

The inevitable transformation of the existing system of consumption into a considerably less harmonious "buyer and seller" relationship means a change in the role of the state in this area, improvement of mechanisms of price control, and different kinds of protection for the lower-income sectors of the population. It will also require a more active role for consumers and the creation by them of sociopolitical spaces that are inherently their own: residential communities and local governments. The existing mechanisms for the articulation of demands, either collectively or individually, have often resulted in institutional initiatives designed to satisfy basic necessities and to resolve the problems of daily life. In the new context that is opening up, steps must be taken to stimulate autonomous initiatives by consumers and greater self-management of community activities.

The Political Dimension

The repeated reference here to the political and ideological consequences of these measures reflects the political-ideological density of Cuba's socialist project. A decade ago the key paradigm was a "true socialism," idealized and considered superior and irreversible, along with a set of other values—nationalism, patriotism, internationalism—organic to popular political culture. Today (1994) the paradigm of "true socialism" no longer exists, and for the ordinary citizen few doubts remain about the supposed superiority and irreversibility not of socialism as a goal (which is perfectly sustainable) but of the experiments east of the Berlin Wall, which were only a mythological construct. At the same time, national reality implies a sequence of ideological transformations such as that represented by the shift of a particular treatise on foreign investment from a favorite target of anti-imperialist rhetoric to a positive option in only five years' time or by the contradiction between the principle of the superiority of a planned socialist economy and the recognition that this economy is in crisis and is increasingly financed by economic actors directly connected to the world capitalist market and therefore beyond the control of state planning. Even from the most optimistic perspective it is clear that we are dealing with information overload.

None of this means that Cuban socialism has exhausted its political or ideological arsenal or that it can ignore this arsenal. Far from it; political and ideological resources are more important than ever, but their effectiveness lies in a direct relationship to the capacity of the system to produce a new discourse and a new political practice, making the call to "resist" an invitation not simply to a holocaust or to inertia but to a new articulation of the national consensus based on participatory and pluralistic foundations. In summary, what is needed is a substantial change in the bipolar relation between politics and ideology such that the former assumes a more determinate role in the production of the latter. This was not the case in the experiments with "true socialism," in which preestablished ideology produced sacred political canons.

Of course, criticisms of the notion of a democratizing and participative experiment in contemporary Cuba abound. Along these lines, for example, there is some support for the idea that moments of crisis have never been fertile ground for serious democratic experiments. In fact, recent world history indicates that the nations that have most successfully met the "export challenge," whatever their ideology, have experienced the spread of authoritarianism and repression—a political price that, from the technocratic point of view, may be considered irrelevant in light of the positive economic results.

At the same time, it should be recalled that the geopolitical reality represented by North American hostility toward Cuba has today become the principal obstacle to the development of democracy, particularly if we take into account that what is really at stake is national independence from the only surviving superpower in world politics. No political strategy in Cuba would be truly democratic if it did not implicitly recognize the exclusive right of the Cuban people to decide their own destiny for themselves without foreign intervention or imposition.

Even taking these adverse circumstances into account, however, the construction of a pluralistic participative democracy seems a precondition for patriotic resistance and for the articulation of a consensus about a path that seems full of obstacles and sacrifices. Probably the most obvious message of the fall of bureaucratic Eastern European socialism has been the necessity to reinterpret the relationship between democracy and governability in a socialist context, recognizing that only the expansion of democracy can ensure the stability of the system. In times in which increase in participation seems irrelevant to the reproduction of capitalism (very dramatically so in the underdeveloped South) and the very term "liberal democracy" has its internal contradictions, the opposite dilemma for a socialist project aims at its superiority as the matrix of a genuinely participative democracy. As a consequence, the capacity of Cuban socialism to guarantee its governability and continuity is directly related to the extent of its democratic construction. In terms of the conceptual framework developed by Therborn (1987: 119), this would amount to the avoidance of a disruption of the relation between qualification and subordination whose stability is vital to the reproduction of any social aggregation, its interruption producing either revolution or resignation.

A first premise of this construction is inevitably the decentralization of political power—a ubiquitous and vulgar theme that has often been reduced to a kind of mercantilist economicism. Certainly it is difficult to conceive of a practical process of decentralization, territorial or functional, that does not involve market relations and even the privatization of certain sectors of the economy, particularly where the public sector has been prominent and inefficient. I have pointed to indications of both the extension of the market and privatization in contemporary Cuba, and these may bring considerable advantages with regard to the creation of a competitive framework that will stimulate the mobilization of resources, improvement in the quality of services, and the production and circulation of more dynamic flows of information between sellers and buyers. This is far from the acceptance of mercantilist-privatizationist dogma, however, and it is important to bear in mind the negative consequences—atomization, the erosion of solidarity, an increase in social and regional inequality, and, as Magdoff and Sweezy (1981) pointed out, the dissemination of criteria different from those that of necessity govern a project as complex and multidimensional as the consolidation of a socialist society. It is precisely in this context that economic planning stands out as a key element of the consensus on the objective of economic growth and social development as a function of the strategic aims of the system.

Cuban socialism cannot abandon the idea that economic development is inseparable from economic planning. Only this scenario can guarantee growth and efficiency under socially optimal conditions. This does not, however, mean confronting the mercantilist proposal with one of centralist bureaucratic bent— creating a choice between, as Lukacs (1989: 39) put it, "the substance of Stalinist methods or the introduction of those in force in the West." The challenge to Cuban socialism lies in showing that between the two extremes may be numerous variations of decentralized planning that are pluralistic and technically and democratically rationalistic, that involve the processing of market signals, and that employ a transparent network of administrative and political circuits and relations of cooperation and competition. Such a scenario would seem to be the most propitious for making decentralization an effective framework for empowering the ordinary citizen—as producer and as consumer—and not simply in a transfer of attributions and functions to bureaucratic and technocratic elites at the level of the enterprise and of government.

On a larger scale, however, decentralization can be initiated only administratively. Scarcely attainable under conditions of subordination to the utilitarian criteria of efficiency, whether governed by the rules of central planning or by the market, it cannot be the distinctive element of the Cuban socialist project. Decentralization therefore calls for the development of popular participation in a framework of increasing self-management, greater autonomous dynamism of civilian society, an expansion of political communication and information at the expense of any monopoly of the production process, and, consequently, the strengthening of conscious social responsibility and the identification of individuals with their opportunities for political participation, whether these be in the workplace, in schools or study centers, or in residential arrangements. And it is precisely this context of decentralization-socialization of power that is the appropriate one for the achievement of what has been missing in Cuban politics: the maturation of a pluralism capable of recognizing the diversity and autonomy of the subject/participants and consequently of understanding conflict as an opportunity for the creation of consensus.

From a logical point of view the problem would seem to be simple: because every society is diverse—made up of different classes, genders, generations, races, and so on—public democratic activity can only be expressed pluralistically. Politically the matter is much more complex because of the uses and abuses to which the concept has been subject, starting with the frequent opposition of liberal political models and "true socialism." One of the most common theoretical vulgarizations in contemporary political sociology is the indiscriminate identification of the pluralist tradition with liberalism when in fact liberalism has manifested itself in only one of its many possible forms: the pluralism that is an active ingredient of a market economic model (MacPherson and Midgley, 1987). Because of this and also because of the political imperatives of socialist or marxist governments in power, important ideological sectors of Marxism have condemned pluralism as a type of liberal perversity. In the case of the Cuban Revolution this situation was also historically conditioned. Although even from the first years political differences existed with regard to particular sectors—the case of women is illustrative—it is undoubtedly true that unity around the concept of the "people" seemed an essential guarantee of the revolutionary agenda and of the defense of national sovereignty against North American aggression. Three decades later this unity continues to be vital, but the political cost of the forced construction of a false consensus cannot be ignored. And in any case it is unlikely that a democratic socialism can be constructed without a pluralist focus or emphasis that is more in tune with the social complexity and diversity that characterize Cuban society.

The intention here is not to reduce the pluralist goal to a multiparty system. As the old refrain goes, confusing the present with the future is more costly in politics than in grammar, and in the Cuban present the introduction of multi-party politics could result in the creation of conditions favorable to the artificial counterrevolutionary currents backed by North American influence and by a Cuban-American community led by an extreme right that dreams of a kind of Versaillian revenge for the Paris Commune. But beyond the short-range question of governability it should be asked whether a multiparty system is indeed the necessary next step in the construction of participative democracy, taking into account not only its meager results in the more advanced liberal democracies themselves but also the Cuban experience of other forms of consensus and Cuban acceptance of the one-party system as the expression of the national will.

Avoiding these well-trodden paths presents a challenge to Cuban socialism, however, with regard to the creation of an institutionalized and participatory democracy based on a one-party system and the requirement that this party allow for more real autonomy of civil society and incorporate all of the cultural and ideological diversity of Cuban society—in short, that it become a Party of the Cuban Nation articulated around a platform of social justice, national inde-pendence, and effective popular participation. Of course I am speaking here of a path that is difficult and full of possibilities for error. In the midst of the neolib-eral euphoria and given the possibility of capitalist restoration symbolized by the fall of the Berlin Wall, it is worthwhile to remember the invitation of Marguerite Duras (impossible to refuse) to "advance, advance more than ever." Certainly this must be a goal located in the stars, but let us remember that it is precisely because of the loftiness of its goals that the socialist ideal has been able to survive the wrath of its detractors, the blows and misfortunes of history, and the incom-petence of its practitioners to remain a viable political alternative.

Notes

1. The relations between business and the central govenment will be omitted here because of space limitations. It should be pointed out, however, that they constitute a central point of the economic restructuring and have profound political and socal impli-cations. By the same token, the fate of the random decentralization that is taking place in the country could produce an informalization of interenterprise relationships, particularly where central planning has lost ground.

2. A case in point is the experience of the Cuban-Spanish hotel Sol Palmeras. The Spanish manager refused to acknowledge the existence of the union until he was per-suaded to do so by the local political authorities. A few months later the investor declared to the Cuban press that the recognition of the union had been a success because, "being well structured, the union and emulation constitute the driving force behind all activity" (*Granma*, 1991). Such a consensus between union and management is unsettling.

6.2

The Future of Democracy in
Cuba: Debates

Joel C. Edelstein and Others

This position essay raises questions about old and new paradigms of political and economic participatory democracy in Cuba. Responses by important scholars of Cuba follow.

THE EXPERIENCE OF LATIN AMERICA, including Cuba, clearly demonstrates that multiparty elections are no guarantee of democracy. The Cuban leadership rejects them in classical Leninist terms and asserts its determination that the counterrevolution not be given any such opportunity to establish itself as open elections would present. It also stresses that, especially in the present crisis, even the appearance of division could invite armed U.S. intervention. My discussions with people on the island suggest that the majority of Cubans agree. However, some Cubans committed to the revolutionary project maintain that the election of a few counterrevolutionaries would be harmless.

The liberal argument for elections is hopelessly abstract because it is not grounded in the needs of the Cuban political economy. Although changes were made possible by the constitutional reforms and the new electoral law, it would be far too much to ask that a practice that advances the functions of representation, negotiation and consensus building among diverse interests, and accountability be created by law alone. Law has a very important role, but it can only be played within a paradigm that will accommodate consensus building. The 1993

First published in *Latin American Perspectives* 87, vol. 22 (4), Sage Publications, Inc. Reprinted with permission from the Latin American Perspectives Collective. Selection from 9–18, 21–42.

election took place under the terms of the new electoral law, born of the Fourth Congress of the Communist Party. However, its context was the paradigm in effect since the 1970s, created in large measure to address the needs of a revolutionary project that has pursued the socialist transformation of a dependent capitalist society.

My examination of the problem of democracy in Cuba proceeds from three points: (1) There is inherent in the revolutionary project a gap between short-term and medium-term interests of individuals and social sectors, on the one hand, and long-term socialist development, on the other. It is this gap that gave rise to the economic and political centralization characteristic of the prevailing paradigm. Centralization was necessary at the outset of the revolution, when its advantages outweighed its unavoidable deficiencies. (2) As a result of both the social development achieved by the revolution and the realities of the global political economy, centralization is no longer viable. A new paradigm that reduced the gap between individual or group interests and socialist development might obviate the need for it. (3) This new paradigm must address the strong tendency of culture and politics to reflect property relations. Power over the means of production through either de jure ownership or de facto control translates into political power. The political arrangements actually available to a given social formation at a particular point in time are determined by the viability of various forms of property. This, in turn, is determined by the particular requirements of the productive activities that prevail in that society and the level of social and political development of its people. A broad distribution of real, direct control over the means of production is most likely to sustain a democratic politics. If that is not feasible, the only democratic alternative is not socialist but a social democracy in which the dominance of concentrated property and market relations is mitigated only by the power of an exceptionally strong and independent workers' political organization.

Democracy, Elections, and Paradigms

The concept of democracy operative in the program and pronouncements of the Cuban Revolution in the 1950s was based on representation through elections. This concept of democracy was appropriate for a project of reformist capitalism based on a broad coalition of class forces, including the patriotic bourgeoisie, in behalf of *los humildes* and national independence. Between 1959 and 1962 the bourgeoisie went into opposition and left the island, and the revolution became the project of workers, peasants, and important elements of the middle sectors. The understanding of democracy was transformed by the historical leadership to another formula not based on institutions. (This transition is examined closely in Edelstein, 1975.) The leadership asserted that an attempt to construct political institutions at that point would be premature. Rather, the degree of democracy was measured by the output of government policy—a political system being democratic to the extent that government policies were oriented toward the benefit of the broad majority, without regard to its institutional arrangements. In this sense, democracy became synonymous with equality, social justice, and development of the economic capacity to meet the needs of society, and these became a central theme in the bargain between the people and the state and a basis of the legitimacy of the political system. Within this conception, democracy exists when the needs of the population are satisfied. When they cannot be satisfied, democracy is found in the equality of sacrifice.

Representation implies that portions of the population present what they perceive to be their particular interests. It requires spaces in which such interests can be formulated without undue influence by central authority, means by which these interests can be articulated, and institutional structures in which they can be asserted and negotiated. However, the paradigm of the revolutionary project has emphasized the primacy of the long-term societal goal of socialist transformation. This interest has generally been given precedence over the immediate interests of particular sectors. Following the hardships of the years leading up to the 1970 harvest and the disorganization of the economy created by that enormous effort to produce 10 million tons of sugar, the nation faced great difficulties. In that instance, the leadership began to acknowledge the existence of immediate interests less than societal in scope. This acknowledgment was based on a previously deemphasized concept that people give greater attention to that which affects them directly. State paternalism came under attack, and community initiative was encouraged in plus-work and other plans for communities to meet their needs by their own labor, with materials provided by the state. Some local decisions such as the allocation of housing were given over to workers' assemblies to avoid the negative consequences of leaving these decisions in the hands of centralized authority. This recognition of interests less than societal in scope then declined until the concept of representation received renewed emphasis in the 1992 constitution.

Centralization and the Construction of Socialism on a Base of Dependent Capitalism

Cuba's relations with the Soviet Union played a role in the development of the paradigm still in effect in Cuba, but at a deeper level this paradigm is a response to a fundamental problem. While some of the socialist revolutions of the present century might be understood as the product of the contradictions of imperialism on a global scale, none has been the result of contradictions of advanced capitalism *within the social formation in which socialist revolutionaries have gained state power.*

At the time of the victory over the dictatorship, Cuba was a dependent capitalist country, enmeshed in an imperialist system that seemed bound to continue to reproduce itself. Cuba produced and exported sugar because it could do so at a lower cost than other countries. It produced little else because it lacked the capital plant and equipment and the skills and experience to do so at a cost below that of imported goods and commodities. Giving private producers the freedom to pursue profit in a competitive market would only perpetuate the pattern of the past. To develop a comparative advantage in other kinds of production would require enormous investment not only in imported technology and machinery but also in human resources, in education and training, and in the creation of a culture comfortable with science and technology. Moreover, the process would be slow, and it would be painfully wasteful of resources because a lack of knowledge and experience would inevitably lead to endless costly mistakes. Finally, because Cuba's level of labor productivity was low, the economic surplus potentially available to invest would be small, and the sacrifice of current consumption to make it possible would be correspondingly great.

Thus, the heritage of dependent capitalist development established a huge gap between the immediate material interests of individuals and sectors of the population and the project of socialist development. The economic transformation needed to create a solid base for national sovereignty and prosperity necessarily would be long and hard, and it would be accompanied by a strong tendency toward the pursuit of individual and group interest, undermining the national project. Moreover, the acute nature of the external threat required that the national interest be paramount. In the early years, this orientation was especially important given Cuba's history of engagement with imperialism.

Against these hard realities, the revolutionary project could be pursued only with an exceptional belief in the power of human will and determination to overcome objective circumstances. Leninist centralization appeared to provide the levers to enable dedicated revolutionaries to lead and direct society in breaking free from the bonds of Cuba's history and to establish the hegemony of the revolutionary socialist project. Taking command of the economy through centralized planning could potentially bring about the diversification and industrialization needed to achieve true economic and political sovereignty. A Leninist political structure—a vanguard party with disciplined cells throughout all the institutions of public life, operating in part to direct mass organizations which incorporated the vast majority of the population—could mobilize the people in the unified pursuit of the national cause that was needed to overcome the challenge of a very real external enemy.

At least in societies in which exchange predominates, voluntary behavior that substantially contradicts immediate material interests is unusual. There may be individuals whose identity is bound up with such behavior. A crisis, such as war or natural disaster, may induce a majority of individuals to perceive the support of collective needs as their highest immediate interest, but this perception is necessarily temporary and tenuous. Pursuit of a long-term or collective interest at the sacrifice of immediate interests disposes us to look for a reason to abandon the sacrifice. We share a tendency to accept and believe information and analysis that support our immediate interests. For example, we may be drawn to conclude that the effort cannot succeed, that sacrifice will achieve no useful purpose. (This is not a departure from accepted social values but only an assessment that they are unattainable.)

The effort to induce sustained behavior in support of long-term or collective goals requires education, persuasion, reinforcement of the importance of doing it—and some promise of success. Consensus is needed because at least the acquiescence, if not the fully voluntary cooperation, of the large majority is required. It can be readily undermined by a noncooperating minority promoting cynicism or asserting the existence of an alternative to cooperation if not actually legitimating noncooperation. Those who avoid sacrifice are exploiting those who do cooperate. This can become an additional reason to believe that the goals cannot be achieved and that sacrifice, if it achieves anything, is merely improving the lot of the noncooperators.

A Leninist form of political organization provides an institutional structure oriented toward the creation and maintenance of this sometimes tenuous consensus. The vanguard is to see clearly and share a disciplined commitment to societal goals. Cells throughout institutions are to promote these goals and to shape the articulation of sectoral interests as subordinate to the national project. This party is to organize supportive communications media and to suppress those that would undermine the consensus and present an alternative. It is to mobilize the people to participate in activities that educate experientially and build identification.

To summarize, when socialist revolutionaries achieve state power in a dependent capitalist society formed by imperialism, the project of socialist development necessarily faces difficulties that call forth both economic and political centralization. In the economic realm, a market economy operating on an economic calculus will tend to reproduce itself, resisting transformation and diversification as well as equality. Politically, pluralism will tend to encourage and reify divisions among diverse sectoral interests as well as conflicts between immediate sectoral interests and the long-term goal of socialist transformation.

Inadequacy of the Centralized Economic Paradigm

These problems of building socialism on a dependent capitalist base are not addressed by prescriptions for democratization that call for unrestrained pluralism; they cannot be resolved by elections alone. Nor is the centralized paradigm viable any longer, and indeed, it may no longer be necessary.

The experience of many societies that have adopted centralization points to both advantages and limits to the centralized paradigm in the economic realm. In the stage of extensive development, centralization serves to redirect and mobilize material resources and labor toward economic transformation, capturing and investing the available economic surplus. In this stage, the degree of efficiency in the use of resources is less important than setting idle resources and labor in motion and diversifying the economy. Moreover, the capacity of centralization to distribute consumption more equitably than an economy driven by the market provides an opportunity to weaken class divisions and increase social mobility.

With the completion of resource mobilization and the transition to the stage of intensive development, the deficiencies of the centralized paradigm become more important. A high rate of investment at the expense of current consumption and a relatively low level of productivity due to waste and inefficiency combine to create a tendency toward excess liquidity. At best, workers are rewarded on the basis of the quality and duration of their individual contributions to production. Too often, the value of this individual effort is lost because of problems in central planning or in enterprise management or a lack of supplies, intermediate goods, electric power, or other resources essential to production. Consequently, wages and salaries paid for work done exceed the value of the goods and services actually produced. When resulting enterprise deficits are covered by central planners, excess liquidity is increased, and the incentive for workers or managers to focus attention on maximizing efficiency and quality is attenuated.

When there is more currency in circulation than there are goods and services available for purchase, a shortage economy is created. Political dynamics tend to limit the use of wage and price policies to maintain monetary balance (Nove, 1983). When consumers accumulate pesos because they cannot find goods they need or want, they tend to purchase what is available regardless of quality. This only adds to the deficiencies of centralization with respect to quality control in producer as well as consumer goods.

In addition, the centralized paradigm is well suited to promoting high-priority projects. However, because it does not provide space or resources for the development of small enterprises to serve the needs of large primary state enterprises, the centralized economy lacks flexibility to adapt to changing conditions and technologies.

At least in the extensive stage of development, the centralized paradigm is capable of producing a rate of economic growth sufficient to improve living conditions and offset the tendency toward excess liquidity. Once the economy begins its transition to the intensive stage, in which efficiency is of critical importance, the weaknesses of centralization become more visible. For Cuba, the situation was obscured somewhat by favorable trade relations, including preferential prices. Also, Cuba functioned primarily within an economic bloc with other societies coping with similar difficulties. Economic centralization is, however, inadequate to provide for continued growth under conditions of reincorporation into the global economy.

In response to the economic crisis, the 1992 constitutional reforms have recognized all forms of property. Foreign private enterprise has been introduced, especially in a dramatic expansion of tourism. Since the parliamentary election of February 1993, individual enterprise *(por cuenta propia)* has been legitimated and a major new cooperativization initiated in agriculture. The dollar has become the de facto basis, if not means, of exchange outside the state sector and has since been recognized in law.

These measures have departed from the centralized paradigm with respect to foreign private capital and to the greater autonomy of Cuban enterprises that relate directly to the world economy. While they have had positive results, the dynamics of the internal economy seem not to have been greatly affected. Both the legislation for the expansion of the cooperative sector and its implementation seem to conform to the earlier paradigm, and I am unaware of significant changes in the rest of the state sector. The most visible attention appears to be directed toward circulation, in particular, the critical problem of excess liquidity.

The loss of trade and preferential prices, the U.S. blockade, and the reincorporation into the global economy of a domestic economy with many difficulties have resulted in negative economic growth. Failure of the state sector to provide for the desires and even some of the basic needs of the population has created a large underground economy. Moreover, the insufficiency of the state sector has led to increasing illicit private appropriation of commodities from it as well as withdrawal of labor in favor of private activities. The economic contradiction is also expressed in a tendency toward corruption because the real conditions of everyday life do not coincide with the reproduction of socialist values, assumptions about the nature of social reality, or ways of analyzing and understanding the world. The leadership teaches that solidarity and sacrifice by all are necessary for the survival of the nation, and the great majority does make sacrifices. Still, the effort to satisfy the immediate needs of the family calls forth the self-concerned mentality of a black market without law or morality.

To revitalize the domestic economy and become internationally competitive, Cuba needs the incentives, the micro-efficiencies, and the discipline that use of a market can provide. A link must be established between the quality and efficiency actually achieved in production and the rewards received for contributions to production.

Inadequacy of the Centralized Political Paradigm

The first years of the 1960s were culminated by the tasks of consolidation and defense. As the upper classes and elements of the middle sectors joined the United States in opposition to the land reform and the urban reform, the revolution became radicalized in order to survive. It defined itself as a project of workers and peasants under the direction of the historical leadership. The long-term goal of socialist development took precedence over short-term needs. Sectoral interests had no legitimacy.

Until 1990, more or less, the leadership sought to obviate the need for the assertion of particular short-term interests by preventing the formation of a variety of coherent classes. With the exception of cooperatives in agriculture and a small number of individual producers, all property was state property. A proliferation of vehicles for popular participation was created at the local level, with strategic decisions reserved for central authority. Opinions expressed in a multitude of consultative meetings held by the mass organizations gave the leadership access to the views of various sectors. These views were considered as the leadership sought to harmonize claims and adapt them to the long-term needs of society. This "consensus" was promoted among the people by the party and the mass and social organizations.

The centralized model has enabled the leadership to act quickly and decisively to meet the many challenges that the revolution has faced. Its potential weaknesses with respect to representation and accountability have mattered little because the attention of the population has been focused on survival of the nation and because of the obvious ability and the incorruptible commitment to the nation and the revolution of the historical leadership. In addition, beginning in the mid-1970s there were gradual improvements in the conditions of daily life. The revolution's legitimacy has been maintained through its achievements with respect to equality, health, education, and secure employment, national sovereignty and dignity, and an active role for Cuba in international solidarity. Moreover, in the past, legitimacy did not require direct representation in policy making. The population socialized before 1959 was formed within an authoritarian political culture in which opportunities for participation on the part of the working class and the peasantry did not exist. In addition, a majority had been denied formal education beyond the primary grades. They readily identified with and supported the government under which they benefited.

Because of many changes in Cuba and in the international environment, the centralized political paradigm is no longer adequate. Economic changes introduced to overcome the economic crisis have opened the way for many different interests to arise in addition to the socioeconomic differentiations of centralized socialism. These include workers in the state sector who have no access to dollars and therefore have seen their pay effectively reduced to the social wage[1] by the loss of purchasing power of the peso. Workers in low-level positions who have benefited from the social guarantees of the revolution, including some who have benefited from state paternalism, have somewhat different immediate interests. Professional-level state employees whose salaries had been significantly above the social wage but are now worth no more than the peso are distinguished from those with access to dollars principally through employment in the tourist industry, cooperativists, people working *por cuenta propia,* and employees in autonomous firms linked to international markets.

This differentiation implies a greater need for the assertion of these diverse immediate interests and consensus building. Even with the ultimate success of the measures taken to deal with the economic crisis, hardships will be unavoidable for some years to come. Moreover, meeting the challenges of survival in the world economy requires the elimination of paternalism and the acceptance of a degree of inequality. It is no longer sufficient to gather the views of various sectors in constructing a set of policies that take these views into consideration and promote the result as a "consensus." The consensus must arise through a process of sometimes conflictive assertion of particular interests. It is in this process that the various individual and social actors experience the necessity of giving up much of what they want in order to gain what is most essential to them and thus recognize that the result is a reflection of the reality of the circumstances of their society. These are times when the society simply lacks the resources to solve many problems and some traditional sources of legitimacy are necessarily attenuated.[2] More direct representation in the process of consensus building is needed to address problems and to preclude the suspicion that the situation is a product of deficiencies of central authority.

In addition, the revolution has succeeded in producing new generations of educated citizens. While Cuban political culture retains some of its heritage of authoritarianism, participation has become an important value (Hernández and Dilla, 1991). More direct access to decision making than the centralized paradigm permits is increasingly expected both within and outside the party.

Finally, with the passage of time it is possible that the people will need greater direct influence over the leadership. It is likely that the importance of the foreign private sector will grow. Given the tendency of economic power to gain political influence, there is the danger that, if the economy becomes dependent on maintaining conditions sufficiently attractive to foreign capital to compete with other host countries, the leadership responsible for the maintenance of economic activity may assume the role of managing society virtually on behalf of foreign interests. Admittedly, the idea that the bulwark of Cuba's revolutionary socialist development and national sovereignty could assume such a role is far-fetched. Yet, the threat will exist to the extent that the economy relies on foreign investment for capital, technology, and access to markets and depends upon exports rather than internal demand (therefore assigning to wages the role of a cost of production rather than that of a significant contributor to the demand on which the economy depends). Although an immediate problem currently being addressed (1995) is the elimination of paternalism and lack of discipline in the workplace, a need may arise for labor organization to differentiate itself from a future state too preoccupied with meeting the demands of foreign capital. If events were to proceed along this road, centralization would obstruct the capacity of the people to guarantee that their interests and the project of socialist development remained primary. . . .

Introducing a New Political Paradigm

Democracy in the United States is popularly understood to mean limited government—limits on what the state can do to a citizen without going through extensive legal procedures. Democracy at the national level is purely formal. Popular control over the economy and foreign policy is nonexistent. Other rich countries with powerful trade union movements do somewhat better. Newly industrialized countries and poor countries generally have still less popular control and weaker protection of civil rights and liberties through due-process requirements. So far, our species has shown only a limited ability to govern itself democratically.

With an economy characterized by a broad distribution of socially owned property, it should be possible for Cuba to establish institutional arrangements that will support higher levels of popular control and protection of civil liberties than prevail in most other societies. Whether there be one party or several, accountability requires that conditions be created for the open representation and negotiation of territorial and sectoral interests within state legislative institutions. Communities of interest, be they territorial communities or others based on socioeconomic location, gender, or other commonality, must be able to articulate their perspectives without interference from central authority. Otherwise, they will not have the capacity to assert potentially conflictive perspectives.[3]

What Is Realistic?

There has never been a successful modern economy with a decentralized political system in which nonstate social property is predominant. Introducing a decentralized paradigm would require that the Cuban political leadership work with all determination to develop the particular structures appropriate to the Cuban popular revolutionary culture. It would involve giving over functions to the people as in the first years of the 1970s, before the impact of Soviet influence, though this time it would be an act of creating a new paradigm. It would involve an acceleration of the direction opened by the 1992 constitution, which removed state functions from the mass and social organizations, eliminated the principle of democratic centralism from the parliament, abolished municipal executive committees, and granted life tenure to judges. And it would mean carrying forward and bringing to fruition the promise of the 1992 electoral law.

If a self-managed, decentralized socialist paradigm were attempted, would individual and sectoral interests enter a war of all against all and each against each, creating a fatal immobilism or leaving the Cuban nation open to direct North American intervention? I believe that by using forms of social property that place workers in contact with the realities of Cuba's current stage of development, bring individual short-term interests into alignment with the needs of national development, and distribute economic power broadly, the tendency toward paralysis or weakness would be much reduced. Economic recuperation would also provide a propitious environment for an opening of political space. Thus, a more democratic economic base would permit the full realization of measures already taken toward political democratization.

To be effective, decentralization would require an opening of the channels of communication. Openness is not an absolute, but the continued pursuit of socialism ultimately must rely upon a popular commitment to the revolutionary project. This commitment can only be based on effective socioeconomic arrangements that coincide with the realities of Cuba's current level of development—arrangements in which the experience of daily life supports the underlying ideology of the project. The state as well as workers would have to leave paternalism behind. The debilitation of the state economy by the crisis of reincorporation into the world economy may have had a single positive effect, calling forth energy and initiative to meet the needs of daily life and preparing most workers to reject state paternalism.

Would this course reproduce what occurred in Eastern Europe in 1989? In the late 1980s, substantial numbers of citizens in the countries of that region rejected centralized systems that provided security but no more—systems in which many felt they were treated like children by their leaders. The ruling parties failed to project a socialist alternative to centralization. Sidney Tarrow has argued that the rebellions constituted a regional social movement, "a collective response to generally expanding political opportunities, in which the costs and risks of collective action lowered and the potential gains increased" (1991: 15). Risks had been reduced by a decline in the suppression of opposition through the 1980s, the growth of a counterculture, and the rise of sheltering institutions such as Solidarity in Poland and the Protestant church in the German Democratic Republic. In terms of perceived potential gains, those opposed to existing governments expected that change would bring the levels of prosperity and social welfare found in the European social democracies. They were encouraged by Gorbachev's policy of nonintervention, the reforms attempted by the respective leaderships, and divisions among party leaders (Edelstein, 1994).

In recent years, the Cuban people have experienced conditions of daily life much worse than those in Eastern Europe in the 1980s. However, the conditions of Tarrow's concept of an expanding opportunity structure do not seem to be present in Cuba. The government appears to be unified and has not tolerated opposition. More important, Cubans have no desire to emulate the ever-growing inequality and social decline experienced elsewhere in Latin America. The reports that many Cubans receive from friends and relatives living in Eastern Europe leave them no illusions about that path. And although there were significant differences among the countries of Eastern Europe, nationalism was generally a force against governments allied with the Soviet Union. In Cuba the government is correctly seen as the defender of the nation, while the prospect of a return of the Miamians in the event of the fall of the government is repugnant to most Cubans.

Change will be difficult and dangerous, but failure to change appears to me to present the prospect of either the reemergence of an authoritarian dependent capitalism or decline into social and political chaos. The feasibility of a decentralized paradigm depends first upon whether the leadership and the party would pursue that course with strength, unity, and determination and second upon whether Cuban revolutionary popular political culture, infused with the inspiration of Martí and developed over thirty-five years of struggle and sacrifice, is capable of confronting the challenges of such an undertaking. Only the Cuban nation and its leadership can make that judgment.

Responses to Edelstein

Edelstein's piece illustrates the numerous lessons offered by the short history of Cuban socialism. It is likely that many of the points contained in this analysis were not unfamiliar to participants in the May 1994 conference in Havana. Indeed, the clash between the raison d'être of Cuban central planning and the immediate need for short-term solutions began to shake the foundations of official thought and discourse in the late 1980s. With critical sensitivity, Edelstein examines the gap between practice and necessity, a gap essential to all paradigmatic shifts and one that, in the Cuban case, lays bare the opportunities lost and the possibilities available.

On the theme of opportunities lost, some thought might be given to the point at which economic and political centralization in Cuba became unnecessary and/or unviable. Edelstein points to the juncture at which intensive development overcame the obstacles of dependent capitalism and placed within reach a more decentralized and balanced system of planning and participation. Others have argued that a much earlier release of citizen power had the potential to fuel more creative solutions during the tumultuous transition from dependent capitalism to an undeveloped socialism. According to this view, institutionalized centralization feeds off a broad definition of "counterrevolution" and the excessive life span of "emergency measures" that remained in place long after U.S. imperialism had been confronted. In the first instance, centralization is limited but central to the paving of a socialist path; in the second instance, it is an obstacle to it. The point at which the conditions for democratic participation have been fulfilled is, of course, a question that must be answered by Cubans. The lesson is that the state should (need?) not be in the position to make the ultimate determination in the absence of widespread dialogue.

The relations of production in the nonstate agricultural sector are instructive.

The tendency of the state to oversee closely the activities of small farmers hindered the autonomous and complete development of a sector committed to the general goals of the revolution. When this did not make sense to farmers, many became cynical and discouraged. The other side of the coin is the position of the state, which acted to mitigate the perceived inefficiencies in and dangers of small-scale farming. The point here is that, even when it was clear that farmers and cooperative members were making valuable contributions, in relation to the state they often were left, unnecessarily, on the opposite side of the coin, though the necessity currently is to draw them in as a valuable resource.

On the theme of possibilities available, the need to act in the face of the present crisis has generated innovative solutions and a rejection of inflexible formulae. Here, both the Cuban state and people have shown their potential, which is why we can still discuss the current stage of Cuban socialism in these pages and talk realistically about Cuba's "pulling through." The emergence of promising and appropriate forms of political organization will teach us even more once their full potential is realized. As Edelstein and others of like mind writing on the topic point out, we must be critical thinkers in this learning process if all of the valuable lessons of Cuban socialism are to be adequately analyzed and appreciated. We might well remember, however, that we are operating with the benefit of hindsight.

Jennifer Abbassi
Randolph-Macon Woman's College

Edelstein writes with great care: I note particularly the cautious phrasing of his mention of the electoral and constitutional reforms of 1992. He speaks of them consistently in terms of their potential for effecting political change rather than as the realization of this change. I am struck, however, by the fact that his (correct) critique of what he terms "the liberal argument for elections" as "hopelessly abstract" could indeed be applied quite well to his own work—both to the formulas and paradigms he uses and to his failure to consider more fully the concrete realities of everyday life in Cuba in 1995. At moments while reading his piece I felt I was listening to Nero fiddle while Rome burned.

One aspect of the problematic he raises is participation. He seems to assume implicitly that democracy, decentralization, and participation are somehow synonymous or, at least, that decentralization and participation lead with some degree of inevitability to democracy. He notes the historically high levels of participation in Cuba and points out that "the skills required for political participation [are] already well developed in Cuba." But he fails to consider the impact of two key issues here.

The first of these has to do with the nature and depth of the current crisis in Cuba (1995). While Edelstein refers throughout his essay to the economic crisis, he seems far less cognizant of the social and political crises and the manner in which the three are intertwined. Most important, they have resulted in a tremendous popular demobilization. People increasingly look to themselves and their family and friendship networks rather than to the state as the guarantors of their survival. There is an increasing sense that there is no collective solution to their problems. As the project of the revolution, which had everything to do with equality, both economic and social, erodes, so too does the level of popular mobilization in support of that project. The desperately needed 1994 October opening of the free agricultural markets—or *agros,* as they are called on the streets—evidences well this shift in reliance from social to individual survival strategies. While the *agros* have palpably diminished the societal tension that has been hiding in Cuba for the past four years, at the same time they mark a new acknowledgment of the state's inability to meet the basic needs of the population and a new plateau in the decline of popular mobilization. Nor can it be expected that new generations, growing up in a society with plummeting possibilities for employment and clear evidence that *any* kind of work, whether legal or illegal, in the dollar sector of the economy offers the best opportunity for survival, will find much meaning in or be attracted by the hauntingly familiar calls for struggle and sacrifce that the leadership continues to issue.

Second, Edelstein does not fully articulate the fact that the existence of an educated and politically sophisticated population has not, even in the recent past, fostered participation at levels other than implementation or in an advisory capacity (usually, if not formally, after decisions have basically been reached). Is there any indication that this is changing or, indeed, that it is likely to change? Some might point to the reformulation of the Popular Power governmental structures in 1992 or to last year's round of workers' parliaments. The problem with both is, in a sense, the same: they reflect, in different ways, the continuing need on the part of the leadership to control the sphere within which political differences and critique, to say nothing of dissent, are permissible.

In the case of Popular Power, this is clearest around the issue of the number of candidates for each deputy position in the new direct elections to the National Assembly. The general informed opinion in Havana is that the decision to have a single candidate per position, despite popular discussions and the opinions of various advisory studies, was made almost entirely on the basis of seeking to exclude the possibility that even one "human rights activist" might be on the ballot, to say nothing about being seated—and this in a body made up of 589 deputies.

In the case of the workers' parliaments, they seem to follow in the footsteps of other nationally organized massive workplace meetings held at other moments—the most recent of which were the 89,000 meetings held during the summer of 1990, preliminary to the party congress. In these meetings as well, workers freely and openly expressed anger and frustration, reacted to possible reforms, and suggested others. Yet, then, as now, if opinions were vented, the general policy measures to be taken had largely already been decided upon: the meetings did little to alter these decisions. Thus, for instance, despite popular rejection in the workers' parliaments of the idea of an income tax, the National Assembly authorized the Council of State to implement such a tax. Nor can the opening of the *agros* be attributed to demands for them evinced in the workers' parliaments. They or their equivalent had been almost universally desired and anxiously awaited for years: this desire was, for instance, clearly expressed in the 1990 round of workplace meetings. Their opening in October had less to do with the call for them in the workers' parliaments than it did with the events of August 1994 and, most particularly, the disturbances of August 5 (when Fidel went to the Central Havana neighborhood in which the rioting began and heard from people in the streets "Tenemos hambre" [We are hungry]). Whatever value these new rounds of workplace meetings have had, they are above all further evidence of the leadership's desire to control the boundaries of dissent and critique and to channel such critique within limits that it itself designates: to determine and to contain, in short, the terrain of contestation.

Yet, simultaneously, it is evident that the leadership will no longer be able to do this. One has only to look in the shadows of current institutions, in the multiple spaces in which a civil society, spurred on by the collapse of old paradigms molded out of necessity and/or ingenuity and made possible by the very achievements of the revolution in producing a politically sophisticated, educated, and tenacious populace, is being shaped and reshaped. Here I mean everything from block-level community development schemes in which neighbors work around, rather than through, the Popular Power bureaucracy to the university faculties now encouraged (in part because of the need for dollar earnings) to make contact with foreign colleagues and the women's groups organized, for example, around professions that, instead of portraying themselves as alternatives to the official women's organization, try to stake out their own territory. (In a sense these groups, in their nascent form, might be analyzed as the equivalent of new social movements elsewhere in Latin America—but this is a separate topic altogether.) It is evident in the active youth culture scene, in which music and dollars play such a central role. It was expressed by the Film Institute members who universally refused to accept banning and censorship (in the 1991 case of *Alicia en el Pueblo de las Maravillas*) and by the pizza parlor *paladares* that offer home delivery service. In the end, it is here where identities and interests will coalesce: in their own spaces rather than in spaces mapped out by the state. The degree to which the present leadership is willing to recognize these spaces and allow them (or rather, not foreclose on or attempt to absorb them) will determine, in part, its continuing relevance.

Carollee Bengelsdorf
Hampshire College

I commend Edelstein for trying to explain current Cuban political-economic realities and future possibilities within a Marxist mode-of-production analysis.

He argues that Cuba's socialist project is now hegemonic and that the populace has numerous opportunties to participate in the workplace and the community. I want to illustrate how Edelstein's formal Marxist approach fails to take every-day reality into account—how civil society, from ordinary folk to high-level officials, has resisted certain conditions imposed by institutional hierarchies through nonsanctioned means. The hegemony of the socialist project has been sabotaged not merely from abroad but domestically, forcing the government to adjust its policies.

Islanders during the special period have defied official regulations, orders, and expectations through a variety of nonsanctioned means that are structurally pat-terned though not structurally predetermined (see my *Back from the Future: Cuba under Castro* [Princeton: Princeton University Press, 1994]).

1. "Exit": Emigration. The most extreme and public expression of disobedi-ence is emigration: opting to "exit," to reject the system altogether. Some island-ers have done so by taking advantage of U.S. travel visas; they take trips from which they never return. Meanwhile, people holding positions of importance in growing numbers have taken advantage of opportunities to travel abroad to defect; they demonstrate a state growing weaker from within. However, the vast majority of people opting out have lacked both these opportunities, turning instead to riskier escapes in unseaworthy craft. The numbers so leaving increased as domestic conditions deteriorated in the 1990s. This mode of exodus reached the proportions of a mass movement during the brief period in the summer of 1994 when the government let it be known that escapees would not be stopped and Washington had not yet decided to deny Cuban refugees automatic citizen-ship rights. Most boat people were able-bodied young men, likely to endure the difficult trip through the Straits of Florida and with little to lose because of declining domestic employment opportunities. Castro preferred that islanders exit rather than rebel; indeed, he opened up the emigration option immediately after a protest involving 1,000–2,000 Cubans erupted in central Havana. Inter-views suggest that boat people were fleeing a crumbling economy more than a political system they despised—that is, that they were rejecting not socialism in principle but socialism as experienced on an everyday basis. How many would opt out, under current circumstances, if given the opportunity and minimal risks no one knows; however, the number is sufficiently large that any analysis of the political and economic effectiveness of Cuban socialism should take their senti-ments into account. Such people do not see institutionalized means within Cuba to bring about the changes they seek.

2. Political protest. Other Cubans dissatisfied with aspects of Cuban life have channeled their grievances into nonsanctioned overt and covert political activity. The large antigovernment protest in 1994 is one example: it was the first such public protest under Castro, and it was immediately repressed. Other islanders have involved themselves in small, unofficial political groupings around such issues as family reunification, artistic freedom, freedom of religious worship, and

democracy. A high-ranking official acknowledged there to be about 50 such groups in 1992, involving some 1,000 people. The numbers involved in such groups and in public protests would undoubtedly be greater were the overt non-sanctioned activity less risky. Activists have been arrested and imprisoned. Because of the risks, islanders channeling discontent politically more often opt for covert means. For example, according to official sources, 7 percent of all islanders and 15 percent of Havana voters registered protest votes in the 1993 election, either spoiling their ballots or casting blank ballots. (Since no outside observers were allowed, the accuracy of these figures cannot be verified.)

3. Cultural resistance. Of greater significance, Cubans in growing numbers have involved themselves in Afro-Cuban cults such as *santería* and other cultural modes of resistance. Syncretic beliefs and rituals reflect cultural resistance to an elite-imposed religious and social order and possibly resistance to culture and social structure more broadly defined. In the 1980s, in response to societal pressures, the officially atheist state became more tolerant of religion. The popularity of such cults has increased since, not only because of this tolerance but because islanders have come to derive more satisfaction from such religious involvements than from alternative institutional life. (Pentecostalism has also increased in popularity.) Music has served as another channel of cultural resistance. Recognizing it as such, the government has denied performance licenses to groups who sing in English and who play rock music. The government, in essence, sees such music as culturally subversive.

4. Labor disobedience. As workers' purchasing power plunged in the special period, they did not publicly rebel. Decades of government and party control over union leadership and union activity explain their seeming acquiescence. Some of their grievances were channeled through formal structures, with some success. For example, the government halted plans to implement an income tax in 1995 after laborers let their anger be known in workers' parliaments. More typically, however, workers have "voted with their feet," and in such numbers as to sabotage production and productivity. Labor, for one, has resisted farmwork, especially but not only in the sugar sector. Farm laborers have fled the fields, and unemployed and underemployed city dwellers have not responded to government exhortations (and enticements) to work in the countryside. This quiet labor disobedience contributed to a fall in export earnings, as the sugar harvest declined by 50 percent, and a domestic subsistence crisis. (The diminition of imports since the collapse of Soviet aid and trade is part of the problem as well.) The government felt pressed to respond to the covert disobedience in a manner entailing—from a Marxist perspective—"capitalist backsliding." The fiscally bankrupt state increased material incentives substantially in the farm sector, transformed state farms into cooperatives, and opened private markets. Faced with an undependable labor force, the government also has turned to the armed forces for assistance. Food, in the words of Raül Castro, had come to be the number one political and ideological as well as economic problem.

Labor problems increased in the service sector as well, to the point that the government had difficulty delivering the very services that had made the Cuban Revolution so distinctive: education and health care. Teacher and nurse absentee rates rose as the real value of peso earnings plunged in the first half of the 1990s. Teachers and nurses also increasingly abandoned their jobs for hard-currency-earning work in tourism, and they took early retirement to draw pensions while setting up businesses. Desertion rates contributed to teacher shortages in key subjects (*Cuba Business,* September 1994).

5. Defiance of the law. During the special period, theft, corruption, specula-tion, and black-marketeering reached record levels. Ordinary citizens up to high-level officials routinely engaged in economic crimes: how they did so typically hinged more on their "structure of opportunities" than on their personal moral-ity. Crop theft became so rampant that rural authorities handed out weapons to "peasant vigilance detachments" on cooperatives, and about 40 percent of farm production sold to the state never reached official outlets. In addition, prostitu-tion proliferated around the hotels, and an illegal dollarization of the economy had such devastating effects on peso-based production that the government legalized usage of the foreign currency in 1993. In decriminalizing dollar posses-sion the government hoped also to rein in a dollarized black market that under-mined state efforts to "equalize sacrifice" through rationing. The value of black market transactions rose from an estimated 2 billion pesos in 1990 to 10 billion pesos three years later. The illicit activity reflected islanders' rejection of state-set rules and regulations and their willingness to defy the state through illegal means. Although people had their own economic interests at heart when defying the law, the effect of much of the illegal activity was a production, distribution, and fiscal crisis of such proportions that the government, in its effort to regain authority and control of the economy, reduced socialist and expanded market-based eco-nomic strategies and institutions.

The full theoretical implications of this analysis cannot be elaborated in the space of a brief commentary. However, I have illustrated the importance of "bringing people back in" to the analysis of state socialism. The way in which islanders have responded to conditions not to their liking has been shaped by institutional arrangements and practices, and their responses are, in essence, pat-terned. They have typically shied away from overt well-coordinated expressions of opposition when these were personally risky, turning under such circum-stances to covert ways to defy authority and improve their lot, such as foot-dragging, hoarding, tax evasion, absenteeism, desertion, pilferage, black-marketeering, ballot destruction, and the like. Such modes of resistance have been veiled behind outward loyalty and deference and certain cooperation and compliance.

The effects of such covert and seemingly uncoordinated activity must be examined independently of the perpetrators' intent and the meaning derived from involvements. The effects in some instances have been so great, however, economically and politically, that the government has modified its policies.

Informal social, political, and economic dynamics are the least analyzed aspect of Castro's Cuba not because of their lack of importance. Rather, they have received little attention because the government does not want to publicize how ineffective its authority is and how unpopular its policies are, and political analysts, Edelstein included, have in the main focused on formal political institutions, formal political behavior, and official discourse. The political system has been taken at face value. But covert forms of defiance have received little attention also because most of the perpetrators of covert activity do not want to draw attention to themselves for fear of reprisals. If the government recognizes the gap between individual and state interests and the failure of institutionalized processes to channel (and effectively contain) people's concerns, so should our academic analyses. The government has been more responsive to the forms of resistance elaborated here than have scholars!

Susan Eckstein
Boston University

Edelstein argues that to spur efficiency and international competitiveness, to narrow the gap between short-term or particular interests and long-term socialist goals, and to achieve genuine political consensus, Cuba needs to jettison its once useful but no longer viable centralist paradigm. It needs a more decentralized socialist economy of market-disciplined and self-managed enterprises and a more decentralized political system that allows interest articulation, representation, and bargaining. He notes that Cuba's crisis has already induced some economic decentralization and that the Cubans have already laid the groundwork for political decentralization, but he calls for more thorough and more rapid change. His criticisms of current Cuban policy are aimed less at the direction than at the extent and timing of change. In discussing these latter, however, he glosses over important issues that merit close attention. Space is too limited for a full examination here; I will only identify some of these issues and indicate how we might think about them differently.

Edelstein would probably agree that, unless some of the economic changes that he proposes and others that are under way can be contained within definite limits, they will undermine rather than bolster long-term socialist goals in Cuba. The question of the extent and limits of change is therefore critical, and he insufficiently addresses it. For example, he calls for an end of economic "paternalism," but this can mean anything from no longer coddling slackers, which would strengthen Cuban socialism, to no longer guaranteeing work or an adequate safety net when work is unavailable. If Cuba's crisis induces a permanent scrapping of such guarantees, Cuban socialism, in any meaningful sense, will be dead.

In this and other instances, Edelstein needs to define more carefully the extent of the changes he is proposing.

Although his analysis of some of the roots and pitfalls of economic centralization is insightful and compelling, his call for more rapid decentralization overlooks the possible value of Cuba's more gradual approach. Centralized economic control, however quickly crumbling, arguably has helped the country avoid fullblown economic disaster in recent years. Without central control, the Cuban regime might not have survived the collapse of Soviet-bloc communism this long or have been able to begin its more or less orderly shift to more decentralized economic mechanisms. Contrary to Edelstein's expectations, moving too rapidly now could result in economic chaos, benefiting no one other than the enemies of the Cuban regime and of socialism.

Edelstein rightly argues that Cuba needs a more decentralized and open political system. Here again, however, in calling for more rapid change he glosses over the importance of timing. It can certainly be argued that considerable centralized political control will remain necessary in Cuba until the country has stabilized its economy and further reestablished its economic ties with the rest of the world and perhaps even until the United States ends or at least moderates its political attacks and its economic blockade against the island. The depth of Cuba's crisis and the severity of the imperialist threat render the timing of any significant political opening critical.

Edelstein wisely shuns prevalent soporifics about the inherent superiority of capitalist economic systems and of multiparty political systems. He admirably attempts a careful appraisal of Cuba's political and economic needs based on its present and likely future realities. He defends socialism in Cuba not with apologetics but with pragmatic suggestions for how the country might successfully navigate between the Scylla of centralist degeneration and the Charybdis of capitalist restoration. Even though he glosses over some important issues, his arguments are laudable for their intent and their intelligence.

Frank T. Fitzgerald
College of Saint Rose

I agree with Edelstein that the centralized political paradigm is no longer adequate and that economic centralization cannot guarantee continued growth under conditions of reincorporation into the global economy. I also agree that there is an urgent need to develop a decentralized socialist project. I will therefore attempt to highlight some failures in Cuba since 1986, mainly in connection with political and economic reforms of the 1990s, that are missing from the Edelstein analysis. In so doing, I will summarize and update the view of the Cuban crisis that I have expressed in several articles and in my latest book, *Will Cuba Fall?* (Rio de Janeiro: Editorial Vozes, 1995).

Signs of the crisis started to appear in 1986, and the Cuban leadership made an effort through the rectification process to return to the Guevarist mystique of the 1960s. Both the chaos that resulted from perestroika and the hope that a coup d'état in the Soviet Union could reestablish the old relationship may help explain the resistance to the changes. They also explain why the convocation of the Fourth Congress of the Cuban Communist Party and the tone of discussions by the masses were more radical than the congress's results.

Since 1989, the Cuban government has been dealing with such enormous challenges as the disintegration of the Eastern bloc, the U.S. blockade, the emergence of a unipolar world led by the United States, the economic and social crises of the South, the "victory" of neoliberalism, and the need to reintegrate Cuba into a new type of global market. Internally, the challenges are to build a new decentralized, capital-intensive model, to maintain legitimacy and credibility in the political realm despite increasing social inequality, to avoid isolation in international relations, and to maintain the morale and strategic strength of the armed forces. In my opinion, the performance has been better in the last two categories than in the political and economic realm, where changes have been rather slow. There has been a tendency to react to social pressures in a piecemeal rather than a systematic way. The economic reform undertaken in 1993 has allowed for the reestablishment of some markets and for some private initiatives that were impossible during the rectification process as well as other ways of dealing with the crisis such as removing sanctions on the use of foreign currency. Although there have been achievements in some aspects of economic reform—foreign investment and coping with the excess of currency, for example—this has been the result not of any overall plan but of a group of measures of mainly financial character. This is why it has proved impossible to revive production, deal with unemployment, and offer the excluded labor force an alternative in either the state or the private economy. Lifting the sanctions against the use of foreign currency has meant the exclusion from consumption, other than that which is rationed, of people who are not receiving money from relatives abroad or large amounts of pesos from dealings in the black market.

I am not opposed to the lifting of sanctions, but to mitigate the effects of the dollarization of the economy a solution should first have been found to the problem of the real salaries of teachers, doctors, and other professionals earning less than waiters or taxi drivers. The result has been to punish the ablest and most revolutionary sectors of Cuban society and reward the black-marketeers and those with relatives in Miami.

The development of the Cuban economy depends not on the excess or lack of currency—although this is an important variable—but on its productive capacity. If this were not the case, the fracture of consensus and the crisis of values that are rapidly developing would lead the country to dependent capitalism or to the type of chaos experienced by many former socialist countries, where the new ruling class is the result of an alliance between the former "socialist" bureaucracy and new sectors of national and foreign capital.

Another important challenge is that of the political order. Even though there have been important political reforms and the leadership has legitimacy, credibility, and the support of the majority of the population, it is necessary to develop this further. In the Cuban political system, participatory democratic practices have not fulfilled their potential, partly because the institutionalization process of the 1970s was contaminated by the Soviet model. In this historical moment, the appeal to personal sacrifice to achieve future prosperity and equality does not mobilize people as it did in the past, among other things because of the impact, especially on the younger generation, of the discrediting of the dogma about the irreversibility of socialism associated with the hardships and increased inequality of the special period. Poverty and marginality today are growing as fast as the resentment of those excluded from the benefits of dollars and power sharing.

I do not see any alternative to a deep structural transformation of the Cuban political system. The paternalistic-vertical model of decision making must give way to decentralization of the decision-making process. Steps should be taken to institutionalize succession to power. The one-party system is not, for the moment, a fundamental issue, but the party must be able to guarantee the representation and expression within its ranks of the Cuban nation and the interests of the new economic, social, and political interest groups that are in the process of developing. It should also make it possible to criticize—within the revolutionary project—and to influence decision makers at the highest levels. If Cuba fails, it will have tragic consequences not only for the island but at a global level, both in the South and in the North. This is why Edelstein's paper is so important. By criticizing some aspects of the prevailing model, he is helping to save the Cuban revolutionary project from present dangers not only from the outside but from the inside as well.

Francisco López Segrera
UNESCO

Edelstein's thoughtful consideration of a decentralized socialism has established some constructive terms for discussing Cuba's future in a world rife with teleological claims about markets and political pluralism. The issues he raises in presenting a historically rooted anticapitalist alternative for Cuba are complex and weighty ones. The matter of "interests" is the point at which I will engage the self-consciously—and importantly—political argument about decentralization and democracy, suggesting several questions for further reflection on the project of reform in Cuba.

Edelstein's analysis accurately assumes that interests are not monolithic in Cuba, notwithstanding the legitimacy-creating achievements of revolutionary centralization or the cohesive force of nationalism to this day. Individuals and sectors are thus granted particular, subnational interests, and, as the argument goes, the immediacy of interests is one measure of the "gap" that renders the old paradigm suspect, of the crisis-induced corruption that affects long-term social-ist ideals, and of the need for a new—electoral—consensus in the 1990s. Indeed, the negotiation of conflict among particular interests is crucial in the decentral-ized paradigm's understanding of democracy as accountable electoral representa-tion. The conception of interests is also critical. Given the needs created by current crisis conditions and timeless assumptions about the meaning of mar-kets, the essay's compelling call for countering liberal abstractions about electoral representation with political-economic realities must push forward on several fronts.

First, what, exactly, are the particular interests and conflicts that will explain the future of representation as a negotiated consensus? Self-managed social prop-erty is the centerpiece of economic decentralization, utilizing market discipline to facilitate the negotiation of interests identified with workplaces and the social relations of production. Socioeconomic location, region, and gender are also embraced with an expandable concept of communities of interest that is key in the new paradigm's accountable representation. Yet material consumption may too easily explain everyone's immediate interests, leaving the scope of conflict and procedures for negotiation underexplored both before and after a change of paradigm. It is not entirely clear, for example, how regional or gender interests fell into the "gap" characteristic of the centralist paradigm or how they and other interests—such as race—will be rescued. If the mechanisms for an upward-moving process of consensus building are a practical concern reminiscent of tra-ditional debates about participatory democracy, the problem of negotiation also faces prevailing perceptions that interests may be perplexingly incommensurate. Negotiation may be essential for reconstituting consensus, but the wheres and hows of negotiation—and thus accountability itself—remain practical and theo-retical issues of a paradigmatic shift in Cuba.

A second, related question is about political interests. Economic recuperation will provide more "political space," Edelstein notes, though much as the pressing realities of survival threaten to make short-term interests the only recognizable ones, recovery might slow the erosion of the centralist paradigm. Rather than conceding either possibility, further exploration of the "political" could support the argument for a new paradigm by uncovering the particular interests imbed-ded in the past legitimacy of the socialist project or foreshadowed in egalitarian, emancipatory ideals. As Edelstein explains, the feasibility of decentralizing change in Cuba is determined by thirty-odd years of social, economic, and politi-cal development. It also depends on the desire for reform on the part of leaders and people. Taking his reference to the Federation of Cuban Women seriously and recalling feminist challenges to conventional conceptions of interests, this and other mass organizations would provide a valuable focus for exploring nego-tiation in terms of sites, the concrete realities of old and newer interests, and the abstractions associated with having or protecting a political space.

A provocative realism that situates the decentralist alternative within Cuban society and revolutionary history sheds other light on these issues of interests and their representation. The simple claim that negotiation will facilitate a recognition of circumstantial limits to the fulfillment of particular—short- and medium-term—interests is, for instance, a striking recasting of the purposes of electoral representation. Edelstein also presumes the role of the "historical leadership" in deciding on change, neatly preempting the idea that decentralization means a broad-scale rejection of all existing institutions. Accepting leadership's power and the maintenance of some significant central responsibilities with regard to planning and policies (such as education and health) of course underscores previous questions about the scope and nature of negotiation. Yet it also entails thinking about a politics that can defend against the exacerbation of "functional" and other inequalities linked to economic reforms, including the privileging of foreign interests. Unlikely as it is that people are unaware of the constraints of their and socialism's survival, imbuing procedures with "defensive" purposes is a vital counterpoint to the theoretical ambiguities—or practical dangers—of democratic consensus building through negotiation. Direct representation in policy making has a quite specific meaning, then, its utility explained by the everyday—concrete—realities of the special period that affect choices, perceptions, and the placing of blame.

Finally, Edelstein's argument about the possibility and necessity of both economic and political change recognizes a "limited space for maneuvering," sensing peril in both forward-moving reforms and centralist recalcitrance. The threat of a revisited dependent capitalist authoritarianism seems clearer, however, than the descent into "social and political chaos" that is associated with a resistance to change. Despite the menacing momentum of the secondary economy that figures prominently in Edelstein's analysis, the remarkable resilience of social and political life within the crisis conditions of the special period finds numerous expressions, including the innovative search for survival that he points out, the countless Cubans who work despite dislocations of every sort, and those who stay put while others leave. Rather than protesting the specter of chaos or belaboring the need for more confrontation of theory with complex realities, a last question joins Edelstein's serious—and welcome—inquiry into the possibilities that exist within Cuban socialism. How do present reforms help or hinder the prospects of a democratic, decentralist future? The leadership is indeed deciding, and consequential change is under way. In the absence of the pluralism of property, autonomy, and self-management that distinguish the new paradigm and its market relations, it is important to know where recent reforms in management thinking, in employment structures, in fiscal policies, and in mass organizations contribute to the dynamics of centralization and decentralization that define the institutional "space for maneuver."

In the end, interests can and should be used to explore the pace, perils, and prospects of all reform—and the absence of reform. Acknowledging that change in Cuban socialism is altering interests is a necessary step to that end, though seeing what is new requires understanding the old. The beginning, therefore, remains a matter of careful consideration of the concrete, historical, and thus circumstantial nature of interests themselves.

Sheryl L. Lutjens
Northern Arizona University

Rejoinder

Joel C. Edelstein

The thoughtful and articulate discussion by Jennifer Abbassi, Carollee Bengelsdorf, Susan Eckstein, Frank Fitzgerald, Francisco López Segrera, and Sheryl Lutjens presents a rich diversity of perspectives. I regret that I can comment on only a few of the issues they raise.

Eckstein offers useful information concerning resistance and defiance. Stating in her opening paragraph that I assert that Cubans have ample opportunities for effective participation, she suggests that I ignore these acts of resistance and defiance, which would occur with frequency only in the absence of such participation. Observing that "the effects [of these acts] in some instances have been so great . . . economically and politically, that the government has modified its policies," she concludes, "The government has been more responsive to the forms of resistance elaborated here than have scholars!" Bengelsdorf emphasizes the popular demobilization that has occurred and the consequent ineffectiveness of further calls by the leadership for struggle and sacrifice. She points out that people now look to themselves, no longer believing in collective solutions. She hears my squeaky fiddle and detects smoke coming from Havana. However, my essay does make reference to behaviors such as withdrawal of labor and theft of property from the state sector and participation in the black market, which register as forms of resistance regardless of underlying motivation. I note that current conditions undermine socialist values and call forth a self-concerned mentality. Eckstein's and Bengelsdorf's comments correct any neglect of these aspects of the situation.

I focus on structural changes that might provide for effective participation. Currently, multiple channels of participation at the local level provide for the articulation of short-term sectoral interests at that level, but central authority incorporates only what can be accommodated to its view of the long-term project. For this reason, while other demands and perspectives are voiced, they are not heard beyond the local level. Consequently, this participation is not effective in forging a consensus through negotiation. I explained that for several reasons space is needed for negotiation of these interests to reach an effective consensus.

My essay attempts to identify the structural roots of a centralization that suppresses immediate sectoral interests. I believe that these roots lie primarily but not exclusively in the contradictions inherent in the project of constructing socialism on a base of dependent capitalism. Abbassi observes unnecessary state intervention in the nonstate agricultural sector unrelated to this heritage. Lutjens makes a very important point that "it is not entirely clear . . . how regional or gender interests fell into the 'gap' characteristic of the centralist paradigm or how they and other interests—such as race—will be rescued." In addition to dependent capitalism, the revolution inherited a history of slavery and a culture marked by machismo. The structures of political centralization also preclude the effective articulation of perspectives that do not conform to the priorities of a leadership that lacks gender and racial balance.

I ask whether over the past thirty-five years the revolution has sufficiently transformed the dependent capitalism that it inherited to undertake a socialist decentralization. I propose an approach that could draw immediate sectoral interests closer to the needs of the long-term project and thus overcome the need for centralization. If adopted, this paradigm shift would not guarantee the resolution of gender and racial issues but would certainly permit a more open assertion of interests.

I am preoccupied with the question of how to bring people into a socialism that can meet the challenge of integration into the global economy. Many who resisted perestroika in the USSR identified socialism with political and economic centralization. For them there was no need for the question of new structures to carry socialist development forward; centralization was the answer. The current Chinese leadership defines socialism as political centralization and maintains it while pursuing a transformation to capitalism. For the owners of capital and their agents, it is too obvious to state that capitalism is the solution that will improve the economic situation, end the crisis, bring the people back in, and guarantee Cubans life, liberty, and the pursuit of happiness.

It seems to me that, as in the first years, a radical and untried course is necessary if the most elementary needs of the majority are not to be forgotten. The revolution came to power seeking to address the urgent needs of *los humildes* and to achieve national sovereignty and dignity through a program of reform within capitalism. When the bourgeoisie in Cuba and its North American senior partner made that program impossible, the leadership responded by radicalizing the revolution and adopting centralized socialism. Although most decisions were responses to daily challenges, in retrospect they appear as consistent steps guided by a coherent strategic framework.

López Segrera observes that the government response to crisis has been characterized by "a tendency to react to social pressures in a piecemeal rather than a systematic way." Unlike the radicalism of the early years, the framework guiding the response to the current crisis appears to be the now-conservative centralized paradigm. With socialism identified with the state sector, the weaknesses of centralization evident in the mid-1980s were not addressed in the rectification. Lacking an alternative concept of socialist relations of production, the major thrust of crisis response has been the use of foreign private capital to compensate for the deficiencies of centralization and actions in the sphere of circulation. As Lutjens observes, "recovery might slow the erosion of the centralist paradigm."

Many policies in response to the crisis induced by the demise of the socialist bloc have been made imperative by the critical lack of foreign exchange and its consequences. Survival has required attracting foreign investment and adopting import substitution measures in energy conservation, food and other agricultural production, and transportation. It has also been imperative to deal with excess liquidity. I agree with Bengelsdorf's characterization of discussions in the National Assembly and the workers' parliaments. They were limited principally to fiscal matters—how to raise government revenues through taxes and state sales of previously rationed alcohol and tobacco products and how to reduce state expenditures. This concern appeared to define the official agenda for the workers' parliaments, limiting them to the sphere of circulation even though many workers raised workplace issues of productive relations. As López Segrera points out, more than resolving the problem of excess liquidity what is required for economic development is improvement of productive capacity. Instruments to deal with the economic crisis that are available in the sphere of circulation are limited to strengthening individual incentives, necessarily increasing and legitimating inequality. A course for recovery that maintains a prospect for socialism must combine measures in both circulation and the social relations of production.

If the leadership pursues recovery mainly on the basis of private capital, foreign and/or domestic, rather than giving strong emphasis to nonstate social property, a meaningful postrecovery political opening will be highly unlikely. This path will represent a partial decentralization but not democratization. It can be expected to result in a configuration of private-sector elites, including many elements of the present central authority, whose economic power will almost surely prevail against working-class organizations in whatever new political arrangements are adopted. My essay presents this possibility while noting that a large-scale cooperativization of agriculture has been undertaken, though real autonomy appears to be lacking. Fitzgerald understands my criticism to be "aimed less at the direction than at the extent and timing of change." To clarify, I have found little evidence that the paradigm shift that I believe is necessary is under way in Cuba.

Bengelsdorf's reference to the growth of spontaneous citizen actions to solve community as well as individual problems resembles Lewin's (1991) description of a similar phenomenon on a much larger scale in the later years of the Soviet Union. She appears to suggest that the Cuban state has lost the initiative and cannot regain it—that it can at best retain its relevance only by accommodating what is developing "in the shadows of current institutions." I believe that a strong leadership committed to a project of transition to self-managed socialism might be able to carry it forward. Prospects would be improved to the degree to which the predominance of nonstate social property was pursued and to the extent to which modest financing could be provided for voluntary cooperative ventures in economic sectors where feasible—particularly in agriculture, services, and manufacturing in support of the tourist industry. Even more important, the full influence of the historical leadership would be required to establish a climate supportive of this radical paradigm transition, placing it at the center of the project for the survival of the nation and the gains of the revolution. This final campaign of central authority in its present form would necessarily include recognizing, while not absorbing, citizen initiatives, vigorously combating resistance among political and economic cadres, and legitimating the struggles for autonomy of cooperatives and other forms of voluntary collectives.

Of course, it is the task of the Cuban people to fashion a solution that preserves the gains for which they have sacrificed so much. They will live with the consequences of the decisions made. It is not their responsibility to pursue the hopes and visions of socialists in other countries.

Notes

1. The social wage refers to goods and services distributed to all Cubans without regard to pay received for work. It includes services provided at no cost such as education and health care. Other goods could also be considered part of the social wage because of their very low cost, such as rent, which is no more than 10 percent of the monthly salary of one occupant, and rationed food and a few other goods available at state distribution centers.

2. These include greater acceptance of inequality, reduced job security, a reduced role in international solidarity, possible reductions in health and education, and the growing presence of relatively privileged foreign tourists, the latter giving some the impression of the subordination of national independence and dignity.

3. In my opinion, the Federación de Mujeres Cubanas offers a strong negative example.

6.3

Sandinismo and the Problem
of Democratic Hegemony

Doug Brown

Writing on the eve of the electoral defeat of the Sandinistas (1990), the author analyzes the problems of political democracy and the precariousness of the revolution.

I T HAS BECOME CLEAR to both experts and casual observers that the Nicaraguan Revolution, after nearly a decade of endless adversity, has an enigmatic character that may well be the basis for its endurance (for a summary of the first eight years, see *Envio*, 1987b). Most of us interested in the process of social change in Nicaragua have by now had to admit that there are dimensions to it that are historically unusual and unique and which, in part, are due to its complexity (see, for example, Martin and Zwerling, 1985). Whether through the proliferation of Nicaraguan literature, the mainstream media, or personal experience, we have become aware of and possibly fixated upon its contradictions. There is clearly both repression and pluralism as well as both popular participation and elitism that inform the practice and ideology of Sandinismo. The following remarks are primarily exploratory but address the revolution's enigmatic quality by outlining a conceptual framework through which we can assess the revolution's democratic character and the extent to which Nicaragua can carve out a novel political-economic model.

Although the revolution is still in its infancy, enough time has elapsed that we

First published in *Latin American Perspectives* 65, vol. 17 (2), Sage Publications, Inc. Reprinted with permission from the Latin American Perspectives Collective.

can make one significant judgment about it: It is one of the first revolutions which has consistently attempted to ground a *socialist* strategy within what Claude Lefort has termed a "politics of human rights." The Nicaraguan Revolution, as witnessed through its ideology of Sandinismo, is explicitly socialist but has not based its political strategy on the economistic view that social and political consciousness is ultimately determined or revealed by one's relation to the means of production. This gives the Sandinista Revolution a unique post-Marxian flavor, and, more important, it forces us to confront some difficult questions regarding this strategy of "socialist populism."

At the theoretical level the American left has been groping toward a new vision of socialist politics, articulated through some notable analytical achievements and exemplified in, among others, the recent works of Albert et al. (1986); Bowles and Gintis (1986); Laclau and Mouffe (1985); Lefort (1986); Bobbio (1987); and Fehér and Heller (1986a; 1986b). Although their terms vary, there is a clear commonality within all of this work. First, the new vision of socialist politics emerges once the last residue of economic determinism is purged from Marxism (for example, Laclau and Mouffe, 1982). For those who have stayed within its fold, what remains of Marxism after all of this is something we have begun to call post-Marxian discourse. For others, what remains is not enough to warrant the label of Marxism. At this stage, whether the approach is post-Marxian, radical democratic, or simply leftist, the issue is a socialist politics without economistic distortion.

Second, the effort to go beyond economistic politics has broken new ground with the appeal to a "discourse of rights." In general, rights discourse is the common context that situates the new socialist politics, and whether it is based on "democratic hegemony," the "completion of formal democracy," or "democratic economics," it is a politics geared to the realities of American capitalism. Its radical democratic vision is premised upon an awareness that a fully democratic society will most likely be achieved by a coalition-building process in which the demands of autonomous social movements are "rooted in the awareness of rights" and "stem from a domain that the state cannot occupy" (Lefort, 1986: 264). This is the understanding that ultimately constitutes a vital dimension of the politics of Sandinismo. In other words, although Sandinismo is not a logically consistent set of ideas consciously formulated by reference to current theories of rights discourse, its evolution has been characterized implicitly by this dimension. A socialist strategy based upon rights discourse is now being played out in Nicaragua, yet the Nicaraguan context is clearly different from that of the advanced capitalist nations for which this strategy seems most appropriate. The following comments are not only an effort to understand Sandinismo but also to clarify the problem of a rights-based political strategy.

Because the Nicaraguan Revolution has not been institutionalized and because it continues to be a process in which even the guiding ideology of Sandinismo is subject to redefinition, we can reasonably argue that the fundamental problematic in which to situate an analysis of Nicaragua is that of hegemony. Consequently, we cannot adequately examine the Nicaraguan economy, church-state relations, or other spheres of activity like that of the mass organizations unless we recognize that they are all in a state of flux and subject to the vagaries of the hegemonic process integral to radical social change. This suggests that Sandinista hegemony is the pivotal variable in unraveling the revolution's paradoxes. More specifically, I conclude that we can distinguish between authoritarian hegemony and democratic hegemony, and to the extent that the process in Nicaragua embodies a political strategy of rights discourse it tendentially encompasses a democratic hegemony. At this point we cannot maintain unequivocally, however, that the Nicaraguan process is a form of democratic hegemony. There are only tendencies in this direction, and consequently my remarks are intended to add some clarification to what is an inherently volatile process subject to contradictory forces that are both democratic and authoritarian. . . .

Sandinismo and Hegemony

Authoritarian hegemony is based upon an economic determinism suggesting that there is in the essence of capitalism (contrary to appearance) a unity of subordinate social groups, all of which are ultimately reducible to the consciousness, interests, and political tasks that the working class *should* have by virtue of its relation to the means of production. Yet the concept of hegemony should be considered a spectrum with democratic hegemony at the opposite end from authoritarian hegemony. For democratic hegemony, there is no essential unity among diverse social groups beyond what can be created through articulation and democratic practice.

To understand Nicaragua's revolution it is necessary to view it as a hegemonic process that is not only situated but also moves along this spectrum between the two poles. Clearly, the FSLN as the major political actor is the hegemonic leader and seeks the "construction of a working consensus supportive of a new political-economic order" (Fagen, 1986: 15). With respect to Gramsci's distinction between rule by coercion and rule by hegemony, it should be apparent from the observable degree of pluralism and its mixed economy that Sandinista Nicaragua is the latter. In other words, it does not have the character of a totalitarian, military dictatorship. Unlike Leninism, Sandinismo is not "dominated by the image of an agent of history, a People-as-One"(Lefort, 1986: 266). However, at issue is the proximity of the FSLN's hegemonic project to the democratic pole of the spectrum. At this point conclusions can only be tentative, because there are several contradictory forces that cause the revolutionary process to vacillate along the spectrum between authoritarian and democratic hegemony. This notwithstanding, there are a few observations that can be made which at least set the parameters for this process.

First, the FSLN has considered itself to be in the role of vanguard of a revolution, and its history since its formation in 1961 is primarily that of a military organization (Vilas, 1986b: 144). This is the context in which hegemony has become the major problematic in Nicaragua. In contrast, the period of armed struggle and popular mobilizaion from 1961 until the 1979 Triumph combined elements of both authoritarian and democratic hegemony. In speaking for the FSLN, Humberto Ortega (currently minister of defense) stated that originally the FSLN viewed mass mobilization as subordinate to the military defeat of the National Guard. On the contrary, "What happened was that it was the guerrillas who provided support for the masses so that they could defeat the enemy by means of insurrection" (Ortega, 1982: 58). This speaks to the dual logic of the pre-Triumph movement. In 1979 the combined membership of the FSLN's three factions—the Tendencia Proletaria (Proletarian Tendency, or TP), the Guerra Popular Prolongada (Prolonged Popular War, or GPP), and the Terceristas—numbered a mere 500 militants, clearly a vanguard party. Yet fundamental to their success was the insurrectional participation of the majority of Nicaragua's people.

It is in this complex dialectic between popular mobilization and vanguard military action that the politics of rights discourse and democratic hegemony are historically situated. More important, a politics of human rights in the context of democratic hegemony appears to have been the effect rather than the cause of the successful FSLN/popular mobilization relationship.

After early failures with the "foco" strategy, which relied on a core of armed professional revolutionaries operating from remote mountain bases, the Sandinistas then pursued a broader approach of building ties with other opposition groups, including the Partido Socialista Nicaragüense (Nicaraguan Socialist Party) and the Frente Estudiantil Revolucionario (Revolutionary Student Front or FER). By the mid-1960s most of the activity was legal and organizational and, like the military "foco" approach, it too had limitations. In 1969 Carlos Fonseca stated that this "did not serve to accumulate forces and that the progress achieved was minimal" (Fonseca, 1986: 175).

Thus, the military strategy resurfaced in the early 1970s but now sought to incorporate popular mobilization as well. "The strategy was to establish 'intermediate organizations' which would be affiliated with the Frente but would not bear its name" (Ruchwarger, 1987: 15). After the FSLN went underground in 1970, mass actions, like the 1971 public transit protest in León, became increasingly important. With Somoza's crackdown on the opposition between 1974 and 1976, the FSLN membership could not agree on a viable strategy and subsequently split into three factions. The GPP had a rural-based guerrilla strategy, while the TP pushed for a mass movement grounded in the urban proletariat and student population. The Terceristas sought a "broad alliance policy" that would cement strategic relations among all Somocista opposition elements including the business sector and the Catholic Church hierarchy (Archbishop

Obando y Bravo). The FSLN's three tendencies suggest that it has not been a monolithic organization, and, moreover, linkage between vanguardism and popular mobilization continued to be a controversial internal issue throughout the 1970s.

The watershed event occurred on January 10, 1978, when Pedro Joaquín Chamorro *(La Prensa's* editor) was assassinated. Even though "isolated revolts had begun to emerge and identify themselves as Sandinista," the massive and spontaneous uprising that resulted from this event went well beyond FSLN orchestration (Ruchwarger, 1987: 23). Over 100,000 demonstrators were at Chamorro's funeral procession, and the Consejo Superior de la Empresa Privada (Higher Council of Private Enterprise, or COSEP) called for a "civil stoppage to demand Somoza's resignation" (Weber, 1986: 195).

In contrast to vanguardism, by mid-1978 there were three distinguishable forces at work against Somoza. First, business opposition had galvanized in a broad opposition alliance called the Frente Amplio de Oposición (FAO). It had the support of Archbishop Obando and also included the Terceristas' "Group of Twelve." The FAO supported a general strike approach to force Somoza's resignation, and with U.S. support it hoped to install a moderate government that excluded the FSLN. Second, the other two FSLN tendencies, which aligned with 22 popular groups in June 1978 in the Movimiento Pueblo Unido (United People's Movement, or UPM), continued throughout 1978 and early 1979 to carry out a variety of military as well as coordinated mass actions, including student strikes and street riots. The Terceristas, with Eden Pastora, also led the seizure of the National Palace in August 1978. The third force was that of the people. In September 1978 the people of Estelí and León mounted a massive insurrection. The FSLN joined in to support it in a violent confrontation with the National Guard. After a week of intense combat, Somoza bombed the cities and forced the FSLN columns into retreat (Weber, 1986: 198). He then enacted "savage reprisals," killing 6,000 people in the bloody aftermath.

Faced with the self-mobilization of the people, Humberto Ortega later claimed that it was "the first national uprising led by the FSLN but that was chiefly due to pressure by the masses" (Ortega, 1982: 68–69). By early 1979 it became clear to most Nicaraguans that Somoza could only be deposed by a combination of both military force and political pressure. Additionally, the people's sacrifices had been too great to accept a moderate, reformist alternative to Somoza (Weber, 1986: 200–205). They consequently turned to the FSLN, instead of the FAO, for leadership. An intense popular organizing drive became a necessity so that the final offensive, combining general strike, popular insurrection, and military assault, could be victorious.

The dynamics of the pre-Triumph mobilization are complex. The best historical analogy may be that of the CIO organizing drives in the late 1930s. Although John L. Lewis and the CIO conducted a vigorous campaign and recruited many Communist Party activists for workplace organizing in many instances this was merely an external stimulus to the self-organizing which industrial workers were simultaneously carrying out.

Similarly, in Nicaragua self-organizing independent of the FSLN occurred. For example, two religious groups, Centro de Fomento Agrario y Educativo (Agrarian Promotion and Educational Center, or CEPA) and "Delegates of the World," began organizing campesinos in the early 1970s (Ruchwarger, 1987: 39). Committees of agricultural workers were formed by these two groups in Carazo and Masaya in the mid-1970s. Then the TP faction of the FSLN joined in these efforts in 1975. The Asociación de Trabajadores del Campo (Rural Workers' Association, or ATC, the primary Sandinista popular organization for peasant representation) emerged in 1977 from a strike at the San Antonio sugar plantation. Yet although it was "promoted by the FSLN," it was "staffed in part by former CEPA organizers" (Ruchwarger, 1987: 40).

Another example is that of housewives who in 1977 had formed "mothers' clubs" to discuss national problems. They subsequently organized themselves nationally as the Asociación de Mujeres ante la Problemática Nacional (Nicaraguan Women Confronting the National Problem, or AMPRONAC). It was composed of middle-class women with a minority of FSLN supporters (Ruchwarger, 1987: 48). In 1978 they participated in the demonstrations protesting Chamorro's assassination, and, with their increased visibility, many new members were recruited. AMPRONAC then joined the ATC in a hunger march in April 1978. Their membership growth culminated in a national convention in which women supporting the FSLN emerged as the dominant faction. They coalesced with the UPM and supported the August 1978 FSLN military offensive. So although AMPRONAC was not FSLN-constituted, after the Triumph AMPRONAC changed its name to Asociación de Mujeres Nicaragüenses "Luisa Amanda Espinoza" (AMNLAE) and ultimately became the major Sandinista popular organization for women's representation (Walker, 1986: 84).

In general the defeat of Somoza involved a web of coalition building between moderate and leftist opposition; an intricate dialectic between vanguardism and popular spontaneism; and a coordinated effort of armed struggle and mass insurrection. The FSLN emerged very late in all of this in a position of hegemonic leadership. It was clearly not the orchestrated coup of a vanguard minority, but the result of a two-decade struggle combining both authoritarian and democratic elements. But "the Frente Sandinista knew how to unite under their leadership all the forces exploited and oppressed by the dictatorship. The contradiction Somocismo/anti-Somocismo could thus be expressed as the contradiction Somocismo/Sandinismo" (Vilas, 1986b: 143). Moreover, the contradiction could be expressed in this way largely because it became within the framework of rights discourse.

The fundamental feature of the revolution is the priority of the poor, yet this unifying theme is expressed in Sandinismo by "a blend of nationalism, pragmatic Marxism, and Catholic humanism" (Walker, 1986: 24). However, since 1979 certain religious and private sector interests have defected from the revolutionary process (for example, Cardinal Obando y Bravo and the Catholic Church hierarchy, COSEP, Alfonso Robelo, Violeta Chamorro, and Eden Pastora), while simultaneously the FSLN has moved to a more democratic practice of hegemony accorded it by its political leadership role in the post-1984 government. It has retained a commitment to the mixed economy and political pluralism, suggesting implicitly that it does not view these two institutions of capitalism as inherently antithetical to a democratic revolution that puts the poor first. This can also be interpreted as a rejection of Marxian economism, which states that they are antithetical to a fully democratic society. In contrast, the FSLN has sought to repress those interests that would maintain a mixed economy and political pluralism in a capitalist form. It has been groping toward something that can be labeled a socialist mixed economy, and this is why many business interests have defected.

For private sector interests the loss of power in the economic sphere has been greater than in the political sphere, where the FSLN governs the National Assembly with a two-thirds majority. The analogous case for the United States would be if the Democratic Party not only shifted to the left but did so with sufficient popular support to win two-thirds majorities in both houses of Congress. Under such circumstances the protests of Republicans and the right would sound much like COSEP in Managua. Because the FSLN is still fighting the contra war (the current Arias peace project notwithstanding), the authoritarianism implicit in a military organization will likely persist and continue to taint its hegemonic efforts. Thus, its political role as the dominant party in the National Assembly should give the FSLN more opportunity to realize a democratic hegemony, yet this is constrained by the military imperatives of the contra war.

Sandinismo and the FSLN have evolved from a complex authoritarian/democratic hegemonic practice. However, the second determinant of its position on the hegemony spectrum is the extent of popular participation in the revolutionary process. The pivotal variable here is the role of the mass organizations as vehicles of popular empowerment. The five principal ones are the Comités de Defensa Sandinista (Sandinista Defense Committees, or CDSs), the Central Sandinista de Trabajadores (Sandinista Workers' Confederation, or CST), the ATC, the Unión Nacional de Agricultores y Ganadores de Nicaragua (National Union of Farmers and Cattle Ranchers, or UNAG), and the AMNLAE. If these organizations were truly autonomous, directly represented their constituency's interests in the revolutionary process, and yet were unified under the hegemonic principle of equal self-determination, then a strong case for democratic hegemony exists.

Popular participation has been a basic theme of the FSLN for more than twenty years and is an integral element of Sandinismo and its hegemonic practice (Vilas, 1986b: 249). Yet, critics argue that the mass organizations are a political tool of the FSLN and a vehicle to spread a repressive Sandinismo hegemony—a political appendage for control. Although it is true that the mass organizations are vehicles of Sandinista hegemony, if this is a democratic hegemony then the criticism is unfounded. . . .

Additionally, since the elections in 1984, the mass organizations are no longer directly represented in the national government (as they were in the previous Council of State between 1979 and 1984), and their autonomy and interest representation have been reduced (Vilas, 1986a). In part this is due to the government's emphasis on control in the face of the contra war, and in part it is due to the replacement of the mass organization's functions by government organs.

The relationship of the mass organizations to democratic hegemony can be summarized in the following way. To the extent that the FSLN is constituted by the mass organizations as an umbrella organization and coalition, hegemony is more democratic than if the FSLN is the constituting force. Also, to the extent that the mass organizations are more a policy-formulating body than a policy-executing body vis-à-vis the FSLN, then hegemony is also more democratic. This issue is clearly complex, and it is not my purpose here to argue definitively for one case or the other but to provide a framework in which to situate the analysis.

Another related question concerns the spectrum of interests represented by the mass organizations. How much pluralism is necessary to constitute a democratic hegemony? Generally, all those interests that are not "with the process" do not have representation comparable to the other mass organizations. Their interests are either repressed or neglected, because, judged by Sandinismo, their interests conflict with putting the poorest segments first; they seek a capitalist mixed economy rather than a socialist one; or they reject subordinating profit making to broader social needs. These group interests, although not part of the hegemonic process, are part of the discourse of rights and continually appeal to "equal" and "human" rights for the legitimacy of their demands. For example, when interviewed in 1987, the leadership of the opposition Partido Social Demócrata (Social Democratic Party, or PSD; founded 1979; member of the Coordinadora and not represented in the National Assembly) admitted to us that they are guaranteed rights to organize and conduct campaigns. They also produced photographs of what appeared to be police brutality at one of their rallies in early 1987. They argued that the Managua police, acting as instruments of Sandinista repression, tried to forcibly break up their legal rally and deny their rights. When questioned, Sandinista representatives claimed they were intentionally provoked into dispersing the crowd. Again, definitive conclusions, as this case indicates, are difficult to make. The political space for opposition parties to extend the boundaries of pluralism has existed yet it is questionable whether this has been adequately utilized by them (see Jenkins, 1986: 522). . . .

The Problem of Democratic Hegemony

The fundamental issue in assessing the Nicaraguan situation is not to be found in the critique of Sandinista economic policy, because this is governed by the broader goal of obtaining hegemony within the revolutionary process and transition. The hegemonic process is publicly symbolized throughout Nicaragua by the copresence of both the blue-and-white national flag and the red-and-black Sandinista flag. Conservative American delegations generally view this as a sign of Leninism and totalitarianism because the implicit message for them is that the state and the party are presented as one. It suggests the existence of the one-party dictatorship.

However, for most Nicaraguans the copresence of national and Sandinista flags represents the populist character of the revolution: "rescuing the nation for the people." Nicaragua, as a formally independent nation, preceded the revolution but did not "belong" to the people. Consequently what Sandinismo represents is the movement to return the nation to the people. It is precisely this type of process that Ernesto Laclau has referred to as socialist populism (Laclau, 1979: 195–198).

Its goal is not a totalitarian society in which central planning and state ownership remove all elements of pluralism and reduce the concept of human rights to something that merely complements socialist society. Such a model, which we associate with Soviet society, is one, according to Lefort (1986: 284),

> which seems to institute itself without divisions, which seems to have mastery of its own organization, a society in which each part seems to be related to every other and imbued by one and the same project of building socialism. It is able to exercise its constraint over every category of the population and to issue instructions which have the status of norms in every sphere of social life.

Sandinismo as a hegemonic ideology is situated within the discourse of rights. Its major appeal for mobilization of the population has been the extension of rights of the poor, women, workers, landless campesinos, and indigenous peoples on the Atlantic coast. It seeks a mixed economy whose socialist character subordinates the rights of business interests (for profit-led growth and market-based allocation) to the broader right of equal self-determination. (It is in spirit what Bowles, Gordon, and Weisskopf suggest as the "Economic Bill of Rights"; see Bowles et al., 1983: 261–390).

Democratic hegemony is therefore the process of achieving a democratized mixed economy (a radical democracy) through the discourse of rights. The question is whether this can be achieved in a Third World nation like Nicaragua.

The new socialist politics based on rights discourse is a product of the Western capitalist experience and is situated within the traditions of stable constitutional democracies. Autonomous social movements in the United States (women, blacks, labor, sexual preference, etc.) are precipitated within a given context of civil liberties, and by taking advantage of these freedoms they are able to pursue their interests through the discourse of rights that precedes their mobilization. Building a radical democracy in the United States by broadening the coalition of autonomous groups is sensible because the autonomy of these groups is less likely to be threatened by centralization than in Nicaragua. Individual social groups and movements in the United States are able to enter coalitions, but because of their established independent histories they can preserve their autonomy, operate within a collective process, and still protect the rights and interests of their members. Therefore, what makes this process entirely different in the advanced capitalist nations is that the revolutionary vigilance function would be minimal for its social groups.

This means, according to Lefort's argument, that they can better cope with the inherent "indeterminacy" of democratization processes that proceed from rights discourse. "Once the rights of man are declared, there arises, so it is said, the fiction of man without determination" (Lefort, 1986: 257). The liberal state is a "theatre of a contestation" of competing and conflicting rights, because rights discourse itself is indeterminate. According to Lefort (1986: 305), modern democratic society

> seems like a society in which power, law and knowledge are exposed to a radical indetermination, a society that has become the theatre of an uncontrollable adventure, so that what is instituted never becomes established, the known remains undermined by the unknown, the present proves to be undefinable, covering many different social times which are staggered in relation to one another within simultaneity—or definable only in terms of some fictitious future; an adventure such that the quest for identity cannot be separated from the experience of division.

Thus the problem of achieving a fully democratic society is one of using rights to both preserve differences and create universal equality in decision-making power. It seeks to subordinate all rights to that of equal self-determination. Democratic hegemony preserves differences and yet homogenizes all particularity under the global right of equal control over social decision-making processes. The dimension of indeterminacy cannot be removed. Given this problematic, the Nicaraguans face grave difficulties in their effort to construct a radical democracy.

The pressures of the contra war, the embryonic state of many of the mass organizations, the volatility of the new state, and the revolution's military dimension, all impede the process of a democratic hegemony and push toward totalitarianism. Why? It is because totalitarianism "tends to weld power and society back together again, to efface all signs of social division, to banish the indetermination that haunts the democratic experience" (Lefort, 1986: 305).

If Lefort is correct, then the inherent problem of indeterminacy in democratization processes will make the realization of the Sandinista vision far more difficult. The scenario of democratic hegemony based upon rights discourse is perhaps most applicable to the advanced capitalist nations. The Arias peace process, if it ultimately leads to an end of the contra war, will advance the prospects for a democratic hegemony. It is also clear that the primary objective of the Reagan administration was to end the Sandinista experiment, and only if this objective can be better served by the Arias peace proposal will such a plan be supported.

In the face of the contra war and the termination of U.S. contra aid, Sandinista resolve has not waned. As O'Brien suggests, this has caused Sandinismo to become more a faith than an ideology. As most Nicaraguans who are with the process understand it, Sandinismo has always been a faith and a commitment to "rescue the nation for the people." This accurately expresses both the nationalism and the socialist populism that are inseparable and yet so vital to Nicaragua's hegemonic process.

6.4

State, Class, and Transition in Nicaragua

David F. Ruccio

This essay examines the role of class and state in the revolutionary transition in progress during the 1980s and notes changing class structure in the evolving mixed economy.

N OT UNLIKE OTHER CASES of peripheral socialist development, the emergence of a "mixed economy" in Nicaragua over the past eight years has been accompanied by both qualitative and quantitative changes in the nature and role of the state (for more detailed analysis, see Ruccio, 1986; 1987).

According to certain well-known indicators (for example, the percentage of gross domestic product [GDP] produced within the "public sector"), there has been a quantitative increase in the role of the state in the Nicaraguan economy and society compared with its role under the Somoza regime (although somewhat less than is commonly believed). In this sense, the Nicaraguan "mixed economy" is characterized, as would be expected, by a general extension of the state into areas previously restricted to private enterprise and other nonstate institutions.

In a qualitative sense, the restructuring of the Nicaraguan state has involved, on the one hand, the maintenance and/or extension of some activities previously performed in and by the state. Thus, for example, the state has increased its participation in such activities as health and education. On the other hand, the Nica-

First published in *Latin American Perspectives* 57, vol. 15 (2), Sage Publications, Inc. Reprinted with permission from the Latin American Perspectives Collective. Selection from 52–57.

raguan state has been transformed by the shifting of traditionally nonstate activities to the state itself. This is true in the case of, for example, the state's near-total control over foreign trade and banking and the production of commodities by state enterprises.

These qualitative changes raise the question of whether or not the current Nicaraguan state exhibits a class structure different from the one that characterized the prerevolutionary state under Somoza. An analysis of the class nature of the state in peripheral socialist economies has traditionally been quite elusive (compare with Saul, 1986: 225). (For a critical review of alternative theories of the state and a fuller elaboration of the Marxian class-analytic approach that informs the present analysis, see Resnick and Wolff, 1983.) One way of getting at this question is to consider the class (and nonclass) processes that can be said to make up the current Nicaraguan state. Toward this end, a few definitions are in order. According to a Marxian framework of analysis, different societies can be distinguished by the mode in which surplus labor is pumped out of the direct producers. This process of performing and extracting surplus labor may be called the "fundamental class process." Thus the feudal fundamental class process, to take one familiar example from history, involves the performance and extraction of surplus labor in the form of feudal rent. This process of surplus-labor appropriation may be distinguished from the "subsumed-class process," the process whereby surplus labor, once appropriated, is distributed. Again, to use a well-known example, the feudal subsumed-class process means that, once the rent is extracted from feudal serfs, it is distributed to a variety of other feudal classes—other feudal lords, the king, the church, and so forth—so that the social conditions for extracting feudal rent are reproduced over time. Finally, "nonclass processes" refer to all other social processes that include neither the performance/ appropriation nor the distribution/receipt of surplus labor.

These class concepts can be used to analyze a peripheral socialist society, as well as any one of the institutions or "sites" in such a society. In the case of Nicaragua, the state, after the fall of Somoza, has continued to be the site of a variety of nonclass and subsumed-class processes; it has also become the site of a fundamental class process. In other words, the state is involved in activities that include (1) the process of extracting surplus labor (the fundamental class process); (2) the process of distributing and receiving already extracted surplus labor (the subsumed-class process); and (3) a variety of other economic, political, and cultural (nonclass) processes.

More concretely, the Nicaraguan state, according to this view, has become the site of the capitalist fundamental class process by virtue of extraction of surplus labor in the form of surplus value within firms that make up the Area of People's Property (APP). The nationalization of the vast holdings of Somoza and his closest allies has meant that a significant number of capitalist enterprises have passed from the private sector to the public sphere. However, the new location of these enterprises does not mean that the extraction of surplus value has ceased to exist.

A radical change in the political process of property ownership does not lead, in any automatic way, to the elimination of the capitalist form of extracting surplus labor. Many other changes would have to occur in order to conclude that the capitalist class process had been eliminated and some other, perhaps communal, process of appropriating surplus labor had emerged.

At the same time, this conclusion does not imply that private and state capitalist enterprises are the same, that they exhibit the same structure or have the same dynamic. In the case of Nicaragua two differences are quite apparent. Directors of state enterprises must be appointed to their positions by state officials (including members of the predominant particular party, the Frente Sandinista de Liberación Nacional [FSLN]), and state enterprises have generally widened the scope of worker participation in the overall running of the enterprises (Ortega, 1985). Without leading to the elimination of the capitalist fundamental class process, at least in the short run, such changes do produce new contradictions and developments in these new sites of surplus-value appropriation.

The Nicaraguan state has also become the site of a wide variety of nonclass economic, political, and cultural processes. For example, the state is involved in economic processes such as the marketing of commodities and credit allocation, in political processes such as lawmaking and law enforcement, and in cultural processes such as education and the dissemination of information in newspapers. Many of these processes have been carried over and even strengthened from the prerevolutionary period. Others are relatively new. More important for the purposes at hand, some of these nonclass processes may be viewed as conditions that reproduce the various modes of extracting surplus labor throughout Nicaraguan society. Surplus labor is extracted in and through a variety of capitalist and noncapitalist fundamental class processes both inside and outside the state—in privately owned and state-owned capitalist enterprises, as well as by individual and cooperative producers of agricultural and industrial goods. (Of the other possible class processes to which Marxists have traditionally directed their attention, slavery has not existed for quite some time and the feudal mode of surplus-labor appropriation has been virtually eliminated in Nicaragua since the downfall of Somoza.) To the extent that the state participates in reproducing the different types of surplus-labor extraction, including its own position as extractor of surplus value, it receives and distributes a portion of the extracted surplus labor and thereby participates in subsumed-class processes.

The Nicaraguan "mixed economy" is thus characterized by a state with a qualitatively new class structure. Viewing the state in this way means that state employees participate in a variety of class and nonclass processes; they occupy a variety of class and nonclass positions. Some state employees occupy the two positions of extractor and distributor of surplus value as the directors of state capitalist enterprises. Other state employees perform the surplus labor that is extracted in the form of surplus value. Still other employees within the state receive distributions of the surplus labor extracted in both state and nonstate enterprises. This is the case, for example, of managers of state capitalist enterprises and recipients within the state of taxes, merchant fees, and interest payments from capitalist and other fundamental class extractors of surplus labor. The state also has a large number of employees who do not perform, extract, distribute, or receive surplus labor. They include military personnel, employees of nonindustrial capitalist enterprises (such as banks and marketing firms), secretaries, judges, and so forth. Thus a large number of state employees hold nonclass positions.

It should be emphasized that the new class structure of the Nicaraguan state, along with the new class positions of state employees, is defined with respect to the processes of surplus labor appropriation and distribution. It is expressly not based on the amount of income received or on the political power that the state or individual members of the state may wield. Individuals may hold considerable political power and yet occupy nonclass positions. The president of the republic and the heads of ministries exercise considerable political power; indeed, they hold power over occupants of both fundamental and subsumed-class positions both inside and outside the state. That power has even become more concentrated in recent years. However, at least under the current arrangement, they do not exploit workers or others, whether inside or outside the state; they occupy nonclass positions. Similarly, unless the incomes received by members of the state include either directly extracted or initially distributed surplus labor, the income-producing position is a nonclass position. The fact that a relatively large number of individuals occupy class positions—fundamental and subsumed—in the current Nicaraguan state, compared to the prerevolutionary state under Somoza, is due in large part to the existence of capitalist enterprises within the APP.

This quantitative and qualitative restructuring of the Nicaraguan state naturally involves a new set of tensions and struggles over the range and nature of the social processes that make up the state. Consider the noneconomic example of state involvement in the "New Education." Since 1979 Nicaraguan education has experienced a large number of changes, including the teaching of anti-imperialist views of history, the integration of military and productive tasks with classroom teaching, and the transformation of traditionally lucrative, individual professional studies like medicine into areas of social responsibility. Therefore, it is not surprising that there has been intense struggle over the nature and effects of the new educational system. Moreover, the struggles that have emerged have involved complex alliances that often cut across the line of social groups such as workers, capitalists, and state officials. For example, members of the church hierarchy in opposition to secular education are joined by other supporters of private religious education. These allies, at least on this issue, include capitalists who see the new public education as producing ideas that undermine capitalist exploitation and workers on the Atlantic Coast who see state education as calling into question regional autonomy. At the same time, capitalists and subsumed-class enterprise managers, both inside and outside the state, support state officials in the latter group's attempt to foster a type of mass education that continues to produce trained productive laborers.

In general, all the social processes that make up the state will have contradictory effects on the class processes of the wider society. State involvement in the cultural process of education, to continue the preceding example, serves to reproduce and/or alter the fundamental class processes; it involves the training of potential workers as well as the dissemination of conceptions of work, life, and so forth. Therefore, state-sponsored education provides some of the cultural conditions whereby one or another mode of appropriating surplus labor is reproduced over time. The provision of mass education, for example, positively affects the productivity of laborers who produce surplus value, thus providing a condition of existence for capitalism. However, the process of education may, and probably does, affect this fundamental class process in contradictory ways: While training productive laborers, educators may disseminate ideas about social life that are in opposition to capitalist exploitation. New ideas may even be produced that foster the emergence of alternative ways of organizing production and social life. Some of the cultural conditions of existence of collective or communal class processes may be fostered in this way. Other social processes performed in and by the state will have similarly contradictory class effects; thus they can be expected to be the objects of tension and struggle on the part of social groups both inside and outside the state.

In the case of Nicaragua, such complex tensions and struggles have emerged over a wide range of state initiatives in addition to education—including property ownership, marketing, price-setting, law enforcement, national defense, and so forth. The outcomes of these struggles will participate in determining future changes in the class structure both of the state and of the wider society.

6.5

Revolution, Counterrevolution, and Imperialism

David Broad

This piece reflects on the counterrevolution and electoral defeat of the Sandinistas in Nicaragua and setbacks to revolution elsewhere.

O N THE MORNING OF February 26, 1990, we learned that after years of hard work and sacrifice the Sandinistas and their supporters had lost Nicaragua's second set of free and fair elections to the U.S.-backed Unión Nacional de Oposición (National Opposition Union—UNO), whose main elements were bourgeois industrialists and landowners. One observer wondered if the contras (counter-revolutionaries), who had been militarily defeated by the Sandinista army, had lost the war but won the elections (Close, 1990).

The initial shock of the Sandinista defeat was similar to that which many experienced following the U.S. invasion of Grenada in 1983. Others will recall Chile in 1973, the Dominican Republic in 1965, and so forth. Bad as the situation is, especially for those directly involved, the only way to move on is to put this latest defeat in historical perspective. In a longer view, revolutionary forces have made great advances since the last century, and this is not the "end of history" (Fukuyama, 1989). Despite the rush to "inter communism and exalt capitalism" (Marzani, 1990), the decline of the latter continues—the more obviously if we accept Lenin's (1915) view that history moves in a spiral.

First published in *Latin American Perspectives* 77, vol. 20 (2), Sage Publications, Inc. Reprinted with permission from the Latin American Perspectives Collective. Selection from 6–7, 10–12, 14–16.

The Longer View

Revolution, counterrevolution, and imperialism are enduring features of the world capitalist system. The transition from feudalism to capitalism in Western Europe occurred as the result of a lengthy struggle between proponents of the new order ("revolutionaries") and those of the old order ("counterrevolutionaries"), with "the masses" pulled in both directions between them (Amin et al., 1990; Arrighi, Hopkins, and Wallerstein, 1989; Kandal, 1989), and from its inception capitalism has been an imperialist enterprise (Koning, 1991). The decline of capitalism also involves a lengthy struggle between revolutionaries and counterrevolutionaries (Sweezy, 1985). The capitalist world system has experienced two distinct phases of revolution with 1789 as the watershed. The French Revolution was at once the pinnacle and the precipice of capitalism. With its call for "liberty, equality, and fraternity," it marked the dawn of struggle for a truly new world order made the more urgent by new forms of exploitation and alienation wrought by the Industrial Revolution and the subsequent "new imperialism."

The European revolutions of 1848 and the Soviet revolution of 1917 were high points of socialist struggle against capitalism (Arrighi, Hopkins, and Wallerstein, 1989). Socialism has had a checkered career, however, and recent events have thrown all but the brashest ideologues into a state of confusion. We are obviously in a historical space of great flux. As Sweezy (1990: 18) has said, "Certain years go down in history as landmarks—the beginning or end of an era, a major turning point. Such years were 1776, 1789, 1848, 1917, 1939. Nineteen eighty-nine promises to be another worthy of addition to the list." Sweezy is, of course, referring primarily to the changes in Eastern Europe, where the old Stalinist regimes fell in rapid succession, the two Germanies were reunited, and capitalist market reforms appear to have become the order of the day. It is also significant that 1989 was the bicentenary of the French Revolution, which Western bourgeoisies have "celebrated" with trivialization and renunciation (Singer, 1989) as they rush toward the integration of the Western European capitalist economies— "Europe 1992."

The year 1989 saw major changes in the Third World as well—a turning point in the struggle between revolutionaries and counterrevolutionaries capped by the 1990 electoral defeat of the Sandinistas in Nicaragua. There has been a significant alteration in post–World War II relations between imperialist and anti-imperialist forces, involving what some (e.g., Gasperini, 1990) see as the disappearance of the "Vietnam Syndrome." After the military defeat of U.S. imperialism in Vietnam in the mid-1970s, U.S. popular opinion and Soviet power constrained the interventionist tendencies of U.S. rulers. The low level of U.S. public opposition to the invasion of Panama and the Gulf War suggests that these constraints are weakening, particularly now that the Soviet Union no longer constitutes an international counterbalance to U.S. hegemony. The fallout from the attempted coup seems to have settled the latter issue, ensured the reintegration of the republics of the former Soviet Union into the capitalist world system, and left even Cuba out in the cold. . . .

A Social Democratic Interlude?

Nicaraguans are not, however, experiencing a return to the status quo ante. As Kahn (1990: 38) points out,

> Gramsci wrote . . . that in periods of static equilibrium in the relationship of forces, both sides acquiesce in a dictator to put a halt to unending and unresolvable civil strife. According to Gramsci, who follows Marx in this observation, such a dictator can lend support, as much as the relationship of forces allows, to either the progressive or reactionary forces.

Substituting "democrat" (read liberal-cum-social democrat) for "dictator" here would produce an approximation of the present situation in Central America (1993). In Nicaragua both sides have acquiesced in the "democracy" of the bourgeois opposition. In El Salvador there are serious negotiations between the ruling class and the opposition forces, with even the Frente Farabundo Martí para la Liberación Nacional (Farabundo Martí National Liberation Front—FMLN) talking about the need for a negotiated settlement and a pluralist politics (Gellen, 1990; Villalobos, 1989). What are the prospects for compromise?

In Nicaragua, the Frente Sandinista de Liberación Nacional (Sandinista National Liberation Front—FSLN) took 41 percent of the vote in 1990 and is the best-organized political movement in the country. There the relationship of forces means that the "democrat," whose own alliance is fractured, must *gain* support from the progressive forces. In El Salvador, the reactionary Alianza Republicana Nacionalista (Republican Nationalist Alliance—ARENA) forces hold the reins of power but even with the support of U.S. imperialism have been unable to defeat the revolutionaries. The FMLN showed its strength and popular support through its recent offensive in the capital (Miles and Ostertag, 1990) and its ability to assault the president's own neighborhood (*Globe and Mail*, 1990a). Again the "democrat" must negotiate with the progressive forces. Regionally, however, the "democrats" are increasingly right-wing, and U.S. imperialism is the wild card. The result, according to Carty (1990), is "low-intensity democracy."

Sweezy (1989: 1) asserts that "the 1990s will witness the disintegration of the worldwide U.S. empire and its probable replacement by a system of competing trade-and-currency blocs." While this is likely, it could mean increasing pressure on Central America as the United States tries to reassert control over its historic "sphere of influence." After Panama, the Nicaraguans could not rule out a direct

U.S. military intervention, and, as the Sandinistas recognize, if the contras refuse to disarm and a civil war erupts, the United States could intervene to save a fledgling "democracy." One FSLN leader, Victor Tirado, has gone so far as to argue that the "cycle of anti-imperialist revolutions is over" and progressive forces will have to come to an accommodation with imperialists and find new ways to achieve revolutionary goals (*Barricada*, 1990).

With the changes in the East, revolutionaries in the Third World can no longer depend on the Soviets for support. Cuba is increasingly placed on the defensive by U.S. belligerence toward its revolution (*Globe and Mail*, 1990b). But invasions of Cuba and Nicaragua would not be as easy as the 1983 invasion of Grenada, and the revolutions have made too many gains to be turned back completely. Even the short experience of "the revo" in Grenada has left its impact, and the people have found the U.S. alternative to be no alternative (McAfee, 1990). The United States apparently could not even invade Panama and overthrow its ruler with impunity: the invaders met stiff opposition (see Becker and Brown, 1990; Leis, 1990; and Petras, 1990a). The FDR leader Rubén Zamora remarked over two years ago that low-intensity warfare was not working for the United States in El Salvador (Calhoun, 1989).

Thus in Nicaragua the new right-wing government must dialogue with the left-wing opposition. In El Salvador both sides have admitted that a military end to the civil war is unlikely, and the FMLN has stated that its November 1989 offensive was intended to push negotiations (Zielinski, 1990). On September 25, 1992, the ARENA government and the FMLN signed an accord bringing the warring parties, as one observer put it, "to the brink of peace" (Tardy, 1991). The upsurge of armed guerrilla activities in Guatemala is intended, according to the Unidad Revolucionaria Nacional de Guatemala (National Revolutionary Union of Guatemala—URNG), to make its "democratic" government more serious about negotiations and encourage the army (which holds the real power) to participate. The most immediate result has been a call from some sectors of the Guatemalan ruling class and the army (some of the most reactionary groups in the hemisphere) for a return to the "total war" of the early 1980s. But the popular sector has rebounded somewhat from that phase of terror, and some communities have even begun to refuse to participate in the so-called civil defense patrols set up by the army to increase its control over the civilian population (see Reed, 1990; Vine, 1990; and *Guatemala Update*, Spring 1990). The ruling class, along with its right-wing counterparts in El Salvador and Nicaragua, is divided over what means will achieve its ends. The balance of forces in the region might suggest a sort of interim social democratic compromise. But even if this turns out to be a possibility, the problems of the region and of the Third World in general are too serious for it to be a long-term solution. The social structures of inequality generated by peripheral capitalism must be tackled head-on, and the counterinsurgency states and death squads constructed to maintain those structures must be dismantled (Marini, 1980).

Again, the wild card is U.S. imperialism, and the Bush administration has shown little sign of favoring compromise. The November 1989 fighting in El Salvador ended Guatemala's "active neutrality" in regional foreign affairs; "a U.S. Air Force Hercules 144 transport plane left Guatemala City for El Salvador, apparently carrying arms or soldiers. The French Press Agency (AFP) reported that 126 of Guatemala's elite counterinsurgency force 'Kaibiles' were transferred to El Salvador" (*Guatemala Update,* Spring 1990). And in Guatemala itself, White House moves appear to have been designed to damage the chances of the Christian Democratic presidential candidate, Alfonso Cabrera, in the fall 1990 elections in favor of one of the more reactionary candidates (Reed, 1990: 11). (The winner was Jorge Serrano Elias, an evangelical businessman.) . . .

Socialism or the End of History?

U.S. rulers are under pressure from various sides. We in the West are informed (more often *mis*informed) about prodemocracy struggles in the East, but there are democratic successes throughout the South as well. Along with the Latin American examples already discussed we should note those of Brazil, where the leftist Workers' Party (Partido Trabalhista, or PT) won 47 percent of the popular vote in the November 1989 presidential elections, and has initiated the São Paulo Forum of regional socialist and social democratic parties and movements to articulate socioeconomic alternatives to neoliberalism; of Mexico, where there is growing popular opposition to the long-reigning Partido Revolucionario Institucional (Institutional Revolutionary Party—PRI) and critics claim that the leftist coalition headed by Cuauhtémoc Cárdenas was cheated out of its 1988 electoral victory by a fraudulent vote count; of Haiti, where slave revolts fought the first independent state in Latin America in 1804 and more recent popular opposition has routed the Duvalier dictatorship and brought liberation theologian Jean-Bertrand Aristide to the presidency; of South Africa, where popular forces and international pressures have pushed the rulers to begin negotiations with the African National Congress over the dismantling of apartheid; of Israel, where another apartheid state has been unable to repress the Palestinian *intifada;* of the Philippines, where Corazón Aquino's "democracy" is subject to coup after coup as the ruling sectors squabble over their inability to squash the New People's Army and other popular forces and the campaign against the presence of U.S. military bases; of Uganda, where the National Resistance Movement under the leadership of Yoweri Museveni has begun to bring "the jewel of Africa" out of a long night of dictatorship (Boyd, 1989); and of Nepal, where a prodemocracy movement that includes communists has forced the thirty-year-old autocratic monarchy into a democratic opening (Sunita, 1990). These struggles may not lead to the socialist conclusion we might have expected some years ago, but even an interim social democratic compromise is a step forward. And "the end of the Cold War" may bring some positive results, as in Ethiopia, where the crumbling of an unpopular Soviet-backed regime gives some breathing space to popular liberation movements such as the Eritrean People's Liberation Front.

The problem is that we do not really know what socialism is. Even in Eastern Europe, where the rhetoric is that of "anticommunism" and "antisocialism," there are neither clear ideas nor consensus on which way to go. While there is movement toward the adoption of market policies and Western ideas, many are cautious about their new relations with the West. In eastern Germany, for example, people are wary about losing social rights such as guaranteed child care for working mothers (Allen, 1990).

In the West as well there are growing popular movements for social justice. Some real innovations in more communal forms have been effected, especially by the most exploited and oppressed sectors of our societies (see, e.g., Sivanandan, 1990), and these experiments will likely increase as ruling classes implement neoconservative/neoliberal policies that lead to a sort of peripheralization of the center, with increasing social inequality, unemployment, and homelessness (Broad, 1988). It is clear that, for growing numbers of people in both center and periphery, capitalism has not delivered the goods (Navarro, 1989), and the argument that socialism is necessary for social well-being has lost none of its validity (Huberman, 1969).

As U.S. imperialism continues to decline and the capitalist world breaks up into rival economic blocs, Petras (1990b: 17) notes a shift on the part of some U.S. rulers "from geopolitical confrontations in the East and South for ideological hegemony, to economic rivalries within the West for global market shares." Their policies give a high profile to state subsidies for exports while continuing to preach deficit reduction. This will mean "cutting social programs to 'remain internationally competitive,'" thus exacerbating the problems of the working class. Growing economic problems combined with already growing demands for disarmament and environmental programs spell a social order very different from capitalism, but constructing this social order will take a long time. It will take "disalienation" (cf. Amin, 1980) to create Che Guevara's socialist "new man." As Magdoff and Sweezy (1990: 16) point out, the possessive individuals of classic political economy "did not just appear one fine day to run the new economy. It took generations to create them."

We live in confused and confusing times, where black and white often seem to blend into grey. With Galeano (1990: 12),

> I sometimes feel as though they have stolen even our words. The term "socialism" is applied in the West as make-up for injustice; in Eastern Europe, it evokes purgatory or maybe hell. . . . In our time, the bureaucrats have stigmatized hope and besmirched the most beautiful of human adventures; but I also believe that socialism is not Stalinism. . . . And today more than ever it is necessary to dream. To dream, together, dreams that undream themselves and become incarnate in mortal matter.

. . . This is my testimony. A dinosaur's confession? Perhaps. In any case, it is the affirmation of one who believes that the human condition is not doomed to selfishness and the obscene pursuit of money, and that socialism did not die, because it had not yet been—that today is the first day of the long life before it.

While many on the left are jumping ship and drifting into "post-Marxism" or some other form of liberalism (cf. Sivanandan, 1990), socialism is still the best term to describe the uncharted waters leading to a better world. Perhaps now that some of the counterfeit and bogus versions of socialism are out of the way we can get on with struggles for the real thing. As global capitalism continues to produce the conditions for militarism, environmental destruction, and destitution of the world's masses, more than ever the choice appears to be between "socialism" and "barbarism."

Conclusion

Looking back on the essays we have chosen for this reader, specific themes emerge that students can relate to the theoretical concerns, issues, and questions raised to this point. First, we were concerned with a definition or conception of development and suggested a variety of approaches to the problem. We identified and characterized political, economic, social, and cultural development and distinguished between development under capitalism and under socialism. We hope students will use these ideas to elaborate a personal approach that examines theoretical perspectives and real situations related to possibilities of providing for people's basic needs and improving their quality of life.

Second, we mentioned earlier the need to look at development theory in relation to nineteenth-century imperialism theory and to twentieth- and twenty-first-century globalization theory. This task involves identifying and understanding the many lines of thinking running through each of these three theoretical directions and comparing and contrasting their approaches. Students should critically assess our central thesis that these bodies of literature and the theories underlying them tend to overlap and even to recycle old questions and debates in the rhetoric of revised and new terminology. This assessment would thus necessitate a look back into historical trends dating to the late nineteenth century.

Once students are able to evaluate these past and present theoretical concerns, it could be useful to focus on the implications of the dependency debates that dominated progressive thinking during the 1960s and 1970s and mainstream social science during the 1980s. An important question is the extent of influence of dependency ideas in contemporary analysis. Academics usually assume that dependency theory is not relevant today, yet the current writing on Latin America is replete with evidence of its use in explaining particular situations. Initially, Latin American intellectuals turned to dependency as a way to understand backwardness and underdevelopment and to counter the prevailing North American belief that capitalism could diffuse into and transform the less-

developed parts of the world. It is important to understand how this confrontation of dependency and diffusionist ideas helped Latin American thinkers in
comprehending why capitalism had not had a progressive influence on their
economies. We could follow the trajectory of the intellectuals who turned, first,
to Marx for the critical tools to combat intransigent ideas and policies that once
prevailed in both left and right political circles and, later, to the creative ideas of
radical thinkers who challenged traditional beliefs such as the notion that feudalism explains backwardness or the notion of the necessity for a national capitalist
class as a means of countering oligarchies. In this way, Latin American radicals
challenged sectarian doctrines emanating from the Soviet Union as well as ethno-
centric theory developed in Western Europe and the United States, in the process
influencing progressive North American scholarship.

Our inquiry into dependency has stimulated many questions. If precapitalist
relations of production have generally disappeared in Latin America, then what
sort of capitalist class has emerged? Is it committed to national development or
linked with international capital? Does it comprise large owners of monopolistic
business and banking capital who have ties with foreign capital? Or nonmonopo-
listic owners of industrial and commercial firms with ties to foreign and national
capital? Or small owners who tend to be nationalist and run artisan industries or
who are independent professionals? We can also examine the role of an agrarian
capitalist class of landowners who run farms with machinery and pay salaries to
workers.

Another line of inquiry could delve into the relationship of dependency to
concepts and theories evolving from a Marxist analysis and ask such questions
as whether Marx offered explanations that may help in analyzing capitalism
today. Marx may have fallen out of favor, yet his analysis of capital in the latter
half of the nineteenth century remains valuable for its method and insights.

Essentially, the task of formulating an understanding of development itself
must go beyond the earlier dependency debates. Various approaches in this
reader, such as neoliberal development, democratic development, and so on,
may help; it would also be useful to explore sustainable development, so fashionable in policy circles. Sustainability involves economic viability, environmental
sensitivity, and social responsiveness, with emphasis on working with and preserving nature and ensuring that natural resources are not depleted.

The search for development must consider the role of the state, given the tradition of a strong central state in Latin America and the more recent neoliberal
tendency toward dismantling and privatizing some state agencies and enterprises. The capitalist class usually is seen as capable of influencing or manipulat-
ing the state in its own interests. Or at times external constraints may inhibit the
state from pursuing interests contrary to capital. Or the state might be envisioned
as a social relation in which capital's interests are brought into play through representation and intervention.

A final consideration, evident in the cases presented in this reader, rests with development following either a capitalist or a socialist path. Capitalism has evolved through historical divisions of labor, in ancient times with the appearance of artisans who produced commodities and exchanged them freely for necessary goods and later with the introduction of money and the appearance of merchants specializing in commerce. Merchant capitalism was an elementary form in which owners appropriated surplus produced by workers and was especially prominent after the fourteenth century in Europe and later in Latin America. As industry was spawned through technology, capitalists evolved in the late nineteenth century in an era of industrial capitalism; later they began to form cartels, trusts, and holding companies through the concentration of finance capital or bank capital that penetrated and dominated industry. After World War II, the export of capital from the advanced nations to the less-developed parts of the world led to the rise of the transnational or multinational firm.

We know less about the transition to socialism, which implies the collective rather than private ownership of the major means of production. This transition involves the replacing of the capitalist state with the workers' state and the provision of the basic needs of all people, usually through a planned economy and ideally through participatory democracy in the struggle to eliminate a money economy, inequality, and the state. We can only begin to comprehend these complex transitional possibilities through awareness of historical experiences and important issues such as the agrarian question: For instance, what changes and reforms can be introduced in the face of large landowners and merchants who dominate the countryside? Once land is available to people in the countryside, should they be organized through state entities, cooperatives, or small subsistence farms? We might question the familiar use of a vanguard party as a mobilizing force in the transition, at the same time recognizing its failings and the tendency toward the hegemony of a powerful minority over the masses and limitations on participation in society. Another question considers whether socialism can evolve through the market, in which choice might depend on both the market and the state in a mixed economy, with some state enterprises existing alongside cooperatives and individually owned businesses but without large-scale private ownership of the means of production.

In addressing these themes, issues, and questions, we recognize that the study of development in Latin America must begin with historical examples and experience, a recognition that various theoretical perspectives affect our understandings, and a willingness to keep an open mind. It is important that we examine different points of view and not be content to settle on established premises. Many questions about Latin America remain largely unanswered and thus allow for interesting and rewarding study. The task ahead may be challenging but not impossible, and we hope that our presentation of different ideas will motivate student readers to take the plunge and discover new understandings through critical inquiry and thinking.

References

Adda, Jacques
  1996 *La mondialisation de l'économie.* 2 vols. Paris: La Découverte.
Albert, Michael et al.
  1986 *Liberating Theory.* Boston: South End Press.
Albrow, Martin
  2000 *The Golden Age: State and Society beyond Modernity.* Stanford, CA: Stanford University Press.
Allen, Bruce
  1990 "Unions in the GDR." *Our Times* 9 (April): 18–21.
Altimir, Oscar
  "Desigualidad, empleo, y pobreza en América Latina." *Desarrollo Económico* 37 (145): 3–30.
Amin, Ash (ed.)
  1966 *Post-Fordism: A Reader.* Oxford: Blackwell.
Amin, Samir
  1974 *Accumulation on a World Scale.* 2 vols. New York: Monthly Review Press.
  1980 *Class and Nation, Historically and in the Current Crisis.* New York: Monthly Review Press.
  1981 *The Future of Maoism.* New York: Monthly Review Press.
  1985 "The prospects for socialism," pp. 16–28 in Milos Nicolic (ed.), *Socialism on the Threshold of the Twenty-first Century.* London: Verso.
Amin, Samir, Giovanni Arrighi, André Gunder Frank, and Immanuel Wallerstein
  1990 *Transforming the Revolution: Social Movements and the World-System.* New York: Monthly Review Press.
Andreff, Wladimir
  1996 *Les multinationales globales.* Paris: La Découverte.
Antunes, Ricardo
  1994 "Recent strikes in Brazil: The main tendencies of the strike movement of the 1980s." *Latin American Perspectives* 21 (1): 24–37.
  1995a *Adeus ao trabalho? Ensaio sobre as metamorfoses e a centralidade do mundo do trabalho.* São Paulo: Cortez/Campinas: Universidad de Campinas.
  1995b *O novo sindicalismo no Brasil.* Campinas: Pontes.

Antunes, Ricardo (ed.)
1997 *Neoliberalismo, trabalho e sindicatos*. São Paulo: Boitempo.
Aricó, Jose
1980 "Mariátegui y la formación del Partido Socialista del Perú." *Socialismo y Participación* 11: 139–167.
Arrighi, Giovanni
1978 *The Geometry of Imperialism: The Limits of Hobson's Paradigm*. London: New Left Books.
Arrighi, Giovanni, Terence K. Hopkins, and Immanuel Wallerstein
1989 *Antisystemic Movements*. London: Verso.
Avelar, Sonia Maria de
1977 "Notas teóricas y metodológicas para el estudio del trabajo industrial a domicilio en México." *Revista Mexicana de Sociología* 39 (4): 1227–1250.
Averitt, Robert T.
1968 *The Dual Economy*. New York: Norton.
Babu, Abdul Mohamed
1981 *African Socialism or Socialist Africa?* London: Zed.
Baer, Werner
1965 *Industrialization and Economic Development in Brazil*. Homewood, IL: R. D. Irwin.
Baerrenson, D. W., M. Carnoy, and J. Grunwald
1965 *Latin American Trade Patterns*. Washington, D.C.: Brookings Institution.
Bahro, Rudolf
1984 *From Red to Green*. London: Verso.
Balibar, Etienne
1970 "The basic concepts of historical materialism," pp. 199–308 in Louis Althusser and Etienne Balibar, *Reading Capital*. London: New Left Books.
Bambirra, Vania
1978 *Teoría de la dependencia*. Mexico City: Ediciones Era.
Baran, Paul
1957 *The Political Economy of Growth*. New York: Monthly Review Press.
Barratt Brown, Michael
1974 *The Economics of Imperialism*. Baltimore: Penguin.
Barricada
1990 "Cycle of anti-imperialist revolutions is over." *The Guardian* 2 (May 2).
Barros, Robert
1986 "The left and democracy: Recent debates in Latin America." *Telos* 68 (Summer): 49–70.
Barroso, Manuel
1991 *Autoestima del venezolano: Democracia o marginalidad*. Caracas: Editorial Galac.
Bartra, Roger
1982 *El reto de la izquierda*. Mexico City: Grijalbo.
Becker, Brian and Esmeralda Brown
1990 "U.S. wields old-style colonial power in Panama." *The Guardian* 42 (March 14).
Becker, David G., Jeff Frieden, Sayre P. Schatz, and Richard L. Sklar
1987 *Postimperialism, International Capitalism, and Development in the Late Twentieth Century*. Boulder, CO: Lynne Rienner.

Beckford, George L.
1972 *Persistent Poverty: Underdevelopment in Plantation Economies of the Third World.* New York: Oxford University Press.
Bell, Daniel
1960 *The End of Ideology.* Glencoe: Free Press.
1976 *The Coming of Post-Industrial Society.* Harmondsworth: Penguin.
Bener ía, Lourdes and Shelley Feldman (eds.)
1992 *Unequal Burden: Economic Crises, Persistent Poverty, and Women's Work.* Boulder, CO: Westview Press.
Benería, Lourdes and Marta Roldán
1987 *The Crossroads of Class and Gender: Industrial Homework, Subcontracting, and Household Dynamics in Mexico City.* Chicago: University of Chicago Press.
Bengelsdorf, Carollee
1985 "Between visions and reality: Democracy in socialist theory and practice." Ph.D. dissertation, Massachusetts Institute of Technology.
Bennholdt-Thomas, Veronika
1981 "Marginalidad en América Latina: Una crítica de la teoría." *Revista Mexicana de Sociología* 43 (4): 1505–1546.
Bernstein, Henry
1979 "Sociology of underdevelopment versus sociology of development," pp. 77–106 in David Lehmann (eds.), *Development Theory: Four Critical Studies.* London: Cass.
Bethencourt, Luisa
1988 "La organización doméstica y la condición de la mujer en los sectores populares." *Cuadernos del CENDES* (September–December): 31–45.
Bettelheim, Charles
1978 *The Transition to Socialist Economy.* Sussex: Harvester.
Bettelheim, Charles and Paul Sweezy
1971 *On the Transition to Socialism.* New York: Monthly Review Press.
Beynon, Huw
1995 *The Changing Practices of Work.* Manchester: International Centre for Labour Studies.
Bihr, Alain
1991 *Du grand soir à l'alternative: Le mouvement ouvrier européen en crise.* Paris: Editions Ouvrières.
Birkbeck, Chris
1978 "Self-employed proletarians in an informal factory: The case of Cali's garbage dump." *World Development* 6 (9–10): 1173–1185.
1979 "Garbage, industry, and the 'vultures' of Cali, Colombia," pp. 161–183 in Ray Bromley and Chris Gerry (eds.), *Casual Work and Poverty in Third World Cities.* New York: John Wiley.
Bitar, Sergio
1979 *Transición, socialismo y democracia: La experiencia Chilena.* Mexico City: Siglo XXI.
Black, George
1981 *Triumph of the People.* London: Zed Press, 2 ed.
Block, Fred
1987 "Political choice and the multiple 'logics' of capital." *Theory and Society* 15: 175–192.

1987 *Revising State Theory: Essays in Politics and Postindustrialism.* Philadelphia: Temple University Press.

Bloom, Alexander
1986 *Prodigal Sons: The New York Intellectuals and Their World.* London: Oxford University Press.

Bluestone, Barry
1972 "Economic crises and the law of uneven development." *Politics and Society* 3 (Fall): 65–82.

Blumberg, Rae Lesser
1984 "A general theory of gender stratification," in Randall Collins (ed.), *Sociological Theory.* San Francisco: Jossey-Bass.
1991 "Income under female versus male control: Hypotheses from a theory of gender stratification and data from the Third World," pp. 97–127 in Rae Lesser Blumberg (ed.), *Gender, Family, and Economy: The Triple Overlap.* Newbury Park, CA: Sage.

Bobbio, Norberto
1987 *The Future of Democracy.* Minneapolis: University of Minnesota Press.

Bodenheimer, Suzanne
1971 "Dependency and imperialism: The roots of Latin American underdevelopment." *Politics and Society* 1 (May): 327–357.
1971 "Dependency and imperialism: The roots of Latin American underdevelopment," pp. 155–181 in K. T. Fann and Donald C. Hodges (eds.), *Readings in U.S. Imperialism.* Boston: Porter Sargent.

Boeninger, Eduardo
1985 "Prólogo," in M. dos Santos (ed.), *Concertación social y democracia.* Santiago: Centro de Estudios de Desarrollo.

Bonefeld, Werner
1998 "150 años: Reflexionando en la Ira." *Cuadernos del Sur* 26 (April).

Boorstein, Edward
1968 *The Economic Transformation of Cuba.* New York: Monthly Review Press.

Bowles, Samuel et al.
1983 *Beyond the Waste Land: Democratic Alternative to Economic Decline.* Garden City, NY: Anchor/Doubleday.

Bowles, Samuel and Herbert Gintis
1986 *Democracy and Capitalism: Property, Community, and the Contradictions of Modern Social Thought.* New York: Basic Books.

Boyd, Rosalind
1989 "The struggle for democracy: Uganda's National Resistance Movement." *Canadian Dimension* 23 (September): 29–35.

Boyer, Robert
1997 "Les mots et les realités," in *Mondialisation: Au-delà des mythes.* Paris: La Découverte.

Braverman, Harry
1974 *Labor and Monopoly Capital: The Degradation of Work in the Twentieth Century.* New York: Monthly Review Press.

Brenner, Robert
1995 "The politics of U.S. decline." *Against the Current* (September–October).

1999 "Beyond state-centrism? Space, territoriality, and geographical scale in globalization studies." *Theory and Society* 28: 39–78.

Brewer, Anthony
1980 *Marxist Theories of Imperialism: A Critical Survey.* London: Routledge & Kegan Paul.

Brezhnev, Leonid
1981 "Report to the 26th Party Congress." *Current Digest of the Soviet Press* 33 (March 25).

Broad, David
1988 "Peripheralization of the centre: W(h)ither Canada?" *Alternate Routes* 8 (Fall): 1–41.

Bromley, Ray
1978b "Organization, regulation, and exploitation in the so-called urban informal sector: The street traders of Cali, Colombia." *World Development* 6 (9–10): 1161–1171.

Brundenius, Claes
1981 *Economic Growth, Basic Needs, and Income Distribution in Revolutionary Cuba.* Lund, Sweden: University of Lund.
1985 *Estrategia del desarrollo industrial en Nicaragua.* Managua: Instituto de Investigationes Económicas y Sociales.

Brutents, Karen
1983 *The Newly Free Countries in the Seventies.* Moscow: Progress.

Bukharin, Nicolai
1971 *La economía mundial y el imperialismo.* Buenos Aires: Pasado y Presente.

Burbach, Roger and William Robinson
1999 "The fin de siècle debate: Globalization as epochal shift." *Science and Society* 63 (Spring): 10–39.

Burgess, Rod
1982 "Helping some to help themselves: Third World housing policies and development strategies," pp. 75–91 in Kosta Marhéy (ed.), *Beyond Self-Help Housing.* London: Mansell.

Calhoun, Jack
1989 "Rubén Zamora: 'Low-intensity warfare hasn't worked for U.S.'" *The Guardian* 40 (March 8): 13.

Calva, José Luis
1993 *El modelo neoliberal mexicano: Costos, vulnerabilidad, alternativas.* Mexico City: Fundación Friedrich Ebert.

Canitrot, Adolfo
1988 "Crecimiento, distribución y democracia," in EURAL (ed.), *Proyectos de cambio: La izquierda democrática en América Latina.* Caracas: Nueva Sociedad.

Carbonetto, Daniel
1985 "La heterogeneidad de la estructura productiva y el sector informal," pp. 47–68 in Daniel Carbonetto et al. (eds.), *El sector informal urbano en los paises andinos.* Quito and Guayaquil: ILDIS/CEPESIU.

Cardoso, Fernando Henrique
1972 "Dependency and development in Latin America." *New Left Review* 74 (July–August): 83–95.

1973a "Imperialism and Dependency in Latin America," pp. 7–16 in Frank Bonilla and Robert Girling (eds.), *Structures of Dependency*. Stanford, CA.

1973b *Clases sociales y crisis política en América Latina*. Mexico City: UNAM, Instituto de Investigaciones Sociales.

1973c "Notas sobre el estado actual de los estudios de la dependencia," pp. 90–125 in his *Problemas del subdesarrollo latinoamericano*. Mexico City: Editorial Nuestro Tiempo.

1973d "As contradições do desenvolvimento-associado." Berlin: Fundaçao Alemã para o Desenvolvimento Internacional, mimeographed.

1977 "The consumption of dependency: Theory in the United States." *Latin American Research Review* 12 (3): 7–24.

1982 "Poulantzas e os partidos do Brasil." *Novos Estudos CEBRAP* 1 (2): 3–7.

Cardoso, Fernando Henrique and E. Falleto

1970 *Dependencia y desarrollo en América Latina*. Mexico City: Siglo XXI.

1979 *Dependency and Development in Latin America*. Translated by Marjory Mattingly Urquidi. Berkeley: University of California Press.

Carranza, Julio

1992 "Cuba: Los retos de la economía." *Cuadernos de Nuestra América* 19 (July–December): 131–158.

Cartaya, Venessa

1987 "El confuso mundo del sector informal." *Nueva Sociedad* (88): 76–88.

Cartaya, Vanessa and Haydée García

1988 *Infancia y pobreza: Los efectos de la recesión en Venezuela*. Caracas: Editorial Nueva Sociedad.

Carty, Bob

1990 "LID: Low-intensity democracy." *This Magazine* 24 (September): 19–21.

Casas Regueira, Julio et al.

1990 *A problemas viejos, soluciones nuevas*. Havana: Editora Política.

Castaneda, Jorge

1980 *Nicaragua: Contradicciones en la revolución*. Mexico City: Siglo XXI.

Castells, Manuel

1983 *The City and the Grassroots*. Berkeley: University of California Press.

1996 *The Rise of the Network Society*. Oxford: Blackwell.

Castro, Raúl

1974 "Principles of people's power." *Granma Weekly Review* (September 8).

Caves, Richard E.

1971 "International corporations: The industrial economics of foreign investment." *Económica* 38 (February): 1–27.

Central única dos Trabalhadores

1991 ¿Negociação ou pacto social? Experiencias recentes do sindicalismo latinoamericano. São Paulo.

Cerroni, Umberto

1973 *Teoría política y socialismo*. Mexico City: Ediciones Era.

Chafetz, Janet Saltzman

1991 "The gender division of labor and the reproduction of female disadvantage: Toward an integrated theory," pp. 74–96 in Rae Lesser Blumberg (ed.), *Gender, Family, and Economy: The Triple Overlap*. Newbury Park, CA: Sage.

Charnas, Rebecca
1999 "Shifting strategies, shifting times: El Barzón, the Mexican debtors' movement, 1995–1999." Senior essay, Yale University.
Chesnais, François
1994 *La mondialisation du capital.* Paris: Syros.
1996 *A mundialização do capital.* São Paulo: Xamã.
1998 "Les dangereux mirages de la relative fonctionnalité de la finance." *Critique Communiste* 151 (Winter).
Chilcote, Ronald H.
1974 "A critical synthesis of the dependency literature." *Latin American Perspectives* 1 (Spring): 4–29.
1984 *Theories of Development and Underdevelopment.* Boulder, CO: Westview Press.
1988 "Capitalist and socialist perspectives in the search for a class theory of the state and democracy." Paper presented to the conference "Comparative Politics: Research Perspectives for the Next Twenty Years," New York City University Graduate School and *Comparative Politics* (September): 7–9.
2000 "Theories of imperialism," chapter 5, pp. 175–251 in his *Theories of Comparative Political Economy.* Boulder, CO: Westview Press.
2002. "Globalization or imperialism?" *Latin American Perspectives* 29 (November): 80–87.
Chilcote, Ronald H. (ed.)
1982 *Dependency and Marxism: Toward a Resolution of Debate.* Latin American Perspectives Series (1). Boulder, CO: Westview Press.
2000a *Imperialism: Theoretical Directions.* Amherst, NY: Humanity Book.
2000b *The Political Economy of Imperialism.* Lanham, MD: Rowman & Littlefield. Cloth edition published by Kluwer Academic Publishers, 1999.
Chilcote, Ronald H. and Joel Edelstein
1974 "Alternative perspectives of development and underdevelopment in Latin America," pp. 1–87 in their *Latin America: The Struggle with Dependency and Beyond.* Cambridge, MA: Schenkman Publishing.
Clarke, Simon
1991 "Crise do fordismo ou crise da social democracia?" *Lua Nova* 24. São Paulo: CEDEC.
Claudín, Fernando
1978 *Eurocommunism and Socialism.* London: NLB.
Close, David
1990 "Counterrevolution, imperialism, and Nicaragua: Did the contras lose the war, but win the election?" Paper presented to the Learned Societies Conference, University of Victoria, Victoria, B.C., May.
Cockcroft, James D., André Gunder Frank, and Dale L. Johnson
1972 *Dependence and Underdevelopment: Latin America's Political Economy.* Garden City, NY: Doubleday/Anchor.
1986 "Immiseration, not marginalization: The case of Mexico," pp. 233–259 in Nora Hamilton and Timothy Harding (eds.), *Modern Mexico: State, Economy, and Social Conflict.* Beverly Hills, CA: Sage.
Cohen, Benjamin J.
1973 *The Question of Imperialism: The Political Economy of Dominance and Dependence.* New York: Basic Books.

Cole, William and Richard Sanders
1972 "A modified dualism model for Latin American economies." *Journal of Developing Areas* 6 (January): 185–198.
Collier, David
1978 *Barriadas y elites: De Odría a Velasco.* Lima: Instituto de Estudios Peruanos.
Cook, Scott and Leigh Binford
1990 *Obliging Need: Rural Petty Industry in Mexican Capitalism.* Austin: University of Texas Press.
Cooney, Terry A.
1986 *The Rise of the New York Intellectuals: Parisian Review and Its Circle.* Madison: University of Wisconsin Press.
CORDIPLAN
1990 *El Gran Viraje: Lineamientos generales del VIII Plan de la Nación.* Caracas: CORDIPLAN.
Coriat, Benjamin
1992a *El taller y el robot: Ensayos sobre el fordismo y la producción en massa en la era de la electrónica.* Mexico City: Siglo XXI.
1992b *Pensar al revés: Trabajo y organización en la empresa japonesa.* Mexico City: Siglo XXI.
Corretjer, Juan Antonio
1977 *La lucha por la independencia de Puerto Rico.* Guaynabo: Cooperativa de Artes Gráficas.
Cotto, Liliana
1993 "The *rescate* movement: An alternative way of doing politics," pp. 119–130 in Edwin Meléndez and Edgardo Meléndez (eds.), *Colonial Dilemma: Critical Perspectives on Contemporary Puerto Rico.* Boston: South End Press.
Coutinho, Carlos Nelson
1979 "Cultura e democracia no Brasil." *Encontros com a Civilização Brasileira* 17 (November).
1979 "A democracia como valor universal." *Encontros com a Civilização Brasileira* 9 (March): 33–47.
1981 *Gramsci.* Porto Alegre: L & PM Editores.
Cueva, Agustín
1976 "A summary of problems and perspectives of dependency theory." *Latin American Perspectives* 3 (4): 12–16.
1979 "Problemas y perspectivas de la teoría de la dependencia," in *Debates sobre la teoría de la dependencia.* San José, Costa Rica: EDUCA.
1984 "El fetichismo de la hegemonia y el imperialismo." *Cuadernos Politicos* 39 (January–March): 31–39.
1986 "Cultura nacional, popular y revolucionaria." *Casa de las Américas* 155–156: 68–73.
CVG (Corporación Venezolana de Guayana)
1963 *Informe anual.* Caracas.
1974 *Desarrollo humano 1963–1973.* Ciudad Guayana.
1979 *Informe quinquenal 1974–1978.* Caracas.
CVG-Sidor (Corporación Venezolana de Guayana Siderúrgica del Orinoco S.A.)
1973 "El trabajo social en Sidor." Paper presented at the First Venezuelan Congress of Social Work, Caracas, Venezuela, June.

Davies, Rob
1979 "Informal sector or subordinate mode of production? A model," pp. 87–104 in Ray Bromley and Chris Gerry (eds.), *Casual Work and Poverty in Third World Cities.* New York: John Wiley.
DAWN/MUDAR (Development Alternatives with Women for a New Era) (eds.)
1990 *Mujer y crisis: Respuestas ante la recesión.* Caracas: Editorial Nueva Sociedad.
Debate
1981 "Comunismo mexicano." 16 (February–March).
De Janvry, Alain
1981 *The Agrarian Question and Reformism in Latin America.* Baltimore: Johns Hopkins University Press.
Delich, Francisco
1983 "La construcción social de la legitimidad política en procesos de transición a la democracia (1)." *Crítica y Utopia* 9: 39–42.
DePalma, Anthony
1995 "U.S. bailout of Mexico verging on success or dramatic failure." *New York Times,* April 2.
De Soto, Hernando
1989 *El otro sendero.* Lima: El Barranco.
Dietz, L. James
1993 "La reinvención del subdesarrollo: Errores fundamentales del proyecto de industrialización," pp. 179–205 in Silvia Alvarez Curbelo and María Elena Rodríguez Castro (eds.), *Del nacionalismo al populismo: Cultura y política en Puerto Rico.* Río Piedras: Editorial Huracán.
Dilla, Haroldo
1992 "Cuba's local governments: An experience beyond the paradigms."*Cuban Studies* 22: 151–172.
Dobb, Maurice
1947 *Studies in the Development of Capitalism.* New York: International Publishers.
Dornbusch, Rüdiger
1990 "Discussant panel," pp. 312–326 in John Williamson (ed.), *Latin American Adjustment.* Washington, D.C.: Institute for International Economics.
Dos Santos, Mario
1985 "Acuerdos sociales y procesos de transición," in Mario dos Santos (ed.), *Concertación social y democracia.* Santiago: Centro de Estudios de Desarrollo.
dos Santos, Theotônio
1968 *El nuevo carácter de la dependencia.* Centro de Estudios Socio-Económicos (CESO), Universidad de Chile, Cuadernos de Estudios Socio-Económicos 10.
1970a "The structure of dependence." *The American Economic Review* 60 (May): 231–236.
1970b *Dependencia y cambio social.* Centro de Estudios Socio-Económicos. Universidad de Chile, Cuadernos de Estudios Socio-Económicos 11.
1970c "El nuevo carácter de la dependencia." *Pensamiento Crítico* 43 (August): 60–106.
1970d "La crisis de la teoría del desarrollo y las relaciones de dependencia en América Latina," pp. 147–187 in Helio Jaguaribe et al., *La dependencia politico-económica de América Latina.* Mexico City: Siglo XXI.

1970e "Dependencia económica y alternativas de cambio en América Latina." *Revista Mexicana de Sociología* 32 (March–April): 417–463.

1971 "The structure of dependence," in K. T. Fann and Donald C. Hodges (eds.), *Readings in U.S. Imperialism.* Boston: Porter Sargent.

1972 *El imperialismo, fase superior del capitalismo.* Peking: Editions in Foreign Languages.

1978 *Imperialismo y dependencia.* Mexico City: Ediciones Era.

Droucopoulos, Vassilis

1976 "Radical in spite of itself: A review of Constantine V. Vaitsos' intercountry income distribution and transnational enterprises." *Latin American Perspectives* 3 (4): 86–96.

Ducatenzeiler, Graciela

1992 "Social *concertación* and democracy in Argentina," in Diane Ethier (ed.), *Democratic Transition and Consolidation in Southern Europe, Latin America, and Southeast Asia.* London: Macmillan.

Dussel, Enrique

1985 *La producción teórica de Marx. Un Comentario a los Gundrisse.* Mexico City: Siglo XXI.

1988 *Hacia un Marx desconocido: Un comentario de los Manuscritos del 61–63.* Mexico City: Siglo XXI and Universidad Autónoma Metropolitana-Iztapalapa.

Eckstein, Susan

1982 *El estado y la pobreza en México.* Mexico City: Siglo XXI.

Edel, Matthew

1972 "Exchange and production: A controversy in anthropology and political economy." Paper presented to American Anthropological Association meetings, Toronto.

Edelman, Marc

1987 "Supportive pragmatism: The USSR and revolutionaries." *NACLA Report on the Americas* 21 (January–February).

Edelstein, Joel C.

1975 *The Evolution of the Thought of Fidel Castro Ruz with Respect to Socialist Development, 1953–1973.* Ann Arbor: University Microfilms.

1994 "Nonviolence and the 1989 revolution in Eastern Europe," pp. 99–124 in Paul Wehr, Heidi Burgess, and Guy Burgess (eds.), *Justice without Violence.* Boulder, CO: Lynne Rienner.

Eisenstein, Zillah R.

1979 "Developing a theory of capitalist patriarchy and socialist feminism," pp. 5–40 in Z. R. Eisenstein (ed.), *Capitalist Patriarchy and the Case for Socialist Feminism.* New York: Monthly Review Press.

Elson, Diane

1992 "From survival strategies to transformation strategies: Women's needs and structural adjustment," pp. 26–48 in L. Benería and S. Feldman (eds.), *Unequal Burden: Economic Crises, Persistent Poverty, and Women's Work.* Boulder, CO: Westview Press.

Emmanuel, Arghiri

1972 *Unequal Exchange: A Study of the Imperialism of Trade.* New York: Monthly Review Press.

Engels, Friedrich
1959 "On authority," pp. 481–485 in Lewis S. Feuer (ed.), *Marx and Engels: Basic Writings on Politics and Philosophy*. Garden City, NY: Anchor.
Epstein, David G.
1973 *Brasília: Plan and Reality*. Berkeley: University of California Press.
Fagen, Richard
1986 "The politics of transition." *Monthly Review* 38 (November): 1–19.
Faria, Graça
1996 "Desfordizando a fábrica fordista." Ph.D. dissertation, IFCH, Universidade de Campinas.
Fehér, Ferenc and Agnes Heller
1986a "Eastern left—Western left. Part I: Reflections on a problematic relationship." *Socialist Review* 16 (September–October): 25–48.
1986b "Eastern left—Western left. Part II: After 1968." *Socialist Review* 16 (November–December): 33–50.
Felix, David
1974 "Technological dualism in late industrializers: On theory, history, and policy." *Journal of Economic History* 34 (March): 194–238.
Ferguson, E. James
1979 *The American Revolution: A General History, 1763–1790*. Homewood, IL: Dorsey.
Fernández, Raúl A.
1979 "Imperialist capitalism in the Third World: Theory and evidence from Colombia." *Latin American Perspectives* 6 (Winter): 38–64.
Fernández, Raul A. and José F. Ocampo
1974 "The Latin American revolution: A theory of imperialism, not dependence." *Latin American Perspectives* 1 (Spring): 30–61.
1975 "The Andean Pact and state capitalism in Colombia." *Latin American Perspectives* 2 (Fall): 19–35.
Fernández-Kelly, M. Patricia, and Anna M. García
1989 "Informalization at the core: Hispanic women, homework, and the advanced capitalist state," pp. 247–264 in Alejandro Portes, Manuel Castells, and Lauren A. Benton (eds.), *The Informal Economy: Studies in Advanced and Less Developed Countries*. Baltimore: Johns Hopkins University Press.
Fernós Isern, Antonio
1996 *Filosofía y doctrina del estadolibrismo puertorriqueño*. San Juan: Libros Homines.
Fieldhouse, D. K.
1961 "'Imperialism': An historical revision." *The Economic History Review* 14 (2): 187–209.
Fitzgerald, Frank T.
1985 "Politics and social structure in revolutionary Cuba: From the demise of the old middle class to the rise of new professionals." Ph.D. dissertation, State University of New York, Binghamton.
1988 "The Sovietization of Cuba thesis revisited," in Andrew Zimbalist (ed.), *Cuban Political Economy: Controversies in Cubanology*. Boulder, CO: Westview.
Flisfisch, Angel
1983 "El surgimiento de una nueva ideología democrática en América Latina." *Crítica y Utopia* 9: 11–29.

Fonseca, Carlos
1986 "Nicaragua: Zero hour," pp. 168–180 in Peter Rosset and John Vandermeer (eds.), *Nicaragua: Unfinished Revolution.* New York: Grove Press.
Foster-Carter, Aidan
1979 "Marxism versus dependency theory? A polemic." University of Leeds, Department of Sociology, Occasional Papers 8, mimeographed.
Fox, Geoffrey (ed.)
1989 *The Homeless Organize.* NACLA Report on the Americas 23 (4).
Frank, André Gunder
1966 "The development of underdevelopment." *Monthly Review* 18 (September): 17–31.
1967 *Capitalism and Underdevelopment in Latin America: Historical Studies of Chile and Brazil.* New York: Monthly Review Press.
1969a "The development of underdevelopment," in *Latin America: Underdevelopment or Revolution.* New York: Monthly Review Press.
1969b *Latin America: Underdevelopment or Revolution.* New York: Monthly Review Press.
1969c "Sociology of development and underdevelopment of sociology" in *Latin America: Underdevelopment or Revolution.* New York: Monthly Review Press.
1970 *Lumpenburguesía: Lumpendesarrollo.* Montevideo: Ediciones de la Banda Oriental.
1971 *Capitalism and Underdevelopment in Latin America: Historical Studies of Brazil and Chile.* London: Pelican.
1972 *Lumpen-Bourgeoisie and Lumpen-Development.* New York: Monthly Review Press.
1974 "Dependency is dead, long live dependence and the class struggle: A reply to critics." *Latin American Perspectives* 1 (Spring): 86–106.
1978a *Dependent Accumulation and Underdevelopment.* London: Macmillan.
1978b *World Accumulation 1492–1789.* London: Macmillan.
Frankel, Boris
1987 *The Post-Industrial Utopians.* Madison: University of Wisconsin Press.
Friedmann, John
1966 *Regional Development Policy: A Case Study of Venezuela.* Cambridge: MIT Press.
Friedmann, John and C. Weaver
1979 *Territory and Function: The Evolution of Regional Planning.* London: Edward Arnold.
Friedman, Milton
1962 *Capitalism and Freedom.* Chicago: University of Chicago Press.
Fukuyama, Francis
1989 "The end of history." *The National Interest* 16 (Summer): 3–17.
Fuller, Linda
1985 "The politics of workers' control in Cuba, 1959–1983: The work center and the national arena." Ph.D. dissertation, University of California, Berkeley.
Furtado, Celso
1970 *Economic Development in Latin America.* Cambridge: Cambridge University Press.
Galeano, Eduardo
1990 "A child lost in the storm." *The Guardian* 42 (May): 1, 12.

Galli, E. Rosemary
1976 "The United Nations development program, 'development,' and multinational corporations." *Latin American Perspectives* 3 (4): 65–85.
García, Jesús
1990 "Caracterización del estado actual del desarrollo de las fuerzas productivas cubanas." MS, Instituto de Filosofía de la Academia de Ciencias, Havana.
García, María-Pilar and Dietrich Kunkel
1991 "Hacia un desarrollo sostenible: El dilema industria-ambiente de la Guayana Venezolana." *Revista Interamericana de Planificación* 24 (94): 99–127.
Garretón, Manuel Antonio
1989 "The ideas of socialist renovation in Chile." *Rethinking Marxism* 2 (Summer): 8–39.
Gasperini, William
1990 "Did end justify means in Panama invasion?" *In These Times* (January 17–23): 11, 22.
Geertz, Clifford
1963 *Peddlers and Princes.* Chicago: University of Chicago Press.
Gellen, Karen
1990 "A Salvadoran rebel on socialism's upheaval." *The Guardian* 42 (March): 15–19.
Gerry, Chris
1987 "Developing economies and the informal sector in historical perspective." *Annals of the American Academy of Political and Social Science* 493: 100–119.
Giddens, Anthony
1975 *The Class Structure of the Advanced Societies.* New York: Harper.
1990 *The Consequences of Modernity.* Cambridge: Polity Press.
Gilbert, Alan and Josef Gugler
1984 *Cities, Poverty, and Development: Urbanization in the Third World.* Oxford: Oxford University Press.
Gilbert, Dennis
1985 "The bourgeoisie," pp. 163–182 in Thomas W. Walker (ed.), *Nicaragua: The First Five Years.* New York: Praeger.
Gilpin, Robert
2002 *The Challenge of Global Capitalism: The World Economy in the 21st Century.* Princeton: Princeton University Press.
Girling, Robert
1976 "Mechanisms of imperialism, technology, and the dependent state: Reflections on the Jamaican case." *Latin American Perspectives* 3 (4): 54–64.
Gitlin, Todd
1987 *The Sixties: Years of Hope, Days of Rage.* New York: Bantam.
Globe and Mail
1990a "Rebels raid near home of Salvadoran leader." May 3.
1990b "Cuba mobilizing in wake of U.S. military exercises." May 4.
Gómez Salgado, Arturo
1994 "Por la distorción de la productividad cayó 7 porciento la ocupación laboral en el último año." *El Financiero,* July 6.
González Casanova, Pablo
1979 *Imperialismo y liberación: Una introducción a la historia contemporánea de América Latina.* Mexico City: Siglo XXI.

González Mendoza, René
1986 "The electoral system in Cuba." *Granma Weekly Review* (September 21): 2.
Gordon, David M.
1972 *Theories of Poverty and Underemployment: Orthodox, Radical, and Dual Labor Market Perspectives.* Lexington, MA: D. C. Heath.
1996 *Fat and Mean.* New York: Free Press.
Gordon, Robert A.
1961 *Business Fluctuations.* 2d ed. New York: Harper.
Gorender, Jacob
1997 "Globalização, tecnología e relações de trabalho." *Estudos Avançados* 29.
Gorz, André
1982 *Farewell to the Working Class.* London: Pluto Press.
1990 "O futuro da classe operária." *Quinzena*, September 16.
Gounet, Thomas
1991 "Luttes concurrentielles et stratégies d'accumulation dans l'industrie automobile." *Études Marxistes* 10.
Graciolli, Edilson
1997 *Um caldeirão chamado CSN.* Uberlândia: EDUFU.
Guidugli, Odeibler Santo and Marta María Barreto G.
1986 "El carácter asistémico de la planificacién en Brasil." *Revista Interamericana de Planificación* 20 (79): 89–103.
Guillén, Mauro
2001 "Is globalization civilizing, destructive, or feeble? A critique of five key debates in the social science literature." *Annual Review of Sociology* 27: 235–60. Retrieved June 7, 2002, from World Wide Web at www.management.wharton.upenn.edu/guillen/docs/GlobalizARS.pdf.
Harding, Timothy F.
1976 "Dependency, nationalism, and the state in Latin America." *Latin American Perspectives* 3 (Fall): 3–11.
Hardoy, Jorge
1982 "The building of Latin American cities," pp. 19–34 in Alan Gilbert (ed.), *Urbanization in Contemporary Latin America.* New York: Wiley.
Hardt, Michael and Antonio Negri
2000 *Empire.* Cambridge: Harvard University Press.
Harnecker, Marta
1986 *Reflexiones acerca del problema de la transición al socialismo.* Managua: Nueva Nicaragua.
Harris, Jerry
1998–99 "Globalization and the technological transformation of capitalism." *Race and Class* 40 (2–3): 21–36.
Harris, Richard L.
1979 "The influence of Marxist structuralism on the Latin American left." *Insurgent Sociologist* 9 (Summer): 62–73.
Harris, Richard and Carlos Vilas
1985 *Nicaragua: A Revolution under Siege.* London: Zed.
Hart, Keith
1973 "Informal income opportunities and urban employment in Ghana." *Journal of Modern African Studies* 11 (1): 61–89.

Hartz, Louis
1964 *The Founding of New Societies.* New York: Harcourt, Brace and World.
Harvey, David
1992 *A condição pós-moderna.* São Paulo: Loyola.
Hayter, Teresa
1971 *Aid as Imperialism.* Harmondsworth: Penguin.
Heilbroner, Robert
1995 *Vision of the Future.* New York: Oxford University Press.
Held, David et al. (eds.)
1999 *Global Transformations: Politics, Economics, Culture.* Stanford, CA: Stanford University Press.
Henríquez Urena, Camila (ed.)
1988 *Eugenio María de Hostos: Obras.* Havana: Casa de las Américas.
Henwood, Doug
1996 "Pos what?" *Monthly Review* 48 (4).
Hernández Cruz, Juan E.
1992 *La invasión de Puerto Rico: Consideraciones históricos-sociológicas.* San Germán Xaguey.
Hernández Rafael and Haroldo Dilla
1991 "Political culture and popular participation in Cuba." *Latin American Perspectives* 18 (Spring): 38–54.
Herzer, Hilda and Pedro Pirez
1991 "Municipal government and popular participation in Latin America." *Environment and Urbanization* 3 (1): 79–95.
Hilton, Rodney et al.
1976 *The Transition from Feudalism to Capitalism.* London: New Left Books.
Hindess, Barry and Paul Hirst
1975 *Pre-Capitalist Modes of Production.* London: Routledge & Kegan Paul.
Hinkelammert, Franz
1970 "Teoría de la dialéctica del desarrollo desigual." *Cuadernos del la Realidad Nacional* 6 (December): 15–220.
Hirata, Helena
1986 "Trabalho, família e relações homem/mulher: Reflexões a partir do caso japonês." *Revista Brasileira de Ciências Sociais* 2(1).
Hirata, Helena (ed.)
1993 *Sobre o modelo japonês.* São Paulo: Editora da Universidade de São Paulo.
Hirsh, Arthur
1981 *The French New Left: An Intellectual History from Sartre to Gorz.* Boston: South End Press.
Hirst, Paul and Grahame Thompson
1996 *Globalization in Question.* Cambridge: Polity Press, 1999.
Hobson, J. A.
1902 *Imperialism: A Study.* London: K. Nisbet & Co.
Hollanda, Heloisa Buarque and Marcos Augusto Gonçalves
1980 *Anos 70: Literatura.* Rio de Janeiro: Europa.
Holloway, John
1998 "El Manifiesto Comunista." *Cuadernos del Sur,* no. 26 (April).

Holston, James
1989 *The Modernist City: An Anthropological Critique of Brasília.* Chicago: University of Chicago Press.
Hopenhayn, Martin
1991 "Crisis de legitimidad en el estado planificador." *Revista Interamericana de Planificación* 24 (96): 5–24.
Horvat, Branko
1982 *The Political Economy of Socialism.* New York: M. E. Sharpe.
Huberman, Leo
1969 "Why socialism is necessary." *Monthly Review* 20 (January): 1–14.
Husson, Michael
1997 "Contre le fetichisme de la finance." *Critique Comuniste* 149 (Summer).
Hymer, Stephen H.
1960 "International operations of national firms—A study of direct foreign investment." Ph.D. dissertation, Massachusetts Institute of Technology.
Ianni, Octavio
1998 "Las ciencias sociales en la época de la globalización." *Revista de Ciencias Sociales* 7/8, Universidad Nacional de Quilmes, Argentina. Retrieved on June 7, 2002, from the World Wide Web at www.argiropolis.comar/documentos/investigacion/publicaciones/cs/7–8/1a.htm.
ILO (International Labor Organization)
1972 *Employment, Income, and Equality: A Strategy for Increasing Productive Employment in Kenya.* Geneva.
Instituto Histórico Centroamericano (Managua)
1985 "Asamblea Nacional: Primeros pasos de un nuevo modelo político." *Envio* 4 (May): 1b–12b.
1987 "The first 3,000 days: Revolution in review." *Envio* 6 (73): 17–48.
Isserman, Maurice
1987 *If I Had a Hammer . . . The Death of the Old Left and the Birth of the New Left.* New York: Basic Books.
Izaguirre, Maritza
1977 *Ciudad Guayana y la estrategia del desarrollo planificado.* Caracas: Ediciones SIAP.
Jacoby, Russell
1987 *The Last Intellectuals: American Culture in the Age of Academe.* New York: Basic Books.
Jaguaribe, Helio
1969 "Dependencia y autonomía en América Latina," in Aldo Ferrer (ed.), *La dependencia político-económica de América Latina.* Mexico City: Siglo XXI.
Jaguaribe, Helio et al.
1970 *La dependencia político-económico de América Latina.* Mexico City: Siglo XXI.
Jameson, Fredric
1984 "Postmodernism, or the cultural logic of late capitalism." *New Left Review* 146 (July–August): 53–92.
1989 "Marxism and postmodernism." *New Left Review* 176 (July–August): 31–67.
1991 *Postmodernism, or the Cultural Logic of Late Capitalism.* Durham, NC: Duke University Press.

Jaquette, Jane
1990 "Gender and justice in economic development," pp. 54–69 in I. Tinker (ed.), *Persistent Inequalities: Women and World Development.* New York: Oxford University Press.

Jenkins, T.
1986 "Nicaragua's disloyal opposition." *The Nation* 242 (April 12): 520–522.

Jessop, Bob
1983 "Accumulation strategies and hegemonic projects." Manuscript.

Jinkings, Nise
1995 *O misterio de fazer dinheiro.* São Paulo: Boitempo.

Jonas, Susanne
1988 "Contradictions of Guatemala's 'political opening.'" *Latin American Perspectives* 15 (3): 26–46.

Kahn, Arthur D.
1990 "Was there no superstructure in ancient Rome?" *Monthly Review* 41 (February): 36–39.

Kandal, Terry R.
1989 "Marx and Engels on international relations, revolution, and counterrevolution," pp. 25–76 in M. T. Martin and T. R. Kandal (eds.), *Studies of Development and Change in the Modern World.* New York: Oxford University Press.

Karl, Terry L.
1987 "Petroleum and political pacts." *Latin American Research Review* 22: 63–94.

Katz, Claudio
1998 "Crisis y revolución tecnológica a fin de siglo." *Realidad Económica* 154 (February–March).

Kaufman, Michael
1985 *Jamaica under Manley: Dilemmas of Socialism and Democracy.* Westport, CT: Lawrence Hill.

Kay, Cristóbal
1989 *Latin American Theories of Development and Underdevelopment.* London: Routledge.

Kellner, Douglas
2002 "Theorizing globalization," pp. 73–108 in Alexandra Suess (ed.), *Globalisierung. ein wissenschaftlicher Diskurs?* Mainz: Passagen Verlag. Retrieved on June 7, 2002, from the World Wide Web at www.gseis.ucla.edu/faculty/kellner/papers/theoryglob.htm.

Kolko, Gabriel
1967 *Triumph of Conservatism: A Reinterpretation of American History, 1900–1916.* New York: Quadrangle Books.

Kondor, Leondro
1980 *A democracia e os comunistas no Brasil.* Rio de Janeiro: Graal.

Koning, Hans
1991 *Columbus: His Enterprise.* New York: Monthly Review Press.

Kotz, David, M.
1994 "Interpreting the social structure of accumulation theory," in D. M. Kotz, T. McDonough, and Michael Reich (eds.), *Social Structures of Accumulation.* New York: Cambridge University Press.

Kowarick, Lucio
1979 "Capitalism and urban marginality in Brazil," pp. 69–85 in Ray Bromley and Chris Gerry (eds.), *Casual Work and Poverty in Third World Cities*. New York: John Wiley.

Kuntz, Sandra
1985 *Presupuestos metódológicos de la cuestión de la dependencia en Marx, en los Grundrisse y el Capital*. Thesis, Facultad de Ciencias Políticas, Universidad Nacional Autónoma de México.

Laclau, Ernesto
1969 "Modos de Producción, económicos y población excedente: Aproximación histórica a los casos argentino y chileno." *Revista Latinoamericana de Sociología* 5 (July): 344–383.
1971 "Feudalism and capitalism in Latin America." *New Left Review* 67 (May–June): 19–38.
1977 *Politics and Ideology in Marxist Theory*. London: New Left Books.
1979 *Politics and Ideology in Marxist Theory*. London: Verso.
1980 "Tesis acerca de la forma hegemónica de la política." Paper presented to the seminar "Hegemonía y Alternativas Populares en América Latina," Morelia, Mexico.

Laclau, Ernesto and Chantal Mouffe
1982 "Recasting Marxism: Hegemony and new political movements." *Socialist Review* 12 (November–December): 91–113.
1985 *Hegemony and Socialist Strategy: Towards a Radical Democratic Politics*. London: Verso.

Lander, Edgardo
1975 "Desarrollo heterogéneo-desigual del capitalismo y lucha de clases." Unpublished thesis, Universidad Central de Venezuela.

Lander, Luis and M. Josefina de Rangel
1970 *La planificación en Venezuela*. Caracas: Sociedad Venezolana de Planificación.

Landi, Oscar
1981 "Sobre lenguajes, identidades y ciudadanías políticas," pp. 11–42 in *Crisis y lenguajes políticos*. Estudios CEDES 4. Buenos Aires: Centro de Estudios de Estado y Sociedad.

Larraín, Jorge
1989 *Theories of Development: Capitalism, Colonialism, and Dependency*. London: Polity Press.

Latin American Perspectives
1976 *Imperialism and the Working Class in Latin America*. 3 (1).
1985 *State and Military in Latin America*. 12 (4).

Lavinas, Lena
1995 "Abismo regional." *Veja*, November 26.

Lechner, Norbert
1985a "De la revolución a la democracia: El debate intelectual en América del Sur." *Opciones* 6 (May–August): 57–72.
1985b "Pacto social: Nos procesos de democratização, la experiência latino-americana." *Novos Estudos CEBRAP* 13 (October): 29–44.

Leeds, Anthony
1971 "The concept of 'culture of poverty': Conceptual, logical, and empirical prob-

lems with perspectives from Brazil and Peru," pp. 226–284 in Eleanor Burke Leacock (ed.), *The Culture of Poverty: A Critique*. New York: Simon and Schuster.

Lefort, Claude
1986 *The Political Forms of Modern Society*. Cambridge, MA: MIT Press.

Lehmann, David
1990 *Democracy and Development in Latin America*. London: Polity Press.

Leis, Raul
1990 "Panama: The other side of midnight." *NACLA Report on the Americas* 23 (April): 4–6.

Lenin, V. I.
1915 *Collected Works*. Vol. 38. Moscow: Progress Publishers.
1916 *Imperialism, the Highest Stage of Capitalism: A Popular Outline*, in V. I. Lenin, *Collected Works*. Vol. 22. Moscow: Progress Publishers, 1964.
1960 *Collected Works*. 45 vols. London: Lawrence and Wilhart.
1967 *Selected Works*. 3 vols. New York: International Publishers.
1968a "Imperialism and the Split in Socialism," in *Marx, Engels, Marxism*. Moscow: Progress Publishers.
1968b *National Liberation, Socialism, and Imperialism*. New York: International Publishers.
1970 *Imperialism, the Highest Stage of Capitalism*. Peking: Foreign Languages Press.
1970a *Karl Marx*. Peking: Foreign Languages Press.
1970b *Left-Wing Communism: An Infantile Disorder*. Peking: Foreign Languages Press.
1973 *El imperialismo, fase superior del capitalismo*. Buenos Aires: De Anteo.
1975 *Selected Works*. Vol. 3. Moscow: Progress.
1976 *Selected Works*. New York: International.

Levine, David P.
1975 "The theory of growth of the capitalist economy." *Economic Development and Cultural Change* 24 (October): 47–74.

Levy, Leonard W.
1963 *Jefferson and Civil Liberties: The Darker Side*. Cambridge: Harvard University Press.

Lewin, Moshe
1991 Expanded edition. *The Gorbachev Phenomenon: A Historical Interpretation*. Berkeley: University of California Press.

Lewis, Oscar
1996 *La Vida: A Puerto Rican Family in the Culture of Poverty*. New York: Random House.

Leys, Colin
1977 "Underdevelopment and dependency: Critical notes." *Journal of Contemporary Asia* 7 (1): 92–107.

Lipton, Michael
1988 "Why poor people stay poor: Urban bias in world development," in Josef Gugler (ed.), *The Urbanization of the Third World*. Oxford: Oxford University Press.

Lojkine, Jean
1990 *A classe operária em mutações*. São Paulo: Oficina de Livros.
1995 *A revolução informacional*. São Paulo: Cortez.

Lukács, Georgy
   1989 *El hombre y la democracia.* Buenos Aires: Editorial Contrapunto.
Luxemburg, Rosa
   1951 *Ausgewählte Reden und Schriften; mit einem Vorwort von Wilhelm Pieck.* Vol. 2. Berlin: Dietz.
   1964 *The Accumulation of Capital.* New York: Monthly Review Press.
   1967 *La acumulación de capital.* Mexico City: Grijalbo.
   1968 *La acumulación del capital.* Buenos Aires: S/E.
   1971 *Selected Political Writings.* New York: Monthly Review Press.
   1972 *The Russian Revolution.* Ann Arbor: University of Michigan Press.
   1984 *The Accumulation of Capital.* New York: Monthly Review Press.
Mackintosh, Maureen
   1981 "The sexual division of labour and the subordination of women," pp. 1–15 in K. Young, C. Wolkowitz, and R. McCullagh (eds.), *Of Marriage and the Market: Women's Subordination in International Perspective.* London: CSE Books.
MacPherson, Stewart and James Midgley
   1987 *Comparative Social Policy and the Third World.* New York: St. Martin's.
Magdoff, Harry and Paul Sweezy
   1981 *The Deepening Crisis of U.S. Capitalism.* New York: Monthly Review Press.
   1990 "Perestroika and the future of socialism, part two." *Monthly Review* 41 (April): 1–17.
Malloy, Mary
   1995 "On Brenner's politics of U.S. decline." *Against the Current* (July–August).
Mandel, Ernest
   1967 *La formación del pensamiento económico de Marx.* Mexico City: Siglo XXI.
   1968 *Marxist Economic Theory.* 2 vols. New York: Monthly Review Press.
   1978 "On the nature of the Soviet state." *New Left Review* 108 (March–April).
   1986 "Marx, la crise actuelle et l'avenir du travail humain." *Quatrième Internationale* 20.
Manley, Michael
   1982 *Jamaica: Struggle in the Periphery.* London: Writers and Readers Publishing Cooperative.
Mann, Micheal et al.
   2001–2002 "The transnational ruling class formation thesis: A symposium." *Science and Society* 65 (Winter): 464–508.
Mao Tse-tung
   1970 *Selected Works.* 4 vols. Peking: Foreign Languages Press.
Marglin, Stephen A.
   1974 "What do bosses do? The origins and functions of hierarchy in capitalist production." *Review of Radical Political Economy* 6 (Summer): 60–112.
Mariátegui, José Carlos
   1928 *Siete ensayos de interpretación de la realidad peruana.* Lima: Amauta.
Marini, Ruy Mauro
   1973 *Dialéctica de la dependencia.* Mexico City: Ediciones Era.
   1980 "The question of the state in the Latin American class struggle." *Contemporary Marxism* 1 (Spring): 1–9.

Márquez, Gustavo
1990 "Venezuela: A country assessment on the role of women in development." *Report to the World Bank.* Caracas, Venezuela.
Mars, Perry
1984 "Destabilization and socialist orientation in the English-speaking Caribbean." *Latin American Perspectives* 42 (Summer): 83–110.
Martin, Connie and Peter Zwerling
1985 *Nicaragua: A New Kind of Revolution.* Westport, CT: Lawrence Hill.
Martinez, Andrea
1998 "Volcado el radio de acción." *El Nuevo Dia,* April 4.
Marx, Karl
1857–1858 *Outlines of the Critique of Political Economy.* [*Grundrisse*] (Rough Draft of 1857–1858 [Second Installment]. In *MECW,* vol. 29. New York: International Publishers, 1987.
1861–1863 *Theories of Surplus-Value.* 3 vols. Translated by Emile Burns. Moscow: Progress Publishers, 1963. Published in Spanish. 3 vols. Mexico City: Fondo de Cultura Económica, 1980.
1867 *Capital.* Vol. 1. Moscow: Progress Publishers, 1965.
1956 *El Capital.* 5 vols. Buenos Aires: Cartago.
1967 *Capital: A Critique of Political Economy.* 3 vols. New York: International Publishers.
1978 *Capital.* Vol. 2. London: Penguin Books.
1973 *El Capital.* Vol. 1. Mexico City: Fondo de Cultura Económica.
1974a *Capital.* Vol. 1. New York: International Publishers.
1974b *Grundrisse: Foundations of the Critique of Political Economy.* Harmondsworth: Penguin Books.
1977 "Results of the immediate process of production," pp. 943–1084 in *Capital.* Vol. 1. New York: Random House.
1994 *Collected Works.* Vol. 34. London: Lawrence and Wishart.
Marx, Karl and Frederick Engels
1958 *Selected Works in Two Volumes.* Moscow: Foreign Language Publishing House.
1967 *El Manifiesto Comunista.* Buenos Aires: Claridad.
1970 *Manifesto of the Communist Party.* Peking: Foreign Languages Press.
1972 *Selected Works.* New York: International Publishers.
Marzani, Carl
1990 "On interring communism and exalting capitalism." *Monthly Review* 41 (January): 1–32.
Mathews, John
1989 *Age of Democracy: The Politics of Post-Fordism.* Melbourne: Oxford University Press.
Mathey, Kosta
1988 "A Cuban interpretation of self-help housing." *Trialog* 18 (3): 24–30.
McAfee, Kathy
1990 "Grenada: The revo in reverse." *NACLA Report on the Americas* 23 (February): 27–32.
McCoy, J. L.
1986–1987 "The politics of adjustment." *Journal of Interamerican Studies* 28: 103–138.

McGee, T. G.

1977 "The persistence of the proto-proletariat: Occupation structures and planning structures of the future in Third World cities," pp. 257–270 in Janet Abu-Lughod and Richard Hay Jr. (eds.), *Third World Urbanization*. Chicago: Maaroufa Press.

McIlroy, John

1997 *Trade Unions in Retreat: Britain since 1979.* Manchester: International Centre for Labour Studies.

MEGA

1972–[1988] *Karl Marx, Friedrich Engels Gesamtausgabe (MEGA).* Edited by the Institute for Marxism-Leninism of the Central Committee of the Communist Party of the Soviet Union and the Institute for Marxism-Leninism of the Central Committee of the Socialist Unity Party of Germany. Berlin: Dietz.

Meier, Gerald M.

1968 *International Trade and Economic Development.* New York: Harper and Row.

Meillassoux, Claude

1981 *Maidens, Meal and Money: Capitalism and the Domestic Community.* London: Cambridge University Press.

Merhav, Meir

1969 *Technological Dependence, Monopoly, and Growth.* Oxford and London: Pergamon Press.

Mészáros, István

1995 *Beyond Capital: Towards a Theory of Transition.* London: Merlin Press.

Mezzera, Jaime

1985 "A puntes sobre la heterogenidad en los mercados de trabajo en América Latina," pp. 29–43 in Daniel Carbonetto et al. (eds.), *El sector informal urbano en los paises andinos.* Quito and Guayaquil: ILDIS/CEPESIU.

1987 "Abundancia como efecto de la escaces: Oferta y demanda en el mercado laboral urban." *Nueva Sociedad* (88): 106–117.

1988 "Excedente de oferta de trabajo y sector informal urbano," pp. 67–96 in Marguerite Berger and Marya Buvinic (eds.), *La mujer en el sector informal: Trabajo femenino y microempresa en América Latina.* Quito: Editorial Nueva Sociedad.

Michalet, Charles Albert

1976 *Le capitalisme mondial.* Paris: PUF.

Mies, María

1986 *Patriarchy and Accumulation on a World Scale: Women in the International Division of Labour.* London: Zed Books.

Miles, Sara and Bob Ostertag

1990 "El Salvador: The offensive in perspective." *NACLA Report on the Americas* 23 (April): 7–9.

Miliband, Ralph

1985 "The new Revisionists in Britain." *New Left Review* 150 (March–April): 5–26.

Miller, James

1987 *"Democracy Is in the Streets: From Port Huron to the Siege of Chicago.* New York: Simon & Schuster.

Mohri, Kenzo

1979 "Marx and 'underdevelopment.' " *Monthly Review* 30 (April): 32–42.

Möller, Alois
1979 "Los vendedores ambulantes en Lima," pp. 415–471 in Victor E. Tokman and Emilio Klein (eds.), *El subempleo en América Latina*. Buenos Aires: El Cid Editores.

Mommer, Bernard
1986 "La renta petrolera, su distribución y las cuentas nacionales: El ejemplo de Venezuela." *Cuadernos del CENDES* 5 (January–April): 189–212.

Monsiváis, Carlos
1987 *Entrada libre: Crónicos de la sociedad que se organiza*. Mexico City: Era.

Montero, Maritza
1983 "La estructura familiar venezolana y la transformación de estereotipos y roles sexuales." Paper presented at the First National Encounter of the Feminist Front of the Movimiento al Socialismo, Caracas, Venezuela.

Montero, Nancy
1990 *Estereotipos sexuales: Matrimonio, divorcio y salud mental*. Caracas: Universidad Central.

Moore, Barrington
1967 *The Social Origins of Dictatorship and Democracy*. New York: Penguin.

Moran, Theodore H.
1973 "Foreign expansion as an 'institutional necessity' for U.S. corporate capitalism: The search for a radical model." *World Politics* 25 (April): 369–386.

Morley, Morris
1980 "Toward a theory of imperial politics: United States policy and the processes of state formation, disintegration and consolidation in Cuba, 1898–1978." Ph.D. dissertation, State University of New York, Binghamton.

Moser, Carolina O. N.
1978 "Informal sector or petty commodity production? Dualism or dependence in urban development?" *World Development* 6 (9–10): 1041–1064.
1994 "The informal sector debate, pt. 1: 1970–1983," pp. 11–30 in Cathy A. Rakowski (ed.), *Contrapunto: The Informal Sector Debate in Latin America*. Albany: State University of New York Press.

Moulian, Tomás
1981 "Por un marxismo secularizado." *Chile-América* 72–73: 100–104.
1983 "Una reflexión sobre intelectuales y política," pp. 7–19 in Tomás Moulian, *Democracia y socialismo en Chile*. Santiago: FLACSO.

Mueller, Willard
1967 Testimony in U.S. Senate, Select Committee on Small Business, Hearings, *States and Future of Small Business*. Washington, D.C.: Government Printing Office.

Munck, Ronaldo with Ricardo Falcón and Bernardo Galitelli
1987 *Argentina, from Anarchism to Peronism: Workers, Unions, and Politics 1855–1985*. London: Zed Books.

Murmis, Miguel
1969 "Tipos de marginalidad y posición en el proceso productivo." *Revista Latinoamericano de Sociología* 5 (July).

Murray, Fergus
1983 "The decentralisation of production: The decline of mass-collective worker." *Capital and Class* 19.

Myer, John
1975 "A crown of thorns: Cardoso and counterrevolution." *Latin American Perspectives* 2 (Spring): 33–48.

Naím, Moisés and Ramón Piñango (eds.)
1984 *El caso de Venezuela: Una ilusión de harmonía.* Caracas: IESA.

Navarro, Vicente
1989 "Historical triumph: Capitalism or socialism?" *Monthly Review* 41 (November): 37–50.

Negrón, Marco
1991 "Realidad multiple de la gran ciudad: Una visión desde Caracas." *Nueva Sociedad* 114: 76–83.

Negroni, Héctor Andrés
1992 *Historia militar de Puerto Rico.* Madrid: Siruela.

Nicolaus, Martin
1967 "Proletariat and middle class in Marx." *Studies on the Left* 7 (January–February): 22–49. Reprinted in James Weinstein and David W. Eakins (eds.), *For a New America.* New York: Random House, 1970.

Nicols, John Spicer
1985 "The media," in Thomas W. Walker (ed.), *Nicaragua: The First Five Years.* New York: Praeger.

Novack, George
1970 "The permanent revolution in Latin America." *Intercontinental Press* 8 (November 16): 978–983.

Nove, Alec
1983 *The Economics of Feasible Socialism.* London: Unwin Hyman.

Nún, José
1969 "Tipos de marginalidad y posición en el proceso productivo." *Revista Latinoamericana de Sociología* 5 (July).
1969a "Marginalidad y participación social: Un planteo introductorio." Mexico City: Simposio sobre la Participación Social en América Latina, mimeographed.
1969b "Sobrepoblación relativa, ejército industrial de reserve y masa marginal." *Revista Latinoamericana de Sociología* 5 (July).
1981 "La rebelión del coro." *Nexos* 146: 19–26.
1984 "Democracia y socialismo: ¿Etapas o niveles?" pp. 249–261 in Fundación Pablo Iglesias, *Caminos de la democracia.* Madrid: Editorial Iglesias.
1987 "La theoría política y la transición democrática," in J. Nún and J. C. Portantiero (eds.), *Ensayos sobre la transición democrática en la Argentina.* Buenos Aires: Puntosur.
1991 "La democracia y la modernización, treinta años después." *Desarrollo Económico* 31 (123): 375–394.

Nun, José, Miguel Murmis, and J. C. Marin
1968 "La marginalidad en América Latina." Buenos Aires: Instituto Di Tella, mimeographed.

Nuñez Soto, Orlando
1986 "Ideology and revolutionary politics in transitional societies," pp. 231–248 in Richard Fagen et al., *Transition and Development: Problems of World Socialism.* New York: Monthly Review Press.

O'Brien, Philip
1973 "Dependency: The new nationalism?" *Latin America Review of Books* [London], 1 (Spring): 35–41.
1975 "A critique of Latin American theories of dependence," in Ivar Oxaal et al., *Beyond the Sociology of Development.* London: Routledge & Kegan Paul.

Ocampo, José F.
1975 "On what's new and what's old in the theory of imperialism." *Latin American Perspectives* 2 (Spring): 59–65.

OCEI (Oficina Central de Estadística e Informática)
1992 *Anuario estadística 1991.* Caracas.

O'Conner, James
1973 *The Fiscal Crisis of the State.* New York: St. Martin's.

O'Donnell, Guillermo, Philippe Schmitter, and Laurence Whitehead (eds.)
1986 *Transitions from Authoritarian Rule.* Baltimore: Johns Hopkins University Press.

OECD (Organization for Economic Co-operation and Development)
1997 *Employment Outlook.* Paris.

Oliveira, Orlanda de and Bryan Roberts
1994 "The many roles of the informal sector in development: Evidence from urban labor market research 1940–1989," pp. 51–74 in Cathy A. Rakowski (ed.), *Contrapunto: The Informal Sector Debate in Latin America.* Albany: State University of New York Press.

Olmedo, Paúl and P. Paz
1972 "El mito del capitalismo post-cíclico y sus efectos ideológicos en la interpretación de la realidad latinoamericana." Paper presented to the X Congreso Latinoamericano de Sociología, Santiago, Chile.

Ortega, Humberto
1982 "Nicaragua—strategy of victory," pp. 53–84 in Tomas Borge et al., *Sandinistas Speak.* New York: Pathfinder Press.

Ortega, Marvin
1985 "Workers' participation in the management of the agro-enterprises of the APP." *Latin American Perspectives* 12 (Spring): 69–81.

Ortiz, Renato
1994 *Mundialização e cultura.* São Paulo: Brasiliense.

Oxaal, Ivar, Tony Barnett, and David Booth (eds.)
1975 *Beyond the Sociology of Development.* London: Routledge & Kegan Paul.

Palma, Gabriel
1978 "Dependency: A formal theory of underdevelopment or a methodology for the analysis of concrete situations of underdevelopment?" *World Development* 6: 881–924.

Pantojas-García, Emilio
1990 *Development Strategies as Ideology: Puerto Rico's Export-led Industrialization Experience.* London: Lynne Rienner.

Papanek, Hanna
1990 "To each less than she needs, from each more than she can do: Allocations, entitlements, and value," pp. 162–184 in I. Tinker (ed.), *Persistent Inequalities: Women and World Development.* New York: Oxford University Press.

Paralitici, José Che
1997 "Encarcelamiento de luchadores anticoloniales: 1898–1958," in Ramón Bosque

Pérez and José Javier Colón Morera (eds.), *Las carpetas: Persecución política y derechos civiles en Puerto Rico*. Río Piedras: Centro para la Investigación y Promoción de los Derechos Civiles.

Peattie, Lisa R.
1981 *Thinking about Development*. New York: Plenum Press.

Pérez, Humberto
1979 *Sobre las dificultades objetivas de la revolución: Lo que el pueblo debe saber*. Havana: Editorial Política.

Pérez Sáinz, Juan Pablo
1991 *Informalidad urbana en América Latina: Enfoques, problemáticas e interrogantes*. Guatemala City: Editorial Nueva Sociedad.

Pérez-Stable, Marifeli
1985 "Politics and conciencia in revolutionary Cuba, 1959–1984." Ph.D. dissertation, State University of New York, Stony Brook.

Perlman, Janice
1976 *The Myth of Marginality: Urban Poverty and Politics in Rio de Janeiro*. Berkeley: University of California Press.

Petras, James
1986 *Latin America: Bankers, Generals, and the Struggle for Social Justice*. Totowa, NJ: Rowman & Littlefield.
1990a "Eight myths about Panama." *In These Times* (January 17–23): 12–13, 22.
1990b "U.S. takes aim at capitalist rivals." *The Guardian* 42 (April 18): 17.

Philon, Dominique
1997 "Les enjeux de la globalisation financière," in *Mondialisation: Au delà des mythes*. Paris: La Découverte.

Phillips, Anne
1977 "The concept of development." *Review of African Political Economy* 8 (January–April): 7–20.

Picó, Fernando
1995 "Aguila Blanca, ¿patriota o bandolero social?" pp. 33–60 in Ivonne Acosta (ed.), *Controversias históricas siglo XX*. San Juan: Editorial Lea.
1998 *Cada guaraguao . . . Galería de oficiales norteamericanos en Puerto Rico (1898–1899)*. Río Piedras: Editorial Huracán.

Pierre-Charles, Gérard
1976 *Genesis de la revolución Cubana*. Mexico City: Siglo XXI.
1979 "Teoría de la dependencia," in *Debates sobre la teoría de la dependencia*. San José, Costa Rica: EDUCA.

Pinto, Aníbal
1968 *Política y desarrollo*. Santiago: Editorial Universitaria.

Placencia, María Mercedes
1988 "Capacitación y crédito para microempresarias," pp. 171–183 in Marguerite Berger and Marya Buvinic (eds.), *La mujer en el sector informal: Trabajo femenino y microempresa en América Latina*. Quito: Editorial Nueva Sociedad.

Portantiero, Juan Carlos
1974 "Dominant classes and political crisis." *Latin American Perspectives* 1 (Fall): 93–120.

1981 "Lo nacional-popular y la alternative democrática en América Latina," pp. 217–240 in Henry Pease García et al., *América Latina 80: Democracia y movimento popular.* Lima: Centro de Estudios y Promoción del Desarrollo (DESCO).

Portantiero, Juan Carlos and Emilio de Ipola
1981 "Lo nacional-popular y los populismos realmente existentes." *Nueva Sociedad* 4: 7–18.

Portes, Alejandro
1983 "The informal sector: Definition, controversy, and relation to national development." *Review* 7 (1): 151–174.

Portes, Alejandro and Lauren Benton
1984 "Industrial development and labor absorption." *Population and Development Review* 10 (4): 589–611.
1987 "Desarrollo industrial y absorción laboral: Una reinterpretación." *Estudios Sociológicos* 5 (13): 111–137.

Portes, Alejandro and Saskia Sassen-Koob
1987 "Making it underground: Comparative material on the informal sector in Western market economies." *American Journal of Sociology* 93 (1): 30–61.

Portes, Alejandro and John Walton
1981 *Labor, Class, and the International System.* New York: Academic Press.

Possan, Magali
1997 *A malha entrecruzada das ações.* Campinas: Centro de Memória, Universidade de Campinas.

Poulantzas, Nicos
1976 *Crisis of the Dictatorships: Portugal, Greece, Spain.* London: NLB.
1978 *State, Power, Socialism.* London: NLB.

PREALC (Programa Regional para Empleo en América Latina y el Caribe)
1979 "Políticas hacia el sector informal urbano," pp. 475–496 in Victor E. Tokman and Emilio Klein (eds.), *El subempleo en América Latina.* Buenos Aires: El Cid Editores.
1991 *Empleo y equidad: El desafío de los 90.* Santiago.

Pryor, Frederic
1986 *Revolutionary Grenada: A Study in Political Economy.* New York: Praeger.

Pulido, Mercedes
1990 Comment made during presentation at the workshop "Women, Education, and Work." Caracas, Venezuela, October.

Quijano, Aníbal
1973 *Imperialismo, clases sociales y estado en el Perú: Seminario sobre clases sociales y crisis política en América Latina,* Oaxaca, Mexico: IIS-UNAM, June.
1974 "The marginal pole of the economy and the marginalized labor force." *Economy and Society* 3: 393–428.
1975 "De la conciliación al enfrentamiento." *Latin American Perspectives* 2 (Spring): 123–135.
1996 "Colonialidad del poder, globalización y democracia." www.urbared.ungs.edu.ar/download/documentos/aquijano2.doc.

Rakowski, Cathy A.
1985 "The planning process and the division of labor in a new industrial city: The case of Ciudad Guayana, Venezuela," pp. 195–223 in John Walton (ed.), *Capital and Labour in the Urbanized World.* London: Sage.

1989 "Evaluating development: Theory, ideology, and planning in Ciudad Guayana, Venezuela." *International Journal of Contemporary Sociology* 26 (January–April): 71–92.

1991 "Gender, family, and economy in a planned industrial city: The working and lower-class households of Ciudad Guayana," pp. 149–172 in Rae Lesser Blumberg (ed.), *Gender, Family, and Economy: The Triple Overlap.* Newbury Park, CA: Sage.

1994 "The informal sector debate, pt. 2: 1984–1993," pp. 31–50 in Cathy A. Rakowski (ed.), *Contrapunto: The Informal Sector Debate in Latin America.* Albany: State University of New York Press.

Ramalho, José Ricardo and Helena de Souza Martins (eds.)
1994 *Terceirização: Diversidade e negociação no mundo do trabalho.* São Paulo: HUC-ITEC.

Rancière, Jacques
1974 *La leçon d'Althusser.* Paris: Gallimard.

Reed, John
1990 "Guatemala's reign of misery." *The Guardian* 42 (April 18): 10–11.

Reich, Michael, David M. Gordon, and Richard C. Edwards
1973 "A theory of labor market segmentation." *American Economic Review* 63 (May): 359–365.

Resnick, Stephen and Richard Wolff
1982 "Classes in Marxian Theory." *Review of Radical Political Economics* 13 (Winter): 1–18.

1983 "A Marxist theory of the state," pp. 121–152 in Larry L. Wade (ed.), *Political Economy: Recent Views.* Boston: Kluwer-Nijhoff.

Rios, Palmira N.
1993 "Export-oriented industrialization and the demand for female labor: Puerto Rican women in the manufacturing sector, 1952–1980," pp. 89–101 in Edwin Meléndez and Edgardo Meléndez (eds.), *Colonial Dilemma: Critical Perspectives on Contemporary Puerto Rico.* Boston: South End Press.

Ritchie, Mark
1996 "Globalization vs. globalism: Giving internationalism a bad name." Paper on the website of the Bureau for Workers' Activities, International Labor Organization, Geneva. Retrieved from the World Wide Web at www.itcilo.it/english/actrav/telearn/global/ilo/globe/kirsh.htm.

Robertson, Roland
1990 *Globalization: Social Theory and Global Culture.* London: Sage.

Robinson, William
1998/99 "Latin America and global capitalism." *Race and Class* 40 (2/3): 111–131.

Robinson, William I.
1996 *Promoting Polyarchy: Globalization, U.S. Intervention, and Hegemony.* Cambridge: Cambridge University Press.

Robinson, William and Jerry Harris
2000 "Towards a global ruling class? Globalization and the transnational capitalist class." *Science and Society* 64 (Spring): 11–54.

Rodríguez, Carlos Rafael
1978 *Cuba en el transito al socialismo (1959–1963).* Mexico City: Siglo XXI.

Rodríguez Gómez, Guadalupe and Gabriel Torres
1994 "El Barzón y COMAGRO: Dos estrategias frente a la modernización neoliberal del campo." *Cuadernos Agrarios* 10: 70–94.

Rodwin, Lloyd et al.
1969 *Planning Urban Growth and Regional Development: The Experience of the Guayana Program in Venezuela.* Cambridge: MIT Press.

Roemer, Michael
1970 *Fishing for Growth: Export-Led Development in Peru, 1950–1967.* Cambridge, MA: Harvard University Press.

Romagnolo, David J.
1975 "The so-called 'law' of uneven and combined development." *Latin American Perspectives* 2 (Spring): 7–31.

Rondinelli, Dennis
1983 *Secondary Cities in Developing Countries: Policies for Diffusing Urbanization.* Beverly Hills, CA: Sage.

Rondinelli, Dennis and Kenneth Ruddle
1978 *Urbanization and Rural Development: A Spatial Policy for Equitable Growth.* New York: Praeger.

Rosenberg, Nathan
1969 "The direction of technological change: Inducement mechanisms and focusing devices." *Economic Development and Cultural Change* 18 (October): 1–24.

Roxborough, Ian
1992 "'Neo-Liberal' offensive in Latin America: Defensive retreat to the trenches for labour?" *South African Labour Bulletin* 16 (4).

Ruccio, David F.
1986a "The state and planning in Nicaragua," pp. 61–82 in Rose J. Spalding (ed.), *The Political Economy of Revolutionary Nicaragua.* Boston: Allen & Unwin.
1987 "The state, planning, and transition in Nicaragua." *Development and Change* 18 (January): 5–27.

Ruchwarger, Gary
1987 *People in Power: Forging a Grassroots Democracy in Nicaragua.* South Hadley, MA: Bergin and Garvey.

Rwcyemamu, Justinian F.
1971 "The causes of poverty in the periphery." *Journal of Modern African Studies* 9 (October): 453–455.

Safá, Helen I.
1982 "Introduction," pp. 3–17 in Helen Safá (ed.), *Toward a Political Economy of Urbanization in the Third World Countries.* Delhi: Oxford University Press.

Sassen, Saskia
1990 [1988] *The Mobility of Labor and Capital: A Study in International Investment and Labor Flow.* New York: Cambridge University Press.

Saul, John S.
1986 "The role of ideology in the transition to socialism," pp. 212–230 in Richard R. Fagen, Carmen Diana Deere, and José Luis Coraggio (eds.), *Transition and Development: Problems of Third World Socialism.* New York: Monthly Review Press.

Schmuckler, Beatriz
1979 "Diversidad de formas de las relaciones capitalistas en la industria Argentina,"

pp. 309–351 in Victor E. Tokman and Emilio Klein (eds.), *El subempleo en América Latina*. Buenos Aires: El did Editores.

Schwarz, Roberto
1977 *Ao vencedor as batatas.* São Paulo: Brasiliense.
1987 *Que horas são?* São Paulo: Duas Cidades.

Segre, Roberto
1978 *Las estructuras ambientales en América Latina.* Havana: University of Havana.

Seligson, Mitchell
1972 "The 'dual society' thesis in Latin America: A reexamination of the Costa Rican case." *Social Forces* 51 (September): 91–98.

Shoumatoff, Alex
1987 *The Capital of Hope: Brasília and Its People.* Albuquerque: University of New Mexico Press.

Singer, Daniel
1989 "On revolution." *Monthly Review* 41 (June): 33–36.

Singer, Hans W.
1950 "The distribution of gains between investing and borrowing countries." *American Economic Review—Papers and Proceedings* 40 (May): 473–485.
1970 "Dualism revisited: A new approach to the problems of the dual society in developing countries." *Journal of Development Studies* 7 (October): 60–75.

Singer, Paul
1973 "Urbanización, dependencia y marginalidad," in Manuel Castells (ed.), *Imperialismo y urbanización en América Latina*. Barcelona: Gustavo Gili.

Sivanandan, A.
1990 "All that melts into air is solid: The hokum of new times." *Race & Class* 31 (January–March): 1–30.
1997 "Capitalism, globalization, and epochal shifts." *Monthly Review* (February).

Sklair, Leslie
2000 "The transnational capitalist class and the discourse of globalization." Excerpts from *The Transnational Class*. Oxford: Blackwell. Retrieved from the World Wide Web at www.globaldimensions.net/articles/sklair/LSklair.html.

Smirnow, Gabriel
1979 *The Revolution Disarmed: Chile 1970–1973.* New York: Monthly Review Press.

Sobel, Lester (ed.)
1974 *Chile and Allende.* New York: Monthly Review Press.

Spalding, Karen
1975 "Hacienda-Village relations in Andean society to 1830." *Latin American Perspectives* 11 (Spring): 49–58.
1992 "Devestation in the Southern Cone: The inheritance of the neo-liberal years." *Latin American Issues* 11: whole issue.

Stavenhagen, Rodolfo
1968 "Seven fallacies about Latin America," pp. 13–31 in James Petras and Maurice Zeitlin (eds.), *Latin America: Reform or Revolution?* Greenwich, CN: Fawcett.

Steenland, Kyle
1975 "Notes on feudalism and capitalism in Chile and Latin America." *Latin American Perspectives* 2 (Spring): 49–58.

Stepan, Alfred (ed.)
  1989 *Democratizing Brazil: Problems of Transition and Consolidation.* New York: Oxford University Press.
Stephens, John
  1986 *The Transition from Capitalism to Socialism.* Urbana: University of Illinois Press.
Sternberg, Marvin
  1974 "Dependency, imperialism and the relations of production." *Latin American Perspectives* 1 (Spring): 75–86.
Streeck, William and Philippe Schmitter
  1985 *Private Interest Government: Beyond Market and State.* London: Sage.
Studies by the Staff of the Cabinet Committee on Price Stability
  1969 Washington, D.C.: Government Printing Office.
Sunita
  1990 "Protesters seize power from Nepal's king." *The Guardian* 42 (May 2): 16.
Sunkel, Osvaldo
  1967 "Política nacional de desarrollo y dependencia externa." *Estudios Internacionales* 1.
Sunkel, Osvaldo and Pedro Paz
  1970 *El subdesarrollo latinoamericano y la teoría del desarrollo.* Mexico City: Instituto Latinamericano de Planificación Económica y Social, Siglo XXI Editores.
Susman, Paul
  1987 "Spatial equality and socialist transformation in Cuba," pp. 250–281 in Dean Forbes and Nigel Thrift (eds.), *The Socialist Third World: Urban Development and Territorial Planning.* Oxford: Basil Blackwell.
Sweezy, Paul
  1967 (1942) *The Theory of Capitalist Development.* New York: Monthly Review Press.
  1980 *Post-Revolutionary Society.* New York: Monthly Review Press.
  1985 "Questions on the transition to socialism." *Studies in Political Economy* 18 (Fall): 9–12.
  1989 "U.S. imperialism in the 1990s." *Monthly Review* 41 (October): 1–17.
  1990 "Nineteen eighty-nine." *Monthly Review* 41 (April): 18–21.
Taino, Susan
  1990 "Maquiladora women: A new category of workers?" pp. 193–224 in Kathryn Ward (ed.), *Women Workers and Global Restructuring.* Ithaca, NY: Cornell University Industrial and Labor Relations Press.
Tardy, Marcella
  1991 "El Salvador on the brink of peace." *The Guardian* 43 (October 9): 10–11.
Tarrow, Sidney
  1991 "'Aiming at a moving target': Social science and the recent rebellions in Eastern Europe." *PS: Political Science and Politics* (March): 12–20.
Taylor, John G.
  1974 "Neo-Marxism and underdevelopment: A sociological phantasy." *Journal of Contemporary Asia* 4 (1): 5–23.
  1979 *From Modernization to Modes of Production: A Critique of the Sociologies of Development and Underdevelopment.* London: Macmillan.
Teixeira, Francisco and Manfredo Oliviera (eds.)
  1996 *Neoliberalismo e reestruturação produtiva.* Fortaleza: Universidade Federal do Ceará/São Paulo: Cortez.

Tinker, Irene
  1990 "A context for the field and the book," pp. 3–13 in I. Tinker (ed.), *Persistent Inequalities: Women and World Development.* New York: Oxford University Press.
Tironi, Eugenio and Ricardo Lagos
  1991 "The social actors and structural adjustment." *CEPAL Review* 44.
Tokman, Victor E.
  1979 "Una exploración sobre la naturaleza de las interrelaciones entre los sectores informal y formal," pp. 203–242 in Victor E. Tokman and Emilio Klein (eds.), *El Subempleo en América Latina.* Buenos Aires: El Cid Editores.
  1987a "El imperativo de actuar: El sector informal hoy." *Nueva Sociedad* (88): 93–105.
  1987b "El sector informal: Quince años después." *El Trimestre Ecónomico* 54 (3): 513–536.
  1989 "Policies for a heterogeneous informal sector in Latin America." *World Development* 17 (7): 1067–1076.
  1992 *Beyond Regulation: The Informal Economy in Latin America.* Boulder, CO: Lynne Rienner.
Torres Negrón, Luis
  1998 "Confirma Filiberto Ojeda el atentado al supertubo." *El Nuevo Dia,* April 22.
Treviño Sillar, Sandra
  1988 "Reflexiones sobre el trabajo domicilio en la zona noreste de Guanajuato." *Estudios Sociológicos* 6 (18): 583–602.
Trías Monge, José
  1997 *Puerto Rico: The Trials of the Oldest Colony of the World.* New Haven, CT: Yale University Press.
Trotsky, Leon
  1969 *La revolución tracionada.* Mexico City: Editores del Sol.
  1972 *Resultados y perspectivas.* Buenos Aires: De Cepe.
  1972 *The Revolution Betrayed.* New York: Pathfinder.
Turner, John F. C. and Robert Fichter (eds.)
  1972 *Freedom to Build.* New York: Macmillan.
UNCTAD (United Nations Conference on Trade and Development)
  1997 *Trade and Development Report.* New York.
UN-ECLA (United Nations-Economic Commission for Latin America)
  1966a *The Process of Industrial Development in Latin America.* New York: United Nations.
  1966b *The Process of Industrial Development in Latin America—Statistical Annex.* New York: United Nations.
Vaitsos, Constantine
  1973 "Policies on foreign direct investments and economic development in Latin America." University of Sussex, Institute of Development Studies.
  1974 *Intercountry Income Distribution and Transnational Enterprises.* Oxford: Clarendon Press.
Valdés, Juan Gabriel
  1989 *La escuela de Chicago: Operación Chile.* Buenos Aires: Editorial Zeta.
Vale, Lawrence J.
  1992 *Architecture, Power and National Identity.* New Haven, CT: Yale University Press.

Valecillos, Hector

1983 "Evolución histórica, situación actual y perspectivas del trabajo de la mujer en Venezuela." Paper presented at the First National Encounter of the Feminist Front of the Movimiento al Socialismo, Caracas, Venezuela.

Valentine, Charles A.

1971 "The 'culture of poverty': Its scientific significance and its implications for action," pp. 193–225 in Eleanor Burke Leacock (ed.), *The Culture of Poverty: A Critique.* New York: Simon and Schuster.

1972 *Culture of Poverty: Critique and Counter-Proposals.* Chicago: University of Chicago Press.

Vasconi, Tomás A.

1990 "Democracy and Socialism in South America." *Latin American Perspectives* 17 (2): 25–38.

Vernon, Raymond

1966 "International investment and international trade in the product cycle." *Quarterly Journal of Economics* 80 (August): 190–207.

Vilas, Carlos M.

1986 *The Sandinista Revolution.* New York: Monthly Review Press.

1986a "The mass organizations in Nicaragua: The current problematic and perspectives for the future." *Monthly Review* 38 (November): 20–31.

1986b *The Sandinista Revolution: National Liberation and Social Transformation in Central America.* New York: Monthly Review Press.

Villalobos, Joaquín

1989 "A democratic revolution for El Salvador." *Foreign Policy* 74 (Spring): 103–122.

Vine, Philip

1990 "Guatemalan army changes tack and targets popular organizations." *Peace Courier* 3: 8–9.

Visser, Jelle

1993 "Syndicalisme et désyndicalisation," in J. Freyssinet (ed.), *Syndicats d'Europe: Le mouvement social 62.* Paris: Editions Ouvrières.

Wachtel, Howard M.

1972 "Capitalism and poverty in America: Paradox or contradiction?" *American Economic Review* 62 (May): 187–194.

Waisman, Carlos

1987 *Reversal of Development in Argentina: Postwar Counterrevolutionary Policies and Their Structural Consequences.* Princeton: Princeton University Press.

Wald, Alan M.

1987 *The New York Intellectuals: The Rise and Decline of the Anti-Stalinist Left from the 1930s to the 1980s.* Chapel Hill: University of North Carolina Press.

Walker, David M.

1980 *The Oxford Companion to Law.* Oxford: Clarendon.

Walker, Thomas W.

1982 *Nicaragua in revolution.* New York: Praeger.

1986 *Nicaragua: The Land of Sandino.* Boulder, CO: Westview Press.

Wallerstein, Immanuel

1974 "Dependence in an interdependent world." *African Studies Review* 17: 1–26.

1975 "The present state of the debate on world inequality," in his *World Inequality: Origins and Perspectives on the World System.* Montreal: Black Rose Books.
1976 *The Modern World-System.* New York: Academic Press.
1979 *The Capitalist World-Economy.* London: Cambridge University Press.

Waters, Mary-Alice (ed.)
1970 *Rosa Luxemburg Speaks.* New York: Pathfinder.

Warren, Bill
1980 *Imperialism: Pioneer of Capitalism.* London: New Left Books.

Water, Malcolm
1995 *Globalization.* London and New York: Routledge.

Weber, Henri
1986 "The struggle for power," pp. 193–207 in Peter Rosset and John Vandermeer (eds.), *Nicaragua: Unfinished Revolution.* New York: Grove Press.

Weeks, John and Elizabeth Dore
1979 "International exchange and the causes of backwardness." *Latin American Perspectives* 6 (Spring): 62–87.

Weffort, Francisco
1971 "Notas sobre la teoría de la dependencia: ¿Teoría de clase o ideología nacional?" *Revista Latinoamericana de Ciencia Política* 1 (December): 389–401.
1984 *Por qué democracia?* São Paulo: Editora Brasiliense.

Wheelock, Jaime
1983 *El gran desafío.* Managua: Nueva Nicaragua.

Williamson, John (ed.)
1990 *Latin American Adjustment: How Much Has Happened?* Washington, D.C.: Institute for International Economics.

Wilson, Tamar Diana
1994 "Garbage pickers: Internal stratification among the 'disguised proletarians' in a Mexicali garbage dump." Paper presented at the 18th International Congress of the Latin American Studies Association, Atlanta, GA, March 10–12.

Wionczek, Miguel
1971 "Hacía el establecimiento de un trato común para la inversión extranjera en el Mercado Común Andino." *El Trimestre Económico* 38 (April–June): 659–702.

Winn, Peter
1986 *Weavers of Revolution: The Yarur Workers and Chile's Road to Socialism.* New York: Oxford University Press.

Wolpe, H. (ed.)
1980 *The Articulation of Modes of Production.* London: Routledge & Kegan Paul.

Wood, Ellen Meiksins
1986 *The Retreat from Class: A New "True" Socialism.* London: Verso.
1997 "Labor, the state, and class struggle." *Monthly Review* 49 (3).

World Bank
1974 *Sites and Services Projects.* Washington, D.C.

Wright, Charles L.
1992 *Fast Wheels Slow Traffic: Urban Transport Choices.* Philadelphia: Temple University Press.

Zabaleta Mercado, René
1974 "Movimento obrero y ciencia social: La revolución democrática de 1952 en Bolivia . . ." *Historia e Sociedad* 3 (Fall): 3–36.

Zhenxing, Su
  1988 "On Latin America's process of democratization." *Latin American Perspectives* 15 (3): 18–25.
Zielinski, Mike
  1990 "A breakthrough for peace in El Salvador?" *The Guardian* 42 (April 18): 12.

Index

About the Contributors

Thomas Angotti is a city planner and a professor in the Graduate Center for Planning and the Environment at Pratt Institute, Brooklyn, New York.

Ricardo Antunes is a professor of sociology at the University of Campinas, São Paulo, and is a participating editor for *Latin American Perspectives.*

David Barkin teaches economics at the Universidad Autónoma Metropolitana, Mexico City, and is a participating editor for *Latin American Perspectives.*

David Broad is a reseacher and coeditor for *The New World Order and the Third World* (Montreal: Black Rose Books, 1992).

Doug Brown is a professor of economics at Northern Arizona University and has visited Nicaragua.

Ronald H. Chilcote is a professer of economics and political science at the University of California, Riverside, and managing editor for *Latin American Perspectives.*

Agustín Cueva was a leading Marxist theorist and Ecuadorean social scientist.

Haroldo Dilla Alfonso was a researcher at the Centro de Estudios sobre America in Havana, Cuba, and is completing his doctoral work in the Dominican Republic.

Enrique Dussel has taught philosophy at the Universidad Nacional Autónoma de México and the Universidad Autónoma Metropolitana (Iztapalapa).

Joel C. Edelstein teaches political science at the University of Colorado and is a participating editor for *Latin American Perspectives.*

Raúl A. Fernández is an economist at the University of California, Irvine.

Frank T. Fitzgerald teaches at the College of Saint Rose and has authored the book *Politics and Social Structures in Revolutionary China.* He is a participating editor for *Latin American Perspectives.*

André Gunder Frank is the author of many books on underdevelopment and world-systems.

Michael González-Cruz is a former president of the Federación Universitaria ProIndependencia in Puerto Rico and at the time his 1998 article originally appeared was a graduate student in sociology at the State University of New York, Binghamton.

Timothy F. Harding is a coordinating editor of *Latin American Perspectives* and a professor of history at California State University, Los Angeles.

Richard L. Harris is coordinating editor for *Latin American Perspectives* and professor of global studies at California State University, Monterey Bay. He is the co-editor and one of the authors of *Critical Perspectives on Globalization and Neoliberalism in the Developing Countries* (Leiden: Brill, 2000).

Keith A. Haynes teaches United States and Latin American history at the College of Saint Rose in Albany, New York.

Colin Henfrey, at the time of writing his article, was a member of the Center for Latin American Studies and the department of sociology at the University of Liverpool.

Claudio Katz is a professor and researcher at the University of Buenos Aires.

Manuel Maldonado-Denis is a Puerto Rican scholar and activist.

Ronaldo Munck is a professor in sociology at the University of Liverpool and a participating editor for *Latin American Perspectives.* He has written widely on Latin America, especially Argentina.

George Novack was a renowned scholar on Marxism and Trotsky.

José Nun has taught political science at the University of Toronto and is a participating editor for *Latin American Perspectives.*

José F. Ocampo is a political economist teaching in Colombia.

Tânia Pellegrini is a professor of Brazilian literature at the State University of São Paulo and a participating editor for *Latin American Perspectives.*

James F. Petras is a professor of sociology at the State University of New York at Binghamton and a participating editor for *Latin American Perspectives.*

Aníbal Quijano, a Peruvian sociologist, is best known for his studies of dependency and of the Peruvian reality.

Cathy A. Rakowski is a professor in rural sociology and women's studies at Ohio State University.

Eduardo Rosenzvaig is a professor of history and director of the Reasearch Institute on Popular Culture at the National University of Tucumán, Argentina.

David F. Ruccio is a professor of economics and director of Latin American studies at the University of Notre Dame.

Rodolfo Stavenhagen is a Mexican anthropologist and author of writings on Latin America.

Frederick Stirton Weaver is a professor and dean at Hampshire College and a participating editor for *Latin American Perspectives.*

Heather Williams teaches political science at Pomona College and is an associate editor for *Latin American Perspectives.*

Tamar Diana Wilson is an associate editor of *Latin American Perspectives* and a researcher on Mexico.